Plots and Prayers

Niki Savva is one of the most senior correspondents in the Canberra Press Gallery. She was twice political correspondent on *The Australian*, and headed up the Canberra bureaus of both *The Herald Sun* and *The Age*. When family tragedy forced a career change, she became Peter Costello's press secretary for six years and was then on John Howard's staff for three years. Her work has brought her into intimate contact with Australia's major political players for more than 35 years. She is a regular columnist for *The Australian*, and often appears on ABC TV's *Insiders*.

In March 2017, the Melbourne Press Club bestowed a lifetime achievement award upon Niki for her 'outstanding coverage of Australian politics as a reporter, columnist and author'. Her previous book, *The Road to Ruin*, was a major bestseller, and won the 2017 General Nonfiction Book of the Year Award at the Australian Book Industry Awards.

Plots and Prayers

MALCOLM TURNBULL'S DEMISE AND
SCOTT MORRISON'S ASCENSION

Niki Savva

SCRIBE
Melbourne • London

Scribe Publications
18–20 Edward St, Brunswick, Victoria 3056, Australia
2 John St, Clerkenwell, London, WC1N 2ES, United Kingdom
3754 Pleasant Ave, Suite 100, Minneapolis, Minnesota 55409, USA

First published by Scribe 2019
Reprinted 2019

Typeset in 12/17pt Adobe Garamond Pro by the publishers

Printed and bound in Australia by Griffin Press, part of Ovato

Scribe Publications is committed to the sustainable use of natural resources and the use of paper products made responsibly from those resources.

9781925849189 (Australian edition)
9781912854646 (UK edition)
9781925693836 (e-book)

Catalogue records for this book are available from the National Library of Australia and the British Library

scribepublications.com.au
scribepublications.co.uk
scribepublications.com

From beginning to end, for Steven and Vincent

Contents

Prologue

The religious overtones were constant and unmissable. They were there before Scott Morrison ascended to the leadership, then continued all the way through to his stunning election victory on 18 May 2019, which he described as a miracle.

Months before that, Malcolm Turnbull was taken aback by a passage in Greg Sheridan's book *God Is Good for You*, which he had launched in early August 2018, only three weeks before his colleagues passed their judgement on him. The passage began with the question, 'And will we face judgement?'

The answer that followed came from Tony Abbott, 'Yes, we will be judged, but I think we will be judged benignly. I think there would be very few people, only people who consistently choose evil, who would find themselves in hell. Maybe only Hitler or Stalin.'

Turnbull was gobsmacked by the morality, or rather what he considered to be the amorality, of the thinking behind Abbott's response. To me, it showed how Abbott had justified his behaviour over the three years since he'd lost the leadership. At his final press conference as prime minister, Abbott had pledged there would be no wrecking, sniping, or undermining, and had then spent every day thereafter doing almost exactly that. And if he didn't do it personally, others did it on his behalf.

Whenever his words were thrown back at him, he would say he had never leaked or briefed – which nobody really believed anyway – but said what he had to say publicly. So backstabbing was sinful, while frontstabbing was acceptable. Or forgivable.

Abbott's destructive path helped demolish Turnbull's prime ministership. The sense of chaos, the instability he created and fuelled, became constant companions. Abbott created the environment that enabled an increasingly frustrated Peter Dutton to make his move.

On 22 August 2018, the day after 35 Liberals MPs cast their vote against Turnbull – enough to spell doom for his leadership – Dutton was making a pitch to Melbourne radio listeners as part of his bid to replace Turnbull. Dutton was asked by Triple M host Wil Anderson to name his favourite AC/DC song. Pleading that he had only had one-and-a-half hours' sleep, Dutton said he couldn't think of one.

As soon as I heard the question, it was obvious – to me, at least – what the answer was: 'Highway to Hell'. That seemed to be where the Liberals were headed. I was not alone in thinking this. So did almost every Liberal MP that day, including Scott Morrison, as he pleaded with Mathias Cormann not to terminate the government. Everything pointed to Armageddon.

Abbott's destabilisation campaign, helped along by his media mates, the betrayals, and the rise of the religious right, who never accepted Turnbull and could not accept the vote on same-sex marriage that he enabled, all contributed to Turnbull's downfall.

So did Turnbull's own poor political judgement. He was a good prime minister and a terrible politician. The good bits of Malcolm were ultimately not enough to make up for the bad Malcolm and the mistakes he made.

The sheer brutality of his removal horrified many Liberals. MPs were traumatised or humiliated by eight days of madness. Men and women cried from the sheer anguish of it. They went to hell, and feared when it was over they would not make it back, and nor would the Liberal Party. But, sustained by his deep faith, fortified by his enormous self-belief, Morrison hoped and prayed that God had other plans.

Turnbull's road ended in disaster, as it was always bound to, and as he always knew it would, as he predicted to me a scant three years before it happened, in a rather wistful, sad way, when I spoke to him for *The Road to Ruin*. Back then, he had felt sorry for Abbott.

But when his end came, when he began the agonising trip down his own Highway to Hell, he could not bear to let go. And then when it was over, he was defiant, fragile – and, yes, at times vengeful.

Based on dozens of interviews, many of them conducted only days or weeks after the coup, *Plots and Prayers* explores the events leading up to Turnbull's demise, the disaster that was the 2016 election, the soap opera surrounding the Nationals leader and deputy prime minister, Barnaby Joyce, the debacle of the energy debate, the chaos of the coup itself, and Scott Morrison's elevation, and then delves in detail into the actions, the motives, the character, and the relationships of those at the centre of the days of madness that led to three prime ministers in three years and the 'miracle' that was Morrison's victory.

CHAPTER ONE

A unique coup

Malcolm Turnbull does not believe that Scott Morrison's stunning election victory vindicated the coup against him. Turnbull remains confident he could have won in 2019, and besides, the revolt by the right was designed to install Peter Dutton, not Morrison, as prime minister. The last person Dutton and his backers wanted to lead the party was Turnbull; the second-last was Morrison.

Turnbull also firmly believes that by holding out against the insurgents during coup week, by delaying a second ballot, he gave Morrison precious time to gather the numbers to triumph over Dutton. If there was any consolation for Turnbull, this was it, particularly as he and those closest to him had warned the plotters that if they persisted, the week would end with Morrison – whom they disliked – being sworn in as prime minister.

It was only a part of Turnbull's strategy that Morrison should succeed. The other part – the primary objective, of course – was to save himself. Morrison, the most astute conservative politician of his generation, did need the extra time that Turnbull bought him, but the plotting and planning by his lieutenants was already well advanced. It is impossible to get to where he got in 24 hours, which is what he later wanted people to believe.

Morrison had done what he could to save Turnbull from himself.

He knew he would be damaged if people thought he had ascended to the Liberal leadership by being disloyal or if he had blood on his hands. The image of him as a cleanskin was vital to his success. This did not stop some of his backers from talking about how it happened, nor his enemies from trying to sully his reputation. He would not allow any of this to distract him from his singular objective of winning an election already deemed lost through the disunity and the despair that had embedded itself in Liberal ranks after the knifing of two prime ministers.

Morrison, who turned 51 five days before the 2019 election, is a complex mix of political cunning and religious conviction who burnishes his image as a daggy dad who loves his beer, loves his footy, and understands what ordinary Australian families need. He is a social conservative with a social conscience. He boosted funding to fight mental-health problems confronting young Australians, and he called royal commissions into the treatment of the aged and the disabled. He has friendships across political and religious divides, including in the Muslim community. He argued in cabinet that the seat-by-seat breakdown of the same-sex marriage vote should not be made public, advocated during the plebiscite for legislation to expand religious freedom, and then abstained from the vote when his own electorate of Cook voted in favour of marriage equality. He was the only other member of the leadership group who supported Turnbull's decision to impose the anti-bonking ban on ministers in the middle of the crisis surrounding Barnaby's doodle.

Labor insiders claimed even before the campaign began that their research showed that Australians thought Morrison was a bit of a 'bible-basher'. They were convinced his religion would be a turn-off for voters. Morrison's decision to invite cameras into his Pentecostal church on Easter Sunday caused disquiet even in Liberal ranks, as unfamiliar pictures of an Australian prime minister praying, swaying, and singing swamped the media. It was a presidential campaign borrowing heavily on the techniques and tactics employed in the United States, crafted solely around him, and accompanying it was another Americanism – the overt insertion by a putative leader of his religion into politics. Other Australian politicians had declared their faith and used it to attract voters, such as Kevin Rudd, who harvested conservative Christian votes from Liberals but offended many with his frequent doorstops outside church on a Sunday. But the footage of Morrison from inside the church was something else again.

There were legitimate questions about how or where Morrison's faith would impact on his role as prime minister. However, Labor leader Bill Shorten's decision in the last days of the campaign to dive into an area where others trod gently and which he had only previously hinted at, in an effort to make Morrison's faith an issue, rebounded on Shorten. He helped Morrison swing people of faith away from Labor and to the Liberal Party in the closing days of the campaign. Later, experienced Labor campaigners mused ruefully that what Morrison had done by unabashedly parading his deep faith was a calculated move to draw conservative believers into the Liberal fold, to make them feel both safe and welcome. Early analysis showed large swings to Liberals in seats with high Christian populations. A procession of senior Labor figures, including Chris Bowen, who suffered a 7 per cent swing in his New South Wales seat of McMahon, urged his party to find ways to speak to people of faith.

However, it was the economy that Morrison, relentlessly and tirelessly, put at the centre of a highly professional, well-executed, and well-resourced campaign. He made it a choice between himself and Shorten, as he emphasised day and night the risks posed by the opposition leader and the billions in extra taxes that he proposed.

Morrison made a virtue out of necessity. It was all about him, not the team, because he didn't really have one, and to give those who remained any prominence, the ones who weren't fighting to retain their seats, would only provide unpleasant reminders of the recent past. He offered little in the way of a third-term agenda beyond Josh Frydenberg's well-received budget, with its promise of a surplus and personal income tax cuts. He won emphatically because he campaigned better and connected better with the voters. He worked hard; he was hungry for it. As a former state director of the New South Wales Liberal Party, he knew the importance of leaders sticking to messages. But he was confident enough to add his own touches. Invoking the language of his faith, he promised Australians, 'I will burn for you.'

Shorten barely mentioned jobs, never talked about aspiration, and ran a campaign that looked as if it had not been adjusted to take account of Turnbull's departure. Shorten railed against the top end of town as if the company tax cuts still existed and the prime minister was still in residence at Point Piper rather than in the Shire, a determinedly middle-class part of Sydney where Morrison lived in a modest house. Shorten pitted young against old, and rich against poor, offending self-funded retirees – many of whom were not wealthy – by promising to remove tax breaks on shares, and he angered young tradies hoping to build wealth through property investment with plans to limit negative gearing. Liberal MPs in the outer suburbs reported swings to them in traditional Labor booths.

Shorten evoked Labor heroes Gough Whitlam and Bob Hawke, who either made him look inept or inadequate. He straddled the barbed-wire fence on coal as Bob Brown's convoy to stop the Adani mine wrecked any chance he might have had of picking up seats in Queensland, and for the first couple of weeks looked like a frightened rabbit. He stopped campaigning 48 hours before the vote, after Hawke's death, believing that the reminders of Hawke's achievements would help him get over the line. He was wrong.

Morrison promised to create 1.25 million jobs over five years, and stuck to his mantra of a fair go for those who had a go. Whatever his early shortcomings as a prime minister, his questionable captain's calls, he was a formidable campaigner. His agenda was threadbare, his team invisible. He never stopped, and he never deviated from a narrative aimed squarely at those he called the 'quiet Australians': Shorten's policies would wreck the economy. On the night before the vote, as he flew to Tasmania for one last visit, Morrison texted his deputy, the treasurer, Josh Frydenberg, to thank him, saying they had done everything they possibly could to unite the party and maintain discipline, adding that it was now 'in God's hands'.

A single-minded, forceful personality, often brusque with colleagues, possessed of enormous self-belief, who works hard, is disciplined, with clear objectives – and who regularly appeals for divine intervention, which often appeared to be heeded – Morrison demolished Shorten, demoralised Labor, and delivered an emphatic victory few thought possible after Turnbull's removal. Including Turnbull.

In those early days after he was deposed, Turnbull blamed plenty of people for his demise. Despite heavy suspicions about Morrison's role and that of his lieutenants, who were active in the field well before Dutton's challenge, initially Morrison was well down on Turnbull's list of guilty parties.

A week after Turnbull gambled his prime ministership and lost, the night before he flew to New York with his wife, Lucy, to seek refuge from the trauma and to escape the by-election campaign for his seat of Warringah, they arrived for dinner at the Hunters Hill home of Craig and Suzie Laundy, with an expensive bottle of French champagne, Ruinart Blanc de Blancs, in hand.

In the words of Arthur Sinodinos, Laundy had provided valuable pastoral care, among other things, to Turnbull in his final days in office. Laundy had issued the invitation to his friend to come to his bayside three-storey home the previous Tuesday at the farewell lunch with Turnbull's staff at the Centennial Hotel in Paddington. Laundy was the only other politician there. He thought it would be good for Turnbull to spend some quiet time in a family setting before he jetted off.

Laundy was not feeling too flash, either. He was gutted by Turnbull's removal. Confronting serious family problems, Laundy had weighed up his future well before the coup and had been inclined to quit. The sheer brutality of that week only confirmed his decision to go. But he was worried about his friend's mental wellbeing. He stayed in regular contact, and even months later wondered if Turnbull would ever get over it or come to terms with what had happened. Laundy would then answer his own question: *No, he wouldn't.*

It was only natural for the pain to linger, but it did eventually subside, allowing the sunnier Malcolm to emerge as he immersed himself in a book about his life, and in new business ventures. It didn't hurt as much to talk about what had happened and those he held responsible for it. He could do it without sounding bitter – he could even make the odd wry joke about it – although forgiveness would be a long time coming. If ever.

That night at the Laundys, their son, Charlie, their daughter Sophie, along with their partners and their youngest daughter, Analise, were the only others there. Suzie had prepared a marinated beef fillet, and Sophie a sticky date pudding. When the youngsters were with them at the dinner table, Malcolm and Lucy were full of questions about their studies, their travel, and their interests. It was relaxed and normal.

But in the hour before that, over drinks, and then after dinner, when the Laundy kids were in the TV room, the conversation was all about what had just happened, when Turnbull's prime ministership had ended in bloodshed and tears.

Turnbull was struggling to come to terms with it. He would say he did not want to relive what had happened, yet that night he kept trying to rationalise it, going through the days of madness, as he called them, although the whole of 2018 had really been his *annus amentia*, a year marked by lunatic events. He would list those he held responsible for bringing him down: Peter Dutton, Rupert Murdoch, Tony Abbott.

Before and after dinner, Turnbull kept coming back to one moment and one man: Mathias Cormann. Turnbull could not help but think he would still have been prime minister if Cormann had not betrayed him. Later still, as he reflected, he seemed to blame Cormann more than Dutton. He had counted on Cormann to protect him, trusting him without hesitation or qualification. Then, much too late, Turnbull came to believe that Cormann had not switched at the last minute, but had been complicit all along, and that his betrayal had been staged and timed at a critical moment to revive Dutton's faltering challenge. Turnbull knew that MPs witnessing Cormann's dramatic defection early on Thursday morning would realise that they would never be able to put the pieces back together again. Which is exactly what the defection was designed to ram home. Turnbull blamed Cormann for destroying a government in which he had played such a constructive role. He found it inexplicable that someone who ranked so highly, and who was held in such high regard, could perpetrate such destruction.

It was as inexplicable as Dutton's plan to challenge, which Turnbull thought was crazy and incredible. Dutton, in Turnbull's view, was utterly unelectable – as if anyone in their right mind could possibly think that Dutton could be leader or prime minister. Turnbull had never given the notion any credence, not even when his best friends in politics warned him the former cop from Queensland was stalking him. He had laughed off those warnings, never believing for one moment that Dutton would challenge, just as he believed that Cormann was too smart and had invested too much in the success of the government to blow it up.

As he tried to piece it all together afterwards, Turnbull complained to friends that there had been a period of what he described as 'radio silence' between him and Cormann during that critical weekend, which only fuelled his suspicions about Cormann's complicity – suspicions already aroused by ministers who told him that Dutton had confided to them that Cormann was aware of and fully on board with his challenge, and had done his numbers.

Despite Cormann's urging of Dutton to tweet his loyalty to Turnbull (which nobody believed) on the Saturday before the coup, when speculation was rife that Dutton was planning a challenge, and which Dutton vehemently denied in conversations with Turnbull – repeatedly professing his loyalty, pooh-poohing the speculation, dismissing it as rubbish, right up until the moment he put his hand up in the party room – Turnbull's conspiracy theories grew. Later, Scott Morrison featured in them prominently, too. You can't blame Turnbull for feeling that way, given what transpired.

Any hope Turnbull had of surviving that week in August, and then possibly long enough to call an election, was scuttled by Cormann's very public defection, which was precipitated by the very high vote against Turnbull at the first party-room meeting – a vote that in turn had been pumped up by the strategic voting of Morrison's supporters, who had war-gamed every possible scenario well in advance, confident that a move on the leadership was imminent. It was as circular as a chainsaw.

Cormann declared to colleagues within seconds after the first vote that Turnbull's position was untenable, and appealed to Turnbull the next day to spare them all the trauma of another challenge by stepping aside to allow Dutton to take over without any further bloodshed. Apart from Turnbull's, that is. Cormann was unsympathetic to Turnbull's complaint that if he did that, it would be tantamount to giving in to terrorism. 'You have to,' Cormann told him. Not for nothing was Cormann nicknamed the Belgian bulldozer.

After having worked so closely with Turnbull, it was remarkable that Cormann did not really know him at all. Cormann wanted a peaceful transition. Dutton knew better. He knew that Turnbull would have to be blasted out.

Only one day before that vote, for the umpteenth time, Cormann had told me he would stick with Turnbull to the bitter end, vowing that if Turnbull went down, he would go down with him. Then, only a matter of hours after standing beside Turnbull and pledging his loyalty, knowing Morrison was on the move, he convinced Mitch Fifield and Michaelia Cash to join him in announcing in the most dramatic, damaging way possible that he was abandoning Turnbull to back Dutton. Cormann was banking on the symbolism as well as the reality of their desertion to shift numbers and momentum to Dutton – whose campaign by then was fraying – hoping it would blunt Morrison's campaign. The mutiny of Turnbull's Praetorian Guard was complete.

As Cormann headed out to announce that he was abandoning Turnbull, Julie Bishop exploded, reminding Turnbull and the remaining members of his leadership group of her warning years before that Cormann could not be trusted.

After she quit the foreign ministry she so loved, and before she left parliament altogether, Bishop described Cormann to me as 'the ultimate seducer and betrayer'. Morrison said later she refused his offer to stay on as foreign minister because she could not bear to be in the same room as Dutton and Cormann. That was true, although she also believed that Morrison – no doubt conscious of the fact that his job would be made easier if a popular female rival was out of the picture – was half-hearted when he made the offer. In any case, by then there were other (unfairly suspected) villains on her long list, including the leader of the moderates, Christopher Pyne.

What made Cormann's betrayal so much more painful was that Turnbull had given him everything he wanted, including despatching George Brandis – who would never have voted for anyone other than Turnbull – to London so that Cormann could take over as government leader in the Senate. One of Turnbull's biggest policy missteps was to keep acceding to Cormann's request, way beyond prudence, for one more chance to get the big-company tax cuts through the Senate. Cormann's evangelical commitment to the tax cuts ensured that they became a ball and chain wrapped around Turnbull's neck.

When the super Saturday by-elections in July turned into a referendum on company tax cuts, Turnbull bitterly regretted that he had reversed a decision he had made in June to dump the unpopular plan. He had relented because Cormann was convinced he could still win over the flip-flopping Pauline Hanson. Turnbull, fully backed by Morrison, had sided with Cormann against Kelly O'Dwyer's spirited advocacy for the company tax cuts to be dropped and replaced by bigger personal income tax cuts.

The rancour over power bills, and the campaign against the Paris emission targets – which Abbott had agreed to as prime minister, and then used relentlessly to undermine Turnbull, only to rediscover the magic of Paris when he was under threat later in his own seat – were lightning rods for disunity. Turnbull battled to frame a new energy policy that changed by the day as he sought to accommodate dissenters, some of whom really only ever wanted one thing: Turnbull's head on a platter. His decision to defer to Cormann and delay dumping the tax cuts, only to then be abandoned by him, combined with his mishandling of the energy debate, contributed to his demise and to his subsequent rage.

With a combination of ambition, ability, and a forceful personality, Cormann made himself one of the most powerful figures in the government, as well as one of the most respected; then, in the space of two days, he became one of the most reviled.

Critical interventions by the then attorney-general, Christian Porter, during those days of madness also helped cruel Turnbull's hopes of surviving until the end of that week and possibly racing off to an election. In a long interview for this book detailing his role in those momentous days, Porter, who was friendly with both Cormann and Dutton, says he divorced his political self from his legal self, gathering every piece of constitutional and legal advice he could as the debate raged about whether Dutton was eligible to remain in parliament. Porter went to a meeting in Turnbull's office armed with his own letter of resignation already typed out. Concerned about the potential for political interference, he had also written to the solicitor-general, Stephen Donoghue, instructing him not to speak to any person in the government – including Turnbull – other than himself. Fearing Turnbull might intercede with the governor-general in an effort to prevent Dutton being sworn in, Porter also emailed Sir Peter Cosgrove, offering to provide him with any advice he felt he might need on matters relating to Dutton.

On the Thursday morning, the day before Turnbull's denouement, Porter told Turnbull that if he said publicly at a press conference what he was saying privately in his office – that the governor-general would be reluctant to commission Dutton because he could be in breach of section 44(v) of the constitution – then he (Porter) would be forced to publicly contradict him and resign as attorney-general.

Porter had obtained advice from departmental solicitors, who had confirmed his view that there were only two issues the governor-general would – or should – consider in commissioning a new prime minister: whether he had the confidence of the House, and whether he could guarantee supply. Porter was confident that Dutton could satisfy both. The fact that Porter, acting on his own initiative, had sought the advice showed how seriously he was taking Turnbull's threat. If Turnbull had followed through, it would have had the potential to trigger a constitutional crisis rivalling that of 1975.

Back then, Sir John Kerr had sacked a Labor government and a Labor prime minister at the urging of the Liberal leader. Turnbull was seeking to have his own government sacked.

Turnbull believed Porter was too close to Dutton, and that this was influencing his judgement. Turnbull formed the conclusion, from which he has never wavered, that Dutton was ineligible. He believed that Donaghue's advice was wrong, and that it was similar to the advice he had given regarding Barnaby Joyce's eligibility, which turned out to be wrong after the High Court found Joyce's dual citizenship rendered him ineligible to sit in parliament.

Turnbull was fully prepared, as the outgoing prime minister, to formally write to the governor-general to advise him that Dutton should not be sworn in. As he fought to hold on to his job, Turnbull told colleagues that Sir Peter would not commission Dutton, threatening to get him on the phone then and there to discuss it. When it was over, after he calmed down a bit, he would acknowledge he did not know what the governor-general would have done, but remained firm in his opinion that the doubts surrounding Dutton's eligibility were both real and relevant.

Although Turnbull was not bluffing with Porter during those days of madness, he pulled back, instead telling a press conference soon after his meeting with Porter that the solicitor-general would advise whether Dutton was eligible or not in time for a party meeting the next day. He also declared that if the spill motion were passed, he would not renominate for the leadership – thereby formally, openly clearing the way for Scott Morrison and Julie Bishop to run.

Turnbull had made the wrenching decision to remove himself, doing his best to protect his legacy with as graceful an exit as possible from the job he had coveted for most of his life. Except, as Pyne was to discover on Thursday afternoon, he had an escape hatch – cars and cops at the ready to take him to the governor-general to dissolve the parliament, even after he had said he would not run if the spill vote in the party room the next day went against him.

Turnbull was prepared for anything and everything. He was convinced that if Dutton won the ballot, he would not win a vote of confidence in the House. He told Rupert Murdoch this in their conversation on Wednesday morning.

Pyne, usually not known for understatements, later observed, 'There was a lot of nonsense going on.'

It was a unique coup against Turnbull. In some respects, it was a self-inflicted coup, brought on by the victim to catch the perpetrator before he could commit his crime, before his plot was fully hatched. Turnbull and Dutton both lost, enabling a cunning Morrison, with the help of his disciplined lieutenants, to emerge victorious. Morrison did not believe Cormann was complicit in Dutton's challenge, and does not care, saying in an interview that, even if he was, it was 'irrelevant'. As you would say, if you were the ultimate beneficiary from such tumultuous events.

After his ascension, there was no doubt that Morrison was helped by the perception that he had clean hands. Not everyone believed that he did – certainly not Dutton and those close to him. Dutton's backers reported that Morrison's men were active well before Dutton challenged Turnbull. Victorian Jason Wood, who had threatened to do the numbers against Turnbull for Dutton, later claimed that Morrison's men had been telling backbenchers before the first ballot that Turnbull was finished. So did Queenslander Ross Vasta.

Nor did those closest to Turnbull believe that Morrison was clean. Turnbull's suspicions also grew, particularly in the light of accusations that while Morrison always appeared to be supportive (such as with Abbott), he was doing everything he could to further his own career.

According to those close to Turnbull, it was Morrison who had fired up the two West Australians, Luke Simpkins and Don Randall, to move the empty-chair spill motion against Abbott in February 2015. There were those who never trusted him and regarded him as a habitual underminer.

After Turnbull's 2015 coup against Abbott, the right had no doubt that Morrison had betrayed Abbott. Abbott had appealed to him on the night of Turnbull's challenge to run as his deputy and to take the treasurer's job held by Hockey. Morrison refused. He did not want to throw Hockey under a bus – plus, on his reckoning, it would not have saved Abbott. Morrison, already set to become Turnbull's treasurer, had concluded well before that night that Abbott was terminal. He spent the remaining hours in his office watching events unfold on television, eating the leftover curry he had made, with his great friend David Gazard. Here, the Turnbullites and the Abbottites were on a unity ticket, convinced that Morrison had been undermining Hockey, background-briefing selected journalists as the 2014 budget tanked.

Morrison was mightily offended a few days after Turnbull succeeded in wresting the leadership when Ray Hadley asked him to swear on a bible that he had not betrayed Abbott. Morrison could see no bible in the Canberra studio, despite Hadley's claim that there was one there – and even if there was, Morrison would not have complied. His faith was a serious matter, and he wasn't going to engage in such a stunt.

So as far as Morrison's detractors were concerned, an unmistakeable pattern of behaviour had been exposed.

Ultimately, though, once Turnbull knew he was done for, his primary objective was to see Dutton go down, even if it meant that Morrison succeeded. Whatever suspicions Turnbull had, he knew full well that Morrison had not initiated the coup. Turnbull's view, shared by Morrison, was that Morrison's best option for realising his ambition was for Turnbull to lead the government to victory in 2019 and then retire midway through the next term, paving the way for Morrison to take over.

Morrison was Australia's seventh prime minister in 11 years, following Malcolm Turnbull, Tony Abbott, Kevin Rudd, Julia Gillard, Kevin Rudd, and John Howard. It cemented Australia's humiliating status as the Italy of the Pacific, the coup capital of the world, exceeding the churn of prime ministers between 1966 when Menzies retired, Harold Holt drowned, and Fraser replaced Whitlam in 1975. Yet voters did not hold it against Morrison. He was determined from the moment he became prime minister to make Bill Shorten his John Hewson. He believed he could replicate Paul Keating's feat in 1993, and win the unwinnable election against Shorten.

Not a single public poll predicted it, and few inside his government dared to hope it was possible, not even the day before it happened. The most they had hoped for was a respectable loss. Everything leading up to it suggested that even this was optimistic.

Turnbull had said repeatedly that he would quit parliament if he were deposed. That was another promise he kept. He told people he had been through such a dark time when he lost the leadership in 2009 that he could not bear to go through something like that again. Pyne said if anyone thought he would stay, they were crazy.

'I remember how he only just pulled himself out of it last time,' Pyne said later. 'He wasn't going to put his health at risk.'

Turnbull's abrupt overthrow, his subsequent failure to openly and publicly endorse Dave Sharma, the man chosen to replace him, helped ensure that the Liberals lost his seat of Wentworth to high-profile independent Dr Kerryn Phelps at the ensuing by-election. Accusations of sabotage were levelled at Turnbull, mainly by people who had worked day and night to sabotage his prime ministership and to obliterate him from the political landscape, who had argued when he was there that he was useless, and then when he was gone that he had an obligation to help the Liberals win.

Three months later, the Victorian election showed that many people who had previously voted Liberal were waiting, not with baseball bats, but bazookas. They were not interested in anything the Liberal Party had to say. It wasn't just that they were still simmering over Turnbull's ousting. It wasn't just that they were furious over the civil war ignited by the overthrow of one more prime minister. It was also because many of them felt that the modern Liberal Party was no longer speaking their language.

As Kelly O'Dwyer famously put it, only months before she announced her retirement from politics, people now regarded the party she had joined as a teenager, attracted by its live-and-let-live credo, as 'homophobic, anti-women climate-change deniers'.

In the wake of the Victorian election, the mad right argued that it didn't matter what happened there, because Queensland would decide who formed government.

That was only partly true. As it turned out, Morrison picked up two seats in Queensland, where Labor's primary vote dropped to a miserable 27 per cent, leaving the party with only six out of 30 seats. But he also managed to hang on to most of the seats at risk in Victoria. It was an extraordinary feat. In January, only a few months before the federal election, the Liberals' private polling showed they were on track to lose between six and eight seats in Victoria alone, including their jewels in the crown of Higgins, Kooyong, and Goldstein. Morrison would have been gone.

On election day, families and young people in Melbourne's leafy suburbs told Liberal candidates on the booths that they didn't mind paying extra tax to fight climate change. Even so, Liberals on smaller margins in the outer suburbs, in seats such as Aston and Deakin that include parts of the state's bible belt – where people actually did mind paying more tax – managed to hold on. Tony Smith, a good local member as well as a great Speaker, had a small swing to him in Casey on the two-party-preferred count. In Kooyong, Frydenberg's primary vote fell by almost 8 per cent, and in Higgins, the two-party-preferred vote fell by just over 6 per cent. Tim Wilson's primary vote dropped by around 3 per cent. They were all saved by their big margins.

Before he lost the leadership, Turnbull had polling which showed that the Liberals were on track to win back seats in Tasmania, and possibly regain Herbert in Queensland. He was confident, given his standing in the southern state, that he would hold on to all seats in Victoria, including the two notional Labor seats of Corangamite and Dunkley, to give him a slightly larger majority than in 2016. It wasn't to be. It could only have worked if the disunity stopped, and there was little hope it ever would while he remained leader. Then, after he left, the Liberals had to fight tooth and nail twice for his seat of Wentworth. Money and volunteers had to be poured into Warringah in what many believed was a futile effort to save Abbott.

Turnbull had obvious cross-party appeal, in those early days before the compromises he made became too pronounced and too frequent, drawing votes to the Liberals from Labor and the Greens. Even that, though, was ultimately used against him, as his enemies spat that he was Labor lite, or that he had lost 'the base', which these days means different things to different people, because the Liberal Party has now become an altogether different beast. In Queensland, Victoria, and Western Australia, moderate Liberals grew increasingly alarmed by the active recruitment of the religious right and their widespread takeover of branches. Lacking their own structures or organisation, these fundamentally socially conservative people, not averse to big spending and big government, found a home under the Liberal banner and then began to take over the brand. Initially, the boost in numbers was welcomed; later, when it became clear what was happening, as preselections were threatened or determined by deeply conservative strongholds hostile to the leadership, there was the beginning of a fightback by more traditional conservative and small l-liberals disturbed by the dramatically changing culture and character of the party.

It remains a battle for another day; however, Morrison, a social conservative whose last act before the final vote was to pray in his office with Stuart Robert, was very much at ease with the new base. He was never happier than when flying solo, so confident was he in his own judgement and his connections to these new members. Turnbull had operated differently as prime minister, making few captain's calls, seeking to make up for his suspect political judgement by treating his ministers as his chief political advisers. He had a good office, with Clive Mathieson as chief of staff, Sally Cray as his principal adviser, David Bold as the contact person for crossbenchers, and a respected media team under Mark Simkin. He restored proper cabinet processes, which had been missing since the Howard era. Inevitably, that slowed down decision-making.

It drove Dutton crazy.

Dutton's discontent had built over time. Towards the end of 2017, Mathias Cormann, his closest friend and confidant in politics, the man Dutton says was like a brother to him, whom he kept informed at all times on all manner of things, had told close friends that while he would stick with Turnbull, he was not sure that Dutton would. Cormann let it drop way back then that Dutton would consider his options around October 2018. When Cormann said this, Turnbull was heading towards the loss of 30 Newspolls in a row – the benchmark he had unwisely set when he launched his challenge against Abbott.

Dutton planned to strike with the release of the 40th losing Newspoll, due around 10 September 2018, which marked the beginning of a scheduled two-week sitting bracket.

'That was D-Day,' he told me later. It was a damn-near perfect fit with the timetable that Cormann had outlined less than a year before. One of those urging Dutton to move against Turnbull, and who was lobbying Queensland MPs to vote against the prime minister, was the then Queensland Liberal National Party president, Gary Spence, who had severed relations with Turnbull after an angry phone conversation. Spence blamed Turnbull and/or his office for unsourced briefings to the media that were highly critical of the Liberal National Party's conduct of the Longman by-election campaign, which had seen the party's primary vote drop below 30 per cent.

Not all Queenslanders were convinced that Dutton was the man for the job. Ross Vasta had become friends with Dutton when he was still a teenager. At the time, the ambitious, enthusiastic 19-year-old Dutton was embarking on a futile mission – to unseat Labor's Tommy Burns in the ultra-safe seat of Lytton. As much as he liked Dutton, Vasta had decided well before August 2018 that Turnbull was finished, and he appealed to his old friend on the Monday night before the first ballot to step aside in favour of Bishop and then to run on a ticket with her as her deputy.

Vasta was convinced that would be a winning combination, more so if they raced off to an early election. A year earlier, when Vasta and Bishop had played the political parlour game on leadership, Bishop had told him that if she ever got there, she would not make the same mistake as Turnbull. She would go to an election during her honeymoon period. Dutton loathed Bishop, and would not countenance being on a ticket with her. He told Vasta that this was 'my time'. It hadn't gone any better for Vasta when he had suggested to Turnbull earlier that same day that the Bishop–Dutton combination had a better chance of winning the next election than he did.

Despite Vasta's reservations about his electoral appeal, Dutton was confident he could breach the divide between right and left once he became leader and neutralised the negatives about him, drawing a pointed contrast in our interview between himself and Morrison's social and religious conservatism.

'I am no further right than Howard and Costello,' he said. 'I am not the evangelical here, not out-and-proud on abortion. I voted for gay marriage, and I wasn't going to bring Tony Abbott back. But you are framed with these things.'

Nevertheless, Turnbull was convinced that Dutton had been persuaded by the Abbottites and the Queensland Liberal National Party to mount the challenge.

Knowing that discontent was growing and that Dutton was coming for him, Turnbull seized control of the timing, deciding to bring on a leadership vote at the party meeting on 21 August, a week after the government's 38th loss in a row in Newspoll. The earlier-than-expected showdown was only one of the critical factors that contributed to Dutton's failure. It caught him and Cormann unprepared; despite all the media backgrounding and urging, and Dutton's intention to move in a few weeks or even that day, they were woefully ill-prepared to mount a coup against a sitting prime minister.

Excitement, chaos, and despair gripped the Dutton camp after the first vote. In the lead-up, Dutton had assured his other good friends, Steve Ciobo and Michael Keenan – such good friends that they holidayed together in Las Vegas – that he had the numbers to topple Turnbull. He told Ciobo that he and Cormann had gamed everything, and that the finance minister was fully on board.

So when the vote of 35 for Dutton was read out, Ciobo and Keenan did not think that Turnbull was finished – unlike others who were blissfully unaware of Dutton's private boasts. They thought that Dutton was, and that in the process they had wrecked their own careers and reputations. Ciobo's hopes of becoming treasurer, which had caused friction with Morrison, were dashed.

Keenan, who disliked Morrison intensely, was left feeling angry and humiliated. They did not know who or what to believe, fearing that Dutton had lied or exaggerated the extent of Cormann's support in order to convince them to come on board. There was a severe rupture in their friendship, which they insist has since been repaired.

In truth, Dutton would not have contemplated a strike against Turnbull without at the very least running it past Cormann. At the most, which is what Dutton told colleagues at the time and then strongly implied to others later, Cormann was intimately involved in its preparation and execution, and had even voted against Turnbull in the first vote on Tuesday.

It is also true that, at the most critical point, Cormann did betray the prime minister, snuffing out any chance he had of holding on.

Cormann, described by Dutton's supporters later as the commander-in-chief, or the general, of the ill-fated challenge, formally assumed the role on the Thursday, after defecting. Cormann publicly justified his defection by claiming that Turnbull was finished and insisting that Dutton had the numbers. Privately, Cormann later gave conflicting accounts about this. To Pyne, over dinner at the Commonwealth Club in Canberra, he said he was convinced that Dutton had had the numbers. To Ciobo, over dinner in Davos during the World Economic Forum, he said he did not believe Dutton had had the numbers, and denied he had helped formulate Dutton's plan.

The other undeniable truth is that many lies were told by many people that week, and that, by their actions, Cormann and Dutton inflicted incalculable damage on themselves, the government, and the Liberal Party.

Dutton's answer to the why-question – Why was Turnbull no longer prime minister? – was typically uncompromising. It carried no whiff whatsoever of regret or remorse. 'He blew himself up,' he said, referring to Turnbull's shock decision to vacate his leadership at that 21 August Liberal Party meeting. 'In his last act, an act of political self-immolation, he demonstrated he had no political judgement.'

Initially, Morrison refused to answer the why-question. Why was Turnbull no longer prime minister? Turnbull had retained a comfortable lead as preferred prime minister over Shorten. The last four Newspolls before his ousting showed that, at 49–51 per cent on a two-party-preferred measure, the government was competitive. Turnbull himself revealed internal Liberal polling that showed the government ahead in critical marginal seats. Assuming a good campaign, the Coalition was on track to do better in 2019 than it had in 2016.

Andrew Bragg, who withdrew from the preselection race for the Wentworth by-election, then later won a prized second spot on the New South Wales Senate ticket, had the most succinct, and probably truest, answer to the why-question: 'They hated him.' There was more to it than that, obviously, but that was a big part of it. There were those convinced, despite the narrowing polls, that the government was headed for a crushing defeat. Queensland MPs, in the main, were worried they would lose their seats. For others, it was a mix of reasons: mainly that he wasn't listening; that his political radar – if it ever existed – was defective; that he deserved it because of what he had done to Abbott or Brendan Nelson; that they feared Abbott's undermining would never stop until they lost; or that they were miffed because he was neglecting them; or whatever.

The Longman by-election, one of five on Super Saturday, 28 July 2018 – four of them because of the dual-citizenship dramas that had plagued the parliament for months as MPs of all colours fell like skittles – was the catalyst, and energy policy was the trigger, although it could have been anything. The two-party-preferred swing that heralded Turnbull's demise was 3.7 per cent in a seat the Liberals had already lost in 2016. In 2001, John Howard retained the seat of Aston despite a swing of 3.6 per cent against the Liberals, yet it heralded his comeback. It was the near 10 per cent drop in the primary vote in Longman that unsettled MPs and made energy policy tougher. Really, though, for Turnbull's enemies, policy was incidental. If it wasn't Longman and energy, it would have surely been the vexed debate over religious freedom (an overflow from the same-sex marriage debate), which Turnbull, being intent on resolving the energy policy, kept delaying. Backbenchers knew that.

Morrison's role, and those of his supporters, in Turnbull's ousting was clever, controversial, and deadly. All along, Morrison stuck to his formula that he had not initiated the change of leadership. That is true. It is also true that Morrison, fearing the demons it would unleash, had not advocated a change. He did not engineer it, and he did what he could to forestall it and to save Turnbull from himself and from his enemies.

But the people closest to Morrison in Canberra, people he lived and prayed with, knew long before that it was coming, and then took full advantage of the opening that the instability created. They were ready, they were highly motivated, they were better organised, and they had worked harder and longer to make sure that Morrison and not Dutton succeeded Turnbull.

Morrison publicly professed his loyalty, telling everyone who asked – and again, many were asking – that he would not run if Turnbull ran. He did not declare his candidacy until he received the all-clear from Turnbull that he could. Morrison says that came on Wednesday evening. A few hours earlier, at one of those memorable moments that often occur in times of high drama, Morrison was asked at a press conference with Turnbull and Cormann if he had leadership ambitions. Morrison, in a premeditated gesture, ostentatiously threw his arm around Turnbull, saying, 'Me? This is my leader, and I'm ambitious for him.' Standing on the other side of Turnbull, at an event to bury the company tax cuts rather than the prime minister, was Cormann. He had tried to get out of attending. Like a cigar-store Indian, Cormann woodenly professed his loyalty in response to questions, saying he would continue to serve Turnbull 'loyally into the future' – a future that did not last beyond the setting of the sun.

Morrison's two Canberra housemates, Stuart Robert and Steve Irons, and his chief numbers man, Alex Hawke, who were also members of a regular prayer group, had not been sitting around twiddling their thumbs. They knew early on that Dutton was on the move. Like him, they had concluded that Turnbull was terminal, so they planned accordingly. Hawke had numbers of who stood where, stored for months in his laptop.

A number of key Morrison backers voted for Dutton in the first ballot, when Turnbull declared his and Julie Bishop's positions vacant, thereby inflating Dutton's numbers as well as his ego. It was not because they wanted Dutton, but because they no longer wanted Turnbull. Ben Morton, who believed in Morrison almost as much as Morrison believed in himself, who later travelled with him, advising him during the election campaign, was one of them; Lucy Wicks, another. For the few days he immersed himself in Morrison's campaign, Morton moved out of the apartment in Kingston he shared with Andrew Hastie, who had signed up to the Dutton campaign. They wanted to preserve their friendship, and thought that was the safest way to do it. It worked. Morton moved back in when it was over. He became a critical figure in all of Morrison's ensuing victories.

Irons gave an enigmatic answer when he was asked who he voted for in that first ballot, while Robert and Hawke insisted they voted for Turnbull. They also say the first they knew that Turnbull would be vacating the leadership was when he announced it in the party room.

Dutton scoffs at this. In an interview for this book conducted in mid-November 2018, Dutton said he had concluded that all of them had voted for him, and that the deputy whip, Bert van Manen, had most likely tipped them off to Turnbull's decision to vacate the leadership that morning. The trick was for enough of Morrison's supporters to vote for Dutton so that Turnbull would be seen by everyone to be terminal. For this to work, the vote against Turnbull had to be in the thirties. That would have required a bit of war-gaming, a confident appreciation of where the numbers lay, and a little bit of notice to implement. They had all three essential ingredients.

Dutton believed that van Manen was an integral part of their ultimately successful strategy. He was a Morrison man, and also a member of the prayer group that they all attended when parliament sat. The chief whip, Nola Marino, and her principal parliamentary adviser, Nathan Winn, had been through enough challenges to know when one was imminent. Marino and Winn (the same Winn who had been despatched by former whip Alex Somlyay years before to wake Abbott from a drunken stupor because he was missing divisions in opposition) decided on Monday to begin preparing the ballot papers.

Twenty minutes before Tuesday's meeting began, Marino told her two deputies, South Australian Rowan Ramsey and van Manen, to get ballot papers ready for a vote on the leadership. They sorted out who would do what inside the meeting. Ramsay swears he did not tell a soul, while van Manen, listed the day after by several media outlets as having voted for Dutton in the first ballot, refused all requests to be interviewed or to answer any questions about what he did that day.

Dutton, believing that Marino had been forewarned rather than forearmed, was certain that van Manen tipped off his friends in advance once Marino told him to get the ballots ready. He certainly had enough time to text his friends or to speak to them.

Dutton was not the only one who was suspicious. Laundy

believed at the time that 10 votes of Morrison's went to Dutton. Turnbull's office did separate tallies of the votes on Tuesday morning before the meeting began, based alternately on Morrison's people voting with the prime minister, and voting against him. Their count with Morrison's people voting against Turnbull was 35, which – surprise, surprise – was the ultimate result.

The Morrison votes boosted the anti-Turnbull vote on Tuesday, and then on Friday ensured passage of the spill motion that was the final nail in Turnbull's prime ministership, all of which adds to the conspiracy theories about Morrison.

Morrison is highly sensitive to the charge, and rejects the proposition that his people voted against Turnbull, even though at least one admits it. He is agitated when he is asked about what his people knew, when they knew it, and how long in advance they had been canvassing votes. Morrison had warned Turnbull the previous weekend, when the speculation about Dutton was rife, not to bring on a leadership vote. He says he warned him the night before the first fateful party meeting that there could be as many as 35 MPs voting against him, made it clear to Cormann that if he defected he would be 'terminating the government', and then urged Turnbull to send everyone home after parliament adjourned to avoid a second ballot that week.

On the surface, he did what he could to save Turnbull. Below ground, Morrison's men did everything they could, whatever they had to do, to get him the leadership.

Morrison insists he was 'shocked' when Turnbull announced in the party room that he was vacating the leadership. In an interview conducted for this book in December 2018, Morrison said he was not given any warning this was about to happen, did not believe his people were tipped off in advance, and maintained that while Turnbull gave him the all-clear on Wednesday night, nothing had been 'activated' at that point.

This skates over the assiduous courting and counting already undertaken by his housemates. He knew that at least one of his senior lieutenants, Stuart Robert, had begun talking to MPs well before that, because Robert had told him he was going to do so.

In discussions that were deeply damaging to Turnbull and would not have helped his vote on Tuesday, Robert was telling MPs on Monday night, hours before the ballot, that Turnbull's prime ministership was terminal. Robert also said in an interview with me that he urged Morrison immediately after Tuesday's party meeting to run, telling him it was his patriotic duty to do so, and that he was going to begin asking colleagues to vote for Morrison over Dutton. Morrison responded to Robert by saying he was supporting Turnbull and was not 'authorising' him to do that. Robert told me, 'We told him we were going to do it. We were not asking permission.'

Robert was onto it within an hour, but it was a continuation, not a beginning.

Dutton reckoned that once Turnbull put it all together, he would retaliate against Morrison and the government in an effort to ensure its certain defeat. Morrison and those close to him were on alert for that very thing, nervously expecting that at some point Turnbull would weigh into the campaign in an effort to derail him and destroy his chances of winning. Turnbull had made a number of unhelpful interventions before the campaign proper began, but once Morrison called it, Turnbull and Lucy flew to New York. He came back the day after, publicly – not privately – congratulated Morrison on his victory, and gave Dutton a flick. 'I'm very glad that in that dreadful time in August he succeeded to the prime ministership rather than Peter Dutton,' he told Channel 7 news. Dutton gave him a flick back, saying they could never have won with Turnbull.

So was Morrison loyal? Define 'loyalty' in politics. It is very complicated.

One experienced Liberal numbers man put it this way, 'The

Dutton camp was plotting; the Morrison camp was planning.' He thought there was a difference. If there was, Ken Wyatt, the first indigenous person to be elected to the House of Representatives, could not see it. 'In politics, you never plan; you always plot,' he said, and laughed. Morrison later appointed him as the first indigenous person to cabinet, and the first to be made responsible for indigenous affairs.

Or it could be a case of those who pray together plot together.

There were definitely differences in what was driving individuals in the two camps. The primary objective of a number of the high-profile monkey-podders, as they were known – the conservatives who met regularly in the monkey-pod room, which derives its name from the wood of its large, highly polished table – the triple-As of Abbott, Eric Abetz, and Kevin Andrews, who attached themselves to Dutton, was to wreck and undermine, to kill Turnbull.

It was not to make Dutton prime minister. Morrison's was a much smaller group, tightly knit, with a singular objective. Although they did not plot to overthrow Turnbull, they knew full well what the others were up to and what the consequences would be, and at critical points they intervened in ways that would help Morrison. They were more than ready, because their primary objective was to make Morrison prime minister.

Contrast this with Dutton's camp, which was ill-equipped, inexperienced, and heavy-handed. Dutton never had the numbers to get there – only enough to terminally wound Turnbull, and only then because of the strategically placed votes of Morrison's men and women.

Turnbull's other mistake was to choose a moment when he was at his weakest to put his leadership on the line.

His strategy, to flush out his enemies, worked too well. There were too many of them to ignore. His support that day, after the continuing debacle of energy policy, was at a low ebb. The high vote against him instantly rendered his position untenable and irretrievable. As he struggled to come to grips with this, he threatened at various times to drive to Yarralumla to ask the governor-general to dissolve parliament so he could call an election, or to call Sir Peter Cosgrove and, as the serving prime minister, advise him that Dutton could not be sworn in as prime minister because he was ineligible to sit in the parliament.

Laundy, Sinodinos, and a few other trusted colleagues and his loyal staff played a vital role in getting him from that position to the agonising point of acceptance, to allow Morrison to take up Dutton's challenge.

From Turnbull's perspective, everybody had ulterior motives. Pyne and the moderates needed Turnbull to accept that it was over so they could mobilise for Morrison to make sure he, and not Dutton, got up. A key part of that strategy involved deliberately sacrificing Bishop, because they calculated that Dutton would beat her – and they could not tolerate him as leader. Morrison, who had pledged not to challenge Turnbull, also needed Turnbull to accept it was over so he could break out and campaign openly with his lieutenants, who had been operating covertly for days, with his knowledge, and who had been collating numbers of who stood where for months.

Dutton was fighting them all, with the majority of the right on his side. He was angry with Turnbull for running the campaign over his eligibility to sit in the parliament, believing this had caused him the most damage. However, the clever manoeuvring by Morrison and his lieutenants, the tough tactics of the moderates, and the loss of two key votes on Friday morning – Mitch Fifield and Scott Ryan – all contributed to Dutton's loss.

Turnbull's strike on Abbott in September 2015 had been surgical. Abbott's revenge fuelled his guerrilla/gorilla campaign that Turnbull later likened to political terrorism, which intensified whenever it looked like the government might stabilise or – heaven forbid – even forge ahead of Labor in the polls. It helped create the climate for Dutton to strike, but it was a half-arsed plot from the outset. Dutton was puffed up by the Bullies and Co., who never got over losing Abbott.

Dutton forgot one of the cardinal rules of politics: never believe your own BS, and never believe the BS fed to you by people who you think are your friends but aren't.

In the view of some in his camp, Dutton made a serious tactical error. They reckon he should have pulled back and waited to make a second strike, rather than immediately insist on another ballot. The next Newspoll would have been horrific, and made backbenchers even more panic-stricken. Yes, that would have given Morrison more time to organise, or for voters to browbeat their MPs into backing off. But Dutton could have used the time, too, if only to put together a proper campaign team and a more credible platform for change. Others thought he was right to keep going, to strike again while the temperature was red-hot.

Dutton also had two almighty drags on his ticket.

Abbott was the first. Dutton had already made it clear to Abbott long before he moved on Turnbull that he would not be Abbott's Trojan horse. What's more, he claimed later, if he succeeded in winning the leadership, he never intended appointing Abbott to his ministry, although Abbott and his supporters believed he was on a promise for that to happen. Dutton told anyone who asked him, and there were plenty asking him, that there was no such promise. They either didn't believe it, or didn't want to risk it. Swinging MPs were fearful of what it implied – that not only would Abbott be restored, but that he would bring his former chief of staff, Peta Credlin, with him. They were anxious that bastardry not be rewarded. They muttered about dire consequences if Abbott returned in any way, shape, or form. So soiled was Abbott internally by then that most of them wanted him to disappear.

Abbott knew that if Turnbull were to win the 2019 election, he would never be leader again. He believed Dutton would win the leadership, then lose the election, and that Liberals would once again turn to him to lead them back from opposition. He forgot to factor in Morrison, never believing he would win, as he fantasised to people that if Morrison lost the election, the party would turn to him again. 'I'm here to serve,' he would say publicly to those who asked if he continued to harbour leadership ambitions. Privately, he was a lot more open about what he thought – or hoped – would happen.

Momentarily, perhaps forgetting again his pledge not to white-ant or undermine, discounting the possibility of a Morrison win or that he might lose his seat, it wasn't long before Abbott was privately retailing unflattering anecdotes about Morrison, and publicly telling journalists he would be available to be drafted as leader after the election. He would say that Morrison's preselection victory in the seat of Cook in 2007, after Michael Towke was dumped as the candidate following allegations of serial branch stacking (later disproved), had tainted Morrison's entry into politics and raised questions about his integrity. An anecdote also surfaced to the effect that Morrison had asked Abbott in 2015 to dump Hockey as treasurer and appoint him because of the failures of the 2014 budget. Morrison denied that it had happened. All fingers pointed to Abbott as the source.

Abbott was aggrieved, but he had long ago lost any right to cast himself as an innocent or as a victim in leadership machinations.

The reward for Abbott's treachery against Turnbull was to have to fight for his life in his own seat against former Olympian turned barrister Zali Steggall, who ran against him as an independent. Liberals in Warringah turned on him in their thousands, with a swing against him of almost 13 per cent on primaries. Mature-age people who had voted Liberal since their youth could not bring themselves to vote for him because of the destruction he had wrought, because he did not support action on climate change, and because he had ignored their wishes and abstained from voting for same-sex marriage. He no longer stood for any of the things they believed in, nor would he even stand up for *them* and the things they believed in.

In what was otherwise a dignified concession speech, Abbott declared on the night that he would rather be a loser than a quitter, which some took to be a dig at Turnbull and others for having resigned from the parliament. He would have spared everyone, including himself, a lot of heartache if he had also resigned after losing the prime ministership. Most of his colleagues breathed a sigh of relief that he was gone. The voters had done what the party couldn't. Despite a thumping win, Morrison still had some rebuilding to do, and the task would be easier without Abbott. For the first time in a long time, no former leader sat in parliament behind the serving leader. It was a clean break.

The second drag on Dutton's ticket was Greg Hunt. One of Dutton's most prominent backers, Michael Sukkar, later remarked he had no idea that Hunt was so unpopular inside the parliamentary party. Although both Sukkar and Hunt hailed from Victoria, it was the other Victorians, led by Dan Tehan, who mobilised against the health minister to make sure he failed, and to make sure that Josh Frydenberg, formerly one of Hunt's best friends, became deputy leader.

Politics is such a cruel business.

Turnbull's denouement remains a sorry saga of betrayal, conspiracy, miscalculation, hubris, and conflicting loyalties and emotions. It involved many characters with a complex web of relationships, both personal and political. Friendships unravelled, reputations were trashed, careers wrecked, resignations hastened, distrust embedded, and respect for the political class even further eroded. It was driven by a thirst for revenge, blind ambition, blind hatred, disappointment, and panic. It triggered premature retirements, accusations of bullying, and lingering regrets. It delivered chaos, disunity, and (threatened) electoral massacre.

The repercussions were immense as the casualties mounted. The leadership of the moderates collapsed. Brandis was long gone. Turnbull quit parliament, as did Bishop and Pyne. Other high-profile moderates, including Kelly O'Dwyer, retired. The right did not escape unscathed. Dutton and Cormann were badly damaged. Best mates Michael Keenan and Steve Ciobo announced within weeks of each other that they were quitting parliament. Friendships and alliances ruptured. Some repaired. Others didn't – either because of lies told or suspected of having been told, or because of positions taken during the challenge.

The departures tore at the fabric and image of the Morrison government and the Liberal Party in the months before the election. After the election, their departures were seen as a blessing for Morrison. A new generation meant a new beginning, although the scars would always be there. Coup plotters, including Cormann, who later tried to tell colleagues and friends that the election win had justified their actions, were soon put in their place.

There was a formidable array of forces inside the party, and powerful spruikers outside it, who had been determined from the moment he became prime minister to destroy Turnbull. The religious right, which had tightened its grip on the Liberal Party, was still raging over same-sex marriage. Bullies and Co. on Fox After Dark, aka Sky, and elsewhere, never forgave him for killing Tony Abbott. Abbott never forgave him. Together, using all available media platforms of print, radio, and television, they conspired to bring him down, no matter the cost, even if the ultimate price turned out to be a Labor victory.

Turnbull's subsequent claim that he was deposed because of fears he would win, and not because of fears he would lose, was not as mad as it sounded. Abbott and his friends were so consumed with destroying Turnbull that they did not care if they destroyed the government in the process.

Party moderates who remained loyal to Turnbull to the end, along with his staff, were not blind to his flaws, but they loved and admired him nonetheless. They surrounded him and sustained him through those difficult final days. While Turnbull did not cry, at least not in front of his colleagues and staff, many of them did – including Pyne, who admitted that on Turnbull's last day he had not shed so many tears since his beloved father had died.

Turnbull was reluctant to let go of the job he had craved for most of his life. It is no small thing to give up a prime ministership, to accept it has ended. Everyone around him understood that, even as they persuaded him to accept the inevitable. It was over from the moment the result of the first ballot was announced, when 35 of his colleagues voted against him.

At the end, only one member of the original group that had helped Turnbull depose Abbott, the G8, was by his side when he walked into his final party-room meeting. Laundy, whose role in 2015 as a fledgling politician could best be described as a plus-one, walked on one side of Turnbull. On the other was Sinodinos, barely back at work after cancer treatment, barely recognisable, whom Turnbull had rung on the Wednesday night, after what he considered to be the ultimate betrayal by Cormann, to ask him to please come to Canberra because there might only be one vote in it.

The other one who stuck, and who was heavily involved both times in the tactics, counting, and planning, was Simon Birmingham. Solid and steady – apart from one brain snap during the long and dirty battle over Catholic school funding – Birmingham had held true to moderate causes, and looks set to emerge as their leading advocate. Pyne was not involved in 2015, but in 2018, he, Birmingham, Paul Fletcher, Marise Payne, and Trent Zimmerman formed a new Praetorian Guard that initially fought to save Turnbull. When they realised he was lost, they sought to convince him he was gone and that he should consider withdrawing from the race. Then they mercilessly cut Bishop loose before coalescing around Morrison to block Dutton. Dutton backers, including Zed Seselja, could not help but be impressed by their ruthless tactics.

Scott Ryan, who voted for Turnbull on Tuesday, and had offered to walk in with him to that final party-room meeting on his last day but never heard back, had been placed in the Dutton camp. Ryan was not intimately involved with Turnbull in the final days. He had also drifted away from Turnbull long before that. Instead, Ryan joined Dan Tehan's campaign to make sure that Frydenberg won the deputy's ballot; and then, after consulting with his close friends, Ryan voted for Morrison.

In 2016, Wyatt Roy had lost his seat of Longman to Labor's Susan Lamb, who was later deemed ineligible to sit in parliament because of her dual citizenship, which forced the by-election that delivered the drop in the LNP's primary vote, which turned Queenslanders violently against Turnbull and precipitated the coup. More karma. Peter Hendy lost the bellwether seat of Eden-Monaro. Mal Brough was forced to quit his ministry in February 2015, and announced he would not be recontesting his seat at the 2016 election. Mitch Fifield joined Cormann in defecting on the Thursday after voting for Turnbull on the Tuesday, and James McGrath voted for Dutton in all ballots that week.

McGrath would later dub it 'The curse of the leadership spill'.

The group, or what was left of it – including Ryan, McGrath, and Sinodinos – had become unsettled by a meeting in Turnbull's office in February 2017. The 2016 election result and everything that flowed from it had been disastrous. McGrath thought it would be a good idea to regroup, or, as he put it to them, 'to get the band back together' to try to work out how to make that year better than the previous one.

They were dismayed when Turnbull reached out to people like Angus Taylor and promoted others who would not only never vote for him, but were suspected of briefing against them and other close allies like Kelly O'Dwyer in an effort to damage them. They had warned Turnbull about Alan Tudge, Michael Sukkar, and Greg Hunt. Turnbull dismissed their concerns, saying that as leader he had to reward people on merit if they deserved it. He had little choice but to bring people in that he knew were opposed to him. McGrath thought it was madness. The old adage was to keep your friends close and your enemies closer.

His friends were beginning to feel alienated, isolated, and ignored, and that he was promoting their enemies at their expense. No good could come from that, and none did.

McGrath, whose methodical cunning, planning, and numbers-counting had been integral to Turnbull's successful 2015 challenge to Abbott, had switched to Dutton.

He was angry at the breakdown of his relationship with Turnbull, and felt sick when he voted for Dutton in the first party-room ballot. He offered advice and moral support, but played no structural role in Dutton's coup attempt. He does not expect to speak to Turnbull again.

A couple of weeks after the coup, when a friend told McGrath there was a 99 per cent chance the government would get smashed at the election, McGrath's black humour sprang back. No, he said, it was more like 95 per cent. For McGrath, it was only ever about Queensland. Again, in his typically sardonic way, he told an anecdote to those who asked him why he had abandoned Turnbull. He would beg Turnbull to visit the regions to spend time there, and Malcolm would say something like, I was only there a few months ago, opening a solar farm. Which Turnbull indeed had, at Barcaldine. He had also visited Birdsville to inspect a telecom cable, but he had not gone on to visit drought-stricken properties. To McGrath, this summed up the problem: Malcolm had his own agenda, and Queenslanders never thought he liked or understood them. And yet, when they saw him, they liked him, and wanted to see more of him. And then, just when McGrath thought his people, including his parents, were beginning to really like him, as opposed to just tolerating him, Longman happened. Suddenly, they wanted him gone.

Dutton had spent polling day in Longman on the booths with the Liberal candidate, Trev Ruthenberg. Big Trev, as they called him, turned out to be a Big Dud who couldn't even get his resumé right, but he was the best the LNP could get to run in a seat they did not believe they could win back from Labor. Nevertheless, on polling day, Dutton was taken aback by the unsolicited character references for the prime minister he was offered. They hate him, he told people later that night. At that point, Dutton felt free to separate from his leader.

Barely three weeks later, on Friday 17 August, the *Daily Telegraph* reported that Dutton was considering a challenge. Later that day, Ray Hadley, with his impeccable contacts, broke into regular programming on 2GB to confirm that Dutton was definitely going to challenge, but was waiting until the next Newspoll. It was not until Saturday, more than 30 hours later – the equivalent of a lifetime in a 24/7 news cycle – after a number of conversations with Turnbull, that Dutton sent out a desultory, fulsome (in the true sense of the word) tweet. The tweet, the wording of which had been agreed with Turnbull, was too little, too late to kill the speculation.

'In relation to media stories today, just to make very clear, the Prime Minister has my support and I support the policies of the government. My position hasn't changed from my comments last Thursday,' Dutton tweeted. This was a reference to an earlier interview with Hadley, when Dutton said the world would know if he had lost faith in Turnbull, because he would resign from his cabinet.

Turnbull, in the words of his friends, had a choice. He knew they were coming for him, and he could either die on his feet or live on his knees. It came as no surprise to them that he chose to bring on the fight. He decided, with Lucy, on Monday night what he would do, and then told his closest adviser, Sally Cray, in a pre-dawn phone call that he was going to bring it on.

It was a fateful call with startling consequences, which threatened to leave the Liberals in ruins. Instead, they found a new saviour, the Messiah from the Shire, as *The Australian* called him – one that few Liberals had any real idea existed, but one with unbounded faith in his ability to deliver. And he did.

CHAPTER TWO

Whine and whispers

When the five-star Westin hotel opened its doors in late April 2018 in Perth, renowned Australian–Italian chef Guy Grossi was waxing lyrical about his new restaurant, Garum, housed within the 368-room hotel.

Who would have thought that Grossi would have become, however briefly, an observer in a discussion full of intrigue and omens, the type that all political tragics toss around a table whenever the urge strikes, whenever the wine flows, or the conversation slows? It happened in the Westin's wine cellar for a specially selected group of Perth's political movers and shakers.

Julian Ambrose, whose company BGC (Australia) Pty Ltd partnered to develop the site, was the host. Grossi was over from Melbourne for the opening, and prepared lunch for the group, a four-course sharing menu beginning with antipasto, followed by pasta, then a choice of fish, veal, or beef, finishing with tiramisu, cheese, and coffee. It was lip-smackingly good food, particularly the Creste di Gallo with pecorino, silver beet, and sultana. How delicious is it that this pasta is so called because its shape resembles the crest of a rooster, which is what some of the lunchers were back then, only to become feather dusters, or plucked and battered deep-fried carcasses, in the space of a few days, only a few months later?

Grossi accepted the invitation of the group to join them for a few minutes for a drink while they ate and drank. Along the way, they devoured the lunches of their Canberra colleagues as well.

Included in the group of 12 was the finance minister, Mathias Cormann; the attorney-general, Christian Porter; the human services minister, Michael Keenan; federal Liberal backbencher and former Western Australia state director, Ben Morton; lobbyist and former state director, Paul Everingham; and Western Australia state Liberal frontbencher and local powerbroker, Peter Collier.

As it always does at these kinds of gatherings, the conversation turned to how the government was travelling. As always, it got around to another popular topic – the prime minister's hearing. Keenan and Porter complained that he had a bit of a tin ear. Cormann defended Turnbull, saying he was getting better and was in fact much better than he had been. That switched the conversation to what, years ago, I described as a political parlour game, when politicians and the media discuss alternatives to the leader if he or she just happened to be run over by a bus, or fall or be pushed under a heavy, fast-moving vehicle. Who was next best after Turnbull, they pondered. There were three possible contenders: Julie Bishop, Peter Dutton, and Scott Morrison.

Everingham said while he thought Bishop was the most electorally appealing and would probably win more seats, he reckoned Morrison was the best of the three. Cormann, whose dislike of Bishop bordered on the pathological (and it was mutual) glared at Everingham.

Neither Porter nor Keenan spoke in support of Bishop. In fact, they were critical of her. Cormann and Porter were both well disposed towards Turnbull.

Keenan had history with Morrison. Keenan had been a junior minister to Morrison when Morrison held the immigration portfolio. Morrison was single-minded in his pursuit of his objective of stopping the asylum-seeker boats. His success gained him a formidable reputation, and not always a favourable one. Keenan thought Morrison treated him like a schoolchild. At that lunch, Keenan let it drop that he thought Morrison was an 'absolute arsehole'.

Porter joined in, saying he did not think Morrison was a team player. Cormann said he had seen Morrison up close now, and, in his opinion, Dutton was better. Cormann and Dutton were best friends. They were political soul mates, so there was a bit of a feeling that he would say that, wouldn't he, but although he didn't spell it out then, Cormann had had a few testy exchanges with Morrison after he had taken over as treasurer from Joe Hockey. Morrison had shouted at Cormann, and after the second time he did it, Cormann – not averse to a bit of forceful talk himself – had told him to cut it out. It didn't happen again.

When they had all finished, Morton, who had been elected to parliament as the member for Tangney in 2016, said he agreed with Everingham. Morrison was the best out of the three. They got cranky with Morton, but he stuck to his guns: Morrison was the best.

People say lots of things over long lunches. One year after Abbott was elected prime minister, Keenan had vowed the Liberals would never do what Labor had done and dispose of a first-term prime minister. Less than a year later, Abbott was gone. After that, Keenan again said they were never going to do that again, and three years later they did, and he was part of it, much to his later shame and fury, as he voted against his leader in the first ballot, publicly pledged his loyalty to him the day after, then resigned the next day and voted against him again the day after that. The events that week were a big factor in his resignation from parliament. Cormann was part of it, too. So was Morton and so was Porter, in ways they could not have imagined back in April.

The roosters, or cocks, had not crowed thrice, but they soon would. They were not to know then exactly how things would unfold, although all of them were acutely aware of how much effort was going into destroying Turnbull, so talk of alternatives was not completely idle.

The poor 2016 election result had meant that Turnbull became even more reliant on Cormann and Dutton, and more beholden to the conservatives in his party. He was hostage to the whims of Pauline Hanson, who had won four Senate seats, and panic-stricken Queensland Nationals like George Christensen, who lived in mortal fear of One Nation and deep loathing of Turnbull, who threatened every other day to cross the floor to bring him down. It emboldened Abbott and those who remained in his orbit, oblivious to his faults or the consequences of the disunity they fostered.

So bad was the result that on election night, an angry Turnbull – the bad Malcolm, who sometimes emerged from the cave – had to be forced to go out to say a few words. His speech was late, it lacked grace, and it presaged a rocky period ahead.

Turnbull had been told early in his prime ministership that he needed to run a strong negative campaign against Bill Shorten and Labor. He was reluctant to do it. He wanted to keep it positive. He believed – wrongly – that he could triumph by seeking to inspire people rather than by playing on their fears.

Andrew Robb, who as federal director had been in charge of two campaigns – the first in 1993 when John Hewson lost the unloseable election because he insisted on trying to sell a great big new tax that he couldn't explain, and the second in 1996 that saw John Howard swept to victory with a classic positive/negative campaign – recalls a conversation with Turnbull a few months after he deposed Abbott.

The two men, who had a chequered history, were having a quiet Christmas drink at Turnbull's home at Point Piper.

As Robb recalls the conversation, Turnbull was posing a series of what-ifs to Robb, who was then in his cabinet as trade minister. What if the budget were brought forward, what if there were a double-dissolution election, what if the campaign went for eight weeks? One of Turnbull's questions was why campaigns had to be so deeply negative – surely there was a better alternative?

Robb had heard it all before from other leaders. It hadn't washed then, either.

Robb told Turnbull it was essential in a campaign that the consequences of electing Labor were fully exposed. People had to have a clear understanding of what they would face. 'If we don't do it, no one else will,' Robb said.

Robb said he had heard that Turnbull had had similar conversations with other colleagues. Later, Robb reflected that Turnbull was acting like he was listening, but wasn't really.

After it went pear-shaped, Robb said the loss of so many seats was 'unforgivable', and laid most of the blame at the door of the then prime minister.

Less than a year after the election, Robb was commissioned by the Liberal Party to conduct a review of the 2016 campaign. He and his fellow inquirers – former Brisbane city councillor Carol Cashman, former federal Liberal minister Chris Ellison, and former New South Wales premier Barry O'Farrell – undertook the assignment on the explicit understanding it would be made public when it was concluded. It wasn't. It has, however, since been made available.

In 2016, the Liberals picked up a solitary lower-house seat in Victoria – that of Chisholm, won by Julia Banks. It lost four in New South Wales, two in Queensland, one in Western Australia, two in South Australia, three in Tasmania, and one in the Northern Territory, to end up with 76 seats and a wafer-thin one-seat majority in the lower house. It lost three Senate seats.

It was a 55-day campaign that concentrated heavily on Turnbull, which was understandable, given he was their best asset. But by the end, it looked like he had run out of puff. Certainly, the party had run out of money. Along the way, just about every campaign rule was forgotten or flouted. While much of the blame can be laid at Turnbull's feet, it was not all his fault, and without the final injection of $1.75 million of his own money it no doubt would have been worse.

Bill Shorten launched Mediscare in the final stages of the campaign. Because of a shortage of money, the Liberals had pared back their research. It took too long to pick up the impact that the scare campaign was having with its central accusation that the government was preparing to privatise Medicare. Consequently, it took too long to respond to it.

The internal post-election review found that this failure to effectively rebut Labor's 'lies' had cost the Coalition six or seven seats.

The 51-page report makes for sobering reading. It contained ominous warnings, some of which were new or unique to 2016, and for which Turnbull was directly responsible, and others that echoed recommendations from earlier reports after other elections with other leaders at the helm, also ignored.

The review found fault everywhere: messaging; the campaign slogan; internal communications between headquarters and state divisions; the failure to run on Shorten's and Labor's negatives; the inadequate use of social media and the latest data-collection techniques; poor candidate selection in a number of seats; deficient fundraising; and bullying and intimidation of candidates at polling booths by people apparently linked to unions and Labor.

The problems for the Coalition and the seeds of the government's demise, according to this hard-headed analysis, began immediately under Abbott after won so handsomely in 2013. It underscored once again that while he and those around him knew what to do to win government, they didn't have a clue what to do once they got there to make sure they stayed there.

The fact that all this needed to be spelled out showed how degraded the Liberals' campaign structure had become. It was not all the fault of Tony Nutt, who had been appointed to replace Brian Loughnane after Turnbull deposed Abbott. The shortage of money meant he initially went without pay, and he only had a few months to try to get the place into shape, but he resigned as the party's federal director after the review was handed over. Pollster Mark 'Tex' Textor retreated to his property at Goulburn.

After they were appointed by Turnbull, the party's new federal president, Nick Greiner, and the new federal director, Andrew Hirst, travelled to each state to talk to divisions about their problems. They actually listened. Greiner agrees that the 2016 election was mostly responsible for Turnbull's problems, but he also thinks it goes slightly further back to his ascension. Greiner thinks the deals he made with the right and with the Nationals on issues like climate change and same-sex marriage constrained his leadership to the extent that he was not the prime minister people thought he would be.

Almost all of 2017, beginning with Cory Bernardi's defection to form Australian Conservatives, was marked by dissension and disunity.

In February, an exasperated Cormann berated Abbott on Sky for his sniping. It sent Abbott into a rage. After the interview, Cormann went into a meeting, and when he got out he found several missed calls from Abbott on his phone. When they finally spoke, Abbott gave him an earful. Cormann's intervention did nothing to stop Abbott. The campaign kept up all year, on every single issue.

At the end of November 2017, only days before the New England by-election, the New South Wales Nationals' leader, John Barilaro, told Alan Jones on 2GB, after some priming from Jones, that Turnbull should do the decent thing and resign by Christmas. The

Bullies and Co., most of whom hosted shows on Sky after the sun went down – hence its nickname, Fox after Dark – had confidently been predicting Turnbull would, in fact, be gone by Christmas that year. They saw it as their mission to help make it happen. Around the same time, Credlin and Bolt claimed that a coalition figure – who turned out to be the Queensland Nationals MP George Christensen, who doesn't actually get a vote in the Liberal leadership – was prepared to cross the floor to bring Turnbull down.

Given Turnbull's one-seat majority, Christensen was aware of his power, and did not use it sparingly. He had been threatening to take drastic action to vote with Labor – along with fellow National Llew O'Brien – to force the government to establish a royal commission into the financial sector.

The issue had been on a slow burn before it got red-hot. Senator John 'Wacka' Williams had been fighting for it for years. He had urged a succession of Coalition leaders —Warren Truss, Tony Abbott, Barnaby Joyce, and then Malcolm Turnbull – to take it on.

In March 2016, when election speculation was rife, Williams, who had initially been sceptical about a double dissolution, changed his mind partly because it would get rid of some of the 'loonies' in the Senate.

He texted Turnbull on 8 March to say:

> PM I support a DD on July 2. We have to clean out that senate. Make sure the ABCC is the trigger. You would be making a great political decision to have a RC into the financial sector that the people want especially after 4 corners last night. Cheers Wacka.

He did not get a response. There was a double dissolution, for which the Australian Building and Construction Commission was the trigger. The commission was subsequently legislated, and then nothing happened about the banks for another 18 months.

There had been a united front in cabinet against a royal commission. Regulations were toughened up and corporate regulators shuffled out. As a former assistant treasurer, and then minister for revenue and financial services, Kelly O'Dwyer had staunchly resisted a royal commission until news broke in August 2017 that the Commonwealth Bank had breached Australia's money-laundering and counter-terrorism regulations 53,000 times.

O'Dwyer thought it was time for a rethink, and spoke to the treasurer, Scott Morrison. Morrison, who had also been having a wobble, relayed O'Dwyer's remarks to Turnbull. He was not budging, and was shirty with O'Dwyer for the one and only time for raising it first with Morrison and not him, and then Morrison hardened up against it again.

Finally, the internal pressure from Coalition MPs and the external pressure from Labor forced the government to cave. Except it wasn't put that way. The major banks approached the government to say that continued resistance was futile, and asked them bring it on.

Around 8.30 am on 29 November 2017, the NAB CEO, Andrew Thorburn, rang Wacka Williams to tell him the banks had asked Turnbull to set up the royal commission to help restore confidence in the sector.

Christensen went public, saying Turnbull had had to be dragged kicking and screaming to agree to the royal commission. Even if true, it was unhelpful, and it was the last straw for Sally Cray. She made a couple of calls. One was to John Barilaro's chief of staff. Then she rang a couple of Nationals MPs close to Christensen. Cray, who, unlike Credlin, seldom bawled people out, let loose on the phones. She pointed out that there were plenty of rumours going around about the character quirks or personal habits of both politicians, which would find their way into the media if they persisted. They quietened down.

In the wake of all this, and as the end of the year approached, Cormann, who was incensed by the continuing destabilisation and the Barilaro/Christensen double-barrel attack, told friends that while he was going down with the ship, the same could not be said of Dutton. Dutton, according to Cormann, would weigh up his options around October–November 2018.

There was one other person Cormann named then as being actively opposed to Turnbull, albeit below the radar. That was the ambitious health minister, Greg Hunt, who figured that any kind of instability would work in his favour.

Despite the turbulence, Turnbull not only made it to Christmas, but managed to finish 2017 on a reasonably positive note, thanks to good results in two by-elections and the legalisation of same-sex marriage.

Barnaby Joyce was re-elected with an improved margin – with a swing to him of more than 7 per cent in New England on 2 December, in a by-election called because of his dual citizenship. John Alexander was also re-elected in a by-election for his seat of Bennelong on 16 December, called for the same reason. Labor had a good candidate – a smart woman with leadership potential, the former New South Wales premier Kristina Kenneally, running against Alexander; however, the Liberals ran an effective campaign, producing a scratchie with Kenneally's photo on it that rubbed away to reveal Bill Shorten.

Worse, in the middle of it, Shorten was forced to tell his friend Sam Dastyari that his services were no longer required in the Senate after yet another transgression involving Chinese connections. Any chance Kenneally had of winning disappeared. She replaced Dastyari in the Senate, and then became captain of the Bill Bus during the 2019 election campaign, where she schmoozed media and fulfilled an occasional attack-dog role, like other Labor women, including Penny Wong and Tanya Plibersek.

Shorten was deemed a liability for Labor during the by-election, and the result in Bennelong – a swing against the Liberals of less than 5 per cent – was interpreted as a sign that after a difficult year, much of which was also taken up with an acrimonious internal debate over same-sex marriage, the Turnbull government was on the road to recovery.

These days, Australian politicians divide their time fighting over two three-letter words ending in x – tax and sex. For obvious reasons, they get more excited about sex – the teaching of it and the practice of it – than they do about tax. It has become a touchstone issue for left and right.

Abbott had agreed to a plebiscite to decide the issue of same-sex marriage (SSM) in the dying days of his prime ministership, probably never thinking he would have to deliver on it, and then did all he could to thwart it when Turnbull was compelled by moderates to press ahead with it.

Labor had refused to support the plebiscite, so the legislation was stalled. Moderate Liberal MPs were threatening to cross the floor to vote with Labor to bring on a private member's bill. Abbott was insisting that Turnbull should simply keep re-presenting the plebiscite idea, confirming in the minds of MPs that he never had any intention of allowing the issue to come to a vote.

Then Peter Dutton, despite his impatience with businesses lobbying for the government to make SSM happen, came up with the idea of a postal ballot. As conservatives, Cormann and Dutton were opposed to same-sex marriage. As members of the cabinet, they were both heavily invested in seeing Turnbull succeed, and SSM had become a serious distraction from core business.

Although Cormann was anxious to have the issue dealt with – even to the extent of contemplating a controlled explosion that would involve accepting Liberal backbenchers crossing the floor to get it voted on and off the agenda – his claim that it was his idea to have the Australian Bureau of Statistics conduct the ballot has been hotly contested.

There were a number of joint submissions to cabinet by Cormann – who was acting special minister of state because of the absence through illness of Scott Ryan – and the then attorney-general, George Brandis. The final one was on 7 August 2017, with the ultimately successful option of getting the Australian Bureau of Statistics to conduct it. That option had come with legal advice from the solicitor-general to Brandis that this process, unlike others, would probably withstand a High Court challenge. This had followed a submission earlier that same month for the Australian Electoral Commission to conduct it, which had foundered on legal grounds. Another option that had been considered was for the Australian Law Reform Commission to run the plebiscite. This, too, was discarded on constitutional grounds on the advice of the solicitor-general.

After Cormann was credited in the media (including by me) with coming up with the idea of the ABS running the ballot, Brandis was indignant, insisting privately that the idea had originated with one of his bright young assistant advisers, Daniel Ward.

Ward, who had studied at Sydney University and Oxford, had begun working for Brandis in October 2015. He had a roving brief, and, come early 2016, realised it was going to be somewhere between difficult and impossible for the government to legislate for the SSM plebiscite.

It occurred to Ward that it might be possible for the government to conduct a ballot under the Census and Statistics Act.

Ward, after discussing it with deputy chief of staff Josh Faulks, sought advice from two eminent Sydney barristers to see if it was legally feasible. They advised in March 2016 that it was. In legal terms, it would be regarded as a statistical research exercise; in practical terms, it would be a vote. Under the act, it was within the remit of the treasurer to direct the ABS to conduct research into various matters. Why not on marriage? Genius.

Time passed. The plebiscite legislation had been bowled up and duly voted down by parliament. Abbott and the capital-C conservatives were delighted by that. Part of Abbott's argument that the government should keep presenting the plebiscite to the parliament was that it was a promise and, of course, all promises were sacred. This was laughable, given Abbott's approach with the 2014 budget, which broke every promise Abbott had made the night before the 2013 election. The moderates were growing increasingly impatient, ramping up their threats to cross the floor. Warren Entsch, once a lone voice in the lower house for the Liberals, was joined by a younger, equally committed, equally articulate crew, including Tim Wilson, Trent Zimmerman, and Trevor Evans (a Dutton protégé), and Dean Smith in the Senate.

In their view, it was untenable to go to the next election still promising a plebiscite. The hard right was insistent that there should not be a conscience vote. Labor and the Greens had no interest in helping Turnbull resolve the issue. They were determined to keep blocking. They wanted SSM to be their legacy, not Turnbull's. Turnbull, fearing the implications for his leadership from the hard-right agitators more than he feared the threatened rebellion by the moderates, would not bend on the free vote. He was willing at that stage to resubmit the plebiscite to an election.

Although, in theory, all Liberal MPs are entitled to a conscience vote on any issue, that applies to an actual bill, not to the procedural votes to bring on a bill to have it debated in the House – a quaint but sometimes effective brake on revolt.

MPs purporting to be conservatives, claiming same-sex marriage would undermine traditional marriage, also threatened to cross the floor to vote against Turnbull if he dared forego a plebiscite in favour of allowing Coalition MPs a conscience vote in the parliament so the issue could be decided. One of those threatening to cross the floor was the Nationals MP Andrew Broad.

In the face of unrelenting pressure from the increasingly impatient moderates, Turnbull eventually told his ministers to come up with a solution to the stalemate. Ward's idea from almost 18 months before, to get the ABS to do it, was dusted off, and then put by Brandis to the solicitor-general, Stephen Donaghue. Donaghue ticked off on it, cabinet approved, and the rest, as they say, is history.

During the plebiscite, there was also some debate in cabinet about how to handle the results. Interestingly, Morrison, whose electorate of Cook subsequently recorded a 55 per cent Yes vote, had argued in cabinet that the seat-by-seat results of the plebiscite should not to be published. Simon Birmingham and Kelly O'Dwyer opposed him. Birmingham said the government should not fear publication, because the results would also reveal Labor seats with a high No vote (which it did, in seats such as Barton, Calwell, and Chifley), and Labor MPs were locked into voting Yes regardless, whereas Liberal MPs would ultimately get a free vote.

Birmingham also knew there were Liberal MPs who would need the cover of the results to justify a Yes vote to their electorates. Turnbull emphatically ruled that the seat-by-seat results should be published.

Despite the reluctance of the SSM lobby to embrace it, and the grumbling from others that the government dared ask people to express a view and cast a vote, including the ludicrous claim by Labor frontbencher Andrew Leigh that young people wouldn't know how to post a letter because they could only send emails, the plebiscite was a huge success. Importantly, it showed that tolerant middle Australia was alive and well. Not that that mattered to the capital-C conservatives. Critically, it also provided Labor with a databank of where the progressive, pluckable Liberal voters were – a valuable tool in the subsequent Victorian election, but not so much in the federal election.

A total of 7.82 million people, or 62 per cent, voted Yes, and 4.87 million, or 38 per cent, voted No during the ballot held between 12 September and 7 November 2017.

On 8 December, only four out of the 150 MPs in the House of Representatives voted against the bill. They were Queensland LNP's Keith Pitt and David Littleproud, who had vowed to vote whichever way his electorate did; Victorian Liberal Russell Broadbent, who, despite being a moderate, had always opposed SSM; and Bob Katter from the Katter Australian Party.

There were nine abstentions: Barnaby Joyce, Tony Abbott, Andrew Hastie, Michael Sukkar, Kevin Andrews, Alex Hawke, George Christensen, Rick Wilson, and Scott Morrison, even though 55 per cent of people in his electorate of Cook voted Yes.

Warringah recorded one of the highest Yes votes in the country, with 75 per cent of Abbott's electors delivering emphatic support to the proposal. Compare that to Groom in Queensland, where 49 per cent voted Yes and 51 per cent voted No, creating a dilemma for the local member, John McVeigh. 'Mate, sucks to be you,' Littleproud told him when they passed in the corridor. McVeigh regarded the vote as statistical line-ball. He consulted religious groups, including the Toowomba Christian Leaders Network, chaired by Pastor Ian Shelton, father of Lyle, the prominent No campaigner and the local mayor, who was a great friend. He spoke to other political contacts, including Philip Ruddock, who was conducting the review into protections for religious freedom. Finally, he talked to his wife of more than 30 years, Anita, and their six adult children. Ultimately, because it was so close locally, with such a big Yes vote nationally showing how Australian opinion had shifted and where it was heading, he decided to vote in favour, and then to do what he could to make sure religious freedoms were protected. He suffered some blowback in his conservative electorate. But, although his preselection was challenged, he fought it off easily, winning 75 per cent of the votes to be re-endorsed.

Abbott could not bring himself to follow through with the wishes of his electorate, and then had the gall later, when his re-election was threatened, to tell his constituents that if it wasn't for him, it would never have happened.

Legalising such an important social reform will remain one of Turnbull's enduring legacies, but it also ensured the enduring enmity of the religious right and the hard right of the Liberal Party, who moved to exact revenge in whatever way they could.

Then, in late December, after speculation had abounded for around a year, Turnbull announced that Brandis would go to London as Australia's high commissioner to the United Kingdom. Brandis had been in two minds about taking up the appointment. He had had a serious wobble in November, and then, after passage of SSM, which he steered through the Senate with considerable aplomb, he decided it was best to go out on a high. Another high came when he rightly upbraided Pauline Hanson for walking into the Senate in a burka. While some on his own side winced, it won him deserved applause and plaudits from the opposition, the Greens crossbenchers, and across the media. But not, of course, from the little foxes.

Brandis's departure meant that Cormann, who had lusted after the job, was able to become leader of the government in the Senate. Turnbull also reshuffled security and border-protection agencies to create the super portfolio of Home Affairs for Dutton.

Julie Bishop was not happy about Brandis going – they were allies and friends – and argued against it. There were suggestions that Brandis had wanted to stay where he was until the election. As well, they were both opposed to the creation of the Home Affairs department. They had been against it when Abbott mooted it for Morrison, and even more so when Turnbull mooted it for Dutton. However, if the prime minister decides it's time for a change, it happens.

Bishop always believed it was a mistake to despatch Brandis, because Brandis would never have voted for anyone other than Turnbull, and she certainly needed one of her friends and allies close by if Cormann and Dutton were to grow even more powerful.

Bishop was Turnbull's deputy, but as foreign minister she was away more often than she was home. She and Turnbull had been friends for a long time, and they would rekindle that friendship towards the end, when their positions were imperilled, and then more so when it was over. However, as is often the way with these things, in between they grew distant. Turnbull needed Cormann and Dutton more than he needed Bishop, and he grew more reliant on them than he ever had been on his deputy for political advice or management of colleagues. Cormann would find ways to swing crossbench votes to get the government's legislation passed through the Senate, and he was an indispensable conduit – along with Dutton – to the conservatives. There was bad blood between Dutton and Bishop, and between Bishop and Cormann.

The dynamics of the leadership group and the lead players around Turnbull around that time are instructive. A former member of that group familiar with its operations said that Cormann looked after governance issues, Dutton was the chief interlocutor with the right or on anything to do with Queensland, and Christopher Pyne looked after everything to do with the parliament. According to this former cabinet minister, Morrison and Dutton loathed one another, while Pyne, as the leading moderate, was close to Morrison – eventually delivering the numbers to make him prime minister. Turnbull sought little advice from Brandis or Bishop, both of whom despised Dutton – and the feeling was mutual – and nor did they trust Morrison. Turnbull grew ever more reliant on Cormann and Dutton.

Dutton always believed that Bishop had been complicit in Abbott's ousting. He was convinced she was actively involved in the plot to remove him, asserting privately at the time that 'she was in it up to her neck'. Cormann was intent on replacing her as the most senior West Australian, immersing himself in the machinations of the local branch to ensure that his people were elected to even the most obscure positions.

Bishop did not trust Cormann, and the enmity between her and Dutton stretched back years. People close to Bishop say it stemmed from her intervention in the preselection battle for the seat of McPherson back in 2009. Dutton had set his sights on shifting there after his own seat of Dickson had been redistributed, making it notionally a Labor one. Bishop had been on a swing through the seat, picked up that Dutton was going to fall a long way short with the preselectors, and plumped for a female candidate, Minna Knight, one of her ex-staffers. The preselection was eventually won by Karen Andrews, but Dutton, who had to fight tooth and nail to hang on to Dickson, had never forgotten nor forgiven.

Cormann and Dutton became indispensable to Turnbull, and they were handsomely rewarded by him as a result; however, hopes that the government was back on track were soon dashed. If the government thought it had begun 2017 badly with the defection of South Australian senator Cory Bernardi to form his own party – a betrayal widely applauded by the delcons, the delusional conservatives – it was nothing compared to the beginning of the 2018 political year.

CHAPTER THREE

Barnaby's doodle

The government crashed into the pits in February, thanks to Barnaby Joyce. Or, more accurately, thanks to Barnaby's doodle, as James McGrath rather delicately described it when it was all over. It was a disaster at every conceivable level – personally for Joyce and his family, politically for him, and for the future wellbeing of the Turnbull government.

There were reverberations all the way through to the election as Joyce sought to reclaim his leadership. He refused to accept that he was part of the problem, and not part of the solution. His successes were overshadowed, particularly among women, by his great lapses. His actions not only put the spotlight on internal divisions; they were a reminder of his unacceptable behaviour.

Joyce's political career had been remarkable. He was a rebel senator who found endless opportunities during the Howard years to vote against the government. In the space of three years, he went from being a senator from Queensland, to winning the lower-house seat of New England in New South Wales, to then becoming the Nationals' leader and the deputy prime minister. His regularly expressed desire to replicate that feat before the 2019 election by reclaiming the leadership and the deputy prime ministership continued to divide the Nationals and damage the government.

Before the election, friends of his drew a mental map of another avenue for his rehabilitation. Just not federally. Given what he had accomplished before, they thought it was not beyond the realms of possibility that if he shifted back to Queensland and got himself into state parliament, he could become premier – a latter-day Joh Bjelke-Petersen minus the corruption.

However, even this fantasy pathway to redemption was upended by his increasingly erratic behaviour, including an unhinged interview during the campaign with Patricia Karvelas on ABC's Radio National. The interview, on water buy-backs, is more impactful in the listening than the writing, but high-pitched attacks on 'Labor, Labor, Labor' sent Coalition campaigners into a spin – more so the next day, when he could not understand why it would be better if he stayed away from a planned media event rather than turn up and kick the affair into the next day. He thought the interview had gone really well. Although the Nationals held all their seats in May 2019, they were beside themselves when their bluest of blue-ribbon seats of Mallee in Victoria recorded a primary vote of 29 per cent. They blamed the plunge on Joyce's water policies and the brand damage caused by him and the outgoing local member, Andrew Broad, with their doodle problems.

Joyce's passage from maverick, to prime political asset, to unqualified liability – especially from the second-highest office in the land to a lowly backbencher over the course of a few weeks, thanks to an extramarital affair – is an extraordinary story.

There had been rumours since early 2017 that Joyce was having an affair with a staffer. One National frontbencher recalls a conversation he had with fellow frontbencher Michael McCormack, who would succeed Joyce in the leadership, that took place around June. It was a few months after the frontbencher had first heard about it. The two men were in furious agreement about what would happen once it got out, as it was bound to do: it would end in tears. There was no sign from McCormack at this stage that he was positioning himself to take over; they were only sharing concerns that once it became public knowledge that the then deputy prime minister was having an affair with his staffer Vikki Campion, who had begun working with him during the 2016 election campaign, everything would go pear-shaped.

The rumours had also reached the prime minister's office early on. Joyce's mood-swings, and the obvious stresses and strains on him, his family, and his staff were obvious, affecting both his performance and the functioning of the government.

Joyce's staff were in an invidious position, caught between him and his wife, and him and the other woman, who also happened to be his media advisor. Dealing with him and the two women was incredibly difficult. The staff suffered collateral damage, as staff always do when the boss crashes and burns. In this case, there were the inevitable questions about how they could have managed the situation better. As if Joyce, a free spirit, could ever be managed.

Many months later, in the wake of criticisms about the performance of staff, his senior media adviser, later chief of staff, Jake Smith, could laugh about it as he relayed to friends the conversation he had with another friend, a senior Queensland National, who had asked him when it was all over, 'Explain to me how the deputy prime minister gets his staffer pregnant, and somehow it's the fault of the gay guy?'

It was an impossible situation, completely unmanageable, partly because of the personalities involved. Campion was very open about her relationship with Joyce – not only to other staff in the office, but to other coalition staff as well, telling them about bushwalking expeditions or other social engagements with her boss. She made no secret of her closeness to Joyce. She would describe him as the loneliest man in the parliament.

Whatever the nature of the relationship in those early stages, and from the very moment she joined the office, staff who were alert to the potential for disaster did their best to keep them apart by trying to arrange separate travel. But what some saw as her frankness, and others, her indiscretion, ensured that the gossip spread quickly through the Coalition. It didn't take long for people to become convinced it had developed beyond the professional, beyond platonic.

Eventually, Joyce's then chief of staff, Di Hallam, along with his friend and colleague Matt Canavan, succeeded in convincing Joyce that Campion could no longer work in his office.

Barnaby's increasingly suspicious wife, Natalie, had been ringing Joyce's ministerial office asking staff probing questions. It put them under enormous pressure, deepening their emotional and ethical conflict, and sorely testing their loyalties. Mrs Joyce, who at that stage had access to her husband's diary and could see the frequency of his travels with Campion, travelled to Canberra in February 2017 to try to find out what was going on. Once in the office, she quizzed an uncomfortable Hallam about her husband's activities, and then threatened to confront Campion.

No matter the circumstances, Hallam, as chief of staff, did not feel it was appropriate for her to allow the minister's wife to tackle a staff member in the office over what was essentially a personal matter. Mrs Joyce chose instead to confront her husband in his office. Staff cringed as doors slammed. They could not hear exactly what was being said, but they could hear the couple yelling, and then saw the distressed expressions on their faces when it was over.

It was awkward and embarrassing. As Joyce's personal life unravelled, it was clear that his professional life would suffer and that the toll would escalate. Staff, including Hallam and Smith, as well as his colleagues, told him he had a choice. If he wanted to remain in his job, let alone save his marriage, Campion had to leave his office.

It is also fair to say that his staff and his other confidants were concerned about the wellbeing of Joyce's family, as much as they were for his political career. Making the situation that much harder, they were all fond of Natalie and the four girls.

Joyce's former chief of staff, the then backbencher Scott Buchholz, also became involved. Buchholz had stayed mates with Joyce, and they would share the odd nightcap here and there. Hallam also sought his advice. Buchholz told her to make sure that all the paperwork dealing with all entitlements was in order. Being a smart operator, Hallam had already done that, seeking reimbursement from Joyce for two claims.

Buchholz also spoke to Joyce. He did not ask him if the rumours were true, figuring it was not his business. Buchholz simply told him he had heard the chatter, as had almost everybody else, and if it erupted, asked Joyce whether he was sure he had the numbers to hang onto his leadership. He suggested to Joyce that he start spending more time with his backbenchers.

When Sally Cray heard the rumours about Joyce and Campion in early 2017, she told Turnbull. Turnbull, who is conventional and prudish about such matters, believing it is always best for couples in trouble to stick together, invited Joyce to dinner at The Lodge soon after. It was just the two of them.

He did not ask Joyce directly if he was having an affair with Campion, but he gave Joyce every opportunity to volunteer the news by asking about his wife, Natalie, and their daughters. There was no hint from Joyce that anything was amiss.

Campion was shifted to Canavan's office in April 2017, which lifted the pressure a bit from Joyce's other staff – although, as it transpired, not enough.

On 11 May, two days after the budget, one of Turnbull's press secretaries, Daniel Meers, took a call from the *Daily Telegraph*'s Sharri Markson. She was checking a tip-off that Joyce had been seen – purportedly by a Labor person – at a medical clinic the day before the budget with Campion, holding an envelope with scans, and that he had then gone into the doctor's consulting rooms with her.

There had also been a bizarre incident the previous weekend when Joyce was acting prime minister. His VIP flight from Whyalla was diverted to Canberra rather than back to Tamworth because of a pending announcement from Buckingham Palace, which turned out to be that Prince Philip was relinquishing royal duties. News reports said that Joyce was cranky he had missed a home-cooked meal.

'I was happily on my way back to Tamworth until my media adviser told me to happily make my way to Canberra and now I'm not very happy,' Joyce was quoted as saying jokingly.

Staffers' eyebrows shot up. There were a few too many 'happy's in there. To them, it seemed like he actually looked forward to spending time away from Tamworth, not in Tamworth.

So a few days later, when staff told Turnbull that journos were querying Joyce's surgery visit with Campion, he asked Joyce to come around to his office. Turnbull told him that media were asking his office about him and Campion visiting the doctor together.

Joyce told him that Campion had been ill, they feared she might have cancer, she was estranged from her family, she had had a terrible upbringing, and he had gone with her to the doctor's as her friend. This time, Turnbull asked Joyce directly if they were having an affair. Joyce said they were not.

Joyce was enraged that word had leaked out about his visit to the surgery with Campion. He was looking for people to blame. He zeroed in on his loyal chief of staff, who happened to be the messenger delivering the request that the prime minister had wanted to see him.

It triggered a blazing row between Joyce and Hallam in his

office. This time, it was so loud that staff in the outer office could hear what was being said. Joyce and Hallam dropped more than their fair share of f-bombs during what was the most fearful row. Hallam, who had been with Joyce for three-and-a-half years, had already decided earlier in the year that she would look for another job. If she needed any confirmation that she had made the right decision, this was it, despite the fact that they made up a few days later.

Not long after the row, Hallam took extended sick leave. She never went back. Her departure fuelled even more rumours and gossip about what had prompted her departure.

Joyce also told other MPs who asked him what was going on, after they, too, had heard that he and Campion had visited the doctor together, that Campion had been ill and he had accompanied her as a friend.

When Canavan resigned from the ministry in late July because of doubts over his eligibility to sit in parliament because of his mother's Italian heritage, Campion was shifted to the office of the Nationals' whip, Damian Drum. Later, whatever Campion's qualifications for the job, this was used against both her and Joyce because it looked like he was finding highly paid employment for his mistress.

Drum says that when Joyce's then chief of staff, Matt Coultan, who had temporarily replaced Hallam, asked him to take Campion on after Canavan's resignation, Coultan told him that there had been a relationship, but it was over. It wasn't all that long after Joyce had appeared at the mid-winter ball with his wife in what later turned out to be a stage-managed appearance worthy of Hollywood. After being told about the affair well before the ball from usually reliable sources, as they say, I had decided to include a paragraph in the updated version of *The Road to Ruin*, released in August 2017.

However, after seeing the pictures of him with his wife, and assuming they were back together, I decided not to name Joyce. Instead, I wrote that if a smart journalist matched up travel entitlements between minister and staffer, they could come up with a story with the potential to wreck careers and shatter the government.

Sharri Markson was already on to it, and she persisted.

It wasn't long before Drum began receiving calls from the media asking if the affair was back on, citing instances where they had been seen together. Drum says he thinks this happened in August, before Joyce's own citizenship came under question.

Drum saw Joyce, who he says by then was staying with his (Joyce's) sister. Drum says he told Joyce he was having to field questions about his relationship with Campion. He says he told Joyce, 'You have to come clean and tell the Australian people you are out of home. You gotta tell them. Then all this stuff is no one's business. You are a single man.'

Joyce said he did not want to do that because it would hurt his children.

Drum warned, 'You are going to hurt them a shitload more if this comes out in front of you and you are not in control of it.' It was blunt, accurate advice, worth heeding. Joyce didn't take it.

The rumours continued, including suggestions that Campion was pregnant. This news puzzled senior Nationals, who believed – apparently after some cryptic comments from the man himself when the rumours were gaining strength – that he had undergone a vasectomy. Joyce had been telling people that he could not have any more children – or words to that effect – leading them to believe he had had minor corrective surgery, or was suffering some other ailment.

While he was grappling with the affair and its likely repercussions on his family, Joyce discovered in August that, by virtue of his father's birth in New Zealand, he was a dual citizen. The New

Zealand high commissioner, Chris Seed, rang Joyce's office on 10 August seeking an urgent one-on-one with him to deliver the bad news. As soon as Seed told him, Joyce said, 'I'm fucked.'

Joyce was prepared to go to a by-election immediately. However, Turnbull thought that was a bad idea, and despite his conviction that Joyce had no problem with his eligibility and that the High Court 'will so rule', the High Court did in fact rule him ineligible.

In early October, Joyce travelled to Inverell, John 'Wacka' Williams' territory, to attend the Sapphire City Festival. The straight-talking Williams, something of a father confessor for Joyce, had known months before that Joyce's marriage was in trouble. Williams had told Joyce back then that he and his wife, Nancy, would not be 'picking sides' between him, Natalie, and their four daughters.

Williams and his wife were close to Natalie and the girls. The Joyce family had stayed with them at their house, so Wacka and Nancy were not going to choose between their friends.

When the official duties were over in Inverell, Williams invited Joyce home for a bite and a cuppa. While Nancy was inside preparing lunch, the two men sat out the back near the barbecue area and talked. It wasn't small talk, either. Joyce told Williams that Vikki was eight weeks' pregnant.

Williams says he said to him, 'Well, of course you would not consider an abortion.' Joyce replied, 'Never.'

'Good,' Williams said to him. 'Whatever happens, it's not the kid's fault.'

Williams then warned Joyce that his daughters would be very upset with him, and that it would take a long time for the wounds to heal.

Williams does not know if at that stage Joyce had told his family that he was going to be a father again. He believes he was one of the first people Joyce told, in confidence. Williams kept his secret.

During his campaign to reclaim his seat of New England, Joyce was not once accompanied by his wife or daughters. He deflected questions relating to his family, saying his personal life was his personal life, further fuelling the speculation that something was definitely wrong.

There was, however, one incident during the campaign. Turnbull flew to Tamworth on 7 November, Melbourne Cup Day, to campaign with Joyce. Screens were set up in a large marquee for spectators to watch the race that supposedly stops the nation. They were working the tent together, but during the running of the race, Joyce slipped away to speak to a visibly upset young woman who had tackled him. She was in tears. It was one of Joyce's daughters. Nine's political reporter, Charles Croucher, spotted the encounter. Croucher decided not to run it after a Nationals MP told him there were health issues involved. Word of the incident soon reached Turnbull's accompanying staff, including Sally Cray and press secretary Daniel Meers.

Joyce won his seat on 2 December with a two-party-preferred swing to him of 7.2 per cent. The afternoon of the vote, Turnbull flew to New England, and then, after the result was clear, in matching checked, open-necked shirts, the rough diamond and the merchant banker shared the stage holding hands up high, positively beaming.

The result would have been very different if word of his affair had seeped out during the by-election campaign – if Joyce had lost his seat, it would have robbed Turnbull of his majority. There were rumours during the campaign, but no proof, and often, unless public monies or other issues are involved, media are reluctant to report on the personal lives of politicians.

Finally, during his speech in the same-sex marriage debate on 7 December, Joyce admitted in one breath that he was no saint and in the next that he and his wife had separated. It was a premeditated confession. Staff and colleagues alike had suggested to Joyce – and he was well aware of this himself – that he could not afford to get up in the debate and moralise. Jake Smith had also reassured the prime minister's office in advance, allaying any concerns that the prime minister and his staff might have had that Joyce would sermonise. Colleagues were already angry that their leader had been unable to campaign full throttle against same-sex marriage because of his messy personal life. It would be even worse if, in parliament, he set himself up as a standard-bearer for traditional marriage while the rumours swirled that his girlfriend was pregnant. The hypocrisy would have provided the excuse that the media needed to break cover on the story.

Drum says Joyce told him in late December that Campion was pregnant. Staff were noticing she was wearing different clothing, and that she was having days off saying she was feeling unwell, so all of them already suspected that she was having a baby.

Jake Smith, who by then held the dual roles of media advisor and chief of staff in Joyce's office, told Sally Cray before Christmas 2017 that Campion was pregnant. A couple of weeks before that, soon after the by-election, Cray had told Smith she was aware Campion was pregnant, but he would not confirm it to her. He later suspected that his predecessor as chief of staff, Simon Price, had already told her. Smith fessed up when Joyce finally gave him permission to tell her. Then, on 12 January, Joyce was due to have a one-on-one meeting with Turnbull in Sydney to discuss charter letters – the formal outline of ministerial responsibilities – following the end-of-year reshuffle caused by the departure of George Brandis. Smith assumed Joyce was going to tell Turnbull about the pregnancy, so, over a coffee, he told Turnbull's chief of staff, Peter Woolcott, and his deputy, Clive Mathieson. They were not in the least surprised. As it transpired, even then Joyce did not tell Turnbull that Campion was pregnant. Nor did Turnbull ask him if she was.

During that ministerial reshuffle, Joyce was described as

especially erratic. He had trouble deciding who to dump and who to keep. He would agree to a promotion or demotion one day, and then change his mind the next, vowing this was it, no changes, it was fixed, only to change his mind again.

He ended up making two formidable enemies. He dumped Darren Chester from cabinet and Keith Pitt as an assistant minister. He wanted to promote David Littleproud to the frontbench, which was fair enough. Littleproud was – and is – a talented addition to the Nationals, with obvious future leadership potential, assuming everything stays on track and he doesn't get derailed. Politics was in Littleproud's genes. His father, Brian, served as a minister in two Nationals governments in Queensland. As a schoolboy, David says he remembers listening in while his father tried to gather the numbers for his friend Mike Ahern to take over the Nationals leadership. He says he also clearly remembers his father taking a call from Joh Bjelke-Petersen asking him to join his government, and his father refusing the offer. Littleproud is proud to recall that, soon after failing to get his father, Russell Cooper, and Ron Borbidge on board, Bjelke-Petersen resigned.

Littleproud says he had known Barnaby Joyce for 20 years. They had worked at competing banks in Charleville, and then at competing banks in St George. When Littleproud put his hand up for Maranoa – which Joyce had wanted before he landed on New England – Joyce supported another candidate.

Despite this, and although Littleproud had only been in parliament for a year, Joyce catapulted him from the backbench straight into cabinet. Joyce told him the day before, at a tourist event in Longreach, that he was going to call him the next day to offer him a slot. He warned Littleproud that the promotion would mean he 'would be in everyone's sights'.

'It was sage advice. I was unknown and untested,' Littleproud admits. He felt the pressure. Turnbull also rang him the next day, and although Littleproud would come to admire him greatly, that first conversation was icy.

Turnbull and Littleproud bonded during Littleproud's handling of the live-sheep drama, when footage of the appalling treatment of the animals on board ships led to demands for the export trade to be abandoned.

A few months after his promotion, Turnbull went to Littleproud's electorate to attend the Bell show and rodeo, which attracted 700 people. Littleproud was bowled over by the reaction to Turnbull. 'They just loved him,' he said. Turnbull visited Maranoa three or four times, and all people wanted – according to Littleproud – was to see more of him.

'I think he was a great prime minister, a great leader. I don't think he was a great communicator, and that's ultimately what brought him undone,' Littleproud said, months after Turnbull's ousting.

'That's the only reason I can give you, because I am a little shocked. He empowered you. We didn't always get along, we didn't always agree on everything, but I had a huge level of admiration for him.'

Littleproud is not your typical National, in the same way that Chester doesn't fit the Nationals' stereotype. Littleproud believes the drift back to One Nation began again in earnest in 2010. That is when he reckons civility disappeared from the federal political scene, to be replaced by rancour. It left people frustrated and disengaged, and looking for an alternative. 'People were disenchanted with the way politicians treated one another,' he says. He readily blames Abbott for changing the political tone of the nation. And not for the better. Littleproud says he tries not to operate like that. He voted against same-sex marriage because his electorate did, but would have voted for it if they had. He talks easily about climate change, because he thinks it's real. His farmers think it's real. They can see the consequences all around them.

However, for a man who doesn't want to make enemies, even among opposition MPs, because he would rather work with people to get things done than fight with them, Littleproud has managed to acquire a few in a short space of time.

Joyce's decision to elevate Littleproud straight into the cabinet at the expense of Chester – while dropping Pitt – was unconventional, put noses out of joint, and was eventually very costly – and not because Littleproud's performance disappointed anyone.

Chester was well suited for the leadership. He was articulate, experienced, presentable. And stable.

Chester was born in Sale, in regional Victoria. There was no Chester political dynasty. His father, Jim, a plumber, and his new bride, Lois, built their first home there from second-hand bricks. Lois still lives there. Sadly, Jim died a year before his son was elected the local federal member in 2008.

As Chester himself says, he is not exactly landed gentry. He was their third child, and then, after a gap of 10 years, two baby sisters arrived. As the much older brother, he helped look after them.

Chester is also a different kind of National Party MP, and while this has won him respect across his electorate and inside parliament, it has cost him, too. He should have been elected leader after Barnaby Joyce went down – he was the most experienced and the best equipped – but there were a couple of reasons it didn't happen. One was his stance on same-sex marriage, and the other was because he had thrown his weight behind a woman and fellow Victorian, senator Bridget McKenzie, to become deputy leader when Fiona Nash was bowled out for being a dual citizen.

In the period leading up to the Irish referendum on marriage equality, Chester had risen in the National Party room a few times to say that he believed the mood in regional Australia was changing in relation to same-sex marriage. He always believed it would have been best if there had been a conscience vote for all members. He urged his colleagues to temper their language when talking about it. He did not personally know of anyone who had taken their life because of their sexuality, but he had heard of it. They all had. Everybody knew somebody who was gay or who had a gay family member.

Chester decided he would go public with his views after the Irish referendum. He held off for a bit at the request of the then leader, Warren Truss – and also because he was feeling unwell – and then, after some negotiating with Sabra Lane, agreed to do an interview with ABC-TV's *7.30*.

A couple of people were so angry after this that they moved to have him disendorsed. That was voted down by 28 to two. He went to an event in Traralgon where a 75-year-old shook his hand and thanked him. He had a son who was gay, and thought it was time the Nationals moved into the 21st century. As did most others who were there that night. Chester believed that every National electorate would vote yes, and in fact his own seat produced a 60 per cent Yes vote. He can't understand the No vote in western Sydney Labor electorates.

'The majority of people have a live-and-let-live attitude,' Chester says. 'Who am I to deny people happiness?'

When MPs fell like skittles during the dual-citizenship crisis, the Nationals' deputy leader, Nash, among them, Chester was still in cabinet. He felt bad that senator McKenzie had been overlooked for promotion, so he mustered the numbers for her for the deputy leadership. Joyce did not object. She was a competent woman. There were too few of them in the Coalition.

People assumed Joyce was angry with Chester over this, because his preferred candidate for deputy, Matt Canavan, missed out. Chester says Joyce quietly encouraged him, and insists that until the day Joyce rang to tell him he was dumping him from the cabinet, they had not exchanged a cross word.

Joyce's actions sent a terrible message to Joyce's colleagues that, regardless of performance, they could be dumped at any time at the whim of the leader. That was not how things were done in the National Party.

Perhaps one reason Chester was dumped was that he had done too good a job when Joyce was absent, fighting to retain New England. Joyce was acting bizarrely even then. Nigel Scullion was made acting leader in his absence, and when Turnbull was due to go overseas, Joyce wanted Scullion, rather than Julie Bishop, to be made acting prime minister. This was preposterous, and not only because the entire population would have wondered again what the hell was going on in Canberra. (No offence to Scullion, who is an interesting character. After a visit to a strip club in St Petersburg in 1998, before his election to parliament, Scullion said that the two life lessons he had learned from the experience were to never let anyone handcuff him to a post, and always to wear clean undies.) Anyway, in the absence of the prime minister and the deputy prime minister – always a National under the Coalition agreement – the convention is that the next person who takes over is the deputy Liberal leader, who happened to be Bishop.

Chester did most of the media and heavy lifting for the Nationals while Joyce was on the campaign trail. Maybe paranoia was setting in.

Turnbull, who got along very well with Chester, was appalled by Joyce's decision to drop him from cabinet, making his displeasure obvious at the press conference where he announced the changes. Joyce, excusing his decision on the grounds of geography (there were too many Victorian Nationals in the cabinet), offered Chester a slot as an assistant, which Chester refused. Chester did not want anyone to think he was okay with what had happened. Looking back, he says he can only assume that Joyce was so rattled or distracted by the turn his personal life had taken that he was not thinking straight.

Proof of just how messy Joyce's private life had become came soon after, on the night of 6 February 2018, just as parliament resumed for the year, when the *Daily Telegraph* published online its front page for the next day, featuring a photo of a heavily pregnant Campion with the headline 'Bundle of Joyce'.

Campion had become aware the day before that she had been snapped by a photographer. She told Joyce, who asked Jake Smith to make inquiries. That evening, Smith spoke to the then editor of the *Telegraph*, Chris Dore, asking him not to run the photo or the story.

Smith's argument to Dore was that there were no public-interest issues at stake. It was a personal matter. Smith told Dore that no taxpayer monies were involved and no policies were affected. Dore had a simple response. What was he, as an editor, supposed to do in a few days or a few weeks, after the deputy prime minister was seen walking down the street with a new baby in his arms? In other words, it was news.

Let me hasten to add here that rumours abound in Parliament House, and always have, about who is on with whom. People talk, if not incessantly, at least frequently, about affairs real or imagined. Sometimes they are irrelevant, and occasionally highly relevant, such as when Laurie Oakes broke the story of Cheryl Kernot's affair with Gareth Evans. One Labor MP walked into the office of another colleague to pick up a notebook he had left behind, only to find a male colleague and another female colleague in flagrante. There were stories about ministers having affairs with each other.

However, for Joyce, the photo of Campion was a career-ending moment. At that point, rumour became fact. Events spiralled. Natalie Joyce released a statement making her displeasure clear. Joyce's position was untenable, yet he believed he could do what no other conservative leader had been able to do and survive such a sequence of events – an angry, betrayed wife who'd gone public, and a visibly pregnant girlfriend.

The Nationals always prided themselves on being like family. The wives of male MPs knew and admired Natalie. MPs were divided on whether he could survive or not, but most thought he could not.

There was a bizarre attempt by Joyce to deny his paternity, which seemed to lend weight to the snip story, but he only further confounded his friends and colleagues when he later said that, yes, indeed he was the father.

Joyce was having a mid-life crisis. Most people get to do it in private. Not the deputy prime minister.

But the Nationals didn't want to vote him out – they wanted him to decide to leave. Chester, Pitt, Barry O'Sullivan, and Michael McCormack met early the following week to weigh up the damage to the party and to the government. They hoped they might be able to manage Joyce's departure without too much trauma. They asked Canavan to speak to him. Joyce wasn't budging.

On 22 February, in an effort to pressure Joyce into resigning, Victorian National Andrew Broad tweeted, 'Quote from the late Billy Graham "when wealth is lost, nothing is lost; when health is lost, something is lost; when character is lost, all is lost" … telling words for the Leadership of the National Party.'

Graham's words of wisdom were designed to ring through the ages. Or so you would think. On 17 December that year, Broad himself first resigned as an assistant minister and then from parliament altogether, following salacious revelations about embarrassingly uncouth text messages he had sent to a young woman living in Hong Kong whom he had first met online and then later visited to try to seduce.

As the Joyce soap opera dragged on, every member of the government hoped Joyce would see sense and fall on his sword to minimise the damage. No such luck.

Like his colleagues, Luke Hartsuyker had reached the conclusion that Joyce could not survive as leader; however, he doubted that Joyce would ever quit. Hartsuyker remembered a speech Joyce had given years before at a Nationals conference that had ignited the coalition's campaign against Kevin Rudd's carbon pollution-reduction scheme. Joyce, who loved historical references and once asked his staff to find out the price of wheat in the time of Jesus, had on this occasion referred to the Spanish conquistador Hernando Cortés ordering that his ships be burned to prevent his troops deserting after the invasion of Peru to loot the Aztec empire. All or nothing, no retreat, no surrender.

However, Turnbull's patience was wearing thin. The government had recovered well over the summer, but was now getting dragged down. Again. The first Newspoll of the year published on 5 February showed that the party-preferred gap between the government and Labor had narrowed to 48 to 52 per cent. Turnbull was way ahead as preferred prime minister. By 19 February, the next Newspoll showed that Turnbull's ratings had crashed, the gap had widened, and most people thought Joyce should quit. The media were not remotely interested in any other story.

Although Joyce was a great retail politician, he was difficult to deal with as the Nationals' leader, and the turmoil only made him more difficult. 'The worst ever,' one Liberal cabinet minister would say later, claiming Joyce would constantly threaten to end the Coalition, to pull the Nationals out of the government, sometimes over trivial issues. Yet here he was, demanding they all pretend there was nothing untoward happening. Everybody did it anyway, didn't they, didn't you, he would ask others. Well, yes and no. Some did; a lot didn't. Joyce always thought it was unfortunate that he was the one who got caught, and that it would soon pass.

Peter Dutton raised the doodle problem with Joyce during a leadership meeting at peak crisis, asking him how he thought it would be resolved, how he saw it playing out. Joyce thought that if they all stuck together, they could ride it out and that people would forget about it.

Centre or centre-left politicians – think of Bob Hawke and Bill Clinton – withstood revelations of marital infidelity. They did so because there were no photos of pregnant girlfriends around, and because, in the face of damning allegations of infidelity or inappropriate behaviour, their wives stuck by them 100 per cent. Hazel Hawke maintained a dignified silence for decades. Hillary Clinton attacked the accusers and stuck by her man. When the photo of the pregnant Campion appeared, Natalie released a statement saying she was hurt and deceived by the affair.

Joyce would sit in leadership meetings, head in hands, getting redder and redder – no wonder they nicknamed him the Beetrooter – while his colleagues talked about him and his mistress and what to do. He would shuffle into the meetings with head bowed, growing more and more depressed. Turnbull was growing increasingly worried about the damage to the government and his own standing, particularly among women, where his support was high.

Turnbull canvassed a so-called bonking ban at a leadership meeting on 14 February. Both Dutton and Cormann had been trying to talk Turnbull out of doing anything. In their view, he was best to stay out of it.

Dutton later described the 'bonking ban' as stupid policy. 'It was Turnbull grandstanding. It made a great enemy of Barnaby. There was no need to do that. He had stood up with him at his by-election. What was to be achieved by that?' he said.

'Mathias and I said in leadership [meeting] to stay out of it. We were against doing anything.'

Pyne also thought it would be a mistake. Morrison was the only cabinet minister who supported it, and according to those who were there, did so enthusiastically.

An exasperated Turnbull decided to bring it to a head. On 15 February, more than a week after the story broke, he announced a new code of conduct that would include a ban on ministers having sex with staff. Turnbull wrote it out himself, incredulous that it needed to be done and that it needed to be put in writing.

'Barnaby [Joyce] made a shocking error of judgement in having an affair with a young woman working in his office. In doing so, he has set off a world of woe for those women, and appalled all of us,' Turnbull said at his press conference.

The head of the Department of Prime Minister and Cabinet, Dr Martin Parkinson, was charged with determining if anything inappropriate had occurred. Where to begin? And where to finish? What could the country's top bureaucrat possibly say? Parkinson didn't have a clue, and was spared further torment when Joyce eventually resigned.

'I never anticipated becoming the ABC' – the Anti-Bonking Commissioner – Parkinson told people when news of his new duties broke.

An infuriated Joyce dug in. Turnbull had given him no warning that he was going to announce the ban. Fuming, he watched him announce it on TV, and then he and Turnbull had a very testy conversation on the phone.

Other Nationals were less than impressed with Turnbull's intervention, which they regarded as unhelpful. As angry as they were with Joyce, they were even angrier when a Liberal tried to tell them or their leader what to do. Eventually, however, they had to take matters into their own hands. The sorry saga dragged on for another 11 days until 26 February, when the story leaked that Catherine Marriott, the former West Australian Rural Woman of the Year, had lodged a sexual-harassment complaint with the National Party against Joyce.

Senior Nationals later surmised that someone in New South

Wales or Western Australia had leaked the Marriott story in an effort to blast Joyce out. Two journalists had already approached Joyce's office, knowing the name of the complainant and details of the alleged incident before any complaint had been lodged.

Whatever happened between Joyce and Marriott – and there are obviously contested accounts – it was the straw that broke the camel's back.

The morning that story broke, Wacka Williams says he texted his friend to say it was time for him to step down. Joyce resigned that day.

Damian Drum believes that if it were not for those allegations, Joyce would have remained as leader. Drum blames the media for Joyce's downfall. He says Joyce was accused of having an extramarital affair, when in fact his marriage had broken down long before that. He does not believe Joyce had done anything wrong – certainly nothing bad enough to warrant his departure as deputy prime minister.

The Joyce soap opera had run for 20 days, dragging the government off message, into a quagmire and down in the polls. It would take months to regain lost ground. As well as robbing the government of momentum, Joyce's departure, all of it completely self-inflicted, robbed Turnbull of something else – a strong protector on his right flank who might have helped him better manage the energy debate, both at the retail end in the bush and internally with the Nationals.

In early April, Turnbull clocked up 30 Newspolls in a row in which the government lagged behind Labor. Much of the blame was laid at Joyce's door. While a few sympathised with Joyce, most of them did not. They were furious with him and his subsequent efforts to paint himself as a victim.

'He enjoyed extraordinary support in the party room, and his fall from grace was all his own doing,' one senior National said.

'He was given every opportunity to succeed in the leadership, and for the first 12 months he did a great job. In the second 12 months, he lost contact with the colleagues. I don't think he had any actual friends in the party.'

This was a harsh assessment, but reflective of Joyce's neglect of his day job.

With Joyce gone, the Nationals had to elect a new leader. Chester was the obvious choice. However, they could not have Victorians as leader and deputy leader; New South Wales and Queensland Nationals would not have it. Chester was not about to shaft McKenzie, and in any case his more conservative northern colleagues were still snarky about his support for same-sex marriage. Chester had skewered himself. He decided to throw his support behind the determinedly uncharismatic Michael McCormack, whose homophobic scribblings during his time in journalism ensured a rocky beginning. Chester was restored to the frontbench. He says he did not ask for it, and that no deal was done with McCormack for his support for the leadership.

So did Chester regret the actions he had taken on both same-sex marriage and Bridget McKenzie, which cost him his own shot at being Nationals' leader and deputy prime minister? Not for a moment.

'It's as good as it gets,' he told me later. 'Sometimes in politics and life you can lead from behind. You can lead from behind in directing votes and support for people who will take the party forward.'

Chester is satisfied with his own conduct. He knows he did the right thing both times, and if he paid a price for that, so be it. He is a rare creature in a cut-throat world.

It took until the budget in May for the government to stabilise; however, it wasn't long before the right fired a few shots across

Turnbull's bow. The reverberations from same-sex marriage played out in a couple of key votes at the party's federal council meeting in June, including the election of Teena McQueen as the federal women's vice-president.

McQueen is not a woman to be trifled with. At a fundraising dinner held at the National Press Club with the then defence minister, Marise Payne, and the defence industry minister, Christopher Pyne, on 19 June 2018, McQueen was asked what her interest was in defence-related matters. McQueen said she owned two guns.

McQueen was on a high after just being elected, and was trying to get a rise out of Pyne. Pyne told her he was untroubled by the vote, even though the woman that McQueen toppled was another progressive from South Australia, the well-regarded former MP Trish Worth. Worth, who had held a marginal seat for 11 years, who knows a thing or two about campaigning and what it takes to make governments tick, and who made telling contributions at executive meetings on the imperative to define Shorten as a captive of unions, was politically acute. Yet she became collateral damage.

McQueen had made no secret over the years of her admiration for Tony Abbott, describing him to friends as her first love (in more graphic language than that), and advertising her disdain for Malcolm Turnbull.

In March 2016, at a black-tie dinner at Parliament House to celebrate 20 years since the election of the Howard government, a group of guests began interjecting during Turnbull's speech. They became so loud and so persistent that another female guest nearby walked over and told one particular woman and her companions to be quiet.

According to eyewitnesses, there was a repeat performance at a tribute dinner in July 2017 for Bill Heffernan, when Turnbull rose to honor the retired senator from New South Wales. The same angry, unimpressed woman began interjecting.

McQueen, who was accused by those present of interjecting at both events, denies it was her, claiming she was the one who told others to be quiet at the Howard dinner.

Her reputation as a Turnbull hater and unabashed Abbott fan was well known, so when she defeated Trish Worth a year later to become federal vice-president, it came as a shock to Turnbull's supporters. It should have been read for the warning it was.

It was the same federal council meeting where an overwhelming majority of delegates, including McQueen, voted in favour of a self-indulgent motion from the young Liberals to privatise the ABC.

When it came to the vice-presidency, their intention, as Michael Sukkar later privately admitted, was to give Pyne a whack. Sukkar saw same-sex marriage as the final battleground for the conservatives – not energy or climate change, but the fight for traditional, cultural values.

Canberra senator Zed Seselja and Sukkar, who were to become prominent in Dutton's coup attempt, were still smarting over the same-sex marriage vote. They were furious that at the previous year's council meeting, Pyne chortled over their diminished influence, saying that progressives had gained the ascendancy in the Turnbull government and were in the winner's circle, and that same-sex marriage would be legislated sooner rather than later.

They figured, wrongly, that Worth was Pyne's candidate. So they did not wound Pyne, as they had hoped, but they did help Abbott by showing that conservatives still had muscle. And, of course, they damaged Turnbull by showing that his had wasted.

A combination of complacency and rodent-like jiggery-pokery (think of Kevin Rudd's description of the Chinese) helped see McQueen elected by 54 votes to 50.

A confident Mathias Cormann had assured Turnbull beforehand that Worth would succeed – the national right was locked in, and would back her over McQueen.

Michael Kroger, the Victorian president, who traded extensively on his status as a so-called power-broker, had also assured the federal president, Nick Greiner, that the Victorians were voting for Worth. Sukkar was to say later that Kroger had done this without prior consultation, which tells you a lot about who really ran the state party then.

When she was talking to Turnbull before the vote, Worth told him she wanted to go and change her jacket and freshen up. Thanks to Kroger's and Cormann's assurances, Turnbull was unfazed, reassuring Worth that she needn't bother, because he had been told there was nothing in the challenge from McQueen.

Later, Worth thought it was strange that Helen Kroger (Michael's first wife) had told her beforehand not to see the vote as something personal against her; rather, it was conservatives wanting to flex their muscle to show Turnbull that they still held influence and power.

Initially, the conservatives had wanted to knock off Greiner as federal president. Greiner, whom Turnbull had chosen, was also a moderate, and also – horror of horrors – supported same-sex marriage. However, they couldn't find a candidate to run against him.

So determined were they to exact some revenge, they backed McQueen to unseat Worth. One of their arguments against Worth, who had made a few sensible comments on the importance of unity after one of Abbott's strategic sniping interventions, was that she had disrespected MPs. This would have been funny if it was not so perverse.

Adding to the false sense of security, Eric Abetz had called Worth when nominations opened to suss her out, complimenting her on her contribution and leaving the clear impression that he and the Tasmanians supported her. Worth took it as a sign that Abetz was mellowing. Wrong. Julie Bishop, who would have voted for

Worth, had to leave the conference early. Other delegates close to Seselja and Sukkar, also simmering over same-sex marriage, voted against Worth, as did a West Australian woman using a proxy vote she had secured for another matter.

There was a widespread belief from the top down that the votes for Worth were locked in. They clearly weren't, and if the political radar of the prime minister, his staff, and his supporters had been more finely tuned, they would have seen it coming.

So a woman well known for her antipathy to Turnbull, passionately devoted to Abbott, joined the party's federal executive. Judging by the email she sent to delegates after the vote, in which she supported the motion to privatise the ABC, insisting that the national broadcaster 'must start paying its own way', she was eager to play a big part in all federal and state election campaigns. Her victory embarrassed the prime minister, and only emboldened Abbott, who around that time was threatening to cross the floor and vote against Turnbull's national energy guarantee if he did not get what he wanted. McQueen leveraged her position to appear regularly on television. She had her followers, but among other members of the federal executive, her appearances were seen as a disaster. She refused all requests to stop appearing on her regular slots, saying she needed the money from Sky.

Ultimately, the vote on SSM was a victory for Turnbull, yet while his role was not bold enough to satisfy its prominent advocates, the ultra-conservatives were determined never to allow him to savour it, and to make him pay for it, one way or another – even though their factional leaders, Cormann and Dutton, had done all they could to help make it happen.

CHAPTER FOUR

A waste of energy

Climate change was the policy that dared not speak its name. Condensed to energy, it became the key issue that precipitated Malcolm Turnbull's decline and fall. Turnbull's handling of the issue lost or bewildered MPs as diverse as Keith Pitt from Bundaberg and Tim Wilson from Brighton. As a National, Pitt didn't have a vote, but his threatened resignation from the frontbench the week before helped contribute to the sense of crisis around Turnbull's leadership. Wilson did vote for Turnbull in the leadership ballots, but he was sorely tested in the lead-up by reports of changes that Turnbull was proposing to the National Energy Guarantee as he sought to convince MPs like Andrew Hastie not to cross the floor to vote against the government.

You can't blame Josh Frydenberg for telling *Insiders* host Barrie Cassidy on 9 September, a fortnight after Malcolm Turnbull's removal, 'It went through the party room three times, so it wasn't the factor in his downfall.' If people did believe it was *the* factor, then they might also believe Frydenberg was in some way complicit in the disaster.

Frydenberg, as the former environment and energy minister, played no part in the undermining of Turnbull, nor in the coup against Abbott in 2015, although that did not stop Abbott from seeking to derail him at every point along the way in his juggernaut campaign to destroy Turnbull. Then Abbott had the gall to ring him and ask him not to run for the deputy leadership against Peter Dutton's running mate, Greg Hunt.

Frydenberg was unable to nail down the National Energy Guarantee (NEG) and perhaps save Turnbull from being dragged down into the mire, because there were people from both the left and right who were determined, for their own reasons, that he should fail. So it may not have been *the* factor, but it was certainly a critical one. And, as Turnbull realised near the end, there was a simpler solution, which if pursued from the beginning might have spared them all a lot of heartache. That was to opt for regulation rather than legislation of the emissions-reductions targets.

It would not have resolved Turnbull's essential problem, which was the determination of his enemies to destroy him, no matter what. If energy was resolved, they would have moved on to religious freedoms. But with the NEG, despite its imperfections, he might have forced combatants in the climate wars, which had wreaked havoc on Australian politics for more than a decade, to lay down their arms, at least for a while. It would have bought him valuable time. But it wasn't to be.

No matter how many meetings were held with premiers, no matter how many experts or industry leaders or lobby groups, from the minerals council to the National Farmers' Federation – all of whom supported the NEG – were lined up to explain to MPs what was involved, there was a clutch of backbenchers who had decided that no resolution would ever be reached under Turnbull.

In 2018, conservatives and moderates alike believed that Turnbull fell into a trap set by his enemies, who succeeded in killing him twice on the same issue. The right argued that Turnbull was making too many concessions in an effort to get Labor premiers on board. The moderates believed he was making too many concessions to keep the right on board.

Frydenberg, as the front man, had spent months trying to convince the public, the premiers, and his own backbenchers that the NEG was the mechanism which would help reduce power prices, provide certainty for investors, and therefore make electricity supply more reliable. Along the way, emissions would be reduced in line with Australia's commitment to the Paris targets that Abbott had signed up to as prime minister – which he then, as a backbencher, advocated should be abolished, because he said his agreement to the targets had come about because he'd been misled by bureaucrats.

As a signatory to the Paris Agreement on climate change, Abbott had committed Australia to reducing its total emissions to 26–28 per cent below 2005 levels by 2030. Later, employing his cut-through communication skills, Abbott managed to turn one word – Paris – into the enemy of cheaper prices, and spearheaded the campaign to follow Donald Trump in abandoning the agreement.

Turnbull's office noted the similarity of the arguments and responses made by Abbott, Jones, Bolt, Credlin, and their attack puppy, Craig Kelly. It was as if they had been issued with the same talking points.

After Turnbull's removal, when Abbott found himself struggling in Warringah against Zali Steggall, whose main policy focus was climate change, Abbott switched positions. Again. Paris was no longer sin city for denialists. Nope, Abbott said during a debate on Sky with Steggall and other opponents, Australia no longer had to quit Paris. And why not, asked moderator David Speers? Well, because there was now a new prime minister and a new energy minister. Mission accomplished. Abbott showed himself to be a man of many convictions, enough to suit any occasion. His camp followers stayed silent.

Only a matter of months before, so critical was this issue to the Liberal Party's future – or so he wanted people to believe – that

Abbott had been threatening to cross the floor to vote against it.

Abbott was keen to present this as similar to Turnbull's vote for Rudd's Carbon Pollution Reduction Scheme; however, there would have been a world of difference between an opposition leader who had committed himself to a policy, lost his leadership because of it, and then voted for it, and a former prime minister in a government with a one-seat majority threatening to vote against that government in the parliament on part of a policy he had constructed. The distinction was lost on Abbott.

Most people – industry, the media (excluding conservative commentators) and Labor, although it withheld support to maximise Turnbull's discomfort – saw the NEG as imperfect, but regarded it as the last, best chance to end the climate wars, which, ironically, would have helped Abbott in his seat.

Abbott and his surrogates, particularly New South Wales backbencher Craig Kelly, whom Frydenberg joked had taken a sleeping bag into the Sky studios, where he appeared at least once a day, saw it as their best chance to blast Turnbull out of office.

As chair of the government's backbench energy committee, Kelly appeared at every critical point to criticise or cast doubt on whatever measure Turnbull and Frydenberg put up. When preselectors in Kelly's seat of Hughes warned him that he faced his own personal emission, Kelly threatened to run as an independent. He defended his speaking out by saying that, unlike Labor MPs, Liberal MPs were not clones, drones, or sheep, which prompted me to describe him in my column in *The Australian* as a more exotic kind of animal, 'part stalking horse, part pet poodle tethered to Tony Abbott'. He gave an involuntary smile when we unexpectedly crossed paths in the press gallery corridor a few hours after Turnbull was deposed, so I asked how his preselection was looking. For once, Kelly had nothing to say, although he did manage later to force Scott Morrison to save him by threatening to sit on the crossbench. One thing poodles do have going for them, other than their reputation as the most pampered of pets, is that they are smart.

Peter Dutton was growing increasingly exasperated by the handling and management of the issue, which he came to call the 'noodle nation NEG', a paraphrasing of the devastating parody of Barry Jones's spaghetti-and-meatballs diagram that Kim Beazley used to launch his Knowledge Nation policy.

'Turnbull's plan was to bring the NEG on [in Parliament],' Dutton later recalled. 'Pyne and I went nuts.'

Dutton acknowledges there are ideological differences between him and Pyne, but they were aligned on this, following what had seemed a successful party meeting on 14 August 2018. Pyne and Dutton agreed that bills which stood no chance of getting passed by parliament – particularly if they threatened to divide the government, as the NEG did – should not be put up for a vote, because they would wreck confidence in the government.

Also, Dutton believed that trying to isolate dissenters by getting Labor on board would only court disaster.

'Malcolm's plan with the NEG was to get the states to agree through COAG [the council comprising leaders of the federal, state, territory, and local governments], then have the states pressure Bill Shorten to support the legislation, and from there what he thought would happen was on one side would be the Liberal Party and the Nationals and Labor. Sitting on the other side would be Tony Abbott and fringe-dwellers', Dutton said later.

'It was never going to happen. There were 20 people on our side who were not going back to their electorates with photos of them sitting next to Tanya Plibersek voting on a motion supporting climate change.

'It would have been a complete disaster for the government. We effectively had the bill pulled.'

Pyne confirms this, saying that he and Dutton convinced

Frydenberg not to introduce the NEG legislation until there was a final, settled position. Frydenberg had lodged the legislation in the Table Office on Tuesday evening, after what had seemed a victory in the party meeting earlier in the day. Pyne had it removed.

A key Morrison supporter, Alex Hawke, thought the NEG was a good attempt, but that the whole thing was a trap.

'And Malcolm fell into the trap again,' he said. 'The states were never going to sign off on it. He was wedged against the base, and was left needing the Labor Party to get it through. That drove me mental.'

The experience of two MPs, one a National from the LNP in Queensland, the other a Victorian Liberal, as different as it is possible for two people to be, who ended up at the same point – angry and confused – showed just how fraught energy policy had become for Turnbull.

Keith Pitt represents one of the poorest electorates in the country, Hinkler, north of Brisbane, which includes the rum-producing town of Bundaberg, where Pitt was born. Tim Wilson represents one of the most prosperous electorates, Goldstein, which includes the bayside suburb of Brighton with its rows of multi-million-dollar mansions looking out over Port Phillip Bay. Wilson was born in the now very trendy inner-Melbourne suburb of Prahran. They were born in and live at opposite ends of the country, and they are as different personally and philosophically as it is possible for two backbenchers to be.

Pitt, an electrical engineer and sugar-cane farmer, has been married to Allison for 20 years. They have three children, Liam, Ruby, and Elisabeth. He was one of four Coalition MPs who voted in the parliament against same-sex marriage. Pitt is a traditional conservative Queenslander.

Wilson, a trade consultant who worked for a conservative think tank, the Institute of Public Affairs, proposed to his partner, Ryan

Bolger, from the floor of the House of Representatives during an emotional speech supporting same-sex marriage. They married at a private family ceremony in March 2018 in Melbourne's Botanic Gardens. Wilson says he doesn't belong to any faction, neither moderate nor conservative, describing himself simply as a Liberal, and later ran for re-election as a 'Modern Liberal'.

On the Friday night before the spill, Pitt, who along the way had threatened to resign his frontbench position, was furious, while Wilson, fearing a 'red line' had been crossed, felt like his head was about to explode.

Pitt has been consistent on energy issues. In June 2015, he had told parliament he would not be supporting the government's renewable energy target, which aimed to have 23.5 per cent of Australia's energy derived from renewables by 2020.

'In my view, the renewable energy target – the RET, the deal the coalition has been forced into with Labor – will achieve only three things,' he said then. 'It will increase the cost of electricity for those who can least afford it, Australian taxpayers will have spent billions of dollars subsidising private enterprise, and, come 2020, environmentalists will have little more to show for it than a warm and fuzzy feeling.'

So it was no surprise he was opposed to the NEG. He did not believe it would deliver lower prices, and he did not believe it would guarantee reliability of supply.

Pitt had written a paper proposing a fund that would provide money to keep existing coal-fired power plants going. He met with Turnbull and Nationals leader Michael McCormack on 28 June to discuss it. He says they were both non-committal.

On Monday 13 August, he told a meeting of National Party MPs that he could not support the mooted energy policy, and that being the case, he would have to resign as assistant minister to the deputy prime minister. He rang Frydenberg to tell him this, and

Frydenberg suggested he speak to the prime minister.

At 4.30 that afternoon, Pitt went to see Turnbull, and told him what he had told his party room. He could not support the NEG. Turnbull told him that if he held to that position, he would have to resign from the frontbench.

Again, Pitt outlined his concerns: it would not deliver what it promised.

Turnbull asked him if he thought the people who had designed the NEG were 'idiots'. Pitt shrugged. Turnbull got Audrey Zibelman, the chief executive officer of the Australian Energy Market Operator, on speaker phone. Pitt had already spoken to her previously, and had not been convinced by her arguments, either.

After half an hour, Pitt left.

Wilson had some sympathy for Turnbull's plight, believing that the Turnbull government had really only existed for six months, and the rest of the time was spent resolving the problems left over from the Abbott government, which in turn were left over from a failure to carry out policy work in the Abbott opposition.

He was concerned that too often when the government was talking about energy, it seemed it was fighting for investor interests rather than for people's. Too often, it got bogged down in fighting for the what, not the who. So when Abbott argued that energy policy should be about 'pensioners, not Paris', he was able to define, with only three words, both the issue and who he was fighting for in accessible language. Wilson thought that was critically important.

In mid-2018, Wilson WhatsApped the prime minister with some advice, urging him to emphasise cheaper prices. Turnbull's arguments were lacking empathy; people wanted to know that their concerns were being addressed and with some sympathy. The messages were not being communicated properly.

Wilson said to Turnbull that the greater task ahead of him was not to devise a policy for all time, but one that would stabilise the market for the next five or 10 years; after that, technology would take over and reduce emissions. He did not think the government should over-invest on the issue; he did not mean this financially. His message was received and read.

Like so many others, Wilson was becoming increasingly concerned that few people understood the NEG.

On Monday 13 August, the night before the joint party-room meeting to finalise the NEG, Abbott had close to the last word at a long, fractious meeting of the energy committee. His former friend Frydenberg went around the table, asking MPs to declare themselves. When he finally got to Abbott, and asked him if he was a yes or a no on the NEG, Abbott replied, 'It's all a crock.' It was an echo of 2009 when he described climate change as 'crap', a comment that as leader he had to disavow. Abbott only joined as a member of the backbench committee that night when he heard of the meeting. He and two others – Craig Kelly and Ken O'Dowd – voted against the NEG, while seven others supported it.

At the next morning's joint party meeting, with Turnbull set to get his energy policy through the party room, Abbott was described by colleagues as looking agitated and sounding belligerent. 'He was right off the reservation,' one said. Another thought Abbott was unhinged. Another thought Abbott's pitch to colleagues that he was the one who knew how to win elections, and knew how the party room ticked, was plain sad.

Even conservative New South Wales senator Jim Molan ended up supporting the NEG, although he did say it was like putting lipstick on a pig.

Pitt sat silently throughout that meeting. That was not unusual. Frontbenchers don't speak unless they are asked a question.

Marginal-seat holders like Sarah Henderson and Julia Banks, who were tired of the conflict and Abbott's divisiveness, decided to have a go. Henderson backed the NEG, but also strongly supported

Barnaby Joyce's call for tougher action against energy suppliers to stop gouging and to keep prices down. Then she turned to Abbott, addressing her remarks directly to him, appealing for unity and telling him that the only way they could win would be if they all fought together. Abbott interjected that he had helped her win. 'You did,' Henderson said. 'But we need to keep winning.'

Banks acknowledged that she didn't have as much experience as others, but did have experience winning a marginal seat. And, although she didn't say so, without Abbott's help. She acknowledged the importance of getting prices down, but also of sticking to the Paris commitment. She also addressed herself to Abbot, appealing for unity outside the confines of the party room, urging him to show respect to all the third parties, from the National Farmers Federation down, which supported the NEG.

Abbott's bitterness, his frustration over yet another humiliating defeat at Turnbull's hands, overflowed. If Labor was looking for an ad, he helped write it for them by describing explanations of the NEG as 'merchant bankers' gobbledygook'. One can only surmise who most voters familiar with rhyming slang would have concluded was the merchant banker in this context.

At the meeting, Craig Kelly and Andrew Hastie announced that they reserved their right to cross the floor, threatening to join Abbott. At that stage, it look like a small band of MPs would be voting in the House with the Greens' Adam Bandt against the government. Labor was also not fully committed to backing the NEG – and thereby backing Turnbull. Labor was enjoying Turnbull's discomfort, and was profiting from the disunity too much to let him off the hook. Not that Labor's support would have helped Turnbull with the hard right. One of the arguments against him was that he spent too much time trying to get Labor premiers on board. They were branding Turnbull as Labor-lite.

In the mix was the possibility that the government would lose the vote on the floor of the House, and then be forced into an early election on power prices.

Turnbull and Frydenberg held a victory press conference after the joint party meeting, which turned out to be embarrassingly premature and only inflamed internal resentment.

A series of meetings was arranged with different groups of backbenchers on the Wednesday as Turnbull, his office, and Frydenberg tried to resolve the differences and to limit the revolt to the few who would never be satisfied.

In what were described as good-faith negotiations, Turnbull met with Joyce and others, to flesh out their concerns, and to see if they could be met. Joyce seemed in some turmoil about which way to go. The mere mention of the word 'climate' set him off. He was not deliberately undermining Turnbull, but neither was he going out of his way to be helpful.

If he had still been leader, he most likely would have found a way through the impasse with the Nationals. Like so much else, it wasn't to be.

When she was leaving around nine o'clock that night, Sally Cray noticed that Dutton's bodyguards were outside Cormann's office. She went in, and staff told her that Dutton was in the dining room. She opened the door, and was surprised to see Dutton and Cormann sharing pizzas and wine with Zed Seselja, Michael Sukkar, and Tasmanian senator John Duniam. They said they were celebrating the defeat of the euthanasia bill in the Senate. Cormann had taken a break from arm-twisting on company tax to rally the numbers against David Leyonhjelm's bill.

They invited her in, and then Cray stayed on with Dutton and Corman when the others left. Dutton told her how bad it had been at a meeting of Queensland MPs earlier in the evening, in what had been their first gathering since Longman. Apart from the fact that it finished late, there was nothing that happened or that was said at the Queenslanders' meeting that was unexpected, except that Luke Howarth, normally one of the saner marginal-seat holders, was agitated, according to what Dutton told Cray.

The next day was ominous. Pitt's threatened resignation had been leaked to *The Australian*. The front-page story on 16 August referred to rebel MPs urging ministers to quit.

The only frontbencher named was Pitt. Backbenchers referred to included Hastie and Tony Pasin, the member for Barker in South Australia, who had already been named as opponents during Tuesday's party meeting. Nevertheless, the leak did what it was designed to do. It built a sense of crisis around the government and Turnbull.

That same morning, Dutton did his infamous interview with Ray Hadley, in which he said he would resign from cabinet if he disagreed with government policy. Cray texted Dutton to ask what was going on. Dutton said he was not causing any trouble, and suggested she read the whole transcript, because it would show Hadley was badgering him. She did, and then showed it to Turnbull in preparation for question time. He underlined a couple of bits, but didn't appear too troubled by it.

Pitt does not know who leaked the story about his threat to resign, swears it wasn't him, and says that the only people who knew were the prime minister and his colleagues in the National Party room – which was more than enough to guarantee it got out. But as Pitt and others argue, if there had been overwhelming support for the NEG, Turnbull would still be prime minister.

Early on, before it got too late, Pitt had a view that if Turnbull had been able to cast the turmoil as a Nationals revolt – given that Andrew Gee, Barry O'Sullivan, John Williams, George Christensen, Ken O'Dowd, and Michelle Landry were not happy with the NEG – he might have been able to get through it. That option was closed off after the 14 August joint party-room meeting.

Turnbull and his office were not oblivious to the problem, but he did not help himself by over-investing in the issue, and ultimately losing more people than he gained by trying to keep people in the tent who would never be satisfied with anything he did.

'Craig Kelly and others we knew were causing a lot of angst,' one senior adviser said. 'In the Nats' party room, it was Keith Pitt. We knew McCormack was having a few problems keeping people together. We knew Abbott was hardening up his position. We knew we were heading for a significant moment with the NEG.'

The internal brawling over the NEG coincided with another period of ascendancy for Bill Shorten. Only the week before, supremely confident Labor apparatchiks had been busily tutoring businesspeople – who had paid more than $1 million to mix with Labor frontbenchers and to hear Shorten speak at a special business forum – on appropriate etiquette. As they worked the room, their advice, only half-jokingly, was that participants should get accustomed to saying 'Prime Minister Shorten'.

Later, at a closed event, a cocky Shorten set aside his prepared speech with a flourish, as if to signal this was one of those times where he could say what he really thought, to deny he was in any way anti-business. All evidence to the contrary, he dismissed this claim as hype from the government, and then couldn't resist a swipe at one of his braver critics, the Business Council of Australia, saying it had been put in the 'naughty corner'.

It was like businessmen and businesswomen had forked out $11,000 each to buy their own tickets to the guillotine. Labor could not be blamed for being so confident then – or business for being either so compliant or so cowardly – about its prospects after watching Liberal Party guerrillas/gorillas commit themselves to killing Turnbull and crippling the government.

Late Thursday afternoon on 16 August, Morrison and Frydenberg met with Turnbull in his office to discuss matters arising from his discussions with backbenchers. It was clear that some MPs would cross the floor if the government legislated the targets. During the discussion, one of Turnbull's economic advisers, Katrina Di Marco, pointed out they didn't have to legislate the target – they could regulate it, with a 'poison pill' attached. That 'poison pill' would be that the minister would not have a licence to change the targets at will, that the minister could not take any action that would increase prices, and that the minister would first have to go to parliament to lay out the reasons for lifting the targets. The minister would also be required to spell out the likely economic impact of any increase.

Turnbull and his staff were cranky that, as the minister, Frydenberg had not canvassed this option previously. Although it's fair to say they were cranky with themselves, too, for not having seen it. All the angst, all the agony, over the legislation of the target could have been – if not avoided – at least mitigated. In fact, there was one view that they could simply put the targets on the Department of Environment website, or record them in the *Government Gazette*, the official repository for proclamations and legislation. That would have driven the greenies mad, but if regulation with appropriate control measures had been the option put to the party room from the outset, it might have spared Turnbull the aggro from the right, and robbed his enemies of one weapon, at least. Unlike a number of his MPs, who were committed body and soul to either one or the other, Turnbull viewed legislating versus regulating as a distinction without a difference. He wanted to nail down the policy, and was focussed on getting as many MPs as he possibly could to support it, knowing all along that he was battling against those who only wanted to 'wreck the joint'.

Later, Turnbull's office concluded that Frydenberg's task of corralling Labor premiers, who had no interest in helping Turnbull, and the Abbottites, who had even less interest in seeing him succeed, was too big for Frydenberg to handle.

In fact, Turnbull's advisers had at one stage suggested diplomatically to Frydenberg to watch out that he did not try to be all things to all people, and to be careful he did not lead them to believe that all their concerns would be met, because clearly they could not.

The Thursday meeting ended with Turnbull, Morrison, and Frydenberg agreeing that regulation was worth considering, so work began on the submission to cabinet to change the policy.

That night, Cray went out to dinner with Turnbull's press secretaries. Pretty soon, all their phones started ringing almost simultaneously, with calls from other media to ask about a story posted online by Sharri Markson in the *Daily Telegraph* saying that Dutton was preparing to challenge Turnbull for the leadership. Again, Cray contacted Dutton. Dutton said he hadn't spoken to Markson; she had been ringing him all day, but he hadn't returned her calls. It was a long way from a denial, and Cray did not see it as one.

The sense of crisis escalated. The NEG was unravelling, and talk of leadership instability was now rife.

On Friday, Hastie was still in Canberra, chairing a meeting of the parliamentary joint committee on intelligence and security. That morning, Justin Bassi, Turnbull's national-security adviser, approached Hastie to ask him if he had heard anything about the leadership. Hastie, who regards Bassi as a friend, told him he had not. Hastie insisted later that he was oblivious to the intrigue sparked by the *Telegraph* story that morning, and that he wasn't even aware the story was running. He told Bassi he was more concerned about the NEG. Hastie was implacably opposed to legislating the targets. In his view, if Shorten wanted to go to the election promising to lift them to 50 per cent, that would be fine. He was confident they could win the argument as to why that would not be a good idea. He swears he did not see it as a leadership issue.

Hastie had to excuse himself from the joint committee meeting at one point after receiving a number of texts from Frydenberg. Frydenberg told Hastie he had spent a couple of hours on the phone talking to his former boss and mentor John Howard about how best to resolve the issue. Frydenberg told Hastie that he and Turnbull were working their way through a number of matters in an effort to resolve the problem, and floated with him the idea of regulating rather than legislating the emission-reduction targets. Hastie thought that was a much better way to go. He says Frydenberg swore him to secrecy.

Later that afternoon, while he was in the Qantas Lounge waiting for his flight back to Perth, Hastie got a call from Turnbull, who also discussed the option of regulation rather than legislation. Hastie told him, 'That sounds good.' He told Turnbull he was willing to move forward and support the government. He assured Turnbull that he 'was not committed to blowing up the government'.

'I was working in good faith,' he told me later. Hastie says someone in the prime minister's office, not from the press office, then suggested to him that he should brief journalists that he was working with Turnbull to resolve the problem. Hastie then texted two senior Fairfax press gallery journalists – Phil Coorey and Peter Hartcher – to tell them he was engaged in constructive discussions with the prime minister's office on the NEG, that the PM was listening, and that good progress had been made. In his texts, he described the leadership speculation to them as 'BS'. Hastie says he did not go into details with them about what changes were being proposed, but he emphasised they had nothing to do with the leadership or politics, and were only about arriving at a good policy.

He ended up sitting next to his housemate and good friend, Ben Morton, on the flight back home. He told Morton he was prepared to back a solution if it could get through cabinet. Hastie was thinking about how he was going to explain his changed position.

He had agreed to be interviewed by Alan Jones on Sky again on the following Tuesday night about the NEG, and the previous week had told him he was prepared to cross the floor over it.

Not long after Hastie's flight took off, one of the journalists that Hastie had contacted, Phil Coorey, and another Fairfax journalist, David Crowe, broke stories online saying that Turnbull was making major changes to the NEG, to regulate rather than legislate the targets, in an effort to contain the threatened backbench revolt amid rumours of an impending challenge from Dutton. Later that night, the Guardian's Katharine Murphy also reported the change. The ABC followed up with a story online saying that the move, which would not require parliament's approval, was designed to head off the prospect of a backbench revolt. Andrew Bolt gleefully reported that Turnbull had panicked and that his leadership was over.

Later that night, with the story out, Turnbull himself outlined the plan to regulate in his speech to the National Party's annual conference in Canberra.

By the time Hastie landed in Perth, the story was everywhere. Hastie was furious. He says he had been sworn to secrecy about the actual change because it supposedly had to go through cabinet, but he got off the plane to read an online story about it in *The Australian* and to scroll through 30 text messages and voicemails, mainly from the media, asking about the compromise.

The headline in *The Weekend Australian* warned, 'Paris retreat may not save PM'. Simon Benson and Joe Kelly wrote:

> Malcolm Turnbull has dumped the government's plans to legislate the 26 per cent Paris emissions-reduction target, in a dramatic capitulation to rebel MPs and ministers threatening to cross the floor and vote it down.
>
> Senior government sources confirmed that Mr Turnbull's praetorian guard had come to the conclusion on Thursday night

> that threats to his leadership were real and that a bold move was needed to head off the growing likelihood of a revolt.

An unauthorised intervention by a prime ministerial staffer; a bit of overbriefing from someone releasing incomplete detail prematurely, without a proper explanation of or emphasis on the 'poison pill' provisions; a highly charged atmosphere, with mounting speculation of a challenge from Dutton; and journos with eggbeaters at 20 paces saw everything spiral. It was a disaster. Attempts to quell a revolt with a policy backflip, supposedly being negotiated quietly, suddenly became public. It exacerbated the tensions. It looked like cabinet was being usurped, while those MPs who had agreed to the NEG on the basis that the targets would be legislated were furious that all their objections and concerns were being overlooked to placate a rebellious few. Perhaps if regulation had been the option from the get-go, it wouldn't have been so bad.

If Hastie was angry, Pitt and Wilson were even angrier. As was Scott Ryan. Unlike Hastie, Pitt thought that regulation rather than legislation was 'adding fuel to the fire'. He thought the prime minister had realised he was in deep trouble and was trying to avoid a showdown with the rebels. Pitt reckons that not only did it make matters worse, but it showed Turnbull's tin ear.

To Wilson, the idea of having a minister determine the target without recourse to parliament, which was how he read the stories on Friday night, was anathema. It would vest enormous power in a minister, giving him or her the power to increase tax rates without getting the necessary legislation through parliament.

Wilson's condition for supporting the NEG was that it would be legislated. He messaged the prime minister, saying it was a 'red line' as far as he was concerned. He made it clear he that was not threatening anything, but it was critical to his continued backing that the NEG be legislated.

'On Friday night when I read it, my head was about to explode,' Wilson said later. 'I spent Saturday trying to get to the bottom of it. I never got clarity.'

On Sunday, Wilson was fielding calls from the media, so he was thinking hard about how to respond to something he regarded as 'quite serious for me'.

'It was a big deal,' he told me later. 'Not just because I felt it was disrespectful. I felt it was a fundamental principle.'

He needn't have worried. Next day, the policy changed again, and then all of them got overtaken by events.

Turnbull had called an urgent meeting of cabinet for Sunday night. By 5.00 pm on Friday, the only two people who had not responded were Dutton and Greg Hunt, with Steve Ciobo also threatening to be a no-show. Turnbull's office told Dutton's office that he had to attend the meeting and that they would be sending a VIP aircraft to get him. They were convinced by then that something was up. Dutton says there was 'no conspiracy' involving him and Ciobo – once regarded as one of Turnbull's closest allies, but who was a close mate of Dutton. Dutton said he had a family event and was always going to catch a 7.00 pm commercial flight. Ciobo's earlier flight had been cancelled, so they were planning to fly down together. Sally Cray told Ciobo there was a seat for him on the VIP to Canberra, too, and that he and Dutton could plot and scheme together all the way to Canberra. She was semi-serious about that. She was deadly serious when she warned him via text that if things blew up, Scott Morrison could end up prime minister by the end of the week.

Ciobo resented the insinuation that he was involved in Dutton's plans, and offered to do what he could to calm things down. While he knew the drums were beating, and while their mutual friend Michael Keenan knew something was afoot and heartily approved, Ciobo insists he was not involved.

Until that flight to Canberra on the Sunday night, that is. Ciobo says Dutton went through it all with him on the way down. He told Ciobo that he had more than 50 per cent of the votes in the party room. He told him he had the numbers to beat Turnbull. Even more importantly, Dutton told Ciobo that he had Cormann's full support.

Dutton insisted to Ciobo that night and the next day that he and Cormann had 'gamed' the whole exercise, that he and Cormann had masterminded the campaign, and that together they had worked out who would go where and what would happen immediately after the coup. Ciobo was to tell people later that this was a critical factor in his decision to support Dutton.

Turnbull had also invited cabinet ministers to dinner at The Lodge that Sunday night before the formal meeting. With leadership speculation at fever pitch, the dinner was switched to the Explorers Room in the cabinet complex at Parliament House so ministers could come and go – or not – without being caught on camera. It was a spectacularly awkward affair in that small room adorned by portraits of famous explorers.

Cormann was a no-show. While that only made Julie Bishop more suspicious about all of them and their motives, the prime minister's office had known in advance that Cormann would not be there, and believed at that stage that his reasons were genuine.

Dutton didn't say much at the cabinet meeting. Pyne says he never heard Dutton say in any private or public forum that he was opposed to the NEG. Other cabinet ministers confirm this.

Pyne was bemused by Dutton's lack of engagement. But he put it down to the fact that Dutton had been a policeman – a typical Queensland cop who thinks everyone is guilty of something, so doesn't talk much, implying that still waters run deep when they don't run all that deep at all.

Pyne and Turnbull had discussed the leadership a number of

times during the week leading up to the emergency cabinet meeting. Pyne thought Dutton was 'utterly unelectable', rating at single digits in the popularity stakes. Like himself. And he bursts out laughing when he tells me this. He could not understand how anybody with such a low rating could even think of launching a challenge. 'None of the normal people in the party room thought they could win with him as leader,' Pyne says. Turnbull shared Pyne's view: Dutton was unelectable. He did not believe for a moment, and never had, that anyone, including Dutton, could seriously think Dutton was leadership material.

Pyne did not like Dutton's Ray Hadley interview on Thursday saying he would quit cabinet if he disagreed with policy; he did not like Friday morning's *Telegraph* story; he did not like the fact that it took so long for Dutton to respond to it; and he did not think Dutton's tweet killed it. He thought it was 'lukewarm' and said the barest-possible minimum.

Pyne had concluded it was time for the government to stop self-lacerating over the NEG. He told his colleagues at the meeting, 'We can keep dragging our bloodied stump across the political firmament, leaving a trail of gore behind us, or we can cut our losses and move on.'

Dutton said nothing. Pyne thought, no, he is not getting away with not being called on to commit to the new cabinet position, which was effectively to abandon the NEG. So Pyne addressed himself directly to Dutton. 'Peter, the one person who has not spoken is you. You are the one person we need to know whether you support the cabinet position or not?' Dutton said he agreed with it.

Pyne also asked Dutton bluntly what he expected them to say when the media asked them about his leadership ambitions. Dutton replied that they should refer them to his tweet, which he reckoned had quashed the story. Others joined in, but Dutton denied anything was happening.

At the cabinet meeting the next day, Julie Bishop also addressed the herd of elephants stampeding around the room. Bishop urged her colleagues to get on with it and to set their differences aside.

Turnbull held a press conference with Morrison and Frydenberg on Monday before question time in parliament to announce that the NEG was on life support, that the emissions component would neither be regulated nor legislated, that the states should press ahead with the reliability guarantee, and that the federal government would concentrate on measures to get prices down, in line with recommendations from the Australian Competition and Consumer Council.

Under questioning, Turnbull said the emission target would be legislated, but would not be presented to parliament while it was obvious that the votes were not there to get it through. In Turnbull's view, this was not tantamount to killing or dumping the NEG, but leaving it as a live option if or when it became clear that the rebellion had been quelled and the numbers were there to pass it.

The press conference wound up with a question to Turnbull, asking him if he had spoken to Dutton and if he had his support.

Turnbull replied, 'Yes, absolutely. Peter Dutton was at our leadership group meeting this morning, and he was at cabinet last night. He's a member of our team; he's given me his absolute support.'

That last bit was a dead-set clue. Whenever a politician pledges his or her absolute support, you definitely know it's on.

It was a mess. The differences in the party appeared irreconcilable. To Trent Zimmerman, it looked like Turnbull was doing everything possible to avoid doing a deal with Labor. 'He was scarred by the events of 2009,' Zimmerman said. He thought Turnbull was being seen to bow too often to the right, and should have ploughed on. 'Make or break would have been better,' he said.

When Zimmerman said that to a cabinet colleague, he was told that Turnbull's strong view was that he did not want to be in a position where he could not rely on his own numbers.

Whereas Zimmerman thought Turnbull was giving in too much to the right, others thought he was giving in to the left: to Ben Morton, it looked like a repeat of 2009, when Turnbull was looking too eager to give in to Labor's demands. After question time that day, under persistent questioning from Labor, during which Turnbull said that the NEG would not be presented because the government didn't have the numbers in the parliament, Morton says he didn't have a clue what the government's energy policy was.

Although most MPs believed the situation was dire, they did not think anything major was imminent. They knew the monkey-podders were agitating, even more than usual, but they did not think Dutton was ready to make his move. While there were those urging him on, others had assumed that the stories over the weekend were beat-ups.

Tim Wilson was the only backbencher I spoke to who thought, as he went into Tuesday's party meeting, that given the choices he faced, Turnbull himself might pull on a leadership spill.

There was one other person who thought Turnbull might bring it on, and that was Peter Dutton.

Dutton knew that Turnbull loved the element of surprise. Dutton rang a couple of close colleagues, including, I believe, Cormann, on Monday night to see what they thought. The consensus view of Dutton's friends was that it was unlikely because, as Dutton so colourfully put it, 'He would blow himself up.'

CHAPTER FIVE

Days of madness

Like every other leader before him who was toppled, Malcolm Turnbull had been warned by friends, and even by people who could no longer be classed as his friends, or maybe never were, that his leadership was under threat. Any number of MPs told him he needed to be wary of Peter Dutton.

George Brandis sounded the alarm as far back as early 2017. Brandis had rung Turnbull early one morning after a major news story appeared on Dutton and the mooted Home Affairs department. A longstanding opponent of the creation of the department, Brandis was not happy about the story, which had appeared in the *Daily Telegraph* and which he suspected had come from Dutton's office. When Turnbull brushed him off, Brandis snapped, 'For God's sake, can't you see this guy is stalking you?'

Turnbull was dismissive. 'Don't be ridiculous, George. As if Dutton is capable of being prime minister.' And he laughed. Brandis told him the two of them might think it was ridiculous, but Dutton most certainly did not think it was. Turnbull told Brandis that Dutton was loyal to him.

'Yes,' Brandis replied. 'Like everyone else in this game, he is loyal until he is not. The day will come when he will come after you, mark my words.'

This echoed another warning to Turnbull from a key supporter of Morrison's soon after the 2016 election not to trust Dutton. Apart from anything else, this showed how early the Morrison camp was alert to the possibility of a Dutton move on the leadership.

In January 2018, Victorian backbencher Jason Wood was so angry with Turnbull for not visiting his electorate of Latrobe and for not taking seriously his concerns about the rise of African gangs that he put Turnbull on notice. Wood told him he would start doing the numbers against him by the end of the year if things did not improve.

A few months later, in May 2018, Turnbull received a friendlier caution from another Victorian Liberal, Russell Broadbent. Broadbent had met with him to discuss two issues pensions, and refugees. On the way out, Broadbent said to him, 'You know your leadership is in trouble?' He told him Dutton was on the move.

Turnbull dismissed Broadbent's warning, saying he had gone through every conceivable scenario that might arise and, according to Broadbent, had concluded he was 'untouchable'. It reminded Broadbent of another occasion when Turnbull had boasted to him that he knew more about a certain issue than anyone else in the parliament. Broadbent pointedly told him that the smartest kid in the room didn't always get the bag of lollies.

Mathias Cormann's regular lunch companion Michael Keenan, also extremely close to Dutton, dropped hints days out – at least to others – that Dutton was preparing to make his move. He had been complaining to people for months about Turnbull's tin ear and accusing him of having no political judgement. He was in no doubt that they were on track to lose the next election, that Dutton was by far the best alternative, and that Dutton would be prime minister by October.

Keenan was one of the few who was aware in advance of Dutton's plans, supportive of his push, and utterly convinced that he had the numbers.

But even after his conversation with Dutton on the VIP flight to Canberra on Sunday, Keenan's very good friend Steve Ciobo needed reassurance from Dutton that he really did have the numbers. Ciobo had begun to draw up his own list, going through every name, and made some calls.

Ciobo rang Ross Vasta, and asked him if he was doing the numbers for Julie Bishop. Vasta in turn spoke to Dutton, and appealed to him not to run for the leader's job, but to run on a ticket with Bishop, as her deputy. Vasta was convinced that ticket could win, particularly if they sped off to an election. Dutton would not hear of it. 'This is my time,' he told Vasta.

Vasta also spoke to Turnbull that night and told him he did not think he could win the next election. He should resign to give Bishop a clear run with Dutton as her deputy. Turnbull was similarly unreceptive.

Ciobo was struggling with the numbers. Finally, he called Dutton to say, Mate, can you come up to my office so we can go through it?

Ciobo wanted to review Dutton's count, name by name. He wanted to know who was a hard-Dutton supporter, who was soft-Dutton, who was hard-Turnbull, and who was soft-Turnbull.

Together, they ran through the entire party room of 85, and at the end concluded that Dutton had 51 votes, give or take one or two. That included Cormann, Fifield, and Cash. It obviously also included diehard Morrison supporters. This was more than enough to topple Turnbull.

As he sought counsel from his friends, Dutton was weighing up whether he should mount his challenge the next day. He had marked a different day in his calendar, two weeks hence, but events were overtaking him.

Ciobo and Keenan spoke again that night. They were perplexed.

How could Dutton have 51 votes and not jump? In their view, it was simple: if you have more than 50 per cent, you do it; if you don't, you don't. It's another golden rule of politics. If you have the numbers, you use them.

That night, if Dutton was ambivalent, Turnbull was resolute.

Two moments in those days of madness sealed Turnbull's fate. The first was when he declared his and Julie Bishop's positions vacant. The second came 48 hours later when Cormann defected.

Turnbull's action at Tuesday morning's Liberal Party meeting was a strategic masterstroke against Dutton. Unfortunately, Turnbull simultaneously inflicted a mortal blow on himself. It flushed out his enemies. It also showed there were too many of them for him to be able to survive.

Turnbull veered from calm, calculating lawyer to cage fighter as he desperately tried to quell the insurrection.

He would alternate between calling his colleagues crazy, angry that they couldn't see that with Newspoll at 49 to 51 per cent they were well placed, even better placed than Howard had ever been at that point in the electoral cycle, to win the next election, and then threatening to go to Yarralumla to bring the election on there and then. As late as Thursday, even after Turnbull had agreed to convene another party meeting to resolve the leadership, as well as committing not to run if the spill motion were carried, cars and cops were on alert. Christopher Pyne says 'friendly sources' told him that Turnbull had C-1, his official limousine, and his close personal protection on standby ready to zip off and visit the governor-general if necessary.

'He wanted to keep all his options open,' Pyne said later. In Simon Birmingham's view, it was untenable to call an election in the middle of such mayhem. 'You can't call an election against your own side,' Birmingham said later.

Others watching the disaster unfold from interstate – including the Victorian Liberal leader, Matthew Guy, who was gearing up to fight a tough campaign, and who had previously warned Turnbull about potentially disloyal ministers in his ranks, including the health minister, Greg Hunt – did privately believe that Turnbull should call an election. Guy believed that Turnbull could have cited as grounds the fact he could not be guaranteed a majority on the floor of the House, although of course that had not been tested.

Events unfolded so quickly, with such lethal consequences, that many of the participants had difficulty later reconstructing what had happened: what days meetings took place, and who said what to whom, when, and where. Different people recalled different elements of the same conversations. Others could not recall them at all. Some of them made notes of critical moments. Turnbull did, and so did Christian Porter.

Julie Bishop had only a few minutes to decide whether to put her deputy leadership on the line after Turnbull told her he was declaring his position vacant. The rest of the week was like that for the woman who had been deputy to four men over 11 years – not much time to think about anything. It was a blur. She was the peoples' choice, the most popular alternative, and the least-favoured by her colleagues, garnering a pitiful 11 votes in the final ballot. Afterwards, feeling wounded, humiliated, and betrayed, she spent months thinking about what she would do next.

There were, of course, repercussions from the differing recollections, particularly over whether Bishop had been told by Pyne that the moderates could not support her because she could not win against Dutton. Many of the moderates had made the threshold decision, most of them as soon as the first vote was announced, that Turnbull could not survive, and that being the case, they would have to back Morrison, because they believed they would not survive under Dutton – they would either lose their seats or lose their cabinet positions.

It was utterly pragmatic, it was completely brutal, and it was gut-wrenching. Cabinet ministers cried later in their offices as they recounted what happened during a week they described as one of the worst in their lives.

On Friday 17 August, after the *Daily Telegraph* exposed Dutton's intention to strike, Victorian frontbencher Michael Sukkar, promoted by Turnbull to the ministry, who would later try to muster the numbers for Dutton – despite having made an earlier vow never to move against a sitting prime minister – and who, along with his then state president, Michael Kroger, would face internal criticism for his behaviour, rang Sharri Markson, one of the authors of the *Telegraph* story, to tell her she had 'over-egged' the story.

Markson assured him she had very good sources. Thinking back, Sukkar reckons it must have come from someone close to Dutton – maybe not Dutton himself, because he wouldn't have wanted his fingerprints on it. Like others, he did not think the story was helpful to Dutton.

Some MPs dismissed the whole thing as preposterous, as a beat-up. Others went into meltdown. Others began to plan or plot in earnest. The ones who weren't already, that is.

After Bishop read the article, she waited for a rebuttal. Bishop's radar had been up well before then. She had been amazed in April when Dutton had confessed to having leadership ambitions. Bishop thought it was extraordinary that a member of the cabinet and the leadership group had made such an admission. She took it seriously, even if Turnbull appeared not to. Bishop noted how Dutton and the Abbott camp, which to her were one and the same thing, were ramping things up.

She rang Turnbull on Saturday morning to impress upon him that he needed to take it seriously, because Dutton was obviously planning to challenge him. Turnbull said he had been in touch with Dutton, and Dutton was going to release a statement.

In fact, Turnbull had contacted Dutton a number of times on Friday and over the weekend. They spoke and texted. Dutton kept reassuring him that he had his support and that he was not planning a challenge. Turnbull told him he had to say so, publicly. Cormann had also been in touch with Dutton. Turnbull and Dutton agreed on the form of words that Dutton eventually tweeted.

According to what Cormann told others in those early stages, he had warned Dutton that the whole thing was crazy, it was silly, and it was their job to keep everybody calm.

Bishop, knowing how tight Cormann and Dutton were, always believed that Cormann was deeply involved, and that the *Telegraph*'s story was well sourced.

Unlike Bishop, another close Turnbull ally, Simon Birmingham, who made three school visits that Friday, didn't think too much about it, and then when he did, thought it was a beat-up. Birmingham remembers that things 'heated up' on Saturday. He says he got a call from Morrison, asking him what he thought about the Dutton stories. Birmingham told Morrison that weekend that in his view the situation was 'saveable', but Dutton had to say something; it could not be left hanging. He says Morrison took it on board.

After talking to Morrison, Birmingham rang Trent Zimmerman to ask him to do a 'health check' of his fellow New South Wales moderates. Zimmerman was confident that Marise Payne, Jason Falinski, Paul Fletcher, and Craig Laundy would all stick. He didn't want to do a big ring-around in case word leaked out to the media. Journalists would have had even more of a field day, writing that Turnbull had been panicked into counting numbers.

Morrison was very active that weekend, ostensibly gathering intelligence to help Turnbull; however, there is no doubt every piece of information he gleaned was useful to him and his lieutenants, who were also speaking to MPs. Morrison spoke to his close allies and numbers men, Alex Hawke and Stuart Robert, a number of times.

Morrison says he also thought initially that the story was a beat-up. By Saturday, he thought it was decidedly odd. He spoke to Cormann, who told him he had spoken to Dutton and that 'there was nothing going on'. Morrison told me later that he trusted Cormann, and did not believe he was involved in or had knowledge of what Dutton was planning – which shows either great naivety or great disingenuousness on his part, given what everyone knows about their friendship and political partnership.

Dutton himself talks about his relationship with Cormann in such a way that the only conclusion capable of being drawn is that Dutton told him everything.

'Mathias and I walk every day,' Dutton told me later, when asked about his confidants, and whose counsel he had sought. 'We were like brothers; we have been very close over a long period of time. I trusted his political judgement. We worked together to keep him [Turnbull] afloat.

'What Mathias probably planned on doing was trying to negotiate a peaceful transition. That was unlikely to ever happen.'

Morrison spoke to Turnbull on Saturday. They talked tactics. Morrison gave Turnbull critical advice that day. He says he told Turnbull, 'Whatever you do, don't call a spill.' He had watched the Howard–Costello wars from a distance, and deduced that one of the reasons Howard survived during tough times was because he never brought on a vote in the party room. Costello himself never dared to bring one on because he knew he didn't have the numbers, and he didn't want to be humiliated – apart from the fact that he did not want to tear down a serving prime minister.

Morrison asked Turnbull that day how many times Howard had called a spill. Morrison says Turnbull seemed to take the point, and he thought that was the end of it. He didn't raise the subject with Turnbull again, but what Morrison also knew was that Dutton was different from Costello in many respects. His attitude to challenging the leader was one of them. Dutton had determined long before, as I recorded in the updated version of *The Road to Ruin*, released in August 2017, that if the opportunity arose, he would not baulk: he would run, and run hard, for the leadership. He would not let anyone get in his way – not Bishop, and not Abbott. And not Morrison either. They were rivals, never friends.

Two days before the 'challenge' became public, Laundy met with Dutton for half an hour. They spent five minutes dealing with an immigration matter, and then the remaining 25 minutes talking about the government's problems – where it was headed and what barnacles had to be removed.

Laundy was a Turnbull supporter to the core, but says he had an open relationship with Dutton. If Dutton thought something was going awry, Laundy says they would discuss it, and if necessary he would lobby Turnbull on Dutton's behalf.

This day, it was a constructive discussion. They were in furious agreement that energy was the big issue that needed fixing, that the immigration debate needed to be recast, and that the company tax cuts needed to be dumped to put the government on the best footing for the next election. Laundy left the meeting believing everything was fine. Certainly, there was no sign from Dutton that Laundy detected which indicated any wavering in Dutton's support for the prime minister.

When the *Daily Telegraph* story appeared two days later, Laundy was puzzled when Dutton did not move immediately to kill off the speculation. Laundy rang Sally Cray, Turnbull's closest adviser, on Saturday. In his view, Dutton was enjoying the attention. He was the only one being talked about as a replacement for Turnbull, and was revelling in it. He told her that Dutton needed to shut down the leadership talk. He offered to speak to Dutton if she wanted him to.

Showing her confidence and trust in Cormann, Cray told Laundy that 'Mathias is handling it'.

By Monday night, offices in Parliament House and restaurant tables in Kingston were dripping with leadership talk. Laundy had organised a regular dinner for the class of 2013, which included Queenslander Luke Howarth, at the Chiang Rai restaurant. Laundy made a fateful call after dinner finished: he rang Cray to warn her he was worried that Howarth might do something 'stupid' the next day. Turnbull, knowing Laundy was having dinner with the group, rang Laundy himself late that night to find out what had happened. Laundy told him what he had told Cray, that he was worried what Howarth might do, that he and Howarth had argued, and that he thought Howarth 'wasn't thinking straight'.

At another table at the Chiang Rai were Morrison's main men: Alex Hawke, Stuart Robert, Steve Irons, and the deputy whip, Bert van Manen.

At the Saffron Middle Eastern restaurant, another Morrison supporter, Ben Morton, was having dinner with Dutton supporters Michael Sukkar, Andrew Hastie, and Tony Pasin. Morton, a politically astute former state director of the party from Western Australia who had been instrumental in putting together winning campaign strategies, had spent much of the weekend pondering what he would do if the leadership came into play. And he had decided long before that if Turnbull went, Morrison was the answer. He had already turned away from Turnbull.

Morton also knew very well the feelings of his dinner companions. Morton had run Hastie's winning campaign for the seat of Canning in 2015, and shared an apartment with the conservative former SAS officer in Canberra. Morton decided it was best to put his cards on the table early, so he told the group that if anything happened, he would be supporting Morrison. He thought that, as minister for immigration, then social services, and then as treasurer, Morrison had shown himself to be the best equipped for the job. He liked it when Morrison talked of a fair go for those who had a go, and he thought he would have the authority to hold the party together. He did not think Dutton was the man for the job.

Later, Morton would say he was not a hater, and that he thought Turnbull was a 'lovely, genuine guy'. But Morton certainly hated that week. He believed the deal-making over the NEG, which in his view looked like Turnbull was more eager to strike a deal with the Labor premiers than with his own backbenchers, showed not only that he had a tin ear, but that each time he had to make a call, it was the wrong one.

Sukkar said afterwards that they dismissed the proposition that anything might happen the next day, and apart from discussing the Fairfax Ipsos poll – which, not surprisingly after the debacle over energy, showed support for the government had crashed – reckons they barely discussed the leadership. Of course not. Who could possibly think plotting was on the menu?

Well, Turnbull and Cray, for starters. They had been told that night that Sukkar was involved up to his eyeballs in promoting leadership speculation.

So widespread was the talk of a challenge that it reached Nationals minister Darren Chester. Chester heard that Dutton was planning a move, probably the next day. Chester was horrified. He texted Dutton around 10.00 pm, pleading with him not to run, saying it would not be in the government's interests. Dutton responded by asking Chester if he thought they could win the next election with Turnbull as leader. Chester was convinced they could, and said so in his reply to Dutton.

Morrison and Turnbull also spoke again late that night. During the day, he and Turnbull had met, and then Morrison had talked to Pyne.

'We were starting to get a little nervous,' Morrison told me. 'Things were a bit weird, and Christopher and I, independently, had gone and tried and worked out, well, if something were to happen, how many votes would they have? And, independently, we both came up with 35. Which was exactly what it was.

'And that night, I just, you know, Malcolm had got home, and I just rang him just to see how he was and, you know, we'd often do that. And he said, "How many [votes] do you think they'd have?" and I said "35". And he didn't think they would have that much. His office was saying to him that it would be in the high teens, 20 at most. And I said, "Well, I don't think that's right."'

In fact, that was not what Turnbull's staff was telling him.

Not knowing that Turnbull had already rung Laundy for a debrief, Cray had decided not to contact Turnbull to tell him about Laundy's exchanges with Howarth at the restaurant. It was late, and she didn't want to wake him.

Besides, she and Turnbull already knew that *The Australian* was running a story the next morning saying that Dutton was getting ready to challenge, probably that week. They had been reliably informed that the 'younger supporters' who would be referred to in *The Australian*'s story, urging Dutton to strike immediately, 'as early as this morning', included Sukkar.

With sleep an unaffordable luxury, Cray went online to read the papers around 4.00 am. *The Australian* headline roared 'Turnbull Braces for Challenge'. Turnbull texted her at 5.20 am to see if she was awake. She called him. He was with Lucy, so he put Cray on speaker phone.

Turnbull told Cray he had decided to call a spill himself at that morning's party meeting. He said the whole thing was ridiculous, and that 'we have to draw a line under it'. He knew they were coming for him. He suspected that Dutton would get either Howarth or Jason Wood, or both of them, to pull something on, and he was not going to sit there and wait for them.

On the one hand, they had supporters and other journalists saying it wasn't real; on the other hand, the craziness had taken hold. They knew Monday had not gone well.

Cray suggested that he should not tell anyone of his plan, he should think about it, and they should look over the numbers when they got to work. It was the calmest she had heard him for days. He was resolved. It might be the right thing to do, she thought, but they needed to make sure they knew what the answer would be.

Around 7.00 am, they were again poring over the numbers in Cray's office. Of course they had lists. Everybody had lists. Previously, it was who sat where on same-sex marriage, or who supported or opposed the NEG. Now it was whether they supported Turnbull or not. From Turnbull's perspective, the swing factor was the Morrison people: Alex Hawke, Stuart Robert, Steve Irons, Lucy Wicks, Chris Crewther, Ann Sudmalis, Bert van Manen, and Morrison himself.

Turnbull's office had calculated the numbers both ways: with Morrison's people, and without Morrison's people. By their count, if Morrison's people were with Turnbull, Dutton would have 28 votes; if they were not, Dutton would have 35. They thought they might be one vote out either way. They did not know at this stage that Ben Morton was with Morrison, and that he would vote for Dutton on Tuesday. Who voted where that day is important because, unlike the Longman by-election, where he needed a three in front, on this day, Turnbull needed a two in front.

As Turnbull's staff were going through their lists that morning, Laundy received a text at 7.11 am from a friend, asking if they still had the numbers. Laundy replied, 'Yes, mate, but I think there is a three in front of their numbers, and a four in front of ours. i.e we live today but I reckon we'll die around 5.10 thurs arvo.'

So whatever confidence Turnbull was showing to other colleagues that his numbers were high enough to save him, his staff and confidantes did not share it, and their calculations did not support it.

Turnbull made a few calls. He rang Queenslander Andrew Laming, who assured Turnbull that if anything happened, he would vote for him. Ken Wyatt says Turnbull called him ahead of the party meeting on Tuesday to ask if he had his support. Wyatt says Turnbull framed it as 'Just asking, just curious.'

'What I don't know is who gave him advice to vacate his position. It lacked logic, and may have been an act of treachery,' Wyatt told me later. Wyatt, not knowing it was Turnbull himself who decided, believed then that whoever advised Turnbull to do it was definitely not trying to help him.

Wyatt also recalled being told a few days previously by fellow West Australian Melissa Price that she had talked to colleagues who believed that Turnbull would be gone by the end of the week. Wyatt suspected that Cormann was one of them.

Turnbull also called Alex Hawke. He asked him if he could count on his support if anything happened. Hawke said he could. Hawke told him that while he liked Dutton, he was not going to back him in: 'No way.' Turnbull had promoted Hawke to the frontbench, so Hawke felt he owed him.

Hawke told Turnbull that things were going badly and that he thought Dutton and his monkey-podders were on the move 'They are coming,' he warned. Turnbull agreed. Hawke says he told Turnbull, 'You are in the 50s.' According to Hawke, Turnbull said, 'No, in the 60s.' They were both way out. In light of the turmoil over energy and the extremely poor result in Longman, there was an unforgiving mood in the party room, which both of them either downplayed or miscalculated.

Hawke was worried that Turnbull and his office were in an ivory tower. He was also frustrated by the constant assaults from the likes of Alan Jones, who admitted to texting MPs to tell them not to vote for Turnbull, and from Abbott-lover Andrew Bolt, making what Hawke described as crazy accusations, saying Turnbull was a Labor plant.

Turnbull rang Stuart Robert on Monday evening, and again on Tuesday morning. On Monday evening, Robert told him it was diabolical in Queensland. 'They are coming for you,' he says he told Turnbull. They were all speaking the same language.

Turnbull asked Robert if he could count on his support. He told Turnbull that, yes, he could.

Robert admitted in an interview with me later that, during that day and evening, he had told colleagues that Turnbull was finished. He says he told them that Dutton was going after Turnbull, and that Turnbull could not win – conversations that were very damaging to Turnbull and conversely helpful to Morrison. Robert's conversations accomplished two objectives: they cemented the notion that Turnbull was terminal, and they planted the seed that Morrison was a viable alternative to both Dutton and Turnbull.

Robert had also had long conversations with his housemates, Irons and Morrison. Robert says he did not know there would be a vote on Tuesday, but he knew that the momentum was with Dutton, and his strong suspicion was that they would engineer something on Tuesday. He figured that Dutton had 30 votes on Sunday, would pick up another five by Tuesday, and would be at 45 by Thursday. That is the way Robert reckons these things have always worked. Once they start, there is no stopping them, and the only question is who wins in the end. Robert, clearly convinced it was over for Turnbull, was determined to do everything he could to ensure he was replaced by Morrison and not Dutton.

Turnbull rang Robert again at 7.13 am on Tuesday. Forgoing greetings, Turnbull said to Robert directly that he had heard he was voting for Dutton. 'Hello, PM, how are you?' Robert asked sarcastically, before again assuring him that he, Hawke, Irons, and others, including van Manen, would not be voting for Dutton.

Hawke says he voted for Turnbull on Tuesday, as does Robert. Irons is reluctant to give a straight answer, to say yes directly and simply to the question, 'Did you vote for Turnbull?', saying only that he always voted for Turnbull. Van Manen, who was listed in the media as voting for Dutton, refused to respond to repeated requests for an interview.

The old saying has it that you can only believe those who say they aren't voting for you. There are sound historical reasons for this. Fibs and fibbers abound in leadership ballots. They are either too devious to play it straight or too cowardly to confess what they are planning. Or plotting.

After Turnbull told Bishop before the start of the usual leadership meeting that he had decided to vacate his position, she told me she did not try to talk him out of it. She says she had no time, only a few minutes before the rest of their colleagues came in for the leadership meeting. She felt she had no choice but to follow suit. She could not see how she could remain in her position if he spilled his, so she agreed to follow suit and vacate the deputy leadership.

The whip, Nola Marino, whose task it was to organise the ballot papers, was also in the prime minister's office when other members of the leadership group arrived. Pyne was surprised when he walked into the prime minister's office and saw her sitting in Cray's office, with Bishop already there. He wondered if something was up. Nobody said anything, so he didn't ask. Often, it's a case of don't ask, don't tell.

Later, Dutton was convinced that the Morrison camp knew in advance, if only by a few minutes – more than enough time to text each other to decide what to do. He deduced that Marino told her deputy, van Manen, so that he could help her prepare and distribute the ballot papers, and that he then alerted his friends.

In fact, Marino had told both her deputies – van Manen, who was part of Morrison's weekly prayer group, and South Australian Rowan Ramsey – to be ready for a ballot. She told them 20 minutes before the meeting began. They sorted out who would do what.

Ramsey swears he did not tell a soul. Van Manen would not answer my questions.

'I'm assuming, and I'm pretty sure it's true, that anyone who was associated with me voted for Malcolm,' Morrison told me in an interview in early December 2018. In fact, that was not true.

He said that the only person who knew in advance of Turnbull's plan was Bishop, even though it had been widely reported that Marino had known beforehand. This turned out to be inaccurate. In fact, after discussing it with her chief adviser, Nathan Winn, on Monday afternoon, Marino concluded that everything was pointing to a showdown in the party room, so they decided it would be prudent have ballot papers ready. She took her deputies into her confidence the next morning, before the meeting began. But few knew that at the time, or subsequently. Everyone assumed she had had inside knowledge, and that Turnbull or his office had tipped her off to his plan.

Morrison told me it was the first he had heard that Marino knew.

'She's a vault. She didn't tell anyone,' he said, adding that it made sense for her to know, so she could get the ballot papers ready. 'But Nola wouldn't have told a soul.'

Me: 'Bert.'

Morrison: 'Well, he's a whip.'

Me: 'Yeah, deputy – but he is also one of your people.'

Morrison insisted: 'None of us knew. I texted Pyne in the meeting, and I texted Mathias and said, "Did you guys know anything about this?" and they said, "No, did you?", and I said, No."'

He further says that none of his people texted him to ask him what they should do. What is obvious, though, is that many people in that room were furiously texting one another, so by the time the ballot papers were distributed, they were able to decide – those who were planning, as well as those who were plotting – what to do, particularly as they were expecting that something would happen, and had planned accordingly.

Nevertheless, Turnbull's announcement was a WTF moment for most of the 84 MPs in the room. (Arthur Sinodinos was still on sick leave.) There was a murmur, quickly followed by another murmur when Dutton stood up to challenge. Birmingham says his heart sank and began beating faster at the same time. Jane Prentice looked across at Dutton as he stood up, as if to say 'What the hell' to him. He gave a slight shrug of his shoulders.

As soon as the vote of 48 for Turnbull and 35 for Dutton was read out, with one MP abstaining, Dutton says his immediate thought was. 'He is dead.'

Ciobo and Michael Keenan did not think Turnbull was dead. They thought Dutton was, and that he should have called it all off then and there.

They had gone into the meeting convinced that if there were a spill, one of their very best mates would emerge prime minister. Then the vote was read out. They couldn't believe it. Thirty-five?! What happened to the 50 or 51 that Ciobo and Dutton had counted up the night before?

Ciobo retreated to his office, wondering what the hell had just happened. He was a cabinet minister who had just voted against his prime minister. He couldn't connect what had happened with what Dutton had assured him would happen. Keenan felt the same.

They couldn't figure out what Cormann was up to, given the reports that he had voted for Turnbull. They were later led to believe he hadn't voted for Turnbull; that he had in fact voted for Dutton. This is hotly disputed by those who remain close to Cormann, saying they have no doubt that on Tuesday he voted for Turnbull, and that he had told others around him in the party room to follow suit. Fifield definitely voted for Turnbull.

Hastie, who sat between Cormann and Christian Porter in the party room, had been planning to get up and speak again on the NEG, because he was still fuming about what had happened on Friday. Then as soon as he heard Turnbull vacate the leadership, he says he had an almighty adrenalin rush. 'We are going straight to a ballot. He's gone nuclear,' Hastie thought.

Just then, Cormann leaned across Hastie and said to Porter, 'This is fucking crazy.' Porter asked Cormann if he knew about it. A clearly angry Cormann said he did not. Ever the military man, Hastie says that when he saw Dutton stand up to challenge, as he buttoned his suit jacket, he thought he had a look about him that he had seen on the face of soldiers getting ready to board the helicopters that would carry them to their missions.

'A mix of adrenalin, courage, and uncertainty,' Hastie would say later. 'I voted for Dutton, and I am not going to be lectured to by people. It's not about revenge. But what's good for the goose is good for the gander, and by the way, you [the prime minister] have declared the position vacant.'

Unlike the despair felt by Ciobo and Keenan, when Hastie heard the vote-count of 35, he thought, 'Wow! For a disorganised, spontaneous vote, that's a pretty big number.' Then he thought there had to be ministers in there, and assumed that a daisy chain of resignations would follow.

Hastie does not criticise Turnbull for bringing it on to take Dutton by surprise, but believes there would have been fewer votes against Turnbull if he had required a spill motion instead. He says that vacating the leadership made it easier for MPs to vote for Dutton, because technically they were not voting against the prime minister. Even so, when asked, he could not say which way he would have voted if the first vote had been on a spill motion. He says that after the meeting, he caught up with colleagues to talk about what had just happened. He kept thinking, 'Holy moly.' Wyatt spotted

Hastie in conversation with Sukkar and South Australian Tony Pasin.

Along with them, Hastie became heavily involved in Dutton's campaign. He acknowledges the criticism of Dutton's putsch as chaotic.

In his defence, he says he did not know Dutton was planning to challenge, nor did his backbench friends. Many of them were encouraging Dutton to run, or asking him if he was going to, yet there was no overt preparation that they were aware of for a challenge that they were all encouraging him to make.

'There wasn't a strong lieutenant working for Peter,' Hastie says.

Turnbull's action worked to the extent that it caught them all by surprise. They were galvanised, but completely uncoordinated.

Hastie, who has a good sense of humour, pokes fun at the media for running stories saying the corridors were abuzz with feverish lobbying. Unlike in the old Parliament House, he says, you look down the corridors of the building they all now occupy, and all you can see are tumbleweeds.

'The chief protagonists are completely separated from the backbench. It all added to the confusion and chaos. There's only so much you can do with Whatsapp,' he says.

He also says Cormann took charge once he came out against Turnbull. He refers to Cormann as 'the General'.

Hastie admits the campaign was nothing like when Turnbull dislodged Abbott. 'The 2015 coup was like the raid on Bin Laden – months of planning in secret, very swiftly done, swiftly executed. Because this was so spontaneous, as a result, to the outside observer it looks very untidy,' he says. Hastie's honesty is commendable, if understated.

Victorian senator James Paterson, whose role would attract some internal criticism, and who would later come to regret his part in events, echoed Hastie's assessment and then some.

He agreed it was 'completely half-arsed'.

'It was shambolic,' he said.

Paterson said there was no one in charge. Dutton had no alternative policy agenda, no campaign manager, and no committee.

Most of them had never been in the middle of a coup before. They did not have a clue what to do or how to go about it.

Hastie was uncertain what would happen after Tuesday's vote. He thought maybe it would die down. He saw Dutton go over and shake Turnbull's hand after the vote was read out, as if they were two captains who had just played a game of football, game over, move on. 'It just seemed really odd,' he said later. 'All I can remember is going to question time, and all the ministers looking very gloomy.'

Surprisingly, there was no formal gathering of the monkey-podders in that room until Thursday afternoon. Before that, they met in clusters in each other's offices, or communicated on their mobile phones.

On Tuesday night, after being interviewed on Sky by Jones, Hastie had a home-cooked meal with ACT senator Zed Seselja and his family. Hastie regarded Seselja as an older brother. Their thinking at that stage was taken up by the prospect of widespread frontbench resignations.

Hastie remembers Seselja feeling weighed down by it, not at all enthusiastic, with neither of them having a clue what would happen next.

Another West Australian, senator Dean Smith, voted for Dutton and against Turnbull both times that week. When Turnbull declared the leadership vacant on Tuesday morning, Smith was both surprised and angry. Sitting between Cormann and Keenan, Smith vented, 'This is an ambush. It's outrageous.'

He is convinced the underlying reason for many in the right voting against Turnbull was his role in the same-sex marriage process. They never forgave him for it. This is not paranoia on

Smith's part. It was also one of the underlying reasons behind Smith's vote against Turnbull. As one of the leaders of the campaign for same-sex marriage, you would think Smith would have been one of the last to vote against Turnbull, but he was dirty with Turnbull over it, nursing grievances over the way he says Turnbull treated him throughout that debate.

Smith was unmoved by Dutton's low approval ratings. He thinks popularity in a leader is over-rated. He still has the original cover of *The Bulletin* magazine featuring John Howard in his first iteration as opposition leader during the early 1980s, when his approval rating dropped to 18 per cent, which prompted *The Bulletin* to pose the question, 'Why does this man bother?'

Dutton had suggested the SSM postal ballot, which Smith did not approve of, but it did help make marriage equality a reality. Then Dutton had voted for the bill – unamended – which was in accordance with the wishes of his electorate, where 65 per cent voted Yes. Smith heartily approved of that.

Smith thought that Turnbull had become a 'lazy campaigner'. He liked Dutton, and liked the fact that he always had to fight to win his seat of Dickson, which he retained with a slim margin of 1.6 per cent after the 2016 election, and won by only 217 votes in the Ruddslide of 2007. Dutton's margin improved slightly to 2 per cent after the 2018 redistribution.

Smith had previously asked Turnbull twice in the party room to arrange for the party's federal director to address them on the 2016 campaign, which he thought was both poorly executed and lazy – just like the 2018 super Saturday by-elections were poorly executed and lazy.

He met with Turnbull in Perth on 10 August to discuss Smith's idea of a population inquiry. Smith remembers that it got testy, and then Smith finished by telling Turnbull that he respected his decision to install five West Australians in the cabinet – Bishop,

Cormann, Cash, Porter, and Keenan – but he needed to do what Ronald Reagan had done with the Russians: trust and verify. In other words, there were people there who could not be trusted.

He told Turnbull he needed to widen his circle of advice. Smith reckons that Turnbull wasn't interested.

After the party meeting on the NEG, Smith had a strong sense that the leadership issue would come to a head, although he says he did not know it would be on the Tuesday.

Bishop and Morrison both subsequently called Smith to seek his vote. He told them both that he would be voting for Dutton. Ever the pragmatist, thinking he could outbid his opponent, Morrison asked him, 'What's he offered you?' Smith replied that Dutton had offered him nothing and that he had asked for nothing.

Smith was convinced that if Turnbull had stayed leader, they would have lost government. 'I was of the view things would get worse for us,' he said.

On Tuesday, Ben Morton voted against Turnbull rather than for Dutton, and then told Morrison after the meeting that he would vote for him if he ran. Morton also told Laundy that Turnbull was finished and that Turnbull needed to know this. He offered to accompany Laundy to see Turnbull to tell him so.

Broadbent, who voted for Turnbull both times in 2018, just as he had voted for Abbott in 2015, texted Turnbull, urging him to sack all the ministers who had voted against him. He did not believe that Tuesday's vote meant Turnbull was terminal. And he did not believe that Turnbull should have said he would not run if the spill motion was passed. He thought that sealed his fate. Quoting Churchill, Broadbent said later, 'You never resign and you never give up.' He did not hear back.

If you ask Broadbent why Turnbull is no longer prime minister, he says, 'I am a great believer in what goes around, comes around. He undermined Abbott to the point of destruction, and he was undermined to the point of destruction.'

Broadbent thought Turnbull had been a good prime minister, but, 'He wasn't good at politics. He allowed himself to be talked out of his leadership.'

Julia Banks was shattered, and went to see Turnbull after the vote on Tuesday. Banks was convinced she would not have won her seat in 2016 if not for him. Even though he had not campaigned there with her before the election – no one thought she could win, and she complained of being starved of money and resources by Victorian campaign headquarters – Turnbull's image had been plastered everywhere in her electorate of Chisholm. She was the only Liberal who won a seat off Labor. She told Turnbull that if Dutton got up, she was out of there – she would quit. Turnbull's office helped her draft a press release announcing her resignation from the Liberal Party.

Inside the party room after the vote, Pyne heard Turnbull say to Dutton, after they shook hands, that he should remain in the cabinet. Dutton replied, 'No, mate.'

As they left the room, Pyne also told Dutton he should stay in the cabinet. Dutton gave the same answer, 'No, mate.' For good measure, Dutton added, 'Malcolm's move was a fatal mistake.' Pyne warned him there could not be a change in leaders – the Australian public would not tolerate it – adding, 'You have to stay in the cabinet.'

Pyne and Dutton had a curious relationship. They were polar opposites in many ways, but because each of them breathed and oozed politics, they also had a healthy pragmatic streak. Dutton reckons he even toyed with the idea of asking Pyne to run as his deputy, which would have been stunning, because Pyne was threatening that if Dutton were victorious, and then dumped him from cabinet, he would quit parliament altogether.

In the days leading up to that week, Turnbull and Pyne were having regular discussions about whether there was anything going on with the leadership, or inside the 'arsehole' faction, as Pyne called the triple-As. Pyne's assessment, which of course changed over the weekend, was that nothing was happening, 'not because people were in love with Malcolm, but because Dutton was utterly unelectable'.

After the party meeting, Birmingham and others told Turnbull to do whatever he had to do to keep Dutton and the ministers who voted for him in the tent. They were convinced that if he was able to do this, he might last out the week, buying enough time for MPs to fly back to their electorates, where they would face the wrath of the voters.

While Pyne, Banks, and Bishop were threatening to quit if Dutton got up, others threatened to go to the crossbench. The government would be plunged into even greater chaos.

As soon as he heard the result of the vote, Chester said he was 'alarmed' that it was so close. In his view, Turnbull had made a mistake to vacate, and the question now was whether Turnbull's leadership was still salvageable. In his view it was, so he decided to do what he could to help Turnbull. Chester decided to front the media on some bogus local issue. His real intent was to send a message to the Liberals that the Coalition would disintegrate and the government would fall. He wanted to demonstrate his unequivocal support for Turnbull.

Chester went public, saying if Dutton was elected leader he would go to the crossbench, as would two other Nationals MPs. Although he did not name them, the other two were another Victorian, Damian Drum, and Kevin Hogan from New South Wales. Of course, the Nationals don't get a vote on the Liberal leadership, but Chester was trying to influence it. And he wanted to exert pressure to avoid a second ballot.

He thinks it might have shifted a couple of votes, but he was convinced that if Turnbull could make it to the end of the week, he might survive.

'The members would realise the public had had a gutful,' Chester said later. 'I believed it was retrievable. Colleagues would realise the folly of their way. There had been a ballot; there was no need for a second vote.

'It wasn't personal against Dutton. It was intentional as a warning to people in the Dutton camp that there was no reason to believe you could continue as a government.

'I thought we were on track to win [with Turnbull]. We just needed to be out there united and selling our achievements,' he says. Despite the disunity, Chester thought the government's record under Turnbull would carry it through. What surprised him during that time of madness was that so few Liberals went out to do what he did that Tuesday.

Although his fellow National MP Kevin Hogan did subsequently shift to the crossbench, Drum did not, and says now that he was never going to. Drum told me he met with Turnbull on Wednesday morning. Turnbull had fulfilled an engagement to catch up with business people from Shepparton in Drum's electorate of Murray.

Turnbull took Drum into his office, and showed him seat-by-seat tracking polling in marginal electorates that he had stored on his desktop computer. The polling of marginal seats in June, after the budget and before the by-elections, when the government appeared to stabilise, had the Coalition at 54 per cent. The final batch of polling in July across the key seats had the Coalition at 52 per cent on a two-party-preferred basis, and Labor at 48 per cent. It looked like they would pick up two seats in Tasmania – Bass and Braddon – and perhaps a third – Lyons. In Victoria, it appeared they would hold on to all seats, including Dunkley and Corangamite. They looked set to pick up at least Lindsay in New South Wales, Herbert in Queensland, and perhaps Cowan in the west. The greatest negative, of course, was the disunity, and the greatest asset for the government, apart from Turnbull himself, was

Bill Shorten. Turnbull was on track to increase his slim majority, if only they would allow him to govern. Which, of course, they wouldn't, because the objective of Abbott and his friends was to destroy him, no matter what.

'We are in a good place. I can't believe they are doing what they are doing. It's madness,' Turnbull told Drum.

Drum agreed. 'It is madness,' he said. Drum liked Dutton. 'I like the role that Dutton plays in the government – the hard-arsed immigration minister protecting our borders, deporting criminals, keeping paedophiles out, and making sure Australia has national-security agencies and border-protection policies that are the envy of the world,' he told me later.

'But to have such a hard-arsed person as leader will never wash with Australians.'

Drum speaks as a southerner, and, as he readily admits, although they are still conservatives, they are different beasts from the northerners. 'The Victorian psyche is very different from rural New South Wales or Queensland,' he says.

Turnbull met with both Cormann and Dutton in his office later on Tuesday. There are differing accounts of what happened over the deputy leadership – whether it was offered by Turnbull, or put up by Dutton and Cormann. Each of them insists it was the other. Ciobo says he tried to set himself up as an 'honest broker' by negotiating between the camps over Bishop's job of deputy leader. He swears he can't remember who came up with the idea of replacing Bishop with Dutton, whether it was Turnbull or Dutton.

One version has it that it was Cormann, already in a meeting with Turnbull in his office before Dutton joined them, who suggested to Turnbull that Dutton could be made deputy leader as a way of breaking the impasse. This at least fits with Cormann's purported desire for an orderly transition.

Turnbull rejected it, pointing out that it was not a gift he could give. It was the gift of the party room. Turnbull has insisted that any suggestion he made the offer to Dutton is a lie; however, there was apparently another conversation after the Longman by-election, when both Cormann and Dutton sounded out Turnbull's advisers about the deputy leadership. Dutton and Cormann, according to one who spoke to them, were concerned that the Turnbull–Bishop combination did not appeal to the base. The leader and his deputy weren't talking to the 'after darkers', Sky's post-sundown audience. The advisers suggested to Dutton that he raise it with Turnbull directly.

Another version is that Turnbull himself had raised the prospect of the deputy leadership with Dutton about a week before the party-room meeting. It was a brief conversation, leaving Dutton convinced that Turnbull had separated from Bishop and that his office was operating on the basis that she was 'moving on'.

Dutton does not think it would have been to Yarralumla to become governor-general, although Turnbull had in fact mentioned to Bishop a while before that there would be a vacancy there shortly.

According to at least one source close to both Turnbull and Bishop, Turnbull was fully intending to offer her the post in the hope she would take it up. As well as believing she would have done a superb job, it would have freed up the deputy's job for Dutton, and the foreign affairs portfolio for Cormann, which he dearly wanted.

Dutton, who by then had set his sights higher, reckons it would have been a 'knights and dames' moment for Turnbull if he had made Bishop governor-general.

In any case, he says it was Turnbull who raised the deputy leadership again with him after the vote. Dutton says he rejected it, telling Turnbull, 'It's untenable because I will be challenging you for the leadership.'

Dutton told Turnbull he could not serve in his cabinet. Dutton reckons that, despite what had transpired, the conversation was cordial. 'Because he wanted me to stay, saying he hoped I would reconsider,' he said.

Dutton did not consider sitting pat and waiting until the next parliamentary sitting bracket to strike again, which at least one member of his camp thought later would have been a better strategy.

'I did not think about pausing. I thought he was terminal, and I thought it had to be resolved. It needed to be done more quickly, rather than stretching it out,' he said.

Ciobo's meeting with Turnbull after the first ballot was tense by comparison. Ciobo offered his resignation, even though he thought Dutton was done for.

Turnbull accused Ciobo of doing Dutton's numbers. He denied it, and then when Turnbull asked him who was doing the numbers, Ciobo told him it was Dutton himself, along with Cormann.

Turnbull disputed the idea that Cormann was involved. He rejected the notion completely, telling Ciobo that Cormann was doing everything he could to talk Dutton out of challenging. Less than 24 hours later, Turnbull would realise how wrong he was.

When Ciobo left Turnbull's office, his head was spinning. Dutton had told him the opposite – that Cormann was doing his numbers. He never thought in a million years that Dutton would lie to him. He kept telling Dutton that Cormann was lying to him [Dutton], and that he was not 'with him'.

Ciobo and Keenan thought none of it made any sense. Pretty soon, they came to realise that they couldn't believe anything anybody was saying. Ciobo concluded that in the 'fog of war and all that', lots of fibs were being told, and it was impossible to know who was telling the truth and who was not.

Pyne, meanwhile, reassured Turnbull after the meeting that bringing on a leadership vote was the right thing to do. 'We can't have those people operating in the shadows in the way they have been. You have to call them out,' he recalled saying.

Weeks later, he still believed it had been the right call. 'Why should he be eaten like a fly-blown sheep, like a bull being stabbed repeatedly with swords by those people? If he was going to go out, he would go out fighting. He did the right thing. Those arseholes, the coup-plotters – I thought that we won.'

Both Bishop and Pyne professed to be happy with Turnbull's vote. Bishop points out that she had been in the thick of five challenges, including one where the winner got there by one vote. That was Abbott against Turnbull in 2009. Birmingham's initial reaction was relief that Turnbull had won the ballot. He was thinking, can we still survive, can we pull it together? They regrouped in Turnbull's office, where Birmingham also told Turnbull he had to speak to Dutton to offer him his position back in the cabinet, and see if he was willing to pledge loyalty.

Pyne reckons there is always one-third of the party that doesn't want the leader, no matter who the leader is, and there were always around 30 who never wanted Turnbull as leader because he wasn't right-wing enough.

'They would have been the people who said to John Howard, why are you encouraging Malcolm Turnbull to stay? This is the National Civic Council, DLP, grouper, Bob Santamaria view of the world,' a clearly upset Pyne said in an interview with me weeks later.

'I lunched with Tony Abbott in Adelaide at the Dynasty Chinese restaurant when I was a backbencher and he was a new parliamentary secretary, and he said in front of me and Christopher Pearson [a writer and close friend of Abbott's], "The DLP is alive and well, and living inside the Liberal Party."'

In fact, the vote of 35 against Turnbull was too high. If it had been in the low 20s, Turnbull would have bought valuable time, dismissing the insurrection as the work of a small band of guerrilla/gorillas. But a vote in the 30s only spurred on his enemies and deepened suspicions in Turnbull's office that Morrison's men had helped inflate Dutton's vote, and that they had in fact helped deliver the mortal blow.

Even among those closest to him, it was painfully clear that Turnbull's chances of survival had been rendered somewhere between zip and zero. Turnbull, however, was far from convinced that it was over. They were difficult days, and he was not the easiest person to handle. Accepting your own political death sentence, even if it is delivered by people you trust, is no small thing. 'Managing Malcolm was a heavy gig,' Laundy was to say later.

Turnbull was angry; he was not going to give up without a fight. When Dutton and his camp demanded another meeting for another ballot, he insisted they had to produce 43 signatures (representing a majority of the party room) before he would call it. They were outraged, and later blamed him for them having to use heavy-handed tactics to try to get the signatures.

Turnbull had a long list of people inside and outside parliament whom he blamed for his predicament. *The Australian* did not editorialise for his removal; however, the news and opinion pages were regularly filled with stories and commentary highly critical of him or, conversely, favourable to Abbott. The little foxes on Sky did not have big viewing audiences – Paul Murray was still the highest, with around 50,000 a night – however, they beamed straight into the homes of conservatives in regional Australia, particularly Queensland. Almost without exception, MPs outside the cities mentioned the war waged by Sky's after-dark presenters against Turnbull.

On Wednesday morning, around 10.00 am, the day after the first vote, Turnbull spoke with News Corps' executive chairman, Rupert Murdoch, who was visiting Australia. Turnbull had been told that Murdoch was peeved Turnbull had not tried to call him, even though the prime minister's chief of staff, Clive Mathieson, a former editor of *The Australian*, had been in touch with Campbell

Reid, who runs corporate affairs for News Corp, to say his boss wanted to catch up with Murdoch.

Murdoch was in Australia coincidentally – although conspiracy theories are much more interesting – mainly to holiday with his two youngest daughters, Chloe and Grace. He was neither peeved, nor upset, nor angry that he had not spoken with Turnbull. He was, in fact, said to have been somewhat relieved. One scheduled call between the two had fallen through because of Murdoch's conflicting appointments, so another was slotted in.

Murdoch knew almost exactly what Turnbull was going to say. He had been well briefed by his editors in advance of his discussion with Turnbull about the prime minister's views on the activities of the various arms of his Australian operations.

Murdoch was, however, later annoyed by suggestions he had told Kerry Stokes, the executive chair of Seven Group, that Turnbull had to go. Through Campbell Reid, Murdoch emphatically denies he said that.

According to one version of events, which I put to Stokes in an email, Stokes had relayed to Turnbull a 'weird' conversation with Murdoch, who had told him that Turnbull 'had to go'. I also put it to Stokes that he had sought to apply pressure to Cormann to stick with Turnbull, and that he had texted at least two other cabinet ministers, backers of Dutton, urging them to vote for Turnbull.

Stokes responded with a carefully worded email, which I quote here verbatim, including spelling mistakes and typos:

> That is complete fabrication. I never spoke to Corman all about any mater before the election of MORRISON.
>
> I never said I had a problem with Murdoch's [sic] at all I did tell Malcolm I thought he had a problem the Aus was strongly against him ALAN Jones was against him on radio and ski News Peta Credlin had strong views.

> Turnbull had ignored Rupert being in Aus for a prolonged period with his children.
>
> I never asked anyone to support Turnbull. What I told him was pretty self-evident.

First, in this emailed reply, Stokes avoided any reference to his purported conversation with Murdoch, which he had apparently relayed to Turnbull; second, I did not say he 'spoke' to Cormann – I said he had sought to apply pressure, which I am assured he did via text.

Also, he texted at least two other cabinet ministers, seeking to convince them to stick with Turnbull. In those texts – the substance of which has been provided to me – he told them that he fully supported Turnbull as prime minister, that no one else had any chance of leading them to victory at the next election, and if there was a change of leader, the party 'will not recover'.

One cabinet minister said emphatically that in the text he received from Stokes, the chair of the Seven Group had 'unequivocally' supported Turnbull and sought to dissuade him from voting for Dutton.

The other part of the conspiracy theory, that Murdoch flew in to help make it happen for Dutton, also falls a bit flat, especially given Murdoch's purported request to editors over dinner to 'remind me again about Dutton and what his policies are'. They had met once. Murdoch's lack of engagement with, and interest in, Australian politics was obvious, particularly as the take-out from some of those present was that Murdoch was actually asking to be reminded who Dutton was.

Turnbull told Murdoch on the Wednesday morning that he could not understand why News Corp – principally *The Australian*, the *Daily Telegraph*, and Sky – had turned against him. He told Murdoch his Australian outlets were running a campaign of destabilisation against him and his government. He said it would end one way and one way only, and that would be with Bill Shorten as prime minister.

He also told Murdoch that if Dutton were elected leader, an election would quickly follow because he would not be able to maintain the confidence of the House.

Turnbull complained more than once during the phone conversation that News Corp was running a campaign against him and the government. Murdoch rejected this, saying that Paul 'Boris' Whittaker, the then editor in chief of *The Australian*, was running his own show. Murdoch said a number of times that he was basically retired, and that he would speak to his son Lachlan, executive co-chair of News Corp, who runs the Australian operations. It was not an angry conversation, and it went for 10 or 15 minutes. Mathieson sat in Turnbull's office during the call.

Around this time, Cormann visited Turnbull in his office to tell him that more ministers had switched to Dutton. Turnbull was convinced that, in fact, the opposite had happened – that Dutton had actually lost votes. Ministers who had voted against him had repledged their loyalty. Other MPs had also had a rethink, particularly after reports that Abbott would be promoted and that Dutton was planning to fiddle with the GST. Turnbull tried desperately to convince Cormann that Dutton's numbers had dropped away. Cormann would not be swayed.

Turnbull insisted his opponents provide proof that votes had shifted to Dutton. A ballot had only just been held. Turnbull was not about to call another meeting just because the plotters said they had the numbers.

If Cormann hadn't defected, thereby allowing Morrison to emerge and seal Turnbull's fate, the woodchucks would still have been walking around with their bits of paper – or, as one female MP cuttingly described them, their 'silly pink folders' – trying to get MPs to sign a petition demanding a second meeting and ballot.

On Wednesday night, with Cormann now in full retreat from Turnbull, Arthur Sinodinos was sitting at home in Sydney watching it all unfold on the television news. Turnbull was standing between Cormann and Morrison burying the reviled company tax cuts, which had finally been voted down in the Senate. A relaxed Morrison threw his arm around Turnbull, vowing he was not budging. Cormann, like a plank of wood, also expressed his loyalty to the prime minister, but in a matter of hours would betray him.

Then it was like the quiz shows when contestants in trouble are offered a lifeline, the option of calling a friend for help. Sinodinos's phone rang. It was Turnbull, asking him if he could please come to Canberra. Turnbull told him there might be another spill, and who knows, he said, there might only be one vote in it. Jeepers creepers, thought Sinodinos, in his typical non-swearing way. He was recovering from a bone-marrow transplant, but next morning at 6.30, his longtime staffer Fiona Brown picked him up in her grey Mazda, and drove him and his media adviser, Craig Regan, to Canberra.

Sinodinos, Brown, and Regan arrived in Canberra mid-morning. They went straight to The Lodge, then got a call to come up to the Hill. What they found was a surface calm, but an inner turmoil.

Turnbull's head told him it was over, but in his heart he hoped it was not true. Later, Sinodinos told me that he thought Turnbull's tactical delays not only allowed Morrison to defeat Dutton, but allowed him to come to terms with his own fate. Not an easy thing.

'Malcolm wanted to hang on, but it became untenable,' Sinodinos recalled.

CHAPTER SIX

Prayers, plots, and plans

The very last thing that Scott Morrison did on Friday before he walked on his own to the party-room meeting that would decide his fate, after all the calls had been made and all the numbers checked, double-checked, and triple-checked, was to pray.

One of the last things that Peter Dutton did was take a call from Scott Ryan, who informed him that if the spill motion succeeded, he would be voting for Morrison. Mitch Fifield had already visited Dutton early that morning to tell him he would be voting for Morrison. Dutton had gone to bed on Thursday night convinced he would be sworn in as prime minister by Friday afternoon. He planned to fly out immediately on the prime ministerial VIP aircraft to visit a drought-stricken farm. Ryan's call at 11.25 am ended those dreams. Before that, Dutton says, he knew he had the numbers.

Showing the attention to detail and the superior organisation of the Morrison camp, Stuart Robert spoke to Morrison's support group to tell them there was no need for them to accompany Morrison on his short walk to the party room. He would go by himself. The optics were much better. Then he and Morrison spent a few quiet moments together in prayer in Morrison's office.

Morrison obviously felt a bit more help from the heavens would not go astray. As he walked out of the office, he said to his young receptionist, Mel, 'Text my family and ask them to pray for me.'

In an interview for this book, I asked Robert about his time alone with Morrison. 'We prayed that righteousness would exalt the nation,' he said. And did he believe, I asked, that righteousness would manifest itself in the form of a Morrison victory? 'Righteousness would mean the right person had won,' Robert replied.

The passage comes from Proverbs 14:34: 'Righteousness exalts a nation, but sin is a reproach to any people.'

Make of that what you will, but the fact is that Robert was part of the small, tight-knit group of conservative MPs – they called themselves the sensible right, while others called them the God Squad – who prayed together, and then worked day and night together to make Morrison prime minister. Outside of his prayer group, inside the parliamentary Liberal Party, Morrison did not have many 'friends', but he and Pyne got along, and that would prove critical to his success.

Only Morrison's group had an uncluttered objective. The moderates had to dump Bishop; they wanted Turnbull to realise he was done for and to pull out; and then they had to convince their colleagues to vote for Morrison – a man not many of them liked. The right was effectively rudderless, leaderless, in despair, and lacked a laser-like focus, divided between those who genuinely wanted Dutton and those grouped around Abbott, who simply wanted Turnbull finished off. Morrison barrelled through the middle to win.

Clearly torn between being impressed and outraged, Abbott later told David Speers, 'Morrison parlayed his half-a-dozen votes into the prime ministership, manoeuvring to (firstly) bring on the spill and (secondly) to then harvest Turnbull votes to get the top job.'

Morrison's impressively tight group did everything together. Robert, from Queensland, and Steve Irons, from Western Australia, shared an apartment with Morrison in Kingston. Their other very good mutual friend was Alex Hawke from New South Wales. Robert, Morrison, Hawke, and Irons were all elected at the 2007 election that saw Kevin Rudd lead Labor to victory, ending more than 11 years of Howard rule. Everyone else was sad or angry about losing, Robert remembers. But they weren't; they were simply hugely excited to be there. They became close friends, like all MPs do who are elected around the same time, but they had the added glue of religion – either Catholics, or Baptists, or, in the case of Morrison and Robert, Pentecostal – to bind them together. Anywhere between five and 10 of them met for bible readings and prayer every Tuesday when parliament sat. All of them, except Luke Howarth, voted for Morrison on Friday.

In their 11 years in parliament to 2018, the class of 2007 had been through enough leadership ructions to know months out when a challenge was brewing. They were neither blind nor stupid.

There are those, including Malcolm Turnbull, who remain deeply suspicious about Morrison's role, particularly in those eight days of madness that climaxed in Morrison's swearing in as prime minister. They are both right and wrong to feel this way.

Morrison did not initiate the move against Turnbull; however, what became obvious was that he and his lieutenants were ready for it and took full advantage of it. They will not admit to plotting, but they will admit to preparing and planning, and then only in that final week, or, in Morrison's case, the final days.

Morrison did what he could to save Turnbull. He told him not to bring on a leadership spill. After Cormann told Turnbull he was quitting, Morrison said it was worth one more shot to try to talk him out of it. He went to see Cormann in his office to tell him, 'You don't have to do this.' Cormann said he did. Morrison was not gone 10 minutes. He went back and told Turnbull, 'He is not for turning.' Then, on Thursday, after parliament had been adjourned, he tried to convince Turnbull and Pyne to send everyone home.

Morrison was astute enough to realise the damage that would be done to the government if another prime minister were removed, and also what a thankless task it would be for his successor to try to put the pieces back together. He was also ambitious enough to do what he could to ensure that he, rather than Dutton, triumphed if Turnbull fell over. He was not about to spurn the chance to become prime minister. Who knew if such an opportunity would ever come again? And his lieutenants were similarly motivated.

In politics, there is a difference, even if it is only a very fine one – a hair's breadth of a line— between plotting and planning, between loyalty and disloyalty. His lieutenants do not believe they crossed that line, which prompts the memorable Mandy Rice-Davies line that they would say that, wouldn't they? Nor do most MPs believe they did; however, there are those who believe they came dangerously close to it, and others still who are convinced they jumped across the demilitarised zone into full combat well before the wounded leader was forced to retire from battle, thereby hastening his demise.

Weeks after the coup, Christopher Pyne had no time for the conspiracy theory, which he described as 'mad'. He firmly believed that Morrison had behaved appropriately at all times during that week, saying he played a straight bat, even arguing for MPs to be sent home on Thursday after Cormann had defected and after parliament had been adjourned, even after Morrison's own candidacy had been publicly announced. The ultimate pragmatist and political animal, Pyne says it's natural in every business to take advantage of a situation, and if Morrison's numbers men were counting before then – well, that was prudent planning.

However, there was no way you could get to where Morrison got to in just 24 hours, from a standing start, which is what he wanted everyone to believe.

Months before that week, Hawke, Morrison's keeper of the numbers, already had a list of who sat where safely stored on his computer, which he kept updating as people identified where they stood on issues like same-sex marriage and energy. There were no bits of paper; everything was electronic.

Morrison's supporters began the counting, canvassing, and courting well ahead of Turnbull's official go-ahead for Morrison to run. Morrison's two flatmates, Robert and Irons, were sussing people out before the Tuesday ballot. It was obvious what was happening, even if it wasn't going to happen that day. They had all discussed it with each other and with Morrison, particularly over the previous weekend.

Hawke says he called MPs from New South Wales, Victoria, and Queensland over the previous weekend, after Dutton's plan had been telegraphed. Hawke said later he was not at that stage assessing numbers for Morrison, but was gathering intel on how people thought the government was travelling, to feed back to Morrison, so he in turn could tell Turnbull – although, clearly, every scrap of information would have been useful to Hawke and Morrison. Hawke says he got the impression that if anything happened, it would be months rather than days away.

Hawke says he believed before the Dutton adventure that Morrison would inherit the leadership from Turnbull after the election – either as prime minister or as opposition leader.

Months before this, Ben Morton had aroused the suspicions of Dutton supporters. He began dropping into the offices of MPs he hadn't spoken to for a long time – some he hadn't spoken to for a year – just to shoot the breeze. They also had been through enough leadership spills to become suspicious when someone was doing what they called a thermometer check, and they knew he wasn't doing it for Turnbull.

'He was clearly taking the temperature. We would have long

discussions about how bad the mood was and what we needed to do,' one Liberal MP said. That's what politicians mean by 'gathering intel' – sussing out who is seduceable, who is a probable conquest, who is a possible conquest, and who is not.

At the start of that week, the thermometer burst. According to one MP, a Dutton backer, Robert told him on Monday night that Turnbull was finished and had to go.

Robert does not dispute this in our interview. Nor does he dispute that he made similar comments to other colleagues. But he casts it in a different context.

As a Queenslander, Robert was familiar with the deep well of dissatisfaction that existed there over Turnbull's leadership. He could see it brewing in the energy debate three months before. He knew Dutton would move because he feared losing his seat. Robert thought the dissent in the party room over the National Energy Guarantee on 14 August was orchestrated by the anti-Turnbull forces; then, when Dutton did his Hadley interview and the *Daily Telegraph* reported he was making a move, he knew it was on.

Robert says Dutton had the weight of the conservative media – 2GB, Sky, and *The Australian* – supporting him. Unlike Hawke, Robert admits he was convinced that Dutton would move during the coming week. On Sunday night, he and Hawke met at their apartment. Morrison had been at the special cabinet meeting, and joined them later. There was only really one topic of conversation: the leadership.

At that stage, Hawke and Robert calculated that Dutton would have 30 votes, but they were convinced his momentum would grow rapidly. 'Every spill starts with 30,' Robert said. They war-gamed everything. Robert thought Dutton or his camp would initiate a 'feint' at Tuesday's meeting, precipitating the resignation of a clutch of ministers, triggering a crisis in the government, enabling Dutton to challenge by Thursday.

They would have to decide who to support, Dutton or Turnbull, so they had a strategic plan in place for any eventuality.

'Scott wasn't running. He always said he would not run against Malcolm,' Robert says. It made no difference, because Robert was convinced Turnbull was finished, so they planned for every eventuality – with Turnbull and without him.

Robert, Irons, and Morrison talked again over breakfast on Monday morning. They all agreed it was 'untidy' and that it would be 'on'. Everyone knows what 'on' means.

When he heard Turnbull declare the leadership vacant on Tuesday, Robert says he texted Morrison inside the party room, 'That's the dumbest thing I have ever seen.' He said Morrison sent a one-word reply, 'Yup.'

Robert insists he voted for Turnbull, because he said he would, and because he was sure that if Dutton got up, the government would collapse. There would be a slew of MPs resigning, Dutton would be forced to call an election, and they would lose.

Morrison, Hawke, and Robert left the party room together. They all agreed that resignations of ministers would follow, and that Dutton would strike again later in the week.

'This is madness,' Robert was saying. 'If Dutton wins, we are in hell.' He told Morrison he had to run. Morrison told him he would not run against Turnbull.

'You have a patriotic duty to run,' Robert insisted. When Morrison said he would not, Robert claims he told him he was going to talk to colleagues to ask them if they would vote for Morrison against Dutton. In fact, he had already begun to do that.

Morrison responded, saying, 'I am not authorising that.'

Robert told me, 'We told him we were going to do it. We were not asking permission.'

So Morrison did not give them a green light. But it most certainly was not a red light, either. Asked about this, Morrison says,

'I didn't ask him to do it. I was saying, "I'm not running, I'm not running I'm not running, I'm not running." And that happened, and that continued. Now, you know, they were all looking at what was going on, they were making their own decisions.'

Morrison said he did everything he could to prevent it. He thought Pyne was wrong to think, 'There, that showed them – that's it.'

'And I thought, "Well, I think it's a lot worse than that. I think that's a pretty bad outcome, and this is going to get very difficult."

'My frame of mind, like Christopher's was, and Mathias's, I believe, was: save Malcolm, because he's the prime minister and this is, this is crazy.

'People can say in hindsight [there was no coming back from that vote], but when you're in the middle of it and you're trying to keep the government on course, as one of the most senior members of the government, you don't go to that place.'

Robert's canvassing continued in earnest immediately after the first vote, concentrating on the Queenslanders – Ross Vasta, Karen Andrews, Ian Macdonald, and Scott Buchholz. He says he made clear to all of them that Morrison would not run against Turnbull, but if Turnbull was out, he wanted to know if they would vote for Morrison over Dutton.

Vasta remembers that conversation with Robert differently. He says it was all based on the assumption that it was over for Turnbull, and that he should think about voting for Morrison over Dutton. It was a full-blooded pitch for Morrison, full stop.

Zed Seselja, a Dutton supporter, said soon after the coup that he did not think Morrison was disloyal. Seselja thought the fact that Morrison won showed how well prepared his backers were, and how smart politically Morrison was to emerge without a stain, and, in those early days at least, to avoid the inevitable transaction costs of a challenge.

Laundy had a very different take. So did Luke Howarth, who had taken a phone call from Morrison the previous Saturday asking him what he was making of things. Howarth did not believe at this point that Morrison was sounding him out for his own purposes, and that he 'had Malcolm's back'.

However, he says he grew highly suspicious on Tuesday, after the first vote, when he saw Robert going up and down the backbenchers' corridor. Howarth texted Morrison on Wednesday morning at 10.55, saying, 'Scott please get behind Peter Dutton and get this done today. We can't have a two week break with Malcolm still there we will bleed to death.'

One minute later, he received a one-word reply, 'No.'

Howarth texted back, telling Morrison that he did not believe he was 'innocent in all this' because he had seen Robert working the hallways. Morrison replied, saying, 'You know me.' Howarth left it at that.

Although Morrison says he got the all-clear from Turnbull on Wednesday night, both Laundy and Sinodinos heard Turnbull say to Morrison and Bishop on Thursday, after Cormann, Cash, and Fifield had held their doorstop to announce their defection, to sort out between them what they did.

As Morrison ran for the door that Thursday morning, he asked Laundy to come and see him.

When Laundy arrived in Morrison's office, Scott Briggs, Morrison's federal electorate chairman, and the suspected conduit to New South Wales moderate powerbroker Michael Photios, was already there. Laundy says he told Morrison he did not want to get too deeply involved because his first priority was to look after his mate. But he said he would be happy to make a few calls. Morrison called Hawke to tell him he had Laundy there with him and that he was willing to provide some help.

Laundy then stopped at Pyne's office after he had also asked to see him. Pyne said they needed to work out who to call. Laundy also told him that he did not want to get too involved, and then made his way to Hawke's office.

He was the first to arrive. There was a long table, with chairs on either side. Soon after, others filed in. Seated around the table were Lucy Wicks, Bert van Manen, Steve Irons, Stuart Robert, Ben Morton, Hawke, and himself. Hawke had his computer out. He asked for intel, any intel at all, to be fed back to him. He then proceeded to go through the rollcall. When they got to Jane Prentice, Stuart Robert said, 'She was with Dutton on Tuesday; she will be with us tomorrow.'

According to Laundy, Wicks responded, 'Same as me.'

Laundy interjected, 'You want intel – that is wrong. She [Prentice] was with us on Tuesday, but you're right – she will be with us tomorrow.' Robert laughed and said to Laundy, 'You and I were on different teams on Tuesday.'

Laundy said nothing in response to Robert. Robert does not dispute this conversation. Unlike Laundy, Robert sees nothing untoward in what passed between them.

Laundy, however, was troubled. He went back to the prime minister's office, where he met up with Cray, Bold, and Mathieson. He told them he thought they had been played, and related what had happened in Hawke's room. Sally looked at him and said, 'We can't tell Malcolm. It will completely kill him.'

It was a devastating moment. Laundy's intel had confirmed for him and Cray their suspicions about the tactics and motives of Morrison's men.

Laundy was torn. 'My heart said it had to be Morrison; my head said it should be Dutton, because when they go down, we can say it was all the fault of the right-wing nut jobs,' he later told me. Laundy was far from alone in thinking the government was doomed.

Cray had always been suspicious of Morrison – more so after

Tuesday's vote, and more so again when she heard that Scott Briggs had called Photios to ask him if the moderates would vote for Morrison. Then she discovered that Briggs was in Canberra. Why?

She asked Morrison directly about the Photios conversation when he was in with Turnbull and Pyne. Morrison told her it was ridiculous, and Turnbull told her to calm down.

Despite the deep suspicions over Briggs and his sudden appearance in Canberra at the beginning of that week, Pyne emphatically denies suggestions that the moderates were dealing with Photios. 'He is a gossip. He carries no weight,' Pyne said later. '[He] was long ago relegated to the second row by the New South Wales moderates. Goodness knows why Scott Briggs was talking to him about the federal moderates. Photios no more speaks for them than you do.'

Morrison and Turnbull were both clear about what they wanted. Morrison's cunning plan was first to ensure Turnbull's survival and to do everything possible to let people know he would not be running if the prime minister was running. His second was to get himself elected if Turnbull was knocked out. Turnbull's plan was to save himself first, and then, when it became clear he could not, to ensure that Dutton got smashed.

On Thursday, the night before the spill, Dutton and Cormann had dinner at Portia's at Kingston, rather than getting takeaway in the office, so they could pore over their numbers to make sure each one was nailed down.

The same night, Michael Keenan tried to get Christian Porter, then up to his eyeballs in legal dramas, to go out for dinner with him and Steve Ciobo. Ciobo and Keenan were sprung at the Ottoman, drinking pink French martinis, by *The Australian*'s 'Margin Call' columnist, Will Glasgow. They were with Sky's Laura Jayes.

Regardless of how it looked, Ciobo and Keenan were not out on the town having an early celebration in anticipation of victory. They were despondent. By then, they knew they were done for. Basically, they had given up. They didn't think that Dutton had the numbers to wrest the leadership, as he was even struggling to get the 43 signatures on the petition for a second spill; Turnbull was irreparably damaged; and – almost certainly – so were they. They had watched the Cormann–Cash–Fifield press conference that morning. They were incredulous. They thought it was surreal. They could not work out what was going on, what the plan was, or if indeed there had ever been one.

The Dutton adventure, misguided in concept and mishandled in execution, was wreaking havoc and misery, even among his closest friends.

Ciobo, who had been trying to run his own campaign for the deputy leadership, had reached the point where he was reluctant to canvass for votes because of the hostility of his colleagues. He did not take it personally. He believed the animosity was directed at what MPs saw as the madness of the whole Dutton exercise. They were either refusing to take Ciobo's calls or, if they answered, used them as an opportunity to give him an earful about it all. Turnbull supporters, particularly, could not understand why Ciobo was involved. When one cabinet colleague asked him why, Ciobo tried to explain that Dutton was one of his best mates – they had been friends for such a long time, sharing a house for more than a decade, going on holidays together, even going to Las Vegas together. Along with their other good friend Michael Keenan.

This minister was scornful, saying the trio thought they were the Australian version of the Rat Pack, the infamous Hollywood celebrities who hung out together in the gambling capital of the world, except in the down-under context their colleagues were placing the emphasis on 'rat'.

The atmosphere was poisonous. It never improved.

Morrison says he first began to get suspicious that Cormann was shifting at the time of the joint press conference with Turnbull on the Wednesday morning.

'He wasn't his usual self,' Morrison says of Cormann, who had tried to get out of appearing.

'That was the one when I put my arm around Malcolm. That was my frame ... you know what I'm like, Niki, that was my frame. I'm with this guy, I'd walked in with him to the parliament the day before with my hand on his shoulder, saying, "This is our guy." I was walking backwards and forwards with him from this office [the prime minister's office, where this interview took place] to the chamber very visibly.

'I was saying, "I'm with him." Because I knew any suggestion that I wasn't would have made the situation worse, and I knew I'd have to be, not just supportive, but in reality that I would have to be very visibly supportive, and that's why I was. And I kept fighting. And after Mathias and I left that press conference, I could see something wasn't right, and he and I spoke a number of times during the course of that afternoon, once or twice, and he's undertaken to me, after about six-ish or thereabouts, that he was starting to indicate that he was of a mind that we have to resolve this, this has to be brought on, this has to be fixed. And I said, "Don't do anything, don't do anything." And he undertook not to do anything that night, which he didn't.'

That night, Morrison says he and Turnbull also discussed what would happen next.

'I said, "Mate, I'm supporting you, I'm supporting you,' and he indicated to me that if this thing goes very bad, you know what you're going to have to do. And I said, "Well, I appreciate that, but that's not where we are.' So nothing had activated at that point. Nothing had activated.

'My view was that, always, that under no circumstances would I be in a ballot with Malcolm Turnbull. Under none. And I had made that clear to everybody who came anywhere near me.

'And it was exactly the same, as you'll recall, when Malcolm rolled Tony. When, in this office [the prime minister's], Tony offered me the deputy leadership, which I wisely declined … and we were talking about whether I'd run, and I said, "I'd never run against you, you're the prime minister. If you're not running, Tony, well, that's a different matter, but if you're running, I'm not."

'And my view was the same with Malcolm. So they'd [Turnbull and his advisers] had lots of discussions themselves and the next day, and, you know, this was my position, and then what we needed to do to sort this out was, we needed to adjourn the House.'

He says he had two meetings with Cormann, Fifield, and Cash on Thursday morning, although he struggles to get the sequence right. One was in Cormann's office, where he went to plead with the three of them.

'I told them, "You cannot do this."

'I said that if you do this … there is no turning back.' He said Cormann was 'totally in control' of the other two. He said they were resolved to do it.

Morrison warned Cormann of the consequences.

'Well, do not kid yourself that by doing this you are not terminating the government,' he told them. 'If you do this, that is exactly what you're doing. Exactly. Don't pretend, oh its heading there anyway. Nup, this is the trigger event, if we go past this.'

Cormann told him they were determined to do it.

At the other meeting with the three of them in a waiting room inside the prime minister's office, Morrison says he not only accompanied Turnbull to witness events, but also because he was worried Turnbull might say something to make matters worse – although how that was possible is not obvious.

'I was also thinking I will need to try and manage him, so if there's any chance of pulling this back, that we won't … nothing happens that the way he handles it precipitates it. But to be fair to Malcolm, it had already got to that point. So I went in there and said exactly what I'd said to them previously.

'Michaelia and Mitch were under enormous pressure. They were heavily affected. Mathias was quite adamant, because Mathias is always like that. But I could see that they were both struggling with it very, very badly, so I kept the pressure up. And anyway, they went and did it.'

Meanwhile, Dutton's people were still walking the petition around, struggling to get to the magic 43 signatures.

The string of ministers who had voted against Turnbull on Tuesday – Steve Ciobo, Michael Keenan, Greg Hunt, Alan Tudge – who repledged their unswerving, unqualified loyalty in parliament after Tuesday's vote, began resigning again on Thursday after Cormann's press conference.

Turnbull and Pyne then took the controversial decision to adjourn the House. They couldn't adjourn the Senate because they didn't have the numbers to do it, but they still had their working majority in the House.

The minister for regional development, John McVeigh, was the duty minister in the House when Pyne came in and told him in a few words what was about to happen.

Instinctively, McVeigh thought it was the wrong thing to do; however, again, there was no time to argue or react. The decision had been made. Labor called a division. Turnbull came into the chamber and took his seat at the table of the House. The significance of the moment was not lost on McVeigh, who offered the second chair at the table to the deputy prime minister and Nationals leader, Michael McCormack. 'No mate, you're fine,' McCormack said. This gesture enabled McVeigh to witness an exchange that helped restore a bit of his faith in the decency of people in that place.

While the vote was being counted, Bill Shorten leaned across and said to Turnbull, 'This is not good for any of us. You could have won this, and we know it.'

Then Shorten added, 'You did not deserve this.'

Turnbull responded, 'Oh, well. I will just fade away now. I will go and look after my children and my grandchildren.'

Shorten said, 'Good on you.' McVeigh filled in the remaining minutes by talking to Turnbull about his family. His daughter had just got engaged. Turnbull responded warmly, and that was that. McVeigh thought Shorten sounded genuine, and he thought the better of him for it.

McVeigh had voted for Turnbull at Tuesday's meeting. Despite this, as Dutton and members of his camp sought to increase the pressure on Turnbull, Dutton suggested to McVeigh that he should resign from the frontbench. McVeigh refused. Then, after Cormann defected, McVeigh became only the 23rd MP to sign the petition. It showed the struggle the Dutton camp was having to get signatures before Cormann's spectacular desertion.

McVeigh did not believe they could leave Canberra without resolving the leadership. He did not sleep on Thursday night, and says he only made up his mind who to vote for as the ballot papers were being handed out on Friday morning. (He won't say who that was.) Dutton had him firmly in his column, and then, after winning the ballot, Morrison dumped him from the ministry. With wry humour, McVeigh says this was so he could spend more time in his electorate. In fact, it was partly because the Nationals wanted to reclaim the regional-development portfolio. McVeigh, son of a politician, the unforgettable Tom, has no hard feelings.

After the House was adjourned, Morrison thought they should all leave town. He says it was clear that Dutton did not have anywhere near the 43 signatures that Turnbull had stipulated were necessary before he'd agree to another party-room meeting on the leadership. Pyne sees this as proof that Morrison was not plotting.

Morrison says, 'I turned to Christopher as we came back here, and I said, "Well, it's Thursday. The House is adjourned, we can all go home.' And I came back in here and said that, and Julie was here, too. I said, "Why don't we just go home?

"We're back in a fortnight, and we'll fight this, slug this thing out over the next two weeks. Yes, it'll be ugly and messy and horrible, and all the rest of it, but, you know, we can."

'And Malcolm took the view not to. He just said that, "No, we're not going to go home" and "they need to get those signatures".

'I think he thought it had progressed to such a level. Maybe he thought he'd – I don't know – tough it out to see if they'd get the signatures, and if they didn't … I mean, there was all, "Oh, it had to be in by that afternoon, or it had to be in by the following morning", and so he'd moved that timetable out, and … just trying to think … he eventually put the timetable out to about Friday lunchtime.

'But this thing, by the Thurs – by the Friday, it had morphed, it had all changed. There were people at that stage – this is why I said, "Let's go home Thursday lunchtime", so this whole madness didn't keep going and it just stopped. Everyone [would have been] back to their electorates, and everyone would have screamed at them, going, "You idiots, what are you doing?", and they'd come back, and hopefully we'd have another crack.'

After Turnbull refused to send everyone home, Morrison, feeling he had done what he could, said, 'I've gotta go.' Laundy couldn't believe the speed with which Morrison exited the room.

Morrison had advised Turnbull not to bring his leadership into play, and had failed. He had tried to convince Cormann to stick, and had failed. He had tried to get Turnbull to send everyone home, and had failed. He then had 24 hours to make that sure he and not Dutton triumphed.

'My position hadn't changed. If he was running, I wasn't

running. But in the event of it being an open ballot, with him not running, then of course I would run.'

Turnbull's two big mistakes that week, according to Morrison, were to initiate the challenge against himself on Tuesday, and then not send everyone home on Thursday. Morrison concedes that Dutton and his camp would not have given up, which was one reason why he said to Turnbull on Saturday, 'How many times did you ever see John Howard call a spill? Never.'

The Cormann–Cash–Fifield press conference triggered a blizzard of meetings, text messages, and phone calls. Dutton's campaign had been faltering after his GST thought-bubble, and MPs were refusing to sign the petition. Cormann changed the dynamics.

Cormann boosted Dutton's numbers, gave his campaign the general that it needed, wrecked any chance of a recovery by Turnbull, and paved the way for Morrison's emergence. The moderates had to move quickly if they were to succeed in blocking Dutton.

Laundy got a call from Zimmerman, who put him on speaker phone. He said he had Simon Birmingham, Marise Payne, David Coleman, and Ann Ruston with him.

Zimmerman asked Laundy, who had just come from a meeting in Turnbull's office, how Turnbull was faring. 'Mate, not good,' Laundy said. Zimmerman told him if Turnbull ran against Dutton, Dutton would win. 'I know, mate,' Laundy replied.

'We need to try to get him to understand that,' Zimmerman urged.

Soon after this conversation, Bishop called Laundy to ask him to vote for her. By then, Morrison's campaign was at full throttle. Laundy told her he was sorry, but he couldn't vote for her. 'The last thing we need is Peter Dutton as prime minister,' he told her. 'You will beat Scott in the first round, but not Dutton in the second round.'

He told her he had to vote for Morrison. He says she thanked him for his honesty. Laundy had just been to a meeting in Paul Fletcher's office, which Zimmerman had also attended, where they war-gamed all options. They were all on the same wavelength. Bishop could beat Morrison, but she could not beat Dutton.

Pyne also recounted in an interview for this book a meeting of the moderates in his office before the House adjourned and after Turnbull had given Bishop and Morrison the green light to run. They went through the numbers, and determined that Bishop could not win. According to Pyne, they then went around to see Turnbull. Bishop also came in. Others present were Marise Payne, Ann Ruston, Simon Birmingham, Paul Fletcher, and Laundy.

Pyne insisted he told Bishop that if the moderates voted for her, she would beat Scott Morrison. He recalls that he said, 'When Scott Morrison's votes go out, my assessment is that not enough will flow to you to beat Peter Dutton. Peter Dutton will beat you. That's not acceptable to us; therefore, unfortunately, the moderates cannot vote for you.'

Pyne remembers Marise Payne saying, 'I agree with that.' Payne does not confirm this, saying she was not present for this conversation.

Later that afternoon, after the House adjourned, Pyne says there was another conversation between him and Bishop. It took place on the phone. Pyne was in his office. Fletcher was in the room, and so was Birmingham. Again, Pyne says he told Bishop, 'If we vote for you, Peter Dutton will win. The Pentecostal Christians will vote for Dutton; they will not vote for you. We will vote for Scott Morrison, but not for you.'

Fletcher remembers this conversation, and so does Birmingham. While their recollections about the conversation in the Turnbull office earlier in the day were fuzzy, both told me later that they definitely recalled the second discussion.

Pyne went through the numbers. He thought Dutton would

have 36, Morrison 39, and Bishop somewhere between 9 and 17, depending on whether Dutton or Morrison fell short of his estimates.

He thought his group could get almost every moderate, except Ross Vasta and Andrew Laming, to vote for Morrison. The question was whether the Morrison people would vote for Bishop. He did not believe that Hawke, Irons, Morton, Robert, van Manen, or Wicks would vote for her.

By Thursday afternoon, despite having had a much later start than Morrison, Bishop told me she had rung many people, including Abbott, seeking their support for her candidacy. Asked to describe the conversation with Abbott, she refuses to go into details of what was said. Instead, she holds her mobile a metre away from her ear.

According to the he-said, she-said accounts published later, Abbott said, after giving her a serve for being disloyal to him, 'Why would I vote for Malcolm in a skirt?', and she replied, 'So I take it I can't count on your vote?'

Bishop insisted she had no conversation with Pyne or anyone else about the numbers for her leadership bid or what the moderates might do.

She showed me a text she had received at 5.01 pm from Pyne to say, 'If you run for deputy leader again, you will win easily. Hunt cannot win.' She was emphatic that she did not receive any other communication from Pyne.

Pyne says in response to this that his text was actually further evidence that he did not think she could win the leadership.

Subsequent revelations of a WhatsApp message from Paul Fletcher telling moderates not to vote for Bishop because it would ensure Dutton's election as leader was a factor – although a long way from the only one – in her later resignation from the frontbench. It was also a factor in the subsequent decision by Julia Banks, the only Liberal to have won a seat from Labor in 2016, who voted for

Bishop at the second party-room meeting, to announce she would not recontest the seat for the Liberals, and would then sit on the crossbenches.

Others, including some of Bishop's dearest friends in parliament, delivered the message to her personally.

When Bishop rang Kelly O'Dwyer to ask for her vote, O'Dwyer headed her off before Bishop could get to the point of asking. O'Dwyer was torn but honest with the woman she so admired.

'You would be great,' O'Dwyer told her. 'I have to tell you I have to think about Victoria. I can't have Dutton, and if I vote for you I think I will get Dutton, and I can't have that on my conscience.'

Nor was it personal against Dutton. O'Dwyer liked him – as did many of his colleagues from whatever faction. She had always had good dealings with him, even during the same-sex marriage plebiscite, which he had helped to facilitate despite his own opposition to it.

But she knew he would be electoral poison in her seat of Higgins, and in others like it. After the final vote, an emotional O'Dwyer went to Bishop's office. She spoke to Bishop's distressed staff, commending them for their years of loyalty and hard work. As a former adviser to Costello, O'Dwyer knew the burdens carried by ministerial staff. Weeks later, tears spilled over as O'Dwyer recounted what happened. It was such an awful week.

On Friday morning, the Speaker, Tony Smith, visited Bishop in her office. She had rung him the night before, seeking his support. Smith regarded Bishop as a friend, and had always admired her work ethic, her professionalism, and how well briefed she always was, particularly when she visited electorates on her many fund-raising expeditions for MPs. Unfortunately, he had to tell her he was not going to vote for her – he was going to vote for Morrison, whom Smith also regarded as a friend. Smith told her he was voting for Morrison because he thought he had a better chance of beating

Dutton in the ballot. She smiled, and thanked him for at least coming over and telling her to her face.

Smith, who worked long and hard with Costello to formulate, sell, and then implement the GST, was dismayed by Dutton's announced intention to remove it from power bills. He was using words like 'buffoon' to colleagues to describe what he thought about Dutton's idea.

Ken Wyatt says he counselled Bishop not to run. After it was over, there were whispers that Wyatt was thinking of jumping ship and joining the ALP. It would have been quite a coup for Labor, and a devastating blow to the government, if it had been able to win over the first Aboriginal person to be elected to the House of Representatives.

In fact, a couple of approaches had been made to him over the years. Kevin Rudd once told him he should join Labor. Wyatt responded by telling Rudd he should join the Liberals. Then Bill Shorten once said to him, when they were sharing a lift, 'I would love you to be in the Labor Party.' Wyatt told him no thanks. He thinks these overtures, plus the fact that he has friendships extending over 40 years with Linda Burney and Pat Dodson, helped fuel the rumours. He also meets regularly with Dodson and Labor's veteran Northern Territory MP Warren Snowdon to talk about indigenous childrens' health.

What was true was that Wyatt was deeply unhappy with the moves against Turnbull. After the first vote, he was inundated with emails from disaffected Liberals, saying they would no longer be voting for the party. He went public, saying that if Dutton was elected leader, he would quit. He told me later that he was deadly serious. Wyatt voted for Turnbull on Tuesday, then against the spill motion on Friday, and when that was passed, he voted for Morrison. He was torn between Bishop and Morrison.

He is a great admirer of Bishop's, but he says he feared what would happen to her. He says he visited her before the Friday ballot and urged her not to nominate.

'There's too much testosterone around,' he warned her. The talk of bullying was rife, and Wyatt was worried that she would get torn apart in a vicious and premeditated campaign by her enemies if she happened to win.

According to Wyatt, she responded by saying, 'You have been talking to Steve Irons.' Wyatt said, 'No, this is what I hear in the corridors.' Bishop does not recall this conversation. Wyatt thinks it's because Bishop went into shock after the vote was read out.

Wyatt expected the same kind of campaign from Dutton's people against Bishop that he believes cost Turnbull his job.

Wyatt says that, to Dutton's credit, half an hour before the ballot on Friday, he called him to tell Wyatt that there would be no hard feelings on Dutton's part if he won the leadership. Wyatt would still have his place on the frontbench – he wanted Wyatt to stay. Wyatt, though, was still prepared to quit and go to the backbench.

'There are some things about people and government that are important,' he says. 'Turnbull gave me my opportunity. I would have been sitting somewhere near Julie Bishop [on the very last row of the backbenches]. I wouldn't serve under Dutton.'

In response to the why-question – Why did Turnbull lose his prime ministership? – Wyatt is clear. 'It was the handiwork of Tony Abbott. You could see it whenever a poll was due. The week before, he would come out with something that impugned Turnbull, that he was incompetent, or weak, or lacked conviction.'

The Liberal Party right, for so long used to running the joint and calling all the shots, was flailing. It was not until Thursday afternoon that the monkey-podders, around 20 of them, held their first meeting, after the House adjourned, and after being summoned by a WhatsApp. Until then, they had been operating pretty much independently, organically. They had to rush to find a projector so they could finally begin to consolidate and count their numbers. None of the junior woodchucks even had a list or a spreadsheet.

The only list they worked off was the one they cobbled together after Hastie's staff bought a projector and attached it to a laptop so everyone could see where they were at.

Finally, Hastie said later, they were able to get a spreadsheet going and to start feeding in information. The hard part was trying to work out who was going with Morrison. He reckoned at this stage that there were 10 votes in it.

'I always thought it was going to be line ball,' he said. Hastie said Abbott was nowhere near the spill, nor the planning for it. He blamed the media for putting an effective 'sub-theme' out there that Dutton was Abbott's stalking horse. He conceded that this cost Dutton votes. As for Hunt, Hastie said he was swayed by his personal relationship with him. He likes him, and he had no idea he was so unpopular in his own state. In any case, he asked, what was the alternative? Many right-wing MPs thought Frydenberg was too damaged by the NEG to be a viable candidate.

James Paterson thought by the end of Thursday that they were ahead, but not by much – and, it turned out, by not so much that it was safe for both Cormann and Dutton to leave the building.

If Cormann and Dutton went to Portia's at Kingston because they thought it was in the bag, Turnbull stopped because he thought it was all over.

On Thursday night, Turnbull had his staff, Laundy, his wife, Suzie, and Arthur Sinodinos and his staff, Fiona Brown and Craig Regan, at The Lodge for drinks and dinner. Turnbull and Laundy peeled off at one stage to watch Laundy's pre-recorded interview on ABC's *7.30*, where he put the case for sticking with Turnbull.

Sinodinos declined Turnbull's invitation to stay at The Lodge. He and his staff went to the supermarket to get toothpaste and clean underwear, and Sinodinos spent the night at his sister's.

They had all stopped counting. In retrospect, given the closeness of the vote the next day on the spill, they feared they had made a mistake. Pyne, Laundy, Birmingham, Cray, and others beat themselves up later for effectively having given up. But by then, everyone, including Turnbull, deep in their heart of hearts, knew it was over.

While Laundy had grown closer to Turnbull in the previous three years, Scott Ryan had grown distant from him. Ryan's counsel was not sought, he had a long period away because of illness, and then he became Senate president after Stephen Parry self-destructed over dual citizenship.

Ryan was another who was concerned about the NEG, particularly by the reports the previous Friday that emission targets would be regulated rather than legislated. He contacted Turnbull and his office over the weekend, but got mixed messages in response. He did not want to make life any more difficult than it already was for Turnbull, but told him he would have to get up in the party room to voice his concerns if this wasn't sorted.

Ryan sensed the change in atmosphere when he arrived in Canberra on Sunday 19 August. There were the Never Turnbulls, as always, but they had been joined by others. His radar told him there was counting going on. Turnbull rang him around ten o'clock on Monday night, but Ryan got no sense that anything was imminent. The next morning, Ryan voted for Turnbull, but, like everybody else, thought the vote of 35 against him was too high, although he thinks that even if it had been in the high 20s, it would still have been too high.

Regardless of whether or not it was retrievable, or the fact that he and Turnbull were estranged, did he believe the government would be better off in any way with the removal of Turnbull? He did not.

However, Ryan, also close to Bishop, still had to make a choice between Dutton and Morrison. Ryan regarded Dutton as a friend, and he was not particularly close to Morrison. He, too, was torn. He went to see Dutton on Thursday, and spoke to Morrison on the phone. He had a drink on Thursday night in Cormann's office, along with Cash and Fifield. Cormann was convinced they had the numbers; however, Ryan says there was no reason for them to think they had his vote, more so because of his views of Greg Hunt, which were unfavourable, to say the least. Ryan had been spending his time rustling up the numbers for Frydenberg.

Two of Ryan's best friends were Michael O'Brien, formerly the shadow treasurer in Victoria, who took over as Liberal leader, and the former leader, Matthew Guy. Ryan and O'Brien had been joint MCs at Guy's wedding. Victoria was heading into an election, and he rang seeking their advice. He also spoke to two other good friends, the Speaker, Tony Smith, and cabinet minister Kelly O'Dwyer. All of them said the same thing. It could not be Dutton.

Ryan still feels the weight of the 2015 coup against Abbott. He knows it was the right thing to do, but like others in that group, he has never bragged about it or been flippant about it. Nevertheless, he was angry over the way Abbott and the others had behaved since then. He did not believe Dutton had been part of any long-term campaign against Turnbull, and in fact had spent a lot of time trying to make his prime ministership work.

It took him a long time to decide who to support. He finally rang Dutton on Friday, about an hour before the party meeting was scheduled to begin, to say he could not vote for him, partly because he was fearful of what would happen in Victoria, and partly because 'bastardry could not be rewarded'.

He told others he would not be voting for the spill on Friday, but if it got up, he would vote for Morrison and Frydenberg. Ryan texted Turnbull to say he had walked in with him in 2015, and he would walk in with him again in 2018 if he wanted. Turnbull did not respond. In fact, they did not speak again until mid-November.

Turnbull rang him to ask how things were looking in the Victorian election. In the immediate aftermath of the coup, the Victorian Liberal vote had crashed.

Ryan says Turnbull lost his prime ministership because he was worn down by the organised, orchestrated, long-term campaign against him, and by his own occasional mistakes.

'The golden rule is that the party that behaves that way will always end this way.'

Warren Entsch insisted on being the last to sign the petition for the party meeting. He wanted his signature to be the 43rd. Then, when he finally signed, on Friday, he wrote beside it, 'For Dr Brendan Nelson.' Entsch wanted an end to the Abbott–Turnbull wars. He was one of those disappointed with Turnbull. 'He just wasn't who he said he would be,' Entsch lamented later. Entsch voted for Turnbull on Tuesday, and then later told Dutton he would vote for him if there was a second ballot. But he changed his mind.

The first reason he gave when we spoke was the interview that Dutton had given in which he canvassed the removal of the GST from power bills. Dutton argues that this was about restarting the conversation on energy and a means of helping the government 'get over the shock of losing another prime minister'. The second problem for Entsch was the story, either spread by Abbott's friends or Abbott's enemies – take your pick – that, as prime minister, Dutton would appoint Abbott to cabinet.

The rumours of Abbott's restoration were rife. On Wednesday, David Speers tweeted, 'Tony Abbott believes he's been assured 110% that he will be included in a Dutton cabinet. Others may have been told otherwise, but that's his understanding.'

Entsch wanted none of that. He was worried about the GST thought-bubble, and he wanted a clean break from the bloody conflicts of the previous decade. He rang Dutton and told him his concerns. Dutton brushed aside the GST issue, and on the subject of

Abbott said, 'No, mate, that's just a rumour.' Dutton said the same thing to Sukkar, and his lieutenants told others, including Scott Ryan, that Abbott would not be on the frontbench.

Entsch told Dutton not long before the Friday ballot that he would not be voting for him after all. He voted against the spill; then, with his heart, in the first ballot for Bishop, 'because I love Jules'; and then in the second, with his head, for Morrison. As for Abbott, Entsch echoed the sentiments of most of his colleagues that he should quit parliament.

Afterwards, Robert thought it incredible that both the Turnbull and Dutton camps had stopped counting, even if for different reasons – Turnbull's, because they thought it was over, and Dutton's, because they thought it was in the bag.

In the Morrison camp, they were taking nothing for granted. They – and Julie Bishop – were still talking to people late into the night. In fact, Bishop rang both Morrison and Stuart Robert after 11.00 pm. Robert gave her points for trying.

Morrison and his men worked until midnight in Morrison's office. Then, satisfied with their work, they went home, and he and Irons and Robert had a quiet whiskey together.

On Friday morning, a group of the moderates – Fletcher, Payne, Zimmerman, and Birmingham – gathered in Cray's office. They were sure it was over. Payne and Fletcher were trying to tell Cray she had to help convince Turnbull that he should resign. It was the only time Cray was close to tears. 'Have you met him?' she asked them. Like, did they not even know who he was?

Then she snapped, asking if Morrison had sent them. Payne, who does a pretty good job of snapping herself, replied, 'I don't get sent by anyone.'

Pyne said later that as the time approached for the party meeting, he was worried that Turnbull would get smashed. He says he did not want him to suffer that kind of humiliation. He decided he had to be the one to suggest to Turnbull that he should consider resigning.

Turnbull was standing, holding on to the back of his chair. He was immovable.

'I have said I will call a spill. If they want to get me out of this office, they will have to vote me out,' he told Pyne.

Pyne told him the spill motion would be carried, and if it was carried overwhelmingly, the far right would be able to claim a huge victory over him, whereas if he stood aside, the last ballot would be the one in which he defeated Dutton.

Pyne and the rest had simply assumed Turnbull would lose the spill motion by a big margin. The moderates had stopped focussing on whether the spill motion would get up, and were concentrating on mustering the numbers for Morrison to defeat Dutton.

In retrospect, Pyne concedes that was a mistake.

As well, that Friday morning, frustration was growing over Turnbull's reluctance to schedule another party meeting until he had sighted the petition with 43 signatures. Former whip Alex Somlyay called Nola Marino's adviser, Nathan Winn, to tell him that, under the rules, if the leader did not call a party meeting, the deputy leader could do so.

Winn walked around to tell Marino, who was in a meeting in Turnbull's office. She broke off to see Winn. After he relayed Somlyay's message, she grabbed his arm and drew him back into Turnbull's office, saying he needed to 'tell Malcolm'. Pyne and Sally Cray were also there. Turnbull was reclining in his chair. Winn relayed Somlyay's message, saying that if he did not call a meeting, Bishop could. 'That's ridiculous,' Turnbull said, and waved his hand dismissively. Pyne was similarly unimpressed. 'That's okay – tell Alex to stick to his golf,' he told Winn.

The petition with the required number of signatures finally arrived, and Marino, who felt for Turnbull but also wanted to ensure that the parliamentary party's interests were best served, was then told by Turnbull to check all the names to ensure they were all genuine. The meeting was finally scheduled for 12.30 pm.

Inside the party meeting, feeling sick at heart, Rowan Ramsey once again handed out ballot papers to his colleagues. Many of them felt as he did; others were excited; and others just wanted it over. Ramsey chose black humour to try to leaven the mood: 'I haven't had this much fun since I ran over my neighbour's dog, then had to tell him what I had done.'

Months later, Ramsey said the mood in his electorate of Grey, which takes in Whyalla, had improved thanks to the revival of the steelworks, plans by billionaire Sanjeev Gupta to power the steelworks with a $700 million solar, battery, and pumped-hydro project, and government infrastructure spending. Even so, people were still asking him 'Why?'

So what was his answer? 'It was a confluence of three different things – one being the former prime minister still causing some issues, the other being the NEG. The big one – Queenslanders panicking about Pauline.'

The spill motion was only carried by 45 votes to 40. If three votes had switched, Turnbull would have won it.

That, however, would not have resolved the leadership turmoil, and what was indisputable was that everyone wanted it resolved. Dutton secured 38 votes in the first round and Morrison 36. Then, with Bishop out after securing only 11 votes, Morrison beat Dutton by 45 votes to 40.

Sinodinos saw Abbott in the party room talking to Ross Vasta. Abbott was about to walk away, so Sinodinos stopped him and put his hand out. They shook hands, but did not really speak.

'He was like a coiled spring. He looked like he was on tenterhooks,' Sinodinos said later. Always level-headed, the devastating turn in his life had given Sinodinos added perspective. When the vote was over, he said to Richard Colbeck and Dan Tehan, 'You understand there's more to life than what happens in this room?' They agreed.

Sinodinos went back to the prime minister's office. 'There were a few tears, they didn't go off the deep end, didn't jump on any tables,' Sinodinos said. He thought Turnbull's staff were very professional and had kept it together well during what had been a very difficult time.

Turnbull had lost patience with them a couple of times, particularly when everyone was trying to tell him what to do, when really sometimes he simply needed space to assimilate what was going on. There were no meltdowns, no tantrums.

Sinodinos did give Turnbull one valuable piece of advice before his final press conference as prime minister.

'I think you have to strike an optimistic note about the country and the future,' Sinodinos told him. 'I think it's always important for people out there to feel, despite what's happened, that you believe in the country and the future of the country.

'It lightens some of the burden, and [shows] you're not out there in a self-pitying way talking about you.'

It was brilliant advice from one of the best chiefs of staff ever to a prime minister. Turnbull took it, at least in his last few hours in office. His press conference was a tour de force. Kevin Rudd had blubbered. Tony Abbott looked like he had had a very hard night. Which he had.

Turnbull was composed. He concentrated on his achievements, beginning with the economy, and deliberately characterising his government as a progressive Liberal coalition. He began by saying, 'It may surprise you on a day like this, but I remain very optimistic and positive about our nation's future', and ended by wishing the new prime minister and his team the very best. When he finished he invited *7.30*'s Laura Tingle to ask the first question. She asked if he regretted having made too many concessions to the conservatives in his party, given that it had frustrated voters and that the right came for him anyway. Turnbull's matter-of-fact response was that he had been trying, as leader, to keep the show together.

He was, at this last outing, at his very best. It punctuated the utter madness of that week. Until his young grandson, Jack, booed the press, providing a potent, heartfelt exclamation mark. When he walked back into his office carrying his granddaughter Alice, Turnbull's staff and his family were in tears. No one saw him cry.

One of the last people to farewell Turnbull from The Lodge on Sunday was the head of his department, Martin Parkinson. They spent 45 minutes, going through the almost three years they had spent working together, the highs and the not-so-highs – the education reforms, the trade treaties, the tax cuts, the same-sex marriage vote, getting the National Disability scheme onto an even keel.

Turnbull had recruited Parkinson after Abbott had sacked him as head of Treasury, which Parkinson says is the job he loved most. In Treasury, there is time to think strategically and to plan ahead. In Prime Minister and Cabinet, problems land on your desk usually because they have gone badly wrong somewhere else. It is short term and reactive, according to Parkinson.

Although he was disappointed when he was sacked from Treasury, he was philosophical. He was in the United States, spending time in Washington and at Princeton University, when a friend texted to say that Turnbull had challenged Abbott.

Soon after, Turnbull himself rang Parkinson and asked him if he would come back to help. Yes, of course, he said, thinking Turnbull might want him to carry out a review of something or other.

He flew back to Australia. He attended a farewell party for his former treasurer, Joe Hockey, who was heading off as US ambassador, one night, and then had a cuppa with Turnbull at Point Piper the next night. Parkinson did not really want to head

Turnbull's department. However, the good Malcolm, the charming, persuasive Malcolm, is hard to resist – even harder if he is prime minister. Before he finally committed, Parkinson also wanted to check that the incumbent, Michael Thawley, appointed by Abbott with the help of John Howard, was not being pushed out. Although Thawley and Turnbull had a bit of history, Thawley was leaving voluntarily. Before he left, he told Parkinson he would sort out the Jamie Briggs matter for him. The young frontbencher had behaved inappropriately with a young diplomat in Hong Kong, was demoted, and then subsequently lost his seat.

Parkinson began the year with his own 'scandal' to sort out, involving another frontbencher, Stuart Robert, who is a magnet for controversies, who also had to be demoted. The year after, he had to sort out the entitlements row involving the health minister, Sussan Ley. Like he said, by the time things landed on his desk, they had usually turned to custard.

Then, the following February, of course he was dragged into the Barnaby Joyce affair.

Not long after, Parkinson and Turnbull went through some testing times. As Parkinson would say later, it was getting harder to keep the bad Malcolm in the cave.

The May budget was well received, but there was no poll bounce from it. The politics of energy proved insoluble. Turnbull was becoming frustrated, and Parkinson seriously considered leaving. Instead, he took a two-week holiday. He went to Bali with his wife, Heather. He came back refreshed and determined to continue. He told Turnbull that he was okay, that he would be staying on. Parkinson thought, like almost everybody else, that Turnbull had managed to get through the 14 August party-room meeting as well as he possibly could.

Parkinson did not think the NEG was perfect, but it provided a framework that could finally provide some certainty for investment, and which both the government and the opposition could work with, if they were to switch roles.

He was incredulous when he read the reports on Friday about Dutton preparing to challenge. He thought it was a beat-up, because he could not see how anyone could think Dutton was electable, let alone why Dutton himself would think he was electable.

Again, like everybody else, when he heard the result of the vote at Tuesday's party-room meeting, he could not see how Turnbull could recover. He thought (as it turned out, like others, such as Morrison did) that maybe Turnbull could make it to the end of the week, after which MPs would go home to be knocked into shape by their constituents and maybe come back in a sober frame of mind.

Nevertheless, he began preparing an incoming brief for a new prime minister. There was a brief for Dutton, a difficult exercise given some of the cockamamie things he was floating, like removing the GST from power bills. There was a brief for the 'other' prime minister.

Within two hours of Morrison's election, Parkinson was in his office presenting that brief, and informing Morrison of the immediate steps that needed to be taken.

First, he had to confirm the Coalition agreement with the National Party. He then had to convince the governor-general, Sir Peter Cosgrove, that as a result of that agreement, he had the confidence of the House. Then he had to be sworn in.

Parkinson also briefed Morrison's chief of staff, John Kunkel, on organising the transition.

So, on the Sunday, he and Turnbull took a little time to reminisce. Turnbull was philosophical, pleased with his achievements, wryly observing that he had never just been fighting Bill Shorten and Labor, but Abbott and his supporters as well. He had had two oppositions and two opposition leaders to contend with.

Parkinson told him it had been an honour to work with him.

CHAPTER SEVEN

My learned friend

As Malcolm Turnbull fought for his political life, he pinned his hopes for survival on questions about Peter Dutton's eligibility to sit in parliament, based on the ownership of child-care centres by Dutton's wife Kirilly, which had received subsidies from the government. Turnbull was convinced there was a strong case for Dutton to be found to be in breach of section 44(v) of the constitution, which prohibits MPs from an office of profit under the Crown.

The section states that any person with 'any direct or indirect pecuniary interest in any agreement with the Public Service of the Commonwealth' is disqualified. Dutton's position was revealed in the audit conducted by Turnbull of all MPs after the dual-citizenship fiasco. The story ran exclusively on Network Ten on Monday night, 19 August, then blew up the next day, after Tuesday's party-room meeting, leaving Dutton convinced it had been leaked by Turnbull's office or supporters in an effort to damage him – to knock him out of the race or out of the parliament. Both Ten and those around Turnbull deny this emphatically.

Turnbull has a brilliant legal mind, but he met his match in those final days with his attorney-general, Christian Porter. Porter had been both treasurer and attorney-general in the Western

Australian government before transferring to the federal seat of Pearce. If he had stayed in state politics, he would have become premier. If he lasts in Canberra, Porter has the qualities and the potential to lead the party and become prime minister. He is bright, has cut-through communication skills, is an effective performer in parliament (recognised by his appointment as leader of the House to replace Christopher Pyne), and is in touch with popular culture. He is a movie buff – a *Star Wars* aficionado – and promised his staff he would get a tattoo if he increased his vote in his marginal seat of Pearce. He doubled his margin to 6 per cent.

Porter had travelled to Canberra on Sunday night, 18 August, with his wife, Jen, and their two young children, Lachlan, two, and five-month-old Florence, hoping that, once the sitting day had ended, he would be able to spend time with them. It didn't happen. To make the week even tougher, his father, Chilla Porter, who won a silver medal in the high jump at the 1956 Melbourne Olympics, was suffering prostate cancer, and in those days underwent his first chemotherapy treatment. It helped Porter put his own ordeal that week into perspective.

As he sought to respond to the extraordinary events, which he later recounted to me in an enthralling narrative combining language befitting both a top-flight lawyer and a tradie, Porter battled to separate his political self from his legal self to ensure that the process surrounding Dutton was scrupulously followed to the letter of the law. He was prepared to abstain from the final vote on the leadership, if necessary, to prove he had been punctilious in the process and observance of the law. He was ready to resign as attorney-general if he had to, but was determined to stay to ensure a fair outcome and to avoid a constitutional crisis unseen in Australia since 1975, because the prime minister was threatening to advise the governor-general that the cloud over Dutton meant he could not be sworn in. Porter told Turnbull he was wrong, and threatened to publicly contradict him and then to quit his post. He had a letter of resignation in his pocket.

Ultimately, despite everything that passed between him and Turnbull, Porter says he voted against the spill that would unseat the prime minister, and then voted for Peter Dutton. He was not convinced in the wake of events, which he described as tumultuous and momentous, that Julie Bishop had the authority within the party to be able to hold the show together. Besides, he and Mathias Cormann had been friends for 22 years, he was also mates with Dutton, and they all had a similar world view.

The week was marked by high-stakes meetings and phone calls, leading Porter to write to the solicitor-general, Stephen Donaghue QC, instructing him neither to speak nor to offer advice to anyone other than himself, including the prime minister. At one meeting on Wednesday 22 August, Porter told Turnbull he should resign – advice not welcomed by the prime minister – and the following day, during a tense meeting, offered his own resignation, which was not accepted by the prime minister, who referred to Porter as 'my learned friend'. It was not a term of endearment.

Porter also called in lawyers from his department and asked them for advice on the legal and constitutional situation if a prime minister refused to surrender his commission, or sought to prevent the commissioning of another person. He feared Turnbull was ready to announce he would advise the governor-general not to swear in Dutton. Porter's view was confirmed that the only interest the governor-general could have was whether the prime minister had the confidence of the House and could be guaranteed supply, and not with questions of a new leader's eligibility to sit in parliament, which Turnbull believed – and hoped – would disqualify Dutton.

Early on Friday morning, Porter sent an email to the governor-general to say he was ready, willing, and able, as was the solicitor-general, to provide any advice Sir Peter Cosgrove might need, or to answer any question he might have. Porter was prepared for anything, including preparing briefing notes to answer every conceivable question in the party meeting, if it came to that.

Porter holds no grudges. He knew he was dealing with a man fighting for his life, with a formidable legal brain, determined to explore every legal avenue in an effort to preserve his own position and eliminate an opponent. That's politics. As attorney-general, Porter was determined to ensure that the letter of the law and the constitution were not breached.

Days of trauma, high stakes, and legal parrying ended on Friday afternoon when Porter shared an emotional embrace with Turnbull's legal adviser, Daniel Ward, by all accounts a brilliant young man – the same Daniel Word who had worked for Brandis – who Porter says behaved with dignity and great common sense. Porter said Ward had a tear in his eye, and confessed that he was moist-eyed himself.

When Porter had arrived in Canberra on the Sunday night, he had no idea what lay ahead. He had dismissed the leadership speculation as just that. Then he got a call that night from Turnbull. They had a seemingly casual conversation, during which Turnbull asked what was happening. Porter's radar went up. It reminded him of a similar call he had received from Turnbull just before he launched his challenge against Abbott in 2015.

Porter told him directly that he had heard nothing about a challenge, that no one had contacted him either by phoning or texting, and that no one had sounded him out. He had no knowledge or forewarning of any coup attempt. He attended Monday's cabinet meeting, which discussed the latest iteration of energy policy. Nothing unusual there.

On Tuesday morning, he strolled down to the party room and sat in his usual seat between Andrew Hastie and Linda Reynolds. When Turnbull declared the leadership positions vacant, he almost fell off his chair. Porter was thinking to himself that no one would take the bait, but when Dutton put his hand up he gasped, and a murmur went around the room. When he heard the vote was 35 against Turnbull, he thought it was inevitable that the process would end with Turnbull no longer prime minister. He was astonished. 'It was the beginning of the end,' he said later.

That night, he had dinner with Cormann at the Italian restaurant Belluci's, a noisy goldfish bowl in Manuka, and a favourite hangout for Cormann.

'I think that we'd both, at that point, formed the view that the likely outcome was that Malcolm couldn't sustain his control of the party room and thereby the prime ministership,' Porter told me subsequently.

'My position was that I would never contemplate voting against a prime minister unless I'd first resigned.

'My sense of it was that the best thing for the party, at that stage, would have been for Malcolm to resign and vacate the field. I think I indicated to Mathias a view that I would be prepared to say that to him [Turnbull] at an appropriate point on the Wednesday. Which I did. And I think at that point, as well, Mathias was contemplating whether he would also have that conversation with him – which conversation would be a much more powerful thing coming from Mathias than it would obviously be from me.'

Porter said it was not an 'I will do this, you do that, type of conversation'. He described it as a 'fluid and dynamic set of circumstances' that they were both trying to digest, as well as trying to work out what they should or could do to resolve it.

'But I volunteered my view that it would probably be necessary at some point over the next day or two that people express a truthful view to Malcolm about the sustainability of the position,' Porter said.

Porter remembers Wednesday as the day that ministers were

falling like flies, punctuated by reports suggesting that Morrison was counting numbers for himself. Turnbull held a press conference with Cormann and Morrison, which Porter thought had been arranged for the prime minister to announce his resignation. Then, in question time, Turnbull was asked if he had sought advice from the solicitor-general about Dutton's eligibility.

Porter recalled that Turnbull leaned over to ask him if he had, and Porter responded that he had not.

After question time, Daniel Ward went to see Porter to tell him that the prime minister wanted advice from the solicitor-general about Dutton's eligibility. Ward said Porter should request the advice, because it would be a bad look if the prime minister requested it.

Porter said he thought that was appropriate, but he wanted to speak to Dutton first to see what advice he had received previously and what documentation he had. As they were speaking, the phone rang. It was Dutton.

Porter went to Dutton's office, and told him it would be useful if he could assist by providing his documents. Dutton agreed, and asked him how long he thought it would take for the advice to be given.

Porter, in his lawyerly way, said there was 'no room for luxury in the timing of it'.

He then texted Cormann to ask 'what on earth' was the press conference all about. He was referring to the now-notorious press conference where Cormann stood beside Turnbull to bury the tax cuts and pledge his allegiance to him.

'I think his response was that they'd had a conversation that morning, where Mathias had put the view that it was unsustainable. That hadn't been met with enthusiasm from Malcolm. So at this point in time, I've understood that Mathias has put a view to Malcolm that he should exit, and do it in a way that was bloodless.'

Porter was feeling despondent. About everything. He had just received a message from his sister with a picture of their father after his first round of chemotherapy. 'And I just, you know, when those things are happening, you just think, "Why the fuck am I here?"

'So I went in see Malcolm, and I guess I just told him what I thought,' he said. 'So I said, first of all, with respect to the s.44(v) issue, I thought my very, very rough assessment was that, generally speaking, that it's never been considered that schemes of general statutory application – things that by legislation effectively transmit welfare – have ever been considered agreements with the public sector, with the Public Service of the Commonwealth under s.44(v). And that whilst here, there would clearly be some form of documentation which registered the child-care provider as an authorised provider – [the] receiver of the child-care subsidy – that, having had the portfolio [Porter had been social services minister for two years], having dealt with childcare, this was a subsidy that went to end-point users who registered individually and became eligible for subsidy to defray the cost, and the child-care centre was the middleman.'

Essentially, Porter did not believe there was a problem with Dutton's eligibility.

'Well, that was a very, very rough view,' he said later. 'But I said, whatever happens, I mean, it will always be equivocal. I mean, by its very nature, this advice, I think I may have said, will take the formulation, "The better view is …" And Malcolm then said, well, you should go out and say that. And I said, no, I won't be doing that.'

Apart from anything else, Porter thought it was 'bad process' to try to pre-empt the solicitor-general.

'Malcolm wanted me to say – the stress that he wanted me to put on – was that the situation was unclear. So he said the words 'you should go out and say that,' meaning that there's a lack of clarity.

'I'm like Spider-Man sensing danger at that point in time. And I thought, well, that indicates here that this is a drowning man looking for a very big plank to hang on to. I said I'm not going to do that.'

Porter told Turnbull he was going to provide written instructions to the solicitor-general after the meeting.

'I said that I wanted to control the process of seeking and receiving the advice, and that I would keep him informed at every step of the way – that my preference was that I alone do that, and not the prime minister or people from the prime minister's office,' he said.

'Now, to be fair to the prime minister, he didn't expressly consent to that, but he didn't raise an alternative view to my preference that I control the process and that I be the one speaking with the solicitor-general formally asking for the advice, receiving the advice, and distributing the advice. Then he said, would I cc him a copy of the request for advice. I said that, no, I would not do that.'

I asked Porter why not. He replied, 'Because I had heard stories about Malcolm, George (the previous attorney-general, George Brandis), and the solicitor-general, and the way in which advice sometimes came into being.

Me: 'So you ask the questions so you get the advice that you …'

Porter: 'Well, worse than that. I think that, you know, it was not merely the asking of the question. How you frame the question can very much influence the sort of response that you get. But, equally, Malcolm is such a bright and talented lawyer and such an influential and persuasive advocate, that if he's looking over drafts or talking about ideas or fleshing out general legal concepts, that I think has the habit of driving the ultimate provider of the advice in a certain direction.

'And I did not want any advice – in what was turning into a pretty high-stakes game – to be anything other than the utterly independent view of the solicitor-general, who was, is, and always remains completely motivated by legal instincts, rather than anything else.'

Porter said that this did not go down well with Turnbull, and it was all downhill from there.

'So the conversation was getting, sort of, terse at this point,' he recalled.

'And I said I also wanted to put a view about the general situation. I said to him, my view is that you should resign.

'I said, this just won't stop. I said, they will keep coming at you. And I said, equally, there's going to be more than one group of people who now appear to be wanting this resolved in a way that doesn't end with you as prime minister. I said I think that you owe it to the next generation of us in the Liberal Party to have an opportunity to try and put together an alternative from this scenario in a way that's as bloodless as possible.

'He ... was not happy at me putting this view.'

After Porter left, Turnbull was fuming, and then suspicious, asking those around him, including Craig Laundy, if they thought Porter had crossed to Dutton. Turnbull knew Porter was close to Dutton and was concerned this might be influencing his opinion about whether or not Dutton had a case to answer.

Laundy was convinced that Porter would play a straight bat, if for no other reason than to protect his integrity. In his view, someone with higher ambitions like Porter would not want such a blot on his record.

Turnbull's dry, rhetorical question to Laundy was simply, 'Didn't you say the same thing about Mathias Cormann?'

Porter set about writing the request for advice from the solicitor-general.

It was after midnight when he got home. 'Everyone's asleep, I crawl into bed, the texts start coming in from Malcolm, the WhatsApp messages at 4.10 am, 4.20 am, when will I get the solicitor-general's advice? I ignored those until a reasonable hour.'

Then he received a call, also very early, from Donaghue. 'He said, "Malcolm's phoned me three or four times." I asked him if he had spoken to him, and he said it was unavoidable after a certain point.

'He said, to be fair, Malcolm wasn't robust or argumentative, or didn't try to influence him, but he put some views about the legal issues at play and was most focussed on when advice would come back.'

Soon after that conversation, Porter was back in his office. The night before, he had researched the Law Officers Act.

'I invoked an ability the attorney-general has to instruct the solicitor-general not to communicate with any other member of the executive government other than me, with respect to a particular matter,' he said. He wrote the letter, signed it, then emailed it straight to Donaghue early Thursday morning. He did not tell Turnbull what he had done.

He then called in Australian government solicitors and constitutional-law experts from his department – whom he would not name – to discuss the process of commissioning a new prime minister.

'It had occurred to me that this could all get very messy, potentially,' he said. His view was confirmed that the governor-general would be concerned only with the new prime minister's ability to guarantee supply and to command the confidence of the House.

In the meantime, he had received a call from Cormann before his resignation press conference with Fifield and Cash. Cormann told him that Turnbull had said in their meeting that the advice from Porter was that Dutton was ineligible to be prime minister, and that Porter had formed a view that the reserve powers would be used to not appoint Dutton.

'That is not at all what had occurred in the meeting on the previous day with Malcolm,' Porter said. 'I felt at that point that I'd been somewhat misrepresented. Now, to give Malcolm the benefit of the doubt, these are stressful, difficult times. People hear different things, and this is third-hand hearsay. It occurred to me that we were somewhere between Chinese whispers and gilding of the lily of my views on these things.'

He continued to receive numerous texts from Turnbull seeking the solicitor-general's advice. Porter went to see him in his office. He had typed out a letter of resignation and put it in his pocket. He did not want to resign, but he would if he had to.

They remained standing during the conversation. Turnbull was pacing, a cup of tea in hand. He was, according to Porter, agitated but not rude. 'It was an unpleasant meeting, right,' Porter said.

'He said to me, "The governor-general will not commission Peter Dutton to be prime minister."

'And I said, "Well, has the governor-general told you that, or is that your perception of his position, or have you told the governor-general that?"

'And Malcolm said that he knows the governor-general, and he will not commission Peter Dutton as prime minister with this doubt hanging over him. Now, I took that to mean the governor-general had not said that, and this is one of the most intelligent, sharp, and strategic men around, finding angle after angle after angle. Like, he's seeing this thing like *The Matrix* at this point in time.'

Again, Turnbull asked Porter when he expected to receive Donaghue's advice. Porter said, 'Well, you tell me – you were talking to him this morning.' He then repeated to Turnbull that he would prefer to be the one speaking to the solicitor-general, but did not inform him that he had written to Donaghue instructing him not to speak to anyone else.

Turnbull went back to discussing the governor-general, telling

Porter he did not understand how serious the situation was.

Porter replied, 'But I am saying to you it would be utterly wrong at law and a total misrepresentation and misunderstanding of the reserve powers if anyone were to instruct the governor-general that there was anything other that he should consider, aside from confidence and supply.

'I went into this meeting having anticipated this angle, and was, as I've noted, very forceful with Malcolm about that fact.

'He then said, "Well, I give the advice to the governor-general."

'I said, "What makes you think that it should merely be your advice in these circumstances?"'

Turnbull replied, 'I am the prime minister.'

'I then said – and Malcolm was about go out and do a press conference – "Well, are you intending to say this publicly in this press conference that you're about to have?"

'And he said, "Yes."

'And I said, "Well, if you did intend to do that, I would feel the need to publicly rebut that proposition."'

Porter told Turnbull, 'If you are not prepared to take my advice on the reserve powers, you can have my resignation if you want it.'

'No, no,' Turnbull said. 'You are my loyally serving attorney-general.' Porter says it was dripping with sarcasm, but he ignored it, and resisted the temptation to bite back against a man literally fighting for his life.

'I felt like saying, mate, they're doing to you what you did to them. Like, have some perspective on it. But I … at that point, it wasn't worth being combative – it would have just been gratuitous.'

Porter said he did not particularly want to resign, but said he could offer a formal resignation 'now' if the prime minister thought the situation was untenable.

Porter recalls Turnbull saying to him, 'You're giving in to terrorists.'

Porter was outraged. 'I think I said to him I've worked my whole life to be in this parliament. Nothing means more to me. I've served you in a very hard-working, loyal way. I've had nothing to do with this, but what's now done can't be undone, and I'm just offering you my honest assessment – the position's untenable.

'I said to him, I've got a father going through chemo back in Perth. I've got a 3.6 per cent seat where I'm constantly out in every spare moment I have, when I'm not working hard as a cabinet minister, going to the opening of every cake stall known to man, and none of this helps me, and I wish it never would have happened, and it has happened.

'And he said words that I won't long forget. He said, well, it's happened because you and people like you are weak, and you've given into terrorists. And I said, well, I won't be staying here to have you call me weak.

'At the end of that meeting … I reiterated that I thought that it would be utterly wrong at law to suggest or provide advice to the governor-general that he couldn't appoint Peter if Peter emerged victorious from the party room, because that would be evidence of confidence and supply.

'And Malcolm was quite close to me when he sort of leaned to me and said, "Well, my learned friend, you'd be quite wrong."'

Porter went back to his office. He stayed glued to his television set, waiting to see what Turnbull would say at his press conference. Turnbull had not been bluffing Porter, but he nonetheless thought better of it, and pulled back at his press conference while still doing his best to cast doubt on Dutton's eligibility.

Porter could not help but be impressed by the way Turnbull responded. 'So clever,' he said.

'He [Turnbull] said that the issue around Peter was one of invalidity of decisions. He did not raise the prospect of putting to the governor-general that Peter would be incapable of being appointed prime minister. He said, the seriousness of this and why he wanted the signatures and why he wanted the advice before any further party-room meeting was that it would be a very serious thing, not merely for a minister to have made decisions which could potentially at some point of time be invalidated, but it was a very, very serious thing if a prime minister was in that position. So he changed tack from can't be chosen, to if he were chosen, it creates a range of difficulties.'

Turnbull was never convinced that the solicitor-general's advice would clear Dutton. He always saw it in the same light as the advice Donaghue had given about Barnaby Joyce's citizenship, which had also suggested the 'better view was' that the High Court would rule Joyce eligible, when in fact the opposite had happened.

Turnbull was determined to ensure that Dutton was thwarted at every point.

In Turnbull's view, it was one thing to have ministers (such as Joyce) continue in their roles while there was a cloud over them, because they could be isolated or separated from whole-of-government decisions, but the prime minister was in a whole different league. Doubt would be thrown over every decision of the government and the cabinet. There would be a legal cloud over everything. However, while he expressed his views clearly to colleagues about what would follow, and while he fully intended to write to the governor-general as the outgoing prime minister formally expressing the view that he could not, or should not, swear in Dutton if he triumphed in the party room, leaving Sir Peter Cosgrove to sort out a constitutional crisis, he was more circumspect in his public comments to media, while still fuelling doubts about Dutton's eligibility.

If Dutton had won Friday's ballot, it would have triggered the most dramatic days in federal politics since November 1975.

Turnbull made it clear at his press conference that he wanted two bits of paper before holding the party-room meeting to resolve the leadership. One was that a letter/petition with 43 signatures seeking another vote on the leadership be presented to him; the other, the advice from the solicitor-general on Dutton's eligibility to sit in the parliament.

He expected to have the advice by the next morning. 'But I cannot underline too much how important it is that anyone who seeks to be prime minister of Australia is eligible to be a member of parliament,' Turnbull told the media.

'But that advice at least will mean the party room is informed, and indeed Mr Dutton is informed. That may impact on his decision to run or not.' Turnbull went on to say that Dutton would have to establish his eligibility, the new leader would have to satisfy the governor-general he commanded a majority on the floor of the House, and he hoped the solicitor-general would be able to deal with the matter conclusively.

Porter spent the rest of the day preparing answers to possible questions from MPs in the party room about the governor-general and the commissioning of a new leader.

His normally orderly office was stacked high with books and notes when his very good friend Michael Keenan decided to drop by.

'I am literally rereading every piece of constitutional law text I can get my hands on about s.44 and s.44(v). Keenan comes into the room and says, "Mate, do you want to come out for dinner?"

'I said, "Mate, are you fucking kidding?" He goes, "Aw, are you doing the s.44 stuff?"

'As it transpires, that was him and Ciobo out at wherever, the Ottoman, drinking champagne cocktails.' He was glad he missed it. Keenan's advice to his good friend Porter was to make sure he was 'on the right side of this thing'.

On Friday morning, Turnbull was on the phone again, trying

to ring Donaghue. The solicitor-general, acting on the instructions from Porter, refused to take his call.

Meanwhile, early that morning, Porter emailed the governor-general's official secretary to say he was 'ready, willing, and able, with or without the assistance of the solicitor-general, to provide any advice you might need throughout the course of the day'.

Porter says he just left it at that, and then waited for Donaghue's advice.

'We are sitting around the table, [and] I have drafted a letter to Malcolm and to Peter,' he said.

'In Malcolm's letter was the cover letter for the advice. I had also, as well as the advice, obtained advice from Australian government solicitors about the proposition that anyone, including the existing prime minister, who advised the governor-general that he couldn't appoint someone who had some level of doubt around their eligibility, was wrong.

'So I provided him with the solicitor-general's advice about s.44(v) with accompanying advice from the Australian government solicitors, saying if you were going to do the thing that you suggested you might do, then that would be quite wrong at law. The PM rang: "Where is it, what does it say?" I said, "PM, I have not had a chance to read it because it has just arrived and I'm on the phone to you, and I'm walking it around now." So I had two staff members walk it round.

'Probably 10 minutes after that, the PM rang me up and, you know, to his credit, I guess, the PM's one of those guys that can have these savagely tense moments with you, and the next moment it's, aw, well, like it's weird, but there you go. "So what do you think of it?" I said, "Well, it is as I suggested, not without its equivocal components, but the better view is that subsidy is not an agreement, and so therefore even if there were a pecuniary interest, there's no agreement."

'But he says there's probably not a pecuniary interest, and with respect to the $15,000 grant, he says it's likely an agreement, but there's no pecuniary interest in it because it just underwrites the cost of a special-needs educator. I said, "You know, there's been two cases heard on this in 120 years, so we can't say anything with absolute certitude, but it is what it is." And I think, at that point, Malcolm sort of gave up on this being a final silver bullet to restore his position.'

Porter then returned a call from Julie Bishop from the night before. He thought she was ringing to ask him to vote for her. In fact, she did not. None of them did. Dutton never called him. Morrison called him, and said basically, '"Mate, whatever happens, I think that you are a good AG and I would like you to be a good AG if I get up", sort of thing, so I said that's nice of you, mate.' But he never asked Porter to vote for him.

Bishop simply pointed out that as she would be running for the leadership, there would be a vacancy for deputy leader, and he should run for it.

He told her what he had told Ben Morton and Bert van Manen when they had suggested the same thing to him the night before.

'It's very kind of you, but no,' he told Bishop. 'I said, (a) I'm dealing with a matter that I think is of substantial importance legally. I said I don't want to get involved with the politics of it. And (b) I don't want to really be sort of in any way seen to be trying to ride a wave of benefit out of a situation that I didn't have anything to do with and I wish had never happened.

'[The] party-room meeting happens. I wander down there, prepared to ask … to be asked and answer a hundred questions. Equally knowing no one might give a shit at that stage. No one cared, because the advice, sort of, you know, was more one way than the other. I was sitting in the row again where I was. I said to Mathias, you know I'm not voting in favour of a spill. I said I'm inclined to vote

Malcolm Turnbull in the boardroom of the National Press Club getting ready to debate Bill Shorten during the 2016 election campaign. Julie Bishop and Lucy Turnbull are chatting, while Patricia Karvelas is commentating.

1 December 2016: Christmas drinks at the Lodge. In his speech that night, Malcolm Turnbull said he might not be the best prime minister Australia had ever had, but he was the happiest.

A grim Barnaby Joyce with Malcolm Turnbull at the Tamworth Racecourse on Melbourne Cup Day during the New England by-election. Joyce won the seat handsomely with more than a 7 per cent swing to him, but it turned into an uncomfortable day for the then deputy prime minister after one of his daughters confronted him at the track. As rumours swirled that he was having an affair with his former staffer, Vikki Campion, neither his wife, Natalie, nor any of his four daughters appeared with him during the campaign. The media decided not to report the confrontation between Joyce and his daughter.

The Three Amigos. At a press conference on Wednesday 22 August 2018, after the government's company tax cuts were voted down in the Senate, Scott Morrison ostentatiously threw his arm around Turnbull, declaring, 'This is my leader and I'm ambitious for him', and Mathias Cormann pledged that he would continue to serve Turnbull 'loyally into the future'. Morrison, it turned out, did have higher ambitions, and as far as Cormann was concerned, the future did not extend beyond the setting of the sun. Later, Morrison told me that it was at this press conference when he first began to suspect that Cormann's allegiance was shifting.
[Alex Ellinghausen/Fairfax]

Arthur Sinodinos and his longtime staffer Fiona Brown at The Lodge before they headed up to Parliament House on Thursday morning after Cormann's defection.

THE HON STEVEN CIOBO MP

Minister for Trade, Tourism and Investment

The Hon Malcolm Turnbull MP
Prime Minister
Parliament House
CANBERRA ACT 2600

Dear Prime Minister

I hereby tender my resignation as Minister for Trade, Tourism and Investment.

It is my considered assessment that regrettably the situation for your Prime Ministership is unsalvageable, following the resignation of the Government's Senate Leader and Deputy Leader and numerous other senior Ministers.

My principal duty is as the representative for the electors of Moncrieff, and more broadly the nation.

I find myself facing conflicting obligations as your Minister for Trade, Tourism and Investment given the circumstances you face, and as such, must ensure my duty to my electors prevails.

It has been an honour to serve the nation in this portfolio, to have negotiated a number of trade agreements, including the Comprehensive and Progressive Agreement for Trans-Pacific Partnership, which will drive economic growth and create employment opportunities for Australians.

Yours sincerely

Steven Ciobo

2 3 AUG 2018

Parliament House Canberra ACT 2600 Australia
Telephone (02) 6277 7420 E-mail Trade.Minister@dfat.gov.au

23 August 2018: Steve Ciobo resigns from his position as minister for trade, tourism and investment after the first party-room ballot, when he voted for Peter Dutton, convinced by Dutton himself that he had the numbers to wrest the leadership from Malcolm Turnbull. Ciobo later decided not to recontest his seat, and left parliament.

Craig Laundy with his wife, Suzie, with Malcolm and Lucy Turnbull at The Lodge on Thursday night, 23 August, the day before Turnbull lost the prime ministership. Turnbull's staff and Arthur Sinodinos were there that night for drinks and dinner.

It is 11.14am, Friday 24 August in the prime minister's inner sanctum. The petition for a second spill has been signed by 43 of Turnbull's colleagues. His fate is sealed. At 12.30 pm, the second party-room meeting that week is held, the spill motion is carried, and his prime ministership ended. From left to right, Lucy Turnbull, Arthur Sinodinos, Turnbull at his desk. Sitting on the long table is the whip, Nola Marino. Standing is Christopher Pyne, who had earlier advised Turnbull to resign rather than recontest and run the risk of getting smashed in the ballot. As it transpired, if three votes had switched, Turnbull would have survived the spill motion.

Arthur Sinodinos (left) and Craig Laundy accompany Turnbull as he walks to the party-room meeting that is about to replace him with Scott Morrison. [Alex Ellinghausen/Fairfax]

Still friends: Peter Dutton, Michael Keenan, and his wife, Georgina, at drinks in Keenan's office after Keenan's valedictory speech on 3 April 2019. Keenan had been convinced Dutton would win the leadership, had a tense relationship with Morrison, and announced in January he was retiring to spend more time with his family.

Scott Morrison with his wife, Jenny, praying inside the Horizon Pentecostal church in Sutherland on Easter Sunday 2019. Although the images caused unease even in Liberal ranks, later analysis showed there had been swings to the government in seats with high percentages of voters identifying as Christian.
[Gary Ramage/Newspix]

Despite employing a giant billboard, Michael Sukkar could not find space for the word 'Liberal' as he fought to retain Deakin. Dave Sharma at least ran as a 'Modern Liberal' to reclaim Wentworth. Tim Wilson also ran as a 'Modern Liberal' in Goldstein.

An Abbott-proof fence is installed over a transit lane during the campaign for Abbott's seat of Warringah.

20 February 2019: in Kelly O'Dwyer's office after her valedictory speech, with her children, Edward and Olivia, Julie Bishop, Simon Birmingham, and, in the white jacket, Julia Banks.

Scott Morrison, with his wife, Jenny, and daughters, Lily and Abbey. Morrison claimed victory, declaring: 'I have always believed in miracles!' [Sam Ruttyn/Newspix]

for Peter, but I'm not voting in favour of a spill. I voted against the spill. I voted Dutton round one, Dutton round two.'

Even after all that, he effectively voted for Turnbull first up. 'Well, yeah. I mean, I just ... I just understand the agony and pressure he was under. I'm not angry at Malcolm. And I'd said to him that if I was, you know, not prepared to resign, he'd always have my support.

'Like, I've spent my life as a lawyer. Somehow or other, I ended up being the Commonwealth attorney-general, and I'm facing down a potential constitutional crisis. Ultimately, one that got to DEFCON 4, and then all the army stood down.

'But, you know, there was a significant likelihood that you might have had Peter Dutton win a ballot in the party room and someone argue to the attorney-general – to the governor-general – that he shouldn't appoint Peter as prime minister, and then Australia wouldn't have had a prime minister.

'Some time after that, I relayed the conversation to Mathias. I said that my view after that meeting had formed that I – if I'd had a view that it would be the right thing to offer a resignation – that I wasn't going to do that again, because it hadn't been accepted and I wasn't going to do that again, because I had a very firm view after that meeting that the best thing I could do was ensure that Australia had an attorney-general through this process.

'Because I thought that if Australia didn't have an attorney-general through the process, that it was likely that someone would be acting in the role of attorney-general, and that the process would not be as fair as it could be.'

Porter walked out of the party room after the vote and headed for home. Before that, he hugged Daniel Ward.

Porter said that he and his 'lads', Tim Wellington [legal] and Will Frost [national security], and Ward had worked very closely together.

Porter empathised. 'And I just – I know that Malcolm can be very, very difficult. Like, I'd experienced it first-hand. I had a very strong sense that they were experiencing it in there as well, because the legal issue became a potential avenue out of a maze for the smartest mouse in the trap.

'He had a little tear in his eye. I may have as well. I just gave him a hug.'

In the aftermath, when Cormann copped so much criticism, Porter felt for his friend. He was keen to cast him in a good light. He said that if Cormann had not resigned and had instead voted against the spill the second time, the 35 votes previously cast meant they would come back in 10 days' time and do it again.

'Now, you know, maybe it was a bad call; maybe it wasn't. But it didn't change the fact that it was over,' Porter said, adding that he did not think his friend was involved in Dutton's plan.

'I think he did his best to resolve it,' he said. 'I think he formed a view Tuesday, Wednesday, that it was unsustainable, and that because of his position of authority in the party room and in the parliament that it was going to fall to him and some others to put a view to Malcolm that it was unsustainable.

'I agreed it was unsustainable. I indicated to Mathias that I was going to put that view to the PM. I did that on Wednesday. At that point, my path diverged from the Morrison camp, from the Dutton camp, from the numbers, from the spreadsheets, because I was just in the 44 vortex.

'I don't hold any ill-will to Malcolm at all, difficult fellow that he could be at times, but I just tried to sort of navigate it as best I could.'

Porter admits he was swayed by Cormann to vote for Dutton, and although he said later that he did not regret it, he admits that Morrison's success was a 'better outcome'.

'It's really hard for someone who's in that conservative wing of the party, whose closest friends are ultimately doing the numbers for Peter Dutton, not to vote for Peter Dutton,' he said. 'And I would say one of the things that I'm most reflective on and maybe a little bit disappointed in myself – maybe this is part of a learning experience – but voting for people because they're from your tribe or that they are your friends, even if that friendship is based on a view about good parts of their character, is not always the best basis for choice.'

As he said later to his wife, Jen, 'I have never voted for someone who has won a leadership contest.'

Clearly, Porter is an intelligent and thoughtful politician, and he spent time in the days after the madness thinking about what had happened. He was disappointed that some of his colleagues refused to admit they might have made a mistake or stuffed up. Michael Keenan did.

When I said I had heard he was distraught, Porter replied, 'Look, he's not in a great way. But I think part of this is because he probably has a feeling that none of us covered ourselves in glory that week, that what happened was not in the national interest. And to the greater or lesser extent that people were involved in what happened, the ones that are most rational say we spend all our lives trying to get here to act in the public interest, and when it was most important, the more involved we were, the less we were acting in the public interest.'

He agreed it was all so unnecessary. 'But, that having been said, you know, anyone who reads the canons of English or ancient Greek literature, if you come to the job by the sword, there is a 92.1 per cent chance that that is how you are going out.'

Even after it was over, Turnbull could not let it go. From New York, he was texting colleagues to tell them that Dutton should be referred to the High Court. Peter Hartcher from the *Sydney Morning Herald* got wind of it, and minutes after his story was posted online,

Turnbull tweeted from New York, saying, 'The point I have made to @ScottMorrisonMP and other colleagues is that given the uncertainty around Peter Dutton's eligibility [to sit in parliament] acknowledged by the solicitor-general, he should be referred to the High Court, as Barnaby was, to clarify the matter.'

It gave his enemies another reason to attack him, and his friends cause for concern. His enemies accused him of trying to destroy the government, while his friends counselled him to preserve his legacy and not become like Abbott, imploring him to behave with dignity and try to let it go.

CHAPTER EIGHT

Oh, Mathias

What made Mathias Cormann's defection hurt all the more, apart from the fact that Malcolm Turnbull and his office trusted him implicitly, was that during the Longman by-election campaign, Turnbull told his advisers he wished he had killed off the second phase of the company tax cuts in June. In fact, he had told his leadership group they had to be either dumped or passed by the time parliament rose on 28 June. The reason they continued to live on, and why his treasurer, Scott Morrison, backed him to head off previous attempts by cabinet ministers to dump or reshape them into cuts in personal income tax, or bigger cuts for small business, was because Cormann kept insisting on having one more chance to get them through the Senate.

When Turnbull imposed that deadline of the final fortnight of the parliamentary sitting, no one in the tight-knit leadership group – more secure in terms of leaks than the cabinet – which met every sitting day in his office, spoke up against it. Not even Cormann. Everyone agreed. Turnbull told the group that the company tax cuts were a barnacle that had to be removed. Several members of the group – which included the prime minister; the deputy Liberal leader, Julie Bishop; Morrison; the Nationals' leader, Michael McCormack; Cormann as finance minister and as leader of the government in the Senate; his deputy, Mitch Fifield; and the leader of the House, Christopher Pyne; plus their most senior staff – recall Turnbull saying this at the beginning of that first sitting week, and then repeating it at the beginning of the second sitting week.

Everyone seemed to be in furious agreement that it was the right call to have them dealt with before parliament got up for the winter recess, and definitely before the five by-elections scheduled for Super Saturday, 28 July. No one demurred when Turnbull issued the edict, but, incredibly, after Pauline Hanson welched on the deal to pass them, Cormann pleaded for yet more time. He was this close, this close, he kept telling Turnbull. He was still confident he could get Hanson and the other crossbenchers across the line. He wanted one more chance. Turnbull, backed by Morrison, relented, and gave it to him, because Cormann had come so tantalisingly close to getting agreement, because Cormann's arguments that governments should stick by their convictions had merit, and because Turnbull's faith in the ability of the finance minister to deliver, given his record with the recalcitrant senators, was so absolute.

There had been attempts before this to kill off the second phase of the package, which had never been popular and which had given the opposition leader, Bill Shorten, a bottomless, poisoned well of choice lines to hurl at the government and the prime minister. The previous deadline was before the May 2018 budget.

The government's narrative, that the tax cuts would boost jobs and growth, was no match for Shorten's cut-through line promising better hospitals and schools, not bigger banks, and that the tax cuts were a gift to the top end of town from the richest occupant of The Lodge there had ever been. One rich man looking after other rich men – particularly the banks and bankers. The government had eventually bowed to the inevitable, allowing a royal commission into the banks to proceed. Day after day, the media were filled with horror stories about the appalling practices of the banks and other financial institutions. There was pressure on the government to excise the banks from the cuts, but they had already had a 0.06 levy imposed on them in the 2017 budget, estimated to raise $16 billion by the time the final phase of the tax cuts was scheduled to be realised. The problem was that nobody remembered the levy. All they knew was that the banks were absolute bastards that ripped people off, all the way to the grave and beyond, and that the government was still planning to reward them.

If Turnbull had followed his instincts and not allowed himself to be swayed by Cormann, history almost surely would have been different.

Research in the immediate aftermath of Longman showed that the most memorable message which stuck with voters from the campaign was the alleged cuts to the local Caboolture hospital, closely followed by the tax cuts for the banks.

Labor's campaign, and its better candidate, combined with the strong presence of One Nation, saw the Liberal primary vote drop almost 10 points to 29.6 per cent. If the government had dumped the big-business tax cuts before polling day, and converted them to small-business tax cuts, it is as near certain as it can be that the LNP primary vote would have had a three in front of it. The government knew from its research that the small-business tax cuts were a vastly more popular proposition, and it would still have been able to maintain its economic argument. That, plus closer attention by Trevor Ruthenberg and the LNP to his resumé, would certainly have resulted in a higher primary vote.

The post-poll internal research pointedly suggested the need for better candidate vetting, something which had been recommended in the 2016 post-poll review by Andrew Robb. There was not much tracking polling done by the LNP during the campaign; however, what was done showed that Labor's candidate, Susan Lamb, added significantly to Labor's vote, while Ruthenberg detracted from the Liberals'.

The research found that while voters did not necessarily believe Shorten's message about cuts to the local hospital, or that it was banks versus health and education – helped along by Mark Latham's robocall on behalf of Pauline Hanson's One Nation, saying Shorten was a liar – it did not deter them from voting Labor. 'They knew they were lies,' one campaigner said later. Nevertheless, showing once again the power of the negative, the truth was not enough to sway them.

Another curious finding came in response to the question to voters of where they had got their messages during the campaign. Both major parties rated closely when it came to TV, radio, and print, but there was a divergence when it came to doorknocking. Labor had a distinct advantage there. Part of the reason for this was put down to the fact that Labor had many more volunteers. The other reason was that while the LNP letterboxed, it didn't knock on doors, so it made less personal contact with voters. More attention to doorknocking had also been recommended in the 2016 review.

It is still unlikely that the government would have won the seat – unlike the public polling by ReachTEL and others, the party's private research never showed it was likely to win, nor that the vote shifted much over the 11-week period. However, a higher primary vote would have had a very different psychological impact on Queensland MPs. And by changing policy, the prime minister would have shown he was more in tune with the voters, thereby minimising his greatest negative – that he was out of touch.

Cormann's obsession with passing the full package was fed by his success in March 2017 when he managed to win over the support of the Nick Xenophon team to get the first stage of the government's company tax cuts through, meaning businesses with turnovers of up to $50 million would pay a rate of 27.5 per cent, which would drop to 25 per cent by 2026–27. The full 10-year plan would cut the rate from 30 per cent to 25 per cent for all companies by 2026–27, at a cost of around $50 billion.

That win against the odds only encouraged Cormann and the government to keep going, and Turnbull to keep supporting him. It got a lot harder after a wrung-out Xenophon announced he was quitting federal parliament to run in the South Australian election. The constant pressure on Xenophon, particularly during the negotiations on the new media laws, when he broke down in private and cried, saying he could not do it anymore, took its toll. His departure robbed the Senate of its sanest independent voice.

Soon after passage of the first stage, Kelly O'Dwyer, the minister for financial services and women, had a brief spell away from the office from mid-April 2017 for the birth of her second child, Edward.

It was not a break as such, and certainly not when Peta Credlin allowed a story to run for a few days before closing it down that a couple of cranky millionaires, upset by changes to superannuation (which, O'Dwyer's friends pointed out, were largely drafted by Morrison but carried publicly by her without complaint), were pressing her to challenge O'Dwyer for preselection. During her brief period of maternity leave away from the Canberra bubble, O'Dwyer began to grow uneasy about sticking with the company tax cuts.

Lower-house MPs are fond of slinging off at their Senate colleagues. They reckon that, because they don't have electorates or constituents as such, senators tend to be more insulated or isolated from the everyday experiences of busy families – even more so if they spend too much time in the echo chamber in Canberra listening to conservative commentators. O'Dwyer thought that Cormann, in particular, suffered from this.

O'Dwyer, both fearless and frank, never holds back in private. In meetings with colleagues, they could always rely on her to say exactly what she thought. They didn't always like it.

O'Dwyer's concerns continued to grow, and by the time preparations were under way in earnest for the May 2018 budget, she was convinced that the company tax cuts were toxic. She felt that Cormann so feared the blow to him personally if they were abandoned that he had lost sight of the bigger picture: the damage that was being done to the government.

She flew to Sydney for a 'deep dive' exercise (an in-depth examination of options) on personal income tax cuts with Turnbull, Morrison, and Cormann on 6 April in preparation for the budget. During the meeting, O'Dwyer suggested they would do better to convert the remaining company tax cuts to larger personal income tax cuts. She said they were a barnacle that needed to be removed.

She argued that, while they had tried hard to get them through, it was time for the government to cut its losses. She argued that no one was asking for them, and posed the simple question, 'Why are we doing this?' More pointedly, she wanted to know why they were continuing to 'flog a dead horse'.

Cormann was not impressed. He argued he was close to getting them through the Senate, they were part of the government's economic plan, essential to their narrative, and 'part of who we are'.

It got willing between them. Back then, Cormann had argued that discipline and unity would help win the 2019 election for the government. That, plus hard work and a relentless determination to convince the hold-outs that his way was the best way. 'I'm not giving up,' he would tell people. 'I will keep at it unless there is genuinely no chance left.'

It was not the only time that O'Dwyer would butt heads with the all-powerful finance minister. O'Dwyer's plan for a business case to examine whether the government should set up a default superannuation fund was also shot down by Cormann before the 2018 budget. O'Dwyer alluded to this in her valedictory speech.

The head of Turnbull's department, Martin Parkinson, had

dropped not-so-subtle hints in the lead-up to the May 2018 budget that the tax cuts should be dumped. He did not directly tell the prime minister to abandon the second phase, but that was the subliminal message from Parkinson as he urged him to think about Plan B if they were voted down. Parkinson was clearly pessimistic about the prospect of getting them passed.

Cormann was unmoved. Turnbull and Morrison were reluctant to countermand him, first because Cormann had exceeded expectations in securing passage of difficult measures, and second because the next phase of the company tax cuts had been woven so tightly into their economic narrative.

A pick-up in revenue meant that Morrison found $114 billion for personal income tax cuts, spread over seven years. That helped ensure that the company tax cuts lived on through the May 2018 budget. However, whatever benefit the government derived from passage of the personal tax cuts through the Senate in the third week of June – again, thanks to Cormann – was shortlived.

After a remarkable series of interviews, when her position changed by the minute, Hanson finally declared on Wednesday 27 June, the day before parliament rose for the winter recess, One Nation's 'firm decision' not to support the tax cuts. 'I've sent a message to minister Cormann this morning, so anyway, he knows,' she said.

Hanson could sniff the wind better than Cormann, and could sense that the company tax cuts would play out very badly during the upcoming by-elections. She didn't care how much the media ridiculed her minute-by-minute flip-flopping, or the fact that she went on a cruise during the campaign.

But still, Cormann – who thought he knew Hanson better than anyone else did, even better than she knew herself and her own mind, who had invited her to his home for dinner, and who had grown familiar with her 'wibble wobbles', as he called them – believed he could swing her around.

Turnbull believed Cormann, and he believed in Cormann, so, backed by Morrison, he agreed to allow the finance minister one last chance to try to weave his magic. He was at that time the government's best performer, bar none. He dominated the economic debate, had enormous influence over the prime minister, and Turnbull and his office trusted him 100 per cent. In my opinon, he was the best finance minister since Labor's legendary Peter Walsh, whom Cormann revered.

Although Cormann never said that the government would win either Longman or Braddon in Tasmania, he did cast the by-elections as a referendum on tax, and made clear the day after Hanson's 'firm decision' to renege that the company tax cuts were still alive and kicking. On 28 June, the day that parliament went into recess, he said the upcoming by-elections would be 'a referendum on who has the better plan for a stronger economy and more jobs'. He appealed to voters in both seats to send Shorten a message that they opposed higher taxes, and then seized on polling showing support among One Nation voters for the government's package.

'I hope that the fact that One Nation voters increasingly appear to be coming on board with our plan for lower business taxes will, over time, help to persuade Senator Hanson this is the right thing to do,' Cormann said.

'We need more time to make our argument to our colleagues on the Senate crossbench – and we, of course, will continue to make our argument in the Australian community. The government remains fully committed to these business tax cuts for all businesses, because it is the right thing to do for working families around Australia.'

Even Dutton was to say later that the tax cuts should have been dumped, despite the confidence of his best friend that he could get them through.

'Turnbull should have had the leadership capacity to make that call,' Dutton told me.

Shorten was not without his problems during the by-election campaigns. Anthony Albanese delivered the annual Whitlam oration on Friday night, 22 June, urging a more business-friendly approach by Labor. It was immediately, rightly, seen as an alternative to Shorten's hostile approach. The government had steadied. The budget had been well received, and the Coalition was coming back in the polls. Turnbull still maintained a better-than-healthy lead over Shorten as preferred prime minister. Media polls were showing that Labor could lose both Longman and Braddon, fuelling speculation about what might happen to Shorten in the wake of a once-in-a-century event.

Around the same time, *Buzzfeed* broke the story that Labor had initiated an internal inquiry into the conduct of one of its backbenchers, following allegations by staff of bullying and inappropriate behaviour. Emma Husar, the member for Lindsay, was a friend of Shorten and his wife, Chloe. Among the charges were that she had made staff walk her son's dog and pick up its poo. Lo and behold, the Seven Network got precious footage of a female staffer doing the dirty deed.

Husar ended up announcing she would not recontest her seat, although she went from alleged perpetrator to victim after one leaked allegation which suggested that she had flashed Labor frontbencher Jason Clare was roundly denied.

Shorten rode through the controversy, and produced his most devastating line of attack during the campaigns: better hospitals and schools, not bigger banks. The combination of Labor's deadly messaging, the lack of a clear one from Turnbull – except to mistakenly cast the contest in one radio interview as a choice between him and Shorten – and the Coalition's poor candidate, coupled with a poor campaign, all contributed to the drop in the LNP vote.

Even on the night of the vote, Cormann was sticking to his guns. It was like the Alec Guinness character in *The Bridge on the*

River Kwai, Lt. Col Nicholson, who lost all perspective when he tried to stop his fellow prisoners of war from blowing up the bridge they had been forced to build for the Japanese. Despite his framing of the contest as a referendum on tax, Cormann argued that he had never thought they would win Longman. Not even the 29 per cent primary vote moved him to rethink his position. When it was put to him late that night that it spelled the end for phase two of the tax cuts, Cormann loudly, reflexively replied, 'No! Why?' Then he again went through all the reasons why the government should stick with them.

Until then, despite wobbles, Dutton had stuck by Turnbull, at least publicly.

Dutton remembers Turnbull twice telling him that the government had only survived thanks to Turnbull himself, Morrison, Cormann, and him – Dutton. This is not in dispute. Turnbull and his office were indebted to Cormann particularly, but then he and Dutton were repaid with serious promotions.

Dutton says they did their best to make up for Turnbull's lack of political judgement.

The questions have persisted around Cormann. Was he duplicitous, plain old disloyal, or did he just try to do his best in an impossible situation?

There are those close to Turnbull, like Sally Cray and David Bold, who had been with him for years and worked closely with Cormann, who do not believe he was duplicitous. They agree, given the closeness of his relationship with Dutton, that Cormann might have been aware of what Dutton was planning, but believe he was not complicit in it.

Cormann had a much better relationship with Turnbull and his office than he ever had with Abbott and his office. Bold worked hand in glove with Cormann in negotiations with the crossbenchers. If Cormann was the closer, Bold was the go-between.

Cray believes that Cormann was not part of Dutton's plan until the Tuesday of coup week. Cormann had been instrumental in getting Dutton to tweet his belated support for the prime minister.

Turnbull would tell friends he had come to conclude that Cormann was complicit. He was mightily suspicious later that Cormann seemed to go quiet over the previous weekend. He was used to exchanging frequent texts with Cormann, but later realised that there had been a period of 'radio silence' between them.

Conversations at the time provide some guidance on, but not necessarily proof of, the extent of Cormann's involvement. As someone who spoke regularly with Cormann, and exchanged text messages with him, I can only say I believed he was genuine when he told me in mid-2017 that if there were any move against Turnbull, he would resign. He pledged to stick by Turnbull till the end. I wrote about this in an additional chapter of *The Road to Ruin*.

And I was not the only one whom Cormann had said this to. He told other close friends – no ifs, no buts – that he would go down with the ship. 'I had an absolute guarantee that he was rusted on, and I believed it until I saw him on TV going to Malcolm's office', one of his close friends said after he watched him walk into the prime minister's office on that Thursday morning.

In preparation for my column for Thursday's *Australian*, I asked Cormann on Monday if he was sticking with Turnbull. He said he was. He also said he had talked it over with his wife, Hayley, and that he would resign if anything happened. He sounded exasperated.

'I am not budging,' he said. 'I am supporting Turnbull.' Until the bitter end? 'Until the bitter end.'

He claimed then not to have known what Dutton was up to, saying he assumed that Dutton had not told him so he would not be compromised – although this was in conflict with what Dutton told other colleagues at the time, and what he said later, and what Cormann himself had told friends in 2017 about Dutton's intentions.

Cormann and I did not speak again. After Turnbull spilled his and Bishop's positions, Cormann claimed that he was too busy to speak. He later ignored all my text messages and calls requesting an interview for this book.

Although Cray refused to believe that Cormann was part of the move against Turnbull until late in the piece, she had begun to worry about what Cormann might do after Ten's Hugh Riminton reported exclusively on Monday evening that Dutton could be rendered ineligible to sit in parliament because of his wife's ownership of child-care centres, which allegedly placed him in breach of section 44 of the Constitution, prohibiting MPs from holding an office of profit under the Crown. The story got huge play the next day, then kept growing.

Dutton and his supporters were convinced that Turnbull or his supporters had leaked the story to Riminton. Riminton emphatically denies this, as do Turnbull and all those around him, saying it was discovered through careful research by himself and his team. Turnbull's office blamed Labor. Riminton says this also is not true.

Riminton told me later that he and his researcher, Kate Doak, had been working on section 44(v) issues for some time, and had done stories involving Queensland senator Barry O'Sullivan. They came across the Dutton issue, and decided to test it by getting an opinion from constitutional-law expert Anne Twomey. Twomey's advice was that Dutton could have a problem. Ten then sought another opinion from another constitutional-law expert, George Williams. He agreed with Twomey.

Twomey, conscious of the mounting conspiracy theories that have since sprung up, went back through her emails after I contacted her for this book, and provided a timeline. She said Riminton had called her the week before on Monday 13 August to outline the Dutton issue. She says she discussed it with two other constitutional-law and citizenship-law colleagues across the corridor from her office. All of them agreed there was 'a real issue', but none of them was completely confident about the legal questions concerning the trust arrangements. She says she conveyed this to Riminton.

The next day, Tuesday, after going through the High Court judgment on former Family First senator Bob Day, who had been ruled ineligible, Twomey told Riminton that Dutton's was a borderline case and that a court could fall one way or the other on it. George Williams replied on 14 August that there was an arguable case against Dutton, but that the outcome was unclear, as it depended on matters that the High Court had not yet determined.

On Wednesday, Twomey recorded an interview with Riminton at the University of Sydney. 'At this stage, I was unaware of any leadership-challenge speculation. I thought it was just another s44 issue, albeit about a minister, so it was likely to be a controversial one,' Twomey wrote in her email to me.

After the leadership speculation erupted on the Friday, she checked with Riminton to see when her interview with him was likely to be aired. Riminton said that they were having it 'legalled' and getting graphics done. At a pinch, Ten could have run the story that night, but Riminton and news executives decided to hold off until the Monday. The reason? Ten had a bigger audience on Monday night. Ten knew it had a good story, it wanted to get it right, it wanted to run it on the night when more people would be watching and when it would have maximum impact. They knew it would play into the biggest political story of the year, but they had begun working on it before Dutton's plan was exposed.

By Monday, when the story aired, as Twomey says, leadership speculation was 'reaching a crescendo'. 'But this was not the context in which the television interview was done,' she says. 'Nor was the issue originally raised in the context of a leadership challenge – it was done much earlier, and completely independent of it.'

At 5.30 pm that day, after Ten went to air, Twomey was attending a legal seminar that the Commonwealth solicitor-general, Stephen Donaghue, was speaking at. 'After it finished, I tipped him off that he would be no doubt asked for advice on the Dutton issue,' she said in her email to me. 'It seemed to be the first he had heard of it.'

Riminton says the only political office he spoke to during the story's preparation was Dutton's, and that was on Monday, when he submitted a series of questions and Dutton denied there was a problem.

Cray knew the story would anger Cormann, and that he would be tempted to believe Turnbull was behind it. She texted him, swearing they had nothing to do with it. Cormann was getting angrier by the minute.

Cormann's suspicion over the Ten story was not eased by Turnbull's decision not to take him into his confidence before Tuesday's party meeting. Cray knew that the story about Dutton's eligibility, which was being picked up by every other news outlet, and getting huge play, would only deepen the distrust, making an extremely difficult situation even worse.

On Wednesday, Cormann had several meetings with Turnbull. At the first, in the morning, Cormann told Turnbull it was looking bad and that the numbers were shifting. He said that another three cabinet ministers had shifted. Two of those turned out to be Mitch Fifield and Michaelia Cash.

Cormann told Turnbull he should step aside to enable a peaceful transition to Dutton. Turnbull, who did not believe that the numbers had shifted to Dutton, and believed that in fact Dutton had lost some, was outraged by Cormann's suggestion that he should simply hand over the prime ministership to Dutton.

'This is terrorism,' he said to Cormann. Cormann agreed it was. 'You are asking me to give in to terrorism,' Turnbull told him.

Cormann replied, 'You have to.'

Cormann was reluctant to appear with Turnbull and Morrison at the press conference after the company tax cuts were voted down by the Senate. He knew he would be asked by the media if he remained loyal to the prime minister. Turnbull insisted that Cormann had to be there. Apart from anything else, Cormann was the one who had insisted they stick with the tax cuts way beyond political prudence, so how could he fail to appear at the press conference supposedly to discuss Plan B?

Cormann stood beside Turnbull and with Morrison on Wednesday to bury them – the tax cuts, that is – and then he pledged publicly to stick with Turnbull. Although it was not as enthusiastic as Morrison's literal embrace of Turnbull, there were no ifs or buts.

Asked if he might shift his support, Cormann replied, 'I was very grateful when Malcolm invited me to serve in his cabinet in September 2015. I have served Malcolm loyally ever since. I will continue to serve him loyally into the future.'

Unfortunately for Turnbull, as far as Cormann was concerned, the future did not extend beyond the setting of the sun.

Later that day, aware that Morrison would run if there was another spill, Cray WhatsApped Cormann to warn him that if Dutton persisted with his challenge, Morrison would be prime minister by the end of the week.

Around eight o'clock that night, just as news was breaking that Cormann was shifting, Cray took off for Cormann's office with a bottle of white wine. She was still hoping she could prevail on him to stick with Turnbull. Cormann was no longer trying to keep things calm. Cray also tried to tell him that Dutton had not gained any numbers – he had in fact lost some, particularly after his thought-bubble on the GST. Cormann said he could no longer hold back the tide. He said that more cabinet ministers were defecting.

To Cray, he seemed in despair.

They talked for 45 minutes. Again, she warned him that the week would end with Morrison as prime minister. Cormann agreed that Morrison was 'up to something'. She tried to convince him that Dutton did not have the numbers and that the people he had surrounded himself with couldn't run a chook raffle. She wasn't angry, and nor was he, but he could not see how the genie was going to be put back into the bottle.

In some perverse way, the prospect of Morrison as prime minister, given that Cormann had decided Turnbull was terminal, and that neither Cormann nor Dutton liked Morrison very much, probably strengthened Cormann's resolve to come out for Dutton.

Despite the public shows of unity and bonhomie, Cormann was not close to Morrison, did not have a high opinion of him, and, according to one person who knew them both well, would have found the idea of Morrison as prime minister 'sickening'. They had a professional working relationship, but that was it.

Next morning, Cormann rang Cray to say he wanted to see the prime minister. She told him that, as he would know, the prime minister was in the usual morning leadership meeting and would see him later, around 9.10 am.

Cormann was impatient. He texted Turnbull, and turned up at his office door around 8.45 am with Fifield and Cash. Cray saw him, and demanded to know why he was there. Furious, she turned on Fifield and Cash, calling them weak.

As soon as Turnbull told Bishop on Thursday that Cormann was coming around to see him, Bishop says she knew what was about to happen. Later, recounting events to me, she was scathing about Cormann. She described him as 'the ultimate seducer and betrayer'. She was convinced he had been part of it all along, that he had never supported Turnbull. She noted he had backed Abbott to the hilt.

On Thursday, after Cormann told Turnbull that he was resigning to vote for Dutton, and that he and Fifield and Cash were about to do a press conference, Bishop exploded. 'I told all of you years ago that this is the most disloyal man and someone you couldn't trust,' Bishop told Turnbull and what remained of his leadership group inside the prime minister's office.

'I was always told I was wrong. I knew one day he would prove me right – I just wish it had not been today.'

Ciobo's reaction was also visceral. As he watched Cormann and company at their doorstop, he was thinking, 'This is without doubt the stupidest thing I have heard in my whole life in politics.'

Before that, Ciobo had thought it was over: Turnbull had won, Dutton was swimming upstream, and had lost support inside the party and outside it with his idea to take the GST off power bills.

He thought the whole thing was a complete debacle, and was angry with Cormann, believing that if he and Cash and Fifield had not walked away from Turnbull, he would still be leader.

'In my mind, it was done, settled,' he said later.

'I genuinely had been trying to be an honest broker. It became very evident to me we were stuck in no man's land. There was now no way on God's green earth we could allow this quagmire to continue through the two non-sitting weeks. It had to be brought to a head.'

Darren Chester was horrified by Cormann's defection, and saddened by the corporate damage it inflicted.

'Your character is tested every day in this place,' he told me later. 'A lot of my colleagues failed the test of character that week. Our collective behaviour that week played directly into the public cynicism about politics in Australia, and whether you can trust any politician whatsoever.'

Chester believes – and who can argue with him? – that it reinforced the view that it was every man and woman for herself. He tweeted to apologise to Australians for what had happened. He had never felt so disappointed or so despondent.

'Malcolm had his faults, but he was the right man to lead our nation, and he didn't deserve to be treated the way he was,' Chester said. 'My personal disappointment at being sacked [as a minister by Joyce in December 2017] was nothing.'

Chester says there was no real policy issue at the core of it. Abbott and Turnbull had been at war for 20 years, dating back to the time of the Republican debate.

So Chester's answer to the why-question, why Turnbull was no longer prime minister, was this: 'Personal animosities within the Liberal Party made it impossible for certain individuals to work in the national interest and put aside personal ambitions.'

Turnbull himself realised that Cormann's actions spelled doom for his prime ministership. His hopes of hanging on plummeted at that point. His government was at a tipping point, and he knew the damaging impact the defection would have on his MPs. He believed it succeeded in doing exactly what Dutton and Cormann intended at the moment their coup was failing, and that was to undermine him and the government to make sure there was no chance he could recover or make it to the end of the week, and perhaps call an election. Turnbull saw it as a deliberate and calculated act of betrayal designed to destroy him and to revive Dutton's challenge.

He knew he would not be able to hold out much longer against another party meeting, that MPs would desert him. He knew they would look at what Cormann had done and say they would never be able to put the pieces back together. But he was determined that if he was not to survive, he would hold on long enough to enable Morrison to succeed rather than Dutton.

Dutton was damaged by his actions, probably everywhere except in Queensland and in the studios of the delcons, the bully boys and girls. If anything, the damage to Cormann's reputation was greater, partly because he had been held in such high esteem and people expected him to not only stick to his word, but to play the adult. Even Cormann's friends could not understand how he could stand beside Turnbull one day and pledge allegiance, then publicly abandon him the next. He not only wrecked Turnbull's prime ministership, but he also he wrecked his own credibility. In the 2016 election campaign, he had been a star player. In 2019, there was room for only one star, Morrison. Cormann had a bit part.

Cormann was personally taken aback by the ferocity of the reaction to his decision, and waited for judgement from the electorate. In those early days, at least, his friends said he was reluctant to go out.

'He did not expect it. When it came, he tried to get out in front of it, then it was like, whoa,' one said.

Less than a week after the coup, there was a high-powered business roundtable in Perth. Woodside CEO Peter Coleman and Wesfarmers chair Michael Chaney were among those who attended. According to one attendee, Coleman, although not a great fan of Turnbull's, made it clear that he was appalled by what had happened. Both Coleman and Chaney wanted stability; they were sick of the revolving leadership door, and believed Turnbull was capable of winning the election.

They were concerned about the prospect of a Shorten prime ministership. And they were particularly scornful about Cormann's role in the coup. All of Cormann's hard work, all his previous successes, melted away.

Cormann justified his actions in interviews with others by pointing to Turnbull's decision to bring the challenge on, Cormann's belief that the 35 votes against Turnbull had rendered his position untenable, and Cormann's conviction that Dutton had the numbers.

CHAPTER NINE

Politically right, personally wrong

It was without doubt one of the worst weeks of senator Mitch Fifield's life. Fifield had been one of the small group of eight that had helped bring down Tony Abbott, thereby restoring Malcolm Turnbull to the leadership. Almost three years later, Fifield was to appear at a press conference with two friends, Mathias Cormann and Michaelia Cash, that would inflict deep wounds on another friend, Malcolm Turnbull.

The decision left Fifield himself distressed, confounded other political friends, and will probably haunt him for the rest of his days. Fifield has reflected long and hard over what happened. It has not been an easy time for him, and, like so many others, he likens it to a grieving process. It is painful, incites bouts of introspection, guilt, deep remorse, and self-laceration.

He has reached a point of some calm. Almost three months after the events, reflecting on what happened, Fifield concluded by saying, 'I did the right thing politically, but I did the wrong thing personally.'

As minister for communications and the arts, and deputy leader of the government in the Senate, Fifield was highly competent and extremely hardworking. He pulled off the seemingly impossible by getting all major media outlets to agree to new ownership laws, then got them through the Senate, ending Paul Keating's outdated prince-of-print, queen-of-screen rules from the 1980s. He was respected by his colleagues and by the crossbenchers. He had a good sense of humour and was a safe pair of hands. Fifield was renowned for his breadth of knowledge and attention to detail.

Fifield had never regretted his part in Abbott's downfall. He had never fallen out with Turnbull, had never had a row with him, had never grown distant from him, and had never had any cause to complain about his treatment. He had never once contemplated defecting from Turnbull, nor ever thought there was a better option than him to lead the government to the election. That was until Tuesday 21 August, when Turnbull vacated the leadership and the vote was read out, revealing that 35 Liberals had voted against him. Fifield voted for Turnbull in that ballot, and he believes that Cormann and Cash did, too.

Fifield had been intrigued by the leadership speculation over the previous weekend, but didn't really think there was much to it until Sunday night's emergency cabinet meeting. Dutton and Steve Ciobo were late getting there, and the pre-meeting dinner was incredibly awkward, marked by desultory conversations. Through it all, Michael Keenan, one of Dutton's best mates, who had dropped strong hints to friends a few days before that Dutton was on the move, said nothing and looked like thunder. The atmospherics were terrible and portentous.

At that meeting, Turnbull and Morrison wanted to announce the decision not to legislate the emissions targets the next day and then announce the acceptance of the ACCC's recommendations to crack down on price-gouging the day after that. Fifield could not see the logic behind separating the two, so suggested that both be announced together, and the package put to a special party-room meeting the next day before the announcement. In Fifield's view, because the situation was so fraught, careful attention should be paid to process, because sometimes faulty process can bring you undone. Ain't that the truth.

Morrison, especially, was opposed to Fifield's idea, saying it was only legislation, not policy, that needed to go to the party room. Turnbull backed him. However, they did eventually agree to announce the two measures together the next day.

In retrospect, convening a special party-room meeting on Monday, where the latest iteration could be explained calmly to everyone at once, and where people would be free to blow off a bit of steam, rather than dropping it all at a press conference, where other issues were bound to intrude and cloud what was already a messy message, or while the government was under attack in parliament – which is what happened – would have been a much better way to go. And if Luke Howarth had followed through with his threat to call for Turnbull's resignation, the likelihood is that he would have been shouted down.

Instead, at the usual Tuesday party meeting, Fifield was listening to Turnbull's speech to MPs. He thought it was good. It was calm, measured, respectful. Then, suddenly, he heard Turnbull say he was vacating the leadership. WTF, he thought.

As soon as the vote was read out, Fifield's heart sank. The vote against Turnbull was way too high. Like dozens of others in that room and elsewhere, he knew immediately that Turnbull would not be able to survive. As Fifield walked out with Cormann, they shared similar emotions. They were cranky that their opinions had not been sought in advance by Turnbull on vacating the leadership. Fifield says they would have done what they could to talk Turnbull out of it. Maybe he doesn't trust us, they thought. And they both concluded that Turnbull's position was untenable. There was only one way it could end.

Fifield and Cash spent some time with Turnbull and Cray that day, offering up whatever intelligence they had, which at that stage was not much.

They were in and out of Cormann's office, too. That night, Fifield attended the FreeTV annual soiree. The next morning, he did interviews on ABC's *AM* and with Kieran Gilbert on Sky, and a doorstop. He avoided answering when he was asked if he thought Turnbull could survive, only making it clear that he had voted for Turnbull and it was time to get on with the people's business.

Subsequently, after the regular leadership meeting in Turnbull's office, Cormann told Fifield that other cabinet ministers had reached the same conclusion they had, which was that Turnbull could not survive. Names swirling around included Dan Tehan, Christian Porter, and Josh Frydenberg.

Cormann wanted to tell Turnbull that he had lost even more cabinet ministers and more backbenchers since the ballot 24 hours before, that his position was not retrievable, and that he should step aside. He asked Fifield if he was okay with that. Fifield told him he was.

Cormann went to give Turnbull the bad news. As previously stated, Turnbull told him this was tantamount to giving in to terrorists, and Cormann replied he knew, but that he had to.

After question time on the Wednesday, after Cormann had appeared with Turnbull at the press conference in the prime minister's courtyard and declared his continuing loyalty to him in response to questions from the media, Fifield and Cash went to see Turnbull, also to tell him the same thing. 'Right, OK,' Turnbull said. 'So you would vote against me in a spill, would you, and vote for Peter Dutton?'

Cash told him it had not got to that. Fifield told him that if it did come to that, he would be prepared to vote for Dutton. 'This has got to come to an end,' he told his friend. 'It's not recoverable;

there has to be an orderly transition.'

This was not the news that Turnbull wanted to hear. He brought up Dutton's eligibility to sit in parliament, insisting that the governor-general would not swear him in. He walked over to his phone, saying he would call the governor-general right then and there to discuss it.

Instead, Cash suggested that Turnbull should 'get Mathias around'. He did. Cormann offered Turnbull his resignation. Turnbull would not accept it, telling him not to be silly, saying there was no need for that. They stood, and he shook them all by the hand, thanking them for their friendship and support up to that point.

'Why are you looking so glum?' Turnbull asked them. 'You should be feeling good. You are working towards what you want – Peter Dutton as leader. I am not glum.'

It took between 10 and 15 minutes. To say it was gut-wrenching is an understatement. Fifield, who had not told his staff or others, including his close friends, what he was planning, wondered how long it would take for it to leak. While Turnbull, Cray, and other staff were hoping to swing Cormann back, word seeped out that evening that Cormann was defecting.

The three of them had not thought beyond the meeting with Turnbull, but now had to think about the next step. Cormann, who was telling his colleagues he was convinced that Dutton had the numbers, said it would all come out, and he would probably have to go out and state his position. Whether Dutton had the numbers or not, the fact is that, at this point, Liberals in each camp believed it was so close that it didn't really change the bottom line, which was that Turnbull's leadership was over.

Cormann was insistent they had to bring it to its inevitable conclusion.

Fifield did not sleep that night. The next morning, Thursday, he rang friends, including the Speaker, Tony Smith, with whom he had worked closely during Costello's years as treasurer, to tell them he was planning to have a press conference with Cormann and Cash so they could announce their decision. Fifield, already dressed and in his office, rang Smith around 6.00 am. Smith was at his home in Canberra, having his first cup of coffee of the morning, watching the news on television. Smith was horrified. He told Fifield he would come in straightaway to see him. Smith was in Fifield's office before 7.00 am. Fifield was looking very stressed. He told Smith that, at their doorstop, they would be announcing they were voting for Dutton.

Smith was brutally frank with his friend. He told him he did not support what they were about to do, and wanted no part of it. He told Fifield that giving in to those determined to destroy Turnbull was both morally wrong and politically stupid – the public would be appalled, and Dutton would be an electoral disaster, particularly in Victoria. It would be like a double Hindenburg, he told his friend. Smith said he would stick with Turnbull and do everything he could to support him and stop Dutton. As far as Smith was concerned, it was nothing personal against Dutton. Smith and Dutton had entered parliament together, and had once shared a flat, but Smith was angry with him and what had occurred, and wanted no part of a 'reckless stampede'.

Smith kept emphasising to Fifield what a really bad idea he thought it was. He urged Fifield to take time to think about it. 'Don't do anything. Just pause,' he advised him. 'Don't go and quit. You have time. Take a bit of time.'

Then he told him to think about what it would mean for his friends, for him in his seat of Casey, and for Kelly O'Dwyer in Higgins.

'You are entitled to do what you want to do, as long as you know you are throwing us into an electoral furnace if you make Dutton leader,' Smith told him. 'If you didn't know it before, you know it now.' Anyone who has spent five minutes watching Smith run proceedings in the House has a rough idea of how direct Smith can be. It is nothing compared to his directness in private.

Fifield was already beginning to regret what he had committed to doing. That deepened as the day wore on, and worsened during the night.

He told Cormann after Smith's visit that he might not do the press conference. Cormann told him he could do it on his own, but he would rather Fifield and Cash were there. He wanted them both standing beside him.

As 9.00 am approached, Smith was getting ready to open proceedings in the House of Representatives. He asked his staff to let him know the minute anything happened.

Jim Chalmers, the shadow finance minister, happened to be on chamber duty that morning. There was hardly anybody else there. Like everyone else in that building, Chalmers was watching events closely. As Cormann's shadow, Chalmers studied Cormann closely. He always thought that Cormann would choose the moment that would have maximum impact to make his announcement. He judged that Cormann liked being at the centre of things, and that whatever he did, he would do in a dramatic way.

Chalmers was scrolling through his phone, when up popped tweets about the trio walking into the prime minister's office. Chalmers rightly assessed that Smith was focussed on what he had to do that moment, rather than on news alerts on his phone. Chalmers, who had also worked for a treasurer, liked Smith and thought him a good Speaker. In fact, even Labor MPs regarded Smith as one of the best speakers of modern times.

Chalmers walked up to the chair, showed him the alerts on his phone, and said quietly to Smith, 'You might like to see these.'

Minutes before, Cormann had texted Sally Cray to say that the three of them needed to see Turnbull. They were told to go in the front door. Cameras stationed at the end of the corridor were able to capture them entering and leaving.

They were ushered into a waiting room. Turnbull entered, closely followed by Morrison saying, 'This isn't a conversation you should be having on your own.'

Angry and disappointed, Turnbull lectured them, saying this was the government of the country, not some university students' association meeting. Again, he said there were issues with Dutton involving section 44 of the constitution that meant he could not be sworn in.

At one point, Fifield suggested another meeting, so they could talk about an orderly transition, but there was no point. They told Turnbull they were going out to do a press conference, and offered their resignations.

Fifield and Cash looked like ghosts. Each of them spoke, each saying the same thing, that Turnbull had lost the support of his colleagues, that there should be an orderly transition, and that Turnbull should call another party meeting so that the matter could be resolved.

When they got back to Cormann's office, the prime minister's office called, seeking their resignations in writing.

At this point, Dutton was the only candidate. Soon, Morrison would formally announce his candidacy, and so would Bishop.

Later that day, Cormann took Fifield around to see Dutton. They went to his office, but were told he wasn't there and that they should look in the monkey-pod room. Dutton wasn't there, either. Fifield walked into the room, saw the projector, and saw that the smallish room dominated by the highly polished table was filled with people who had worked for three years to destroy Turnbull. His brain began to throb. Did he really want to be aligned with them? Fifield was not alone in thinking this. Others had also told

Dutton that they could not vote for him because of Abbott.

Fifield received a text message from Morrison that evening, asking for his support. He received other text messages, including one from Christopher Pyne, also imploring him not to throw him into the furnace by voting for Dutton. Pyne was threatening to quit his seat if Dutton was elected and then sought to punish Pyne by dumping him from cabinet. Julia Banks was getting help from the prime minister's office to write her letter of resignation. Pyne also asked other friends of Fifield's to intervene, to see if they could talk him around.

His Victorian colleagues from the lower house, particularly Smith and Kelly O'Dwyer, were shattered, not only fearing that their own seats would fall if Dutton were elected leader, but wondering how all of them would fare at the hands of voters appalled by what was happening. They were nowhere near as shattered as Fifield. He was distraught.

Smith texted Fifield around 7.30 pm, then went back to see him again around 9.00 pm. He wanted to have one more go at talking him around. He didn't stay long. 'You heard everything I said this morning,' he said to Fifield, and then asked him for an undertaking he would think about it overnight. Fifield pledged that he would.

Fifield spent another sleepless night. Early on Friday morning, he spoke to two people whose wise counsel he valued. The first was his partner, and the other was Smith again. He had pretty much resolved in his mind not to vote for Dutton, that he would switch his vote to Morrison. He then had to tell everyone.

He ducked across the corridor to Cormann's office first to tell him. Cormann said it looked like he could not change Fifield's mind. Fifield confirmed he could not. He told him that Morrison had not been in the race when they made their announcement, and he had to do what he thought was best electorally. He was particularly worried about what would happen in Victoria.

Then he went to see Dutton, who had people in the room with him. Dutton ushered them out. After Fifield told him his decision, Dutton was disappointed, but remained calm and professional. He asked if Fifield was taking anyone else with him. Fifield had not sought to sway any others. They shook hands. Dutton told him that no matter what happened, he would want Fifield in his cabinet.

His next stop was the office of the defence minister, Marise Payne, to tell her his decision. The two have been friends for decades. 'In the 30 years we have been friends, I have never wanted to throttle you until yesterday,' she told him. They hugged and wiped away tears.

Then he went to see Simon Birmingham. They worked closely together in the Senate, and they had worked closely together to plan Turnbull's coup against Abbott.

His final stop was Morrison's office. He also had people with him, and ushered them out. His numbers men – Alex Hawke, Steve Irons, and Stuart Robert – were clustered around a laptop in another adviser's office.

As Fifield walked into the treasurer's office, the place he had spent so many hours in another life, Morrison said to him, 'Come home, Mitch.'

Before Morrison could give him his spiel, Fifield told him he had been to see Dutton to tell him he would not be voting for him. 'I am voting for you,' Fifield said.

Morrison, not quite believing his luck, or mishearing what Fifield had said, asked, 'Are you going to tell Duts?'

Fifield replied, 'I already have.'

Morrison asked him if he was going to put out a statement. Fifield hadn't thought about it, and it soon became immaterial anyway. Before Fifield had made the short walk back to his office, Sky was already reporting that he had switched his vote and would be supporting Morrison.

Fifield voted for the spill motion on the Friday, and then supported Morrison in the leadership.

Fifield was not the only MP traumatised by the events of that week, nor the only one to regret his actions.

His answer to the why-question – Why did Turnbull lose the prime ministership? – also echoes his colleagues. 'A combination of reasons. There was internal agitation and a group of people who never accepted him as prime minister. That and political misjudgement in the final week by Malcolm. A large number of colleagues, in the face of those facts, determined the situation was untenable and irretrievable.'

After the election, Fifield had to make a tough choice – to either stay in cabinet as communications minister and as manager of government business in the Senate, or to go to New York to become Australia's ambassador to the United Nations. Morrison had made it clear to him that he could do either. Fifield decided the best thing for him and his family was to go to New York.

CHAPTER TEN

A touch of the Keatings

Two days after the coup that toppled Malcolm Turnbull, Peter Dutton was unrepentant and utterly remorseless. Dutton's actions destroyed Turnbull, destabilised the government, damaged his own standing, and threatened to send them all into oblivion. In the immediate aftermath, colleagues surveying the wreckage – particularly those who had ambitions of their own – predicted he would never lead the Liberal Party, so angry were they with him for the demons he had unleashed, and so nervous were they about the electoral consequences.

In the months leading up to the election, Dutton remained defiant. The mood in Queensland had lifted. Up there, unlike down south, he reported they were glad that Turnbull was gone. After the election, he felt vindicated. Yes, his leadership bid had been thwarted, but he had succeeded in eliminating Turnbull, and by his reckoning this had saved the government. The Liberal National Party had regained the seats of Longman and Herbert. The further north you went, the higher the swings to sitting MPs. Dutton's primary vote in Dickson went up by more than 1 per cent, while his two-party-preferred margin rose to 2.4 per cent. Labor's use of him down south as the bogeyman appeared to have little impact on the Liberal vote. He remained insistent that Turnbull could never have won the election, and that his own actions were justified.

Even so, there were tinges of regret. He was supremely confident he could have won the election as leader, but he had been outmanoeuvred by Malcolm Turnbull and Scott Morrison, and undercut by Tony Abbott's few friends and many enemies.

Dutton was particularly stung that people thought he was Abbott's stooge. It was one of the biggest drags on his numbers. When word seeped out that Abbott would be back on the frontbench if Dutton won, Dutton lost votes.

Dutton wanted to be seen as his own man, making his own decisions; however, to some, it looked like he was being used by Abbott and his acolytes to wreck Turnbull's prime ministership, and was, intentionally or not, providing a back door for Abbott's resurrection. Dutton was mightily insulted by the notion that he was Abbott's surrogate.

However it might have looked to those on the outside, Dutton insists he took steps well before August 2018 to make it clear to Abbott that he was never going to act as his proxy. Ultimately, this made little difference to some of his colleagues, even those who liked Dutton, who thought that a victory for Dutton would mean a victory for the years of bastardry by Abbott and his acolytes – not to mention the prospect of a wipe-out at the election.

Dutton tried to separate from Abbott, although he was careful never to be overly critical of him publicly. He told Abbott he would never be his Trojan horse. Abbott was upset, but Dutton didn't care. He said later he didn't even want Abbott in his cabinet, and would not have wanted him there if he had won. This differs from what Abbott's friends were telling people. According to them, Abbott 'absolutely' had an undertaking from Dutton that he would be appointed to the frontbench. When it became clear that this prospect was costing him votes in the party room, Dutton told journalists who were asking that no promises had been made. He told colleagues who were also asking that Abbott would not be on his frontbench.

Like most of his colleagues, Dutton would have been happiest if Abbott had just disappeared. So while Dutton was not the Trojan horse for Abbott, Abbott was the riderless, stalking horse for Dutton. He created the environment for Dutton to act. He did the dirty work, creating the constant sense of crisis that ensured Turnbull never got ahead in the polls, enabling Dutton to inflict a killer blow. Abbott's behaviour repulsed so many Liberal MPs that it cost Dutton the votes he needed to succeed. His running mate, Greg Hunt, as unpopular in his own way as Abbott, also cost Dutton precious votes.

Dutton was hearing what everyone else was hearing: Abbott saw him as a vehicle to return him to the leadership. One backbencher planning to do media the next day texted Dutton on the Sunday night, asking him if he was planning anything on the leadership so he could couch his answers carefully. Despite all the signs to the contrary, and in keeping with his denials to Turnbull and others, Dutton assured him he wasn't. Regardless, this MP, who liked Dutton, took the opportunity to warn him that if he did, it would look as if he had been put up to it by Abbott and Co., and it would end badly for him.

Peta Credlin had reportedly told friends – what one associate called a fantasy option – that Dutton would wrest the leadership from Turnbull, he would go on to lose the election, then Abbott would regain the opposition leadership, and – *simsalabim* – go on to repeat history by destroying a Shorten Labor government and becoming prime minister again himself. Credlin was utterly convinced that Dutton would be the one to replace Turnbull, just as she seemed convinced that Shorten would win the election.

Reviewing the period, Dutton was disenchanted with both Abbott and Turnbull: 'They were in a death embrace. For 10 years. I would talk to Abbott when he was PM, and he would go on about Turnbull. I would say, "For fuck's sake, stop obsessing about Turnbull." Then when Turnbull was PM, he would go on about Abbott and I would say, "For fuck's sake, stop obsessing about Abbott." They were obsessed with each other. It was debilitating. It couldn't go on.

'A long time ago, I told Tony Abbott I would never be his proxy, never be his Trojan horse. That upset him at the time. If people think I am some shrinking violet ...

'I don't take direction from anyone. I did my level best to make that government work. I formed a judgement in Queensland and elsewhere, that just as they did with Abbott, they could not connect with him [Turnbull].'

Months later, after he had had a little time to reflect on what had happened, when he spoke to me for this book – and before he unloaded to NewsCorp tabloids about Turnbull – he was still comfortable with what he had done. He had no remorse, no regrets. At least, none that he cared to share.

He had over that time, however, concluded that Turnbull had played Morrison, stringing him along, never intending to support him, and that equally Morrison had played Turnbull, publicly standing by him while privately allowing his lieutenants to muster the numbers to depose him. In the end, of course, that meant Dutton got played, too.

Neither of them will regard this as a compliment: there is a touch of the Paul Keatings about Peter Dutton. It is not intended as an insult. Well, not entirely.

Keating was confronting, colourful, polarising, thoughtful, funny, alarmingly frank, loved by the party's base and by his rusted-ons in caucus, and, ultimately, at his peak, a ruthless cut-through politician. So is Dutton. Keating could not and, even now, cannot be ignored. Nor could Dutton.

When Dutton told the chair of Qantas, Alan Joyce, and other business people lobbying heavily for same-sex marriage to stick to their knitting, it was deeply evocative of Keating's determinedly un-PC observation many years before that no one could ever convince him that two men and a cocker spaniel were a family.

There is one critical difference. Although Dutton has friends across the factional divide in the Liberal Party – certainly more than Morrison ever had, being infinitely more popular in the party room than Morrison ever was – he has not managed to breach the great divide between his base and elite opinion, from the battlers to educated suburbanites and lifetime subscribers of the Opera House. And who knows now if he will ever get the chance – although if we have learned anything over the past dozen years, it is to expect the unexpected. Having crossover appeal in these days of vitriol and polarisation could be overrated; but in a compulsory preferential-voting system, it is critical to have some appeal south of the Queensland border and beyond the narrow confines of the party base. And beyond the right-wing media pack, whose first preference was always Abbott. It would have been easier for Dutton to remake himself as prime minister – like Morrison, for instance, has been able to do.

Colleagues such as Jane Prentice and others urged him to get out of the immigration portfolio, but he was reluctant to let it go. Initially, it was because he wanted to see the last of the refugees rehoused from the detention centres on Manus Island and Nauru, and then later because it dealt with issues close to the heart of the Liberal base.

The thing about Dutton, which some people find confounding, is that he is generally well liked by colleagues outside the right. Prentice, who lost her preselection to a man, describes him as a sweet, nice guy.

The party's federal president, Nick Greiner, was incredulous that

Dutton had challenged Turnbull, and agreed with those who said that if Dutton was the answer, it was a pretty strange question. However, after getting to know Dutton better, Greiner liked him, regarded him as intelligent and much more nuanced than he had realised.

Dutton and leading moderate Marise Payne had worked together for 20 years. He regarded her as a friend. After it was over, they had a drink in his office, went through what had happened, and then, he says, they 'hugged it out'.

The private Dutton is a very different persona from the public Dutton.

When he became home affairs minister – a portfolio created for him by Turnbull over the objections of Julie Bishop and George Brandis – there was an opportunity for him to branch out more into areas of national security. He zeroed in on African gangs in Melbourne, which won him the support of Jason Wood, who held Latrobe for the Liberals, but his language dwelled on conflict rather than reconciliation. While that won him the votes of the Woods of the world, it alienated others.

Gangs are a serious problem in many Australian communities, whether they are bikies, Vietnamese, Lebanese, Greek, or Chinese. The debate on immigration was getting a nasty edge – not just subliminally, but also in overtly racist or bigoted ways, as politicians such as Fraser Anning and Pauline Hanson competed for the vote of the maddies with ever-more-extreme positions. It panicked hard-right Liberals and Nationals from the deep north into trying to compete for their votes, and gave a unsavoury tone to the debate on immigration targets.

There was a debate to be had about migrant numbers and congestion in cities, and about how to get new arrivals to settle in regions or places such as Adelaide or Tasmania, but there were those who overstepped the mark – including Labor's leader in New South

Wales, Michael Daley, caught on tape saying that educated Chinese were taking the jobs of Australians, forcing young people to flee Sydney. Daley's offensive remarks cost Labor votes during the state election, and continued to reverberate during the federal election.

Dutton never went that far, but he was not prone to nuances in his public statements. He saw it as his mission to sharpen the contrasts and to keep the base on side. 'The base loves that stuff,' he would say after particularly torrid interventions by him in debates.

It bought him some grief after the massacres in two mosques in New Zealand by a white Australian supremacist.

It was Keating who told me years before that he could easily flick the switch to vaudeville; but if you have seen the classic Hollywood movie that prompted him to say this, you have to be singing and tap-dancing while you do it, and not skip a beat.

Keating and Dutton have this in common, too: a disarming frankness, particularly when they are dissecting their enemies, wherever they might reside. Two days after the coup, I spoke to Dutton, just after an *Insiders* episode had finished screening. Calling back in response to an earlier message from me, he asked if I had been on the show. I wasn't, but Barrie Cassidy hadn't been able to resist re-running my prediction from my previous appearance on 12 August, when I had immodestly pointed out I was the journalist who first said we were in danger of becoming the Italy of the Pacific because of the churn in prime ministers.

'It could be time to say *arrivederci* to all that,' I had enthused, showing my mastery of Italian as well as forecasting. 'Malcolm Turnbull will clock up 1,100 days in office on 18 September, making him Australia's longest-serving prime minister in 11 years, zipping past Kevin Rudd both times, Julia Gillard, and Tony Abbott.' Cassidy said this was like the kiss of death.

When I told Dutton, he laughed and said, 'Thanks for that. You jinxed him.' The thought had occurred to me, too.

Dutton, pledging to be 100 per cent behind Morrison, was keen to keep everything he had. 'I don't need to change my image in that respect. The best thing I can do is continue to appeal to older Australians' concerns about borders, visa cancellations, law and order,' he said.

Later that same day, Morrison took immigration off him and gave it to David Coleman. For some, this was a sign that concerns remained about Dutton's eligibility. His enemies not only thought he was too divisive in that portfolio, but they believed he was shifted because of fears that the many decisions made by him as immigration minister could be subject to challenge. Coleman was uncontroversial and safe.

Despite Turnbull's insistence that he had not been aware of questions surrounding Dutton and section 44(v) until they blew up in the media, Dutton was certain the whole question of his eligibility had been dredged up by Turnbull in that week to try to discredit him, because the prime minister's office had had access to the files on his family's financial interests for months after all MPs conducted audits during the chaos over citizenship, when politicians fell like skittles.

Not long after this, after the same-sex marriage plebiscite, Dutton confided to Cormann that he would look at his options mid-term. He did that, preparing to strike after Turnbull had lost the 40th Newspoll in a row. 'That was D-Day,' he told me.

That would have been either during the next sitting brackets around mid-September 2018 or early October, which, strangely enough, fitted the timetable that Cormann had outlined to people in December 2017, when he told them that Dutton would assess his position.

Even before the Longman by-election, Dutton was becoming exasperated with Turnbull.

'He couldn't make a decision. He debated around for too long on every issue. Every political opportunity passed us by,' he says.

'All the talk about good cabinet government was a backhander for Abbott, which was fine. He wanted consensus.'

Although he gives credit to Turnbull for instituting proper cabinet processes, he complained that at times a discussion would be interminable, with no decision made and no conclusion reached.

'You had 13 ministers who resigned. He lost 14 seats at the last election. We were still talking about noodle nation NEG, and people didn't understand it. He couldn't succinctly put a message. He was one of the brightest people. He was a terrible campaigner. He ran the worst campaign in Liberal history.

'He restored integrity to the prime minister's office – the whole cabinet government process was a contrast to Abbott,' he said.

'But it was code, or cover, for not being able to make a decision. I was assistant treasurer to Costello, and in cabinet, he or Howard would say here is this issue, it's a tough one for us, here are the options. [In the Turnbull cabinet] all of our discussions were rambling, they just went on and on and on. Nothing leaked, not even from the last one. I did my best to make it work. We were going to get smashed. No question, in my mind.'

Dutton harks back to the cabinet discussion in July 2016 on whether the Australian government would support Kevin Rudd's nomination to run for UN secretary-general.

'He had obviously been playing footsies with Rudd on the United Nations,' he says.

'The room was split 50–50 as to whether Rudd should receive the support of the government. He walked out saying we would have to give further consideration. He couldn't make the call. He couldn't make the call himself, because ultimately he was not a Liberal at heart.

'Howard and Costello were on a different part of the spectrum. They were instinctive Liberals; they could make decisions. Malcolm saw the Liberal Party as a vehicle to become prime minister. He was a barrister who could argue the brief for either side.'

Dutton says that colleagues, both in Queensland and in marginal seats, were going into meltdown, pressing him to do something.

He accuses Turnbull of having built up expectations in Longman – unlike Morrison, who downplayed them in the by-election for Turnbull's seat of Wentworth.

'Nobody in the country thought we could win Wentworth,' he said. 'We could have won if Turnbull hadn't sabotaged us. There would have been wind in our sails. Because we lost it, Morrison lost some momentum.

'I remember saying to him [Turnbull] in Longman, we have to be careful about expectations, because if we lose this, they are going to start talking about leadership again. You will be on your way to 40 Newspolls, and back in the mire.'

'He said to me on two occasions, this government doesn't survive without Mathias, Morrison, you, and me. We are the only four people who make it work.'

Dutton described himself, Morrison, and Cormann as the 'Karl Roves' of the government (a reference to the US guru instrumental in George W Bush's presidential successes).

Dutton describes their relationship as 'excellent', including during the last crazy days of trying to sort through 'the NEG 10.0'.

'In leadership meetings, in NSC, cabinet, I did absolutely everything to make that government work,' he says.

Dutton says the 2016 election campaign was the worst he had ever seen. He subsequently lost all hope that the government would be re-elected.

'We lost 14 seats in 2016. He had to be coaxed out to make a statement [on election night].

'All of this said to me we were on target to lose 14 more. Those who are criticising us now would say when there was annihilation, why did you allow it to happen?

'And Malcolm would have been in New York, and would never have looked back – you know, it was Tony Abbott, it was ministers, it was blah blah blah.

'I saw what the campaign was last time. There was not one element of improvement since. His decision-making, his decisiveness, none of that improved.

'We needed to find a slogan somewhere between three words and 3,000 words. He just couldn't communicate.

'The residual hope was that people didn't hate him. But they kept saying we are so disappointed in him. He saved us from Tony Abbott, but I don't know what he stands for.

'While they didn't hate him, there was a prospect of turning it around, but it never improved.

'You are at 38 Newspolls, 49–51, it was wipe-out territory.

'Going around the electorate, people were saying we love your work locally, but we can't vote for you. I would say we have done this and that, and they would say, you should get rid of him, or we will,' Dutton recalled.

'It's exactly how it was in '07 with Howard, and with Newman in the state election. Our numbers only held up because Shorten was there. Once we got into the campaign proper, we would be smashed. We were going to get smashed.'

He dismisses Turnbull's claims that marginal-seat polling showed the government ahead. 'Nobody saw this polling. It's bullshit. People were over us, and they were over him. People had already made a decision. The numbers were artificially inflated because of Shorten.'

He says that at the time the *Daily Telegraph* and Ray Hadley told the world he was making a move on the leadership, he was 'working up in my mind what was feasible'.

'After Longman, the debacle of the NEG, I started to conclude that the wheels were well and truly coming off. All the marginal-seat people thought they were going to be wiped out.

'What was going to happen with the NEG, his signature policy? We couldn't get it through the parliament. We would still be talking about it today.'

He also believes that the company tax cuts should have been dumped at the end of June, even though his very good friend Mathias Cormann was still committed to them.

'They should have been dropped. Mathias thought he could get them through. Turnbull should have had the leadership capacity to make that call.' Again, in Dutton's view, this was proof that Turnbull couldn't make the hard decisions.

More and more MPs were going to him, he says. Not to Abbott. While Dutton had told Abbott long before that he would never be his stalking horse, he had also told him he 'didn't need to be out there doing stuff'.

'Tony could never help himself. Abbott, Abetz, and Andrews were never in the inner sanctum. I wasn't a proxy for him; I find that insulting. I talked to people whose political judgement I trusted, and senior people within the government.'

When the *Daily Telegraph* story broke, he dismisses his delay in responding as inconsequential. He had two choices. 'Those things, you either feed them or you ignore them. I thought making comment would just feed it.'

Asked if he meant what he said in the tweet, he said, 'Yes, I did.'

However, he does admit he was talking to people that weekend. 'I was sounding people out, to see where they were at. Trying to inform myself where the mood was at.'

There was a lot more than that, of course, as his conversation on the VIP plane with Steve Ciobo showed.

Dutton also admits he had spoken to the Liberal National Party president, Gary Spence. 'He thought Turnbull had to turn things around quickly, or there had to be a change,' he says. In fact, by then, Spence wanted Turnbull gone.

Dutton is mightily suspicious about the sequence of events the following week, and outlines how he believes they unfolded. 'Turnbull tells Julie Bishop he is going to open the leadership, but doesn't tell anyone else,' he says. 'But he also tells the whip, Nola Marino, who has to prepare the ballots.'

Dutton then points out that the deputy whip was Bert van Manen, part of the Morrison bible group.

'He [van Manen] would have known, he could have given them notice,' he says, naming them: 'Stuart Robert, Alex Hawke, Bert van Manen, Steve Irons.' He says he has no proof, but he has 'no doubt' they did not vote for Turnbull, and in fact voted for him in that first ballot.

Thanks to media reports at the time, Dutton got it slightly wrong on Nola Marino. She and her principal adviser, Nathan Winn, figured something would happen, so decided on Monday to begin preparing the ballot papers. She did tell her deputies in advance, and his theory that van Manen then told other Morrison supporters to prepare is eminently plausible, especially in light of van Manen's refusal to discuss what he did that day.

Dutton did not hesitate to challenge when Turnbull pulled his surprise spill. 'I would have looked weak and impotent if I had not,' he says, but bridles at suggestions that his campaign was chaotic.

Dutton was reluctant to say which colleagues he took into his confidence or whose counsel he sought on his challenge, beyond emphasising his closeness with Cormann. However, there were others who thought it might have been better if he had at least waited after the ballot on Tuesday, and partly stuck to his original timetable of striking again after the 40th losing Newspoll. However, that also would have given Morrison's people more time to organise.

Both the government and Turnbull would have bled to death.

Trusting his instinct that Turnbull was 'dead' after the first vote, Dutton determined to go hell for leather to bring Turnbull down. 'I did not think about pausing,' he says. 'I thought he was terminal, and I thought it had to be resolved. It needed to be done more quickly, rather than stretching it out.'

Dutton surmises that Turnbull's plan was to try to get to Friday, and then call an election as soon as he possibly could. The government would get smashed – as it was always going to, under him – and then he would blame the instability and Dutton for it.

'He was playing for time,' Dutton said. 'He was playing Scott, and Scott was playing him. He was saying to Morrison and Bishop, you work it out. Morrison was in the same leadership meetings, NSC meetings, as me. He knew he [Turnbull] was hopeless. He could read it was leading to a crescendo.

'Turnbull was hoping 43 signatures wouldn't come up, he was leaning on the solicitor-general, and Hunt lost a couple of votes. The damage to me was done by section 44.

'Turnbull was playing for time. I don't think he was supporting Morrison for prime minister. The vote would never have been brought on if we had not got to 43.'

Dutton says Morrison never had the numbers on the conservative side. 'He brought the "anybody-but-Dutton bloc," Dutton says, fully aware of the fears of some of the moderates.

He is snippy that his plan to remove the GST from power bills was 'mispresented' by Morrison. 'I thought there was a complete market failure in energy. The government had to do a few things to distinguish itself from Labor, and to get over the shock of losing another prime minister – something tangible on energy prices.

'I thought it was necessary to try and restart the conversation. What was important was the 24 hours to frame it. I had planned to go straight to a drought-affected community.'

He also dismisses claims of bullying by his supporters. 'People lean on people,' he says. 'We are not shrinking violets. People put their arguments.'

When I suggest that Michael Sukkar threatened Jane Hume's preselection, Dutton seems surprised. 'Not at my urging,' he says.

Dutton knew on the Friday morning it was slipping away from him when Mitch Fifield visited to give him the bad news in person, and then knew that he was done for a couple of hours later when Scott Ryan rang to tell him he would not be voting for him.

He was happy with the reaction from punters later. 'Almost without exception, people would say, good on you for getting rid of him, sorry you didn't get there, don't give up.'

Back then, he was confident about his personal future, and what he could have offered if he had succeeded in his leadership bid, making a subtle criticism of Morrison's religious and social conservatism.

'I thought I could campaign well,' he said. 'I knew what would work in marginal seats.' That part was certainly true, given how he had managed to hold onto Dickson.

'The stars aligned for me as best they could. I could have campaigned on law and order. I had credibility in that space. Negatives would have neutralised.

'I am no further right than Howard and Costello. I am not the evangelical here, not out-and-proud on abortion, I voted for gay marriage, and I wasn't going to bring Tony Abbott back. But you are framed with these things.'

As for why Turnbull was no longer prime minister, Dutton does not hesitate. It was all his own fault.

'He blew himself up. In his last act, an act of political self-immolation, he demonstrated he had no political judgement.'

It has to be said that Dutton also made a number of fundamental errors. Instead of operating under the radar, he told people who told other people what he was planning, and they put it in the newspaper or broadcast it on radio, so Turnbull had plenty of warning and prepared accordingly. So did Morrison.

Because the first spill was brought on so abruptly by Turnbull, only a few of Dutton's closest friends even knew of his plan. As a result, some of those who signed up to his campaign instantaneously after Tuesday's vote treated it like student politics, or sought to heavy their colleagues. They seemed not to know or care that it is no small thing to remove a sitting prime minister. It requires meticulous planning and a deft touch with colleagues.

Others inside the Dutton camp described Cormann as the commander-in-chief of Dutton's campaign.

'He did attend meetings in the monkey-pod room, and was clearly in charge of operations. Mathias was certainly in control. Cormann dodged a bullet [afterwards] because a number of people involved kept their positions or were promoted, notwithstanding their behaviour,' one said.

'They would project numbers onto the screen and say they had the numbers, but they didn't.

'There was no structure, no planning.'

Others found the bloodlust off-putting. James McGrath says there was a level of joy back in 2015 at tearing Tony Abbott down, which disturbed him at the time.

'I kept thinking this is pretty bad, what we are doing. It's why Mitch [Fifield], Scott [Ryan] and I got Maccas and went home after the spill.

'Some of Dutton's people might have been more turned on by the kill, in getting rid of Malcolm rather than making Dutton prime minister. They were driven to get rid of Turnbull, when they should have been trying to sell Dutton. They didn't give people a sense he would save their seats at the election. It was about killing Malcolm.

'It also didn't help him that Abetz, Andrews, and Abbott were doing media. They should have shut up and let the young Turks do it.'

Dutton's supporters had no time to prepare – they'd been kept in the dark, they were given little direction, their confidence was misplaced, and then later they feared they had been misled.

At one point, Greg Hunt fed in intel that Josh Frydenberg would vote for Dutton. Frydenberg insists this was never the case.

Dutton now realises that Hunt was a bad choice of his for deputy. The Victorians were particularly unimpressed. Not only did most of them not want Dutton, fearing they would be wiped out at the election if he was leader, but they certainly did not want Hunt, even though he was a fellow Victorian.

Hunt was an effective energy minister and a dedicated health minister, charged with reversing some of the damage caused to the Coalition in the 2016 campaign over its health record and the Mediscare campaign. Almost every weekend as health minister, he would release details of new drugs, to fight cancer or arthritis or what felt like every other conceivable illness, which the government would be listing on the Pharmaceutical Benefits List to make them affordable for patients.

Previous health ministers would release the names of listed drugs en masse during the working week with little fanfare, receiving little or no publicity. Hunt knew how to get attention.

But he had a terrible temper.

A few months before the coup, Hunt was compelled to make a public apology to the mayor of Katherine, Fay Miller, for swearing at her during a meeting and pointing his finger in her face. Hunt twice dropped the f-bomb on Ms Miller, who later described his behaviour as misogynistic.

The charge of misogyny is hotly disputed by male colleagues. They, too, have been on the receiving end over the years, where Hunt has lost his temper and abused them in front of others. 'He can be very nasty,' one said.

Hunt was also widely suspected of briefing against colleagues and of persistently, covertly seeking to undermine Turnbull.

There was one notorious story from late 2015 that Hunt had made disparaging remarks about Turnbull to Australia's ambassador in France, not long before the prime minister arrived in Paris. The ambassador, Stephen Brady, thought it prudent to inform Turnbull. Turnbull's allies would remind him of this whenever they thought he needed to be on guard about enemies within. They related the story after the days of madness when, along with several other ministers, Hunt voted for Dutton, then pledged loyalty to Turnbull in parliament, then resigned, and then voted against him in the spill.

The former Victorian Liberal leader Matthew Guy had also warned Turnbull about Hunt. Around mid-2017, when Guy raised a local political problem with him, Turnbull suggested to Guy that he should ask Hunt to help him sort it. Guy was astonished, and told Turnbull he did not think this was a good idea. He asked Turnbull if he was sure he could trust Hunt to be his point man in Victoria, and if he believed him to be loyal to him. Turnbull said yes. Guy tried to tell him to remember who his friends were.

Ultimately, Dutton says he had little choice but to go with Hunt. He needed a Victorian, even though he was confident his strong stand on law and order would see his position improve there. His contacts on *The Australian* had told him that when it came to poll ratings, he was strongest in Queensland, followed by Western Australia, followed by Victoria.

Dutton had thought initially about asking Pyne to run as his deputy, because, in spite of everything, they got on reasonably well. He thought Pyne was pragmatic and would bring moderates with him. Pyne, whose office adjoins the monkey-pod room, and who says he could hear them talking through the connecting wall, thought this idea was hilarious. He says he heard Cormann say, 'I will go and talk to Pyne about being deputy leader.' He never did. He also heard them talking about courting Ann Sudmalis and Rowan Ramsey, so Pyne made sure the moderates got to them first.

Dutton would have preferred a woman as deputy, but the most senior Victorian female was Kelly O'Dwyer, and although he liked her, he believed she lacked gravitas. She never would have agreed, in any case. He also thought Frydenberg had been damaged by the NEG, and was aware of a non-aggression pact between Frydenberg and Hunt, so thought Hunt the best available option.

'He didn't bring any votes,' Dutton said later. 'It probably cost votes. That was a mistake.'

It most certainly was.

There had been speculation some time before that Hunt would be Dutton's running mate. Dan Tehan saw it reported again in the weekend papers. On the Monday afternoon, when the corridors were exploding with talk of a leadership challenge, Tehan rang Josh Frydenberg.

Tehan told him that if anything happened, he should run for the deputy's job. Tehan didn't know at this stage who would be leader, but whoever it was, he would rather Frydenberg was deputy.

Tehan had some history with Morrison. He had been chief of staff to the tourism minister, Fran Bailey, when Morrison ran Tourism Australia and was responsible for launching young model Lara Bingle onto the world stage in the 'Where the bloody hell are you?' advertising campaign.

There was tension between Bailey and Morrison, and Tehan often had to act as a bridge between them. In one small historical footnote, Tehan and I helped make sure that Morrison and his crew were gazumped by Bailey in one of those minor battles that often occur between politicians and outsiders in the hunt for publicity. It happened after Bailey's office got wind that Nine's *A Current Affair* was doing a package, focussing on Morrison, on the decision by the British to ban the advertisement because of the use of that most offensive swear word, 'bloody'.

It was March 2006, and one of my tasks back then, as a staffer in the cabinet policy unit, which came under prime minister John Howard's office, was to help co-ordinate ministers and their media appearances. Tehan came seeking my advice about how his minister should handle the looming story on *A Current Affair*.

It occurred to me that the greatest journalist in the press gallery, Laurie Oakes, who loved nothing better than a scoop, might also not be averse to scooping another program in his own stable. I called Oakes, asking him if he was interested in doing a story that would feature an exclusive interview with the minister on the Poms. His report would obviously air on the Nine news before *A Current Affair* could screen its version. Oakes did not hesitate, and on 9 March 2006 there was Fran Bailey on the national news ridiculing the British for banning the ad.

'This is, of course, from the country that gave us Benny Hill and the Two Ronnies and Ali G, so I'm a bit bemused,' Bailey said. Bailey then took off for England, accompanied by Tehan and Bingle. Bailey had some friendly advice for Bingle: 'Now, darling, you just sit there and smile, and I will do all the talking.'

Lots of shots of the beautiful Bingle; no sign of Morrison. Soon after, there was no sign of Morrison at all at Tourism Australia. He had been sacked.

It was only a minor setback for Morrison, with no hard feelings, hey – except that after he became prime minister, he gave Tehan the education portfolio in his ministry, charging him with resolving the conflict with Catholic Education over funding.

Tehan stuck with Turnbull during coup week – although, along the way, after Cormann told Turnbull that three other ministers had deserted him, Turnbull and his office thought that either Frydenberg or Tehan were included in the defections. Tehan had gone quiet, for reasons which would soon become obvious. Laundy rang Tehan, and asked if he could come and see him. He apologised for asking, but wanted to know if Tehan was still with them. Tehan said he was. The prime minister's office believed him, and concluded that Cormann was lying.

Like others, Tehan's assessment was that the vote on the Tuesday would not resolve the leadership, but initially he thought Turnbull would make it to the end of the week. He was hoping that things would settle down – even though, as he is fond of saying, modern politics is a funny beast. It takes on a life of its own.

'It's like sheep on a boat,' was his way of describing it. 'One or two go to one side, then more and more, and the ship starts to tilt.'

Tehan had another tricky task ahead, with Frydenberg challenging Hunt. Frydenberg and Hunt are – or were – best mates. Hunt was a groomsman at Frydenberg's wedding, Frydenberg was best man at Hunt's wedding, and they are godfathers to each other's daughters.

Frydenberg and Hunt had discussed their leadership ambitions over the years. Because Hunt had got into parliament first, because he had been there longer and was more senior, they both assumed he would be the first to make headway, and that he would do it with Frydenberg's support. So assured did this seem that Frydenberg had once told his friend, 'If you run, I can't see myself running against you.'

Hunt was highly ambitious. Cormann had confided to people at the end of 2017 that no one was agitating against Turnbull (even though he also confided that Dutton was reserving his options for later in 2018), except Hunt. Hunt's theory was that instability might work in his favour.

It did him no good with his colleagues, particularly the ones who suspected that he regularly briefed against them.

Tehan and the other Victorians would not wear Hunt. Tony Smith, Scott Ryan, and Kelly O'Dwyer all rang Frydenberg to urge him to run, and pledged to support him. They quickly coalesced.

On Thursday, when it became clear that Morrison and Bishop were both running, and that the petition was getting to the magic 43 required for another party-room meeting, Tehan told Frydenberg he had to run.

Frydenberg said he had to do something first. He had to go and speak to Hunt; he had to tell his friend face to face that he was going to run against him. It was an extremely difficult conversation. Hunt reminded Frydenberg of his words a few years before, and asked Frydenberg not to run against him. Frydenberg argued that they were now dealing with completely unexpected events. He said he would remain loyal to Turnbull until the end, but if the spill motion got up, and if Bishop did not run for the deputy's job again, he would put his hand up. He felt he could make a contribution.

So much had happened since they had made their pact. Frydenberg seized his opportunity. This was nothing personal; it was politics. Frydenberg then rang people, such as Arthur Sinodinos, whom he had worked with in Howard's office, and whom he regarded as a mentor, to seek his advice. He also asked for his vote.

Frydenberg asked for Melissa Price (later rewarded with a promotion to cabinet as environment minister) and Scott Ryan to be brought in to help with his campaign.

On Wednesday, Dutton's friend Steve Ciobo began his own campaign for the deputy leadership. He thought it made no sense to have Frydenberg, because of the problems with the NEG.

Ciobo reached an agreement with Hunt that if Dutton were elected, he (Ciobo) would not run. What he neglected to do was make another deal with Hunt that if Dutton were not elected, Hunt would pull out. Ciobo on his own would have stood a better chance against Frydenberg.

On Thursday afternoon, with only hours to go, Frydenberg was in his office with a spreadsheet, sorting the numbers. He was surrounded by Tehan, Ryan, Price, and Karen Andrews, when who should stick his head in to say hello but Michael Kroger? Talk about awkward. This was *the* Michael Kroger, the Victorian president of the Liberal Party, who was now backing Dutton and Hunt, who had previously touted Frydenberg as a future leader, whose behaviour and interventions, either privately with MPs or in the media commenting on events that week, was considered inappropriate. As soon as he realised what he had stumbled into, Kroger quickly withdrew.

Later, Frydenberg told those helping him that Tony Abbott had called him and asked him not to run. Abbott was smart enough to know that Frydenberg would cost Dutton and Hunt votes, but not smart enough to realise that all his destabilising statements and behaviour to do with the NEG meant he was the last person that Frydenberg would listen to.

Frydenberg's helpers divided up their lists, and began calling. By the time of the ballot the next day, Frydenberg had spoken to almost every Liberal MP. One of the points he made was that he was not running on anyone's ticket: he was running as an independent.

There were around half-a-dozen people who voted for Dutton as leader who did not vote for Hunt as deputy, but voted for Frydenberg. The vote showed that he had drawn support from moderates and conservatives.

Frydenberg demolished Hunt. It was an utter humiliation for Hunt, delivered by his friend with the help of his enemies.

Frydenberg won on the first ballot with 46 votes. Ciobo came in second with 20, and Hunt came third with 19.

When his former boss John Howard rang to congratulate Frydenberg on winning the deputy leadership, Howard asked, tongue firmly in cheek, 'What took you so long?' Howard had become Malcolm Fraser's treasurer in 1977 when he was 38 years old. By comparison, Frydenberg was an ancient 47.

Hunt was crushed by the vote. Afterwards, although he stayed active, making almost daily announcements about new drugs on the PBS, stakeholders from professional groups reported that he had lost interest. They began to bypass him, preferring to seek help on health matters from other senior advisers in the government, particularly Peter Conran, who had come out of retirement to run the cabinet policy unit again. Hunt's colleagues noticed that he sounded beaten in private.

He spent the election campaign hunkered down in his seat of Flinders, beating off a stiff challenge from Labor and newly minted independent Julia Banks. Banks received 14 per cent of the vote, but there was a swing of only 3.65 per cent on primaries against Hunt.

CHAPTER ELEVEN

Queensland: perfect one day, shitty the next

They had different reasons for taking the decisions they did, and they got there in different ways. For a few, like Abbott and his small band of followers who despised Turnbull, his removal was a time for rejoicing. For others, it was incredibly tough. Men and women cried. Julie Bishop was visibly upset as her staff broke down in tears around her in her office after her humiliation. When they spoke in the days and weeks afterwards about what had happened, and what they did, their emotions were raw.

Luke Howarth, who had helped precipitate Turnbull's decision to vacate his leadership, ducked out of the party room after the final vote on Friday, slipped into his office across the corridor, closed the door, and wept. 'The whole week was pretty shitty,' he told me later. Anne Ruston walked into Michaelia Cash's office, stood before one of her staff, and said, 'Tell her I am disappointed in her and with what she has done to us.' Ruston then burst into tears and walked out.

The discontent had crystallised in Queensland with the disastrous primary vote in the Longman by-election, was stoked by Abbott in the debate over the NEG, and was accentuated by the continuing dispute with the Catholic education sector, which was taking months to resolve.

Queensland, where there was lingering distrust of Turnbull, was the epicentre, and the state's most senior party official fuelled the discontent.

The Liberal National Party state president, Gary Spence, was a chief urger behind the scenes for Turnbull's removal. Spence had become convinced that the prime minister and/or his office was background-briefing the media that Longman had been lost because of a bad campaign. I have no direct knowledge of this; however, I do know that Liberals from Queensland to Tasmania were attributing the loss to four factors: a poor choice of candidate; a poor campaign; no money to match Labor's big spend in the last week; and the raising of expectations that a victory was possible.

Nevertheless, Spence blamed Turnbull and/or his office for briefings against the LNP's campaign, and swore to get even. Malcolm Turnbull did not help himself by casting the by-election as a contest between himself and Bill Shorten, Mathias Cormann framed it as a referendum on tax, and the media pumped out a plethora of unreliable polls showing that the government had a once-in-a-century chance of winning a seat from the opposition.

Expectations were wildly out of control, and there was no reining them in. The member for Brisbane, Trevor Evans, whose family hails from Longman, attended branch meetings in his electorate where enthusiastic young LNP members were convinced they could win. He kept trying to hose them down, but they wouldn't listen. Like others, he had rung around a few people trying to get a better candidate. No one wanted to run. Attempts were made to recruit former state MP Lisa France. As someone with strong local connections, she would have been ideal; however, since she had lost her seat of Pumicestone in 2015, France had secured a well-paid career in the corporate world and was reluctant to return to politics. She summed up the problem faced by the Coalition in recruiting women: those who support the conservative side of politics tend to be in small business or the professions. At least, they used to be. It is difficult to persuade them to give up that life, disrupt their families, take a pay cut for the uncertainties of politics, deal with the hostilities that go with it, and submit to rigid party structures.

Ruthenberg was simply the best they could get. Evans, whose first election campaign had been as a volunteer for Peter Dutton against star Labor recruit Cheryl Kernot in Dickson, and then went on to work for Dutton as his chief of staff, said in an interview for this book that he was not even surprised by the near–10 per cent drop in the primary vote. It was exactly what he had expected.

What Evans did not expect, or welcome, was what it triggered, which he later described as bordering on traumatic. Like his colleagues, he faced a difficult choice. Dutton was his former employer, friend, and mentor, whom Evans describes as a decent person. As an openly gay man in an inner-suburban electorate, which he describes as similar to Wentworth for its diversity, Evans felt that his best chances for re-election lay with Turnbull. All the candidates courted him, and fellow moderates tried to sway him. He refused to sign the petition for the second meeting, and he would not tell his friends from the class of 2016, fellow newbie MPs, which way he voted. He has not told family or staff; however, although he was philosophically aligned with Turnbull, he was open about looking to the future. He was open to persuasion about which candidate was best equipped to secure that future. No one was absolutely confident they knew where he stood. He did participate in one early tactical meeting with Sally Cray, leading the Turnbull camp to believe he had voted for the prime minister in the first ballot on the Tuesday. Later, both the Morrison and Turnbull camps had him in the Dutton column.

Unlike Trevor Evans, fellow Queenslander Luke Howarth made his views, if not his explicit intentions, well known.

The class of 2013 – MPs elected in the great Abbott victory – held Monday-night dinner rituals during sitting weeks. On the night of 20 August, Luke Howarth, Craig Laundy, Sarah Henderson, Melissa Price, and David Coleman gathered at the Chiang Rai at Kingston.

Laundy didn't think much of it at the time, but they all saw another group of MPs walk in and head for another part of the restaurant: Stuart Robert, Steve Irons, and Alex Hawke. The Morrison men. It clicked later.

For the class of 2013, leadership was on the menu, and Laundy was keen to know what Howarth was thinking. Howarth had decided to get up in the party meeting the next day to ask both Turnbull and Abbott to resign.

He insisted after it was over that Dutton had not asked him to do this, and that he was acting on his own. He says he had not consulted anyone, and that he directly told only one person about his plan, and that was his office manager, who had been with him for five years and who he said was 100 per cent trustworthy.

Howarth says he told Laundy over dinner that he thought Peter Dutton would make a good prime minister. He thought he was tough and could carry a message. He was the only one at the table who thought this. Testy exchanges followed. Laundy pleaded with Howarth to think of what would happen in seats like his own of Reid, with a margin of 3.3 per cent. He said those who wanted change were a pack of dills.

Laundy says Howarth was convinced the government was 'fucked'. 'We are gone, Turnbull is gone, your mate's gone.' Laundy says the conversation was feral.

Howarth says that Henderson, whose seat of Corangamite had become notionally Labor after the redistribution and sat next to him in the House, could barely bring herself to speak to him the next day. Henderson disputes this, saying she was not offended by or put off by what Howarth had said over dinner, even though she says she strongly disagreed with him. She regarded him as a friend, and still does.

Howarth found the whole thing very difficult. He complained that Turnbull had not met any of his own KPIs (key performance indicators), particularly on Newspoll, and that he had not taken seriously the result in Longman. He says now he can't remember exactly what he said at dinner. He thinks he said he would have preferred Turnbull to step aside. He had no doubt that Laundy would report his comments to the prime minister's office. Which he did.

Although Howarth swears he did not tell his colleagues that night exactly what he planned to do the next day, he said enough to set off alarm bells for Laundy, who later that night debriefed Turnbull and Sally Cray on his conversation.

'I definitely did not say he would be a suicide bomber, but I had real concerns he could do something stupid in the party room,' Laundy says. 'I was very clear with them [the prime minister's office] that I was extremely concerned, given the anger and venom Luke showed, that he would do something stupid.'

That piece of intelligence confirmed Turnbull's thinking to bring the spill on. And, as it turned out, Laundy was right. Howarth was definitely planning to do something.

Howarth's seat of Petrie borders Longman, as does Dutton's. They have known one another for 20 years. Howarth's wife, Louise, whom he married in 1999, is a first cousin of Dutton's. (Their fathers were brothers.) In 2011, Howarth's pest-extermination business was doing well, so he pulled his three young sons out of school and went on a family road trip for five months. The business continued to do well without him. By the time he got to Western Australia, he decided it was time to give politics a real go, having unsuccessfully stood for a state seat in 2001. He rang Dutton and told him he wanted to run in either Petrie – where he grew up – or Lilley. In the end, along with 12 others, he ran for preselection for Petrie. Dutton helped him, while John Howard vouched for another high-profile candidate. Howarth won that battle by one vote.

So, as well as being family, Howarth also regarded Dutton as a friend and mentor.

It was the feeding frenzy that erupted in the wake of the Longman by-election which rocked Howarth. However, there had been no sign of panic or despair from him on the night of the by-election. I texted him at 9.37 that night (28 July) to say I was doing *Insiders* the next morning, and to ask what he made of the result.

He responded:

> Gary Spence LNP President summed it up well. Difficult for a government to win bi-elections history statistically shows this. Australians are over the dual citizenship issues and have returned everyone on both sides.
>
> Disappointing the primary swing in Longman, Wyatt Roy still had a strong following and part of his vote has gone to one nation and labor. Labor definitely lied again, there are NO cuts to CABOOLTURE hospital funding is going up if you could ask the media to fact check claims in future.
>
> Me: What does it mean for general election?
>
> Howarth: Not a lot. It's next year. Longman may even get a swing back next time. Labor's campaigning is effective, obviously, but it's disappointing because a lot of it is based on lies, and it's not good for our country.
>
> They may eventually get in Labor 2019, 2022, but government with higher taxing policies that they have will be very bad for the country.

However, by 10 August, Howarth's anxiety levels had risen. He texted Turnbull to say that he and Julie Bishop needed to do more media interviews with conservative commentators like Paul Murray and Ray Hadley. He understood why they would not do interviews with either Jones or Credlin. He was worried that conservative Liberal voters were shifting to One Nation and independents, and that only a small percentage of them were coming back via preferences.

Although Howarth thought the company tax cuts were good policy, he suggested they should be put up in the Senate for a vote, and then, when they went down, they should be dumped. He also wanted the prime minister to be doing more on the drought. He was not thinking about regime change. It wasn't even the energy wars that caused him to change his thinking, even though he had been warning for a long time of the impact of power-price increases. But he said people were 'going feral'. They were even telling him he shouldn't run again.

Turnbull texted him back, thanking him for his 'good advice', assuring him that he would be talking about some of those things 'today'.

A couple of days later, reports surfaced that Turnbull had done a deal with Liberal Democrat senator David Leyonhjelm on euthanasia to get the Australian Building and Construction Commission legislation through. Howarth was again worried that this would trigger another outbreak of disunity. This faded after the Senate voted against Leyonhjelm's Bill to grant territories the right to make their own laws.

On Friday 17 August, Howarth received a message from Turnbull saying he had been working intensively on the energy policy, and that he wanted to run a few things past him.

Howarth did not return Turnbull's call. Instead, he called Dutton.

He had flown home from Canberra that day, and when he landed, checked with his office to see what was happening. He says they told him that Ray Hadley, who was seen as close to Dutton, had gone on air urging people to ring their MPs to tell them Turnbull had to go.

What Hadley had actually done that day was break into Chris Smith's 2GB program at 2.10 pm to confirm '100 per cent' that Dutton would challenge Turnbull for the leadership. It would be after the Newspoll scheduled for Monday week (27 August), and not because of another losing Newspoll, but because of the dispute over energy. He also predicted a push by 'disaffected conservative constituents who talk to you, me, and Alan, and our colleagues all the time, they will be saying to those constituents, "I want you to ring your local member, you know, the pants-wetters, I want you to tell them that unless there is a change in leadership we won't be voting for you."'

A few days later, Hadley sharpened up his campaign to influence MPs by publishing their email addresses, just to help the push along. But Hadley's Friday message, garbled though it was, registered with listeners in Howarth's electorate. Howarth says his office got something like 20 calls.

After getting the message from his office and from listeners, Howarth rang Dutton to ask him if anything was happening. Dutton, despite Hadley's certainty, told him it wasn't, and that Hadley had done it 'off his own bat' – although Howarth got the distinct impression that Dutton was not unhappy that the idea of a challenge was now out there. Howarth told me that Dutton did not tell him he was planning to challenge.

Howarth spoke to a few people after that. He spoke to Spence, and asked him what he thought about it all. Spence told him he would be happy if there was a change, and that he would support a change.

Howarth spoke to Bert van Manen, who was close to Morrison. Then Morrison himself rang Howarth on Saturday asking, 'What do you think?'

Howarth told him, 'Well, I think if there was some sort of challenge, I would vote for Dutton.'

Nevertheless, Howarth says he decided, on his own initiative, to get up at Tuesday's party meeting to tell Turnbull – and Abbott – to resign. Again, he says he did not tell Dutton what he was planning, nor did he tell his dinner companions on Monday night.

As is now well known, Turnbull got in before Howarth was able to call on him to resign, declaring both his and Julie Bishop's positions vacant.

Howarth voted for Dutton in Tuesday's ballot, and then sent Turnbull a message via WhatsApp. In it, he said, verbatim:

> PM I was going to ask you to resign before the poll. You set the KPI of 30 opinion polls we are now nearly at 40. You have lost the base in Qld and the support of the LNP. We can't win without the base. We will lose the next election as Abbott will continue to wreck. You and Abbott both need to go at the next election.
>
> What's the point of hanging on as PM for nine months, you could of retired gracefully.
>
> I won't be out in media actively encouraging this I hope we can unite but I seriously doubt it.

He received a four-word reply from Turnbull: 'United is the key.'

Howarth showed the text to Laundy after that first vote. Laundy had ducked into Howarth's office to use his loo because it was the closest one to the party room. Laundy pleaded with Howarth to stop, 'for all our sakes'. Howarth replied, 'Craig, you are too close to him. You don't get it, we need a change.'

The events of that mad week took a toll on Howarth, as they did on everyone else. He said then, like many of them did, that the experience was much worse for him than when Turnbull deposed Abbott.

On the Friday, after the vote and after the speeches, when Morrison emerged triumphant, Howarth was touched by Morrison's call for unity and regeneration. Howarth sought refuge in his own office, just across the corridor.

After breaking down in his office, Howarth took a few minutes to compose himself, before going back into the party room to shake hands with both Morrison and Frydenberg. 'It was the enormity of it,' he said later. 'It was upsetting. The whole week was pretty shitty.'

Although the putsch had originated in Queensland, support for it was far from unanimous, and not everyone was happy with Spence's intervention to campaign actively against Turnbull and for Dutton.

Spence says he had supported Turnbull, and then fell out badly with him in the wake of Longman. He was angered by commentary after the by-election that canned the Liberal National Party's campaign. He claimed that the commentary only came from Canberra-based columnists (including yours truly), *The Australian*'s Paul Kelly, and others from interstate. According to Spence, locally based reporters knew better and reported differently. He rang one of those Canberra-based columnists (not yours truly) to tackle them about it. According to Spence, this correspondent told him that the information had been sourced from 'the highest office in the land'.

That was it for Spence. He got on to senator James McGrath, once a key numbers man for Turnbull, to get him to deliver a message to the Turnbull office.

McGrath was having his own problems with Turnbull. They had grown distant, and his relationship with Sally Cray had ruptured. He didn't think they understood Queensland, and he felt they weren't listening to him.

McGrath rang Turnbull's chief of staff, Clive Mathieson, and told him that the prime minister had to speak to Spence.

Turnbull tried to ring Spence soon after. They played a bit of phone tag, and then, when they finally hooked up, it was a hostile conversation that lasted about half an hour. Spence told me subsequently that this occurred around two weeks after the by-election. He says Turnbull told him he had not briefed against the LNP, and nor had his office. Spence did not believe him.

On such things are lasting enmities built, with devastating consequences. After that, as far as Spence was concerned, whatever relationship he had had with Turnbull was fractured beyond repair.

However, perhaps before declaring war on Turnbull, Spence should have spoken to the former president of the Queensland Liberal Party, Paul Everingham, who was appalled that Ruthenberg had not been properly vetted and that the medal mix-up had not been corrected. (Ruthenberg had been pinged during the campaign for wrongly claiming he had been awarded the more prestigious Australian Service Medal rather than the lower-order Australian Defence Medal.)

Or to senator Richard Colbeck, who was intimately involved in the Braddon by-election campaign in Tasmania, where the former member, Brett Whiteley, almost succeeded in winning back the seat. Colbeck contrasted the Braddon campaign, which was disciplined and well run, with Longman. The swing against Whiteley on primaries was 1.9 per cent —almost half that of the swing against Labor, thanks to a strong local independent and a sliver of a 0.1 per cent two-party-preferred swing to Labor's candidate Justine Keay. If the Liberals had won that seat, it might not have appeased the Queenslanders, but at least it would have mitigated Longman's loss and created a more sustainable environment for Turnbull.

While in the south the mood was relatively benign – despite

Georgina Downer's inability to regain Mayo from independent Rebekha Sharkie – it didn't matter, because it was toxic in Queensland. As Dutton would say later, it didn't matter what happened in Tasmania, the election would be won or lost in his home state.

When the story broke about Dutton, Spence – who spoke to me for this book – says he was called by some Queensland MPs, asking him what he thought they should do. He also admitted he spoke to Dutton. He will not reveal exactly what was said between them, although it is obvious he encouraged Dutton to run. He said he told the MPs who called him that if there was a spill, they should not vote for Turnbull – they should vote for Dutton. At this stage, Morrison had not announced he was running, and Spence told Queenslanders that with Dutton they would hold on to their seats.

He also admitted that he initiated some calls himself to tell MPs the same thing. He reckons he spoke to five or six MPs.

Then someone dobbed Spence in to Sky daytime host Laura Jayes, whose reporting during the week of the challenge showed the breadth of her contacts in the coalition.

'The you-know-what hit the fan,' Spence said.

Spence rebuts suggestions that he circulated polling in marginal seats showing the LNP was way behind under Turnbull. He says the cash-strapped organisation did two polls during Longman. The first, at the beginning of the campaign, showed that Ruthenberg was way behind, at 42 per cent to Labor's 58 per cent; the second, two weeks out, showed that he had made up some ground to reach to 47 per cent to 53 per cent. (Labor held the seat with a 54.5 to 45.6 per cent margin.)

He was adamant that they were never going to win the seat, and he blamed Turnbull for raising expectations that they would.

One of the cardinal rules in politics is to keep your friends close and your enemies closer. Turnbull did the latter and neglected the former, as the breakdown in the relationship between him and McGrath showed.

Turnbull had been introduced to McGrath by pollster Mark Textor. After a meeting at his home in Point Piper, and before he lost the opposition leadership in 2009, Turnbull ensured McGrath was appointed the federal Liberal deputy director, to work with the director, Brian Loughnane. That did not end well. After Loughnane sacked McGrath, the Queenslander headed home, where he became state campaign director in 2010. He was at the helm when Campbell Newman had one of the biggest wins in Australian electoral history.

McGrath is completely eccentric and unconventional in many ways – witness the figurine of a polar bear in his office cradling an empty bottle of Bundaberg rum, the photo of Margaret Thatcher on the wall, and the shoes and socks strewn across the floor as he walks around barefoot in a business shirt and shorts after a nap on the couch – but he is a complete genius on Queensland and what it takes to win there.

He knows southerners think that Queenslanders are mad. He also concedes that they do get mad very quickly, often for no real reason. He reckons they get cranky and go off. He doesn't care. He argues, and there is evidence to support, if not prove, his proposition, that if the Coalition can't win Queensland, it can't win government. All you have to do, he says, is just give them something, pay them some attention – lots of attention, actually – and be very nice to them.

McGrath not only helped elect Newman, but he was a key member of the group that restored Turnbull to the leadership in 2015.

The messiness of his personal surrounds stands in stark contrast to the meticulous planning of his political life. His attention to detail in the 2015 coup was incredible. It left scars that are still obvious. He got no pleasure from Abbott's removal, but he had one clear motive, and that was to prevent Bill Shorten from becoming prime minister in 2016, which he remains convinced would have happened if Abbott had been left in the job.

In mid-2018, McGrath thought Turnbull was making good headway. McGrath thought Turnbull's speech to the LNP annual conference around that time was brilliant. It was self-deprecating and confident, and he made jokes about Big Trev. He thought it was Malcolm at his best. Three days later, Turnbull gave a very different kind of speech to the Queensland Media Club on energy and electricity, which McGrath also thought was very good, even though he didn't think anybody understood it. It was obvious that Turnbull knew more than anybody else about the subject; however, the message was not getting through.

After Longman, everything turned to custard.

McGrath had an angry phone conversation with Turnbull. He told people that the prime minister basically blamed him – as the patron senator for the seat – for the loss, and along the way called the LNP a bunch of dickheads. McGrath reminded him that the only reason he was prime minister was because of the Queensland LNP.

McGrath dismisses claims it was a poor campaign in Longman. Rather, he says, it was a poorly funded campaign. They had no money. McGrath had tried but failed to get a woman to run in the seat, which is what Turnbull wanted, particularly after one of his closest supporters, Jane Prentice, had lost her preselection in Ryan to a male former staffer.

Turnbull couldn't understand why it took so long to find a candidate. McGrath reckons it was because those approached either didn't like Turnbull or didn't think the government was going to win the election. The delay in finding a candidate contributed to the lateness in announcing the date for the by-election, and then there was another long campaign period, which also did not help the vote. Labor had more money, more volunteers, and ran hard on banks and company tax, and on the alleged funding cuts for the Caboolture hospital.

McGrath defends Ruthenberg as a decent person who had worked for charities all his life, who, thanks to the campaign, became unemployable. 'He is a good person who made a mistake,' McGrath says, referring to the medal muddle.

McGrath believes that the LNP never liked Turnbull because of what happened in 2009, when Abbott wrested the leadership from him by one vote because of Turnbull's support for Labor's Carbon Pollution Reduction Scheme. After 2015, McGrath spent a lot of his political capital telling people that Turnbull was like Howard and Menzies – terrible first time around, but someone who had learned from his mistakes.

Early on in Turnbull's tenure, there was angst over the revival of plans, later abandoned, to increase the rate of the GST. The eight-week-plus 2016 election campaign also caused angst. As did Turnbull's speech on election night. Turnbull was late appearing – at close to midnight – by which time McGrath reckons only party members were watching, and they didn't like what they heard.

After Longman, sentiment in Queensland soured abruptly. McGrath noticed it was immediate, it was brutal, and it was across the state, not just rural and regional.

McGrath had a terrible weekend in early August. He went to three events in three electorates, beginning with his launch of Luke Howarth's volunteers' campaign at Clontarf, with a barbecue on the esplanade. He couldn't get over how many of those present told him he had to get rid of Malcolm. They said they were prepared to help Howarth, but would not vote for him, 'because we don't want Malcolm'. It terrified McGrath that they were saying that to him, because if they were doing that, what were they saying to their friends and family?

Deeply worried, he called Dutton after the Howarth event to tell him that party members were not going to vote for 'us'. Dutton said he was getting the same message. Dutton said that what people didn't understand was if they lost the next election, they would be out for 10 years – it wouldn't just be for one term.

The same weekend, McGrath went to the Hervey Bay seafood festival in the electorate of Wide Bay, which he attends every year. Same thing. People were coming up, asking him when they were going to get rid of Malcolm. They didn't like Turnbull because they didn't think he was one of them, they were terrified that Bill Shorten would end up prime minister, and they were angry with the LNP for not doing anything to stop him.

His last gig was a branch meeting in Stanthorpe on the Darling Downs in the electorate of Maranoa, where 60 people turned up. All of them wanted to tell McGrath how angry they were with Turnbull and the NEG.

McGrath described Longman as a movie trailer. It was a preview of what the next election would be like.

When McGrath returned to Brisbane on Sunday 12 August, he tapped out a long, detailed WhatsApp, which he sent to Turnbull, telling him that Queensland had 'turned against us',

In the message, he told Turnbull that people were disappointed, that they wanted the government to be better, and that they were terrified of Shorten. He said the government should dump the company tax cuts for banks, and dump the tax cuts for the big end of town.

He said at the Stanthorpe meeting, branch members had 'unanimously' called for the tax cuts to be dumped. He told Turnbull that few people understood the NEG, or how it would work to cut power prices. He feared that at the upcoming party meeting on Tuesday, Abbott's theme of 'If you don't understand it, don't support it' would resonate.

McGrath said his parents were pensioners who could not afford to put their heating on. 'It may sound mad to you but they are not alone,' he told Turnbull.

'Not one person I spoke to thinks we can win.'

Turnbull's response was unsympathetic, and dripped with sarcasm. 'With your support, I fear no challenge,' he replied.

Turnbull went on to reassure McGrath that the tax cuts would be sorted shortly. He told him he should understand the NEG, and asked whether he had read the available material. Turnbull said he needed McGrath to 'understand it and sell it'.

The next message McGrath got from Turnbull was on Saturday 18 August. They spoke that day. Turnbull was keen to know if McGrath was hearing 'anything' – code for 'anything happening on the leadership'.

McGrath said he hadn't, but he did fill him in on what had happened at the usual meeting of Queensland MPs in the monkey-pod room on the previous Wednesday night. The Liberal's federal director, Andrew Hirst, was due to deliver a post-mortem on Longman. Before Hirst appeared, there was a discussion among the MPs, which McGrath later described as brutal.

George Christensen, Michelle Landry, Luke Howarth, and Warren Entsch all spoke. They were either worried they would lose their seats, or angry that the prime minister was not listening to them or not getting back to them about their concerns. In a room full of crankiness and complaints, they realised they all felt pretty much the same.

'They were basically pooing themselves they were next in line to lose their seats,' one attendee said later.

Hirst's presentation showed they had been outcampaigned by Labor. Labor had clearer, sharper messages that cut through, like the alleged cuts to Caboolture hospital. Exit polling showed that even though not everyone believed it, close to 90 per cent could remember the claim. There was also blowback against Ruthenberg. Hirst's slide show also told them that the party had made up a lot of ground during the campaign, which, given the result, did little to lessen their anxiety.

McGrath spoke to Dutton and Howarth the weekend before Tuesday's party-room meeting, but claims not to recall any discussion of a challenge.

At the meeting, McGrath thought Turnbull had made a pretty good speech, and then heard him finish up by declaring the leadership vacant. McGrath was, as usual, sitting next to Dutton. He turned to him, saying, WTF, did you know about this? No, Dutton said. McGrath told him he would vote for him.

It was clear that the Dutton camp was in chaos. They had been caught completely unprepared by Turnbull's decision to bring a spill on, and it showed. McGrath went first to Dutton's office to offer him material as well as moral support. Around 5.00 pm, he went to Turnbull's office to offer him his resignation.

Turnbull asked McGrath if he wanted him to accept it, then asked what he could do to keep him. McGrath told him it was all about Queensland, it was about Turnbull not visiting a drought area after going to a solar farm at Barcaldine, about not getting dust on his boots, and it was about him – McGrath – not having a relationship with a key member of Turnbull's staff. Bottom line: they didn't understand Queensland. McGrath agreed to think about his position.

Turnbull had described the Dutton forces as terrorists. They were wreckers, tearing down the government. McGrath felt terrible, sick to his stomach. But after what had happened in 2015 (when Turnbull overthrew Abbott with McGrath's help), he wasn't going to take any lectures from Malcolm.

'I always thought it would end in tears. I didn't think it would end in bloody tears,' he would say later.

That night, McGrath took his staff to the Kingston Hotel for steak, chips, and a beer, because he knew pretty soon they would be out of work.

The next day, McGrath decided to force the issue. He went to see Turnbull's diary secretary, Jenny Brennan, and asked to see the prime minister.

Turnbull called out to him, 'Yes, James?'

McGrath said, 'Prime Minister, I would like you to accept my resignation.'

Turnbull replied, 'Yes, OK.'

McGrath thinks they shook hands, but can't remember exactly, and as Turnbull was closing the door after him, told McGrath he would write to the governor-general in the morning to inform him.

McGrath reckons they are the last words he and Turnbull will ever exchange.

McGrath insists he did not make a single phone call to enlist support for Dutton, nor did he walk the petition around. He went to meetings in the monkey-pod room and in Dutton's office, providing advice and intelligence on where people were at, and how people should be deployed.

He was touched when Simon Birmingham told him that whatever happened that week, friendships were very important.

McGrath was not surprised when Morrison won the ballot on the Friday. Despite the braggadocio of the Dutton camp, he was never convinced they had the numbers. They were too disorganised, and he suspected that the Morrison camp had been gathering intel for months.

He thinks it was a major strategic error on Dutton's part to insist on another meeting that week. He thinks he should have pulled back, waited, and had another go later, a la Keating, who made two strikes against Hawke, months apart. While Turnbull and his supporters thought delay might have helped them, McGrath believed delay would have only helped Dutton. The government and Turnbull would have continued to bleed, strengthening sentiment among backbenchers that he had to go.

On the day after Morrison won the ballot, McGrath went to the Kingaroy baconfest. Talk about happy as pigs in the proverbial. People were coming up to him saying they were really angry with what had happened in Canberra, but they were happy Turnbull was gone. It was the same at a party meeting at Dalby. People there were telling him they were very angry with what he did, but 'you should have done it sooner'.

McGrath reckons it was bipolar. He still feels terrible about it; he does not, however, regret it, even though he is convinced they will never speak again. He was furious with Turnbull for not helping out later in the Wentworth by-election.

McGrath has one sentence, a cruel one, on why Turnbull lost the prime ministership: 'He was never one of us – and all the more reason he should have listened.'

McGrath's fellow Queenslander Ross Vasta, who voted for Turnbull in 2015, has connections with Peter Dutton going back to when Dutton was 19. They were both hooked on politics, were Young Liberals together, and then lost touch after Dutton joined the police force. They met again by chance at a gathering at a party official's house more than a decade later. They renewed their friendship. Vasta's then girlfriend had a friend called Kirilly, who worked as PA to businesswoman Serena Russo. She wanted to introduce her friend to Dutton because she thought they would hit it off. Vasta later split up with his girlfriend. Dutton married her friend, Kirilly, in 2003.

Despite their friendship, Vasta did not see Dutton as the solution to the government's problems.

When Jason Wood rang Vasta – he believes it was on Thursday 9 August – to ask him if he knew anything about Dutton running against Turnbull, Vasta, who had already concluded that Turnbull could not win, said he was not thinking about Dutton. He told him that he believed their best chance of retaining government was to replace Turnbull with Bishop. She was popular, an effective fundraiser, and a good campaigner. She could call an early election, and with her they could win it. They simply could not afford to allow Bill Shorten to get elected. He said the same thing to Bert van Manen at the weekend, and to Tony Abbott, who had been up in Queensland telling Young Liberals and others they should back Dutton for the leadership.

Vasta believed Turnbull should step aside. 'Those who live by the sword die by the sword,' he told fellow MPs.

On Monday, he told Steve Ciobo that it could not be Dutton, and that Dutton would do better if he moved to another portfolio.

Then Turnbull asked to see Vasta. Turnbull told him the whole thing was 'madness' and that there was no way they could win with Dutton. Vasta agreed with that, but also thought they could not win with Turnbull. Vasta told Turnbull he thought the government would do better with Bishop as leader and Dutton as her deputy. He said the continuing 'negativity' from people like Alan Jones was starting to hurt, that people in his electorate were not renewing their membership and were deserting the party. Turnbull offered to visit to help him with a recruiting drive. Vasta said that would not be enough. The negativity had to stop, and Turnbull needed to sort it out with Jones.

That night, Vasta also spoke to Dutton. Vasta told him he should stand aside and run as Bishop's deputy; that way, they could win the election. Dutton would not countenance it. He told Vasta he could not work with her. The next day, Vasta voted against Turnbull rather than for Dutton, and then on Friday was one of the 11 who voted for Bishop in the first ballot, and then for Dutton in the second.

Warren Entsch is another eccentric Queenslander. It often seems there is no other kind. Entsch was also unhappy. He had spent time with Turnbull's chief of staff, Clive Mathieson, on the Monday, the day before Turnbull declared his position vacant, going through unresolved issues. 'The problem we have here is we have a prime minister who is elected, but has absolutely no authority,' Entsch says he told Mathieson.

Entsch has been able to survive in the deep north while maintaining his small-l liberal credentials. He says he hates being called a conservative. He is anything but. And he is proud of the causes he has championed. More recently, it was same-sex marriage. Before that, it was mental health. And weird exchanges on this issue with Tony Abbott were what convinced him that the former prime minister should get out of parliament.

At Turnbull's request, Entsch decided to renominate for his seat of Leichardt. Entsch has kept every clipping of himself since 1996, so he asked staff to dig out a few things for him. He needed a dossier of achievements to put to the voters. In the Howard years, when Abbott was health minister, Entsch made a point of getting up at every party meeting to highlight the desperate need for more money for mental health.

As Entsch said, it killed at least one person a week: either mentally ill people were killed by others, they killed others, or they killed themselves. Finally, before one of the weekly meetings, Howard asked him not to raise the subject that day, because something was about to happen. Something did: the government announced a $1.9 billion mental-health package.

So, when it came to May 2018, Entsch wrote to both Howard and Abbott seeking letters commending him for his efforts in securing funding for mental health.

Abbott texted back. 'Mate, I got your letter. Yes you did a fine job getting money … that's done a lot of good, I am happy to say that. For the life of me though, I can't understand why you opposed me and I would probably want to put that in too.'

Sure enough, the letter came back 10 days later on 25 May, paying tribute to Entsch for having worked so hard to draw attention to the hidden epidemic of mental illness: 'We need more people in the parliament who aren't afraid ... except for a period in August–September 2015, we always got on well.'

That two-month period covered the contentious same-sex marriage debate in the party room, when Abbott dudded Entsch, followed soon after by the challenge from Turnbull, when Entsch voted for Turnbull. Entsch has never shied away from difficult policies or tough choices.

Entsch had been bitterly disappointed with Turnbull's third-reading speech in parliament to legalise same-sex marriage. He had pocketed his own speech, giving up his spot to speak to the prime minister, because he thought it was the right thing to do. He thought Turnbull's speech was terrible. He felt deflated. Then the NEG debate became, as he said, a dog's breakfast. The majority of MPs had taken a stand on a difficult problem, only to have the ground move under them.

On the day before the challenge, when speculation was rife, he had a message for Mathieson about Turnbull's critical problem, as he saw it.

'He is a fence sitter, and where I come from, the top wire is barbed, and if he is pushed one way or another, we know what's going to be left hanging on the wire,' Entsch warned.

The next morning, Entsch walked into the party meeting with Dutton. 'I hope you are not going to pull anything on today,' Entsch said to him. Dutton replied, 'Mate, I am not.'

Turnbull's decision to declare the two leadership positions vacant took them all by surprise. Sitting between Ken Wyatt and Andrew Laming, Entsch said to them, 'This is crazy. If he doesn't get well over 60 votes, he is fucked.' Entsch voted for Turnbull in that first ballot because, 'Fifty metres before the finishing line, you don't change your jockey.'

When the vote was read out, Entsch thought, 'He is dead. He can't recover.' Entsch then rang Dutton and told him, 'He has killed himself. If there is another vote and you are running, I will support you.'

However, before the vote, as outlined earlier, Entsch switched.

Another Queenslander, Scott Buchholz, approached his decision very differently. Buchholz was a fully signed-up member of the monkey-podders. He attended the regular meetings, he was a conservative, and he regarded Dutton as a great mate. Unlike many of his colleagues, Buchholz says he had not spent time in the lead-up to Tuesday's meeting talking about the leadership. Like all of them, he was stunned when Turnbull moved, and stunned even more when the vote was so high. 'Holy shit,' he thought when the number was read out. Then he turned to his sitting companions and advised them not to say who they voted for, because they would be branded with it.

Buchholz says he voted for Turnbull. He says that reports suggesting he voted for Dutton were wrong, so he is happy to correct the record. When Dutton rang him after Tuesday's meeting to ask for his vote, Buchholz was up-front. He told him he had no reason in the world to be supporting the prime minister, because Turnbull had sacked him as chief whip after he wrested the leadership from Abbott. But Buchholz said he would be supporting Turnbull, because he thought people were sick of the revolving door of prime ministers.

Dutton said he respected that.

On the Thursday afternoon, Buchholz organised a phone hook-up of his branch presidents and the two state MPs whose electorates overlapped his. He had two questions for them: first, should he sign the petition calling for another meeting to resolve the leadership question; and, second, if the spill motion were successful, who should he vote for.

The unanimous view of the 10 people on his hook-up was that he should sign the petition, so he did, writing beside his name in brackets, 'I support the office of the Prime Minister.'

Their answers to the second question were interesting. Two said to vote for Julie Bishop, two said to vote for Dutton, but the majority – 70 per cent – said he should vote for Morrison. So that is what he did.

'Maybe my people backed in Morrison because he is the first prime minister in a decade that doesn't have blood on his hands,' he said later.

Buchholz also voted for Josh Frydenberg for the deputy leadership. He had earlier committed to Greg Hunt, but when Frydenberg entered the race, he changed his mind. He rang Hunt and told him of this, even though he knew he didn't have to.

'Someone told me once that the only people you can believe are those who tell you they're not voting for you,' he told Hunt. He didn't want Hunt to tally up his numbers inaccurately.

Andrew Laming was another Queenslander who did not blame Turnbull for Longman. Instead, Laming laid most of the blame at the feet of the candidate, Big Trev Ruthenberg. Laming said later that even his mother, Estelle, was reluctant to help out in the seat after the news hit that Ruthenberg had claimed he had been awarded one military medal when in fact he had received another.

Laming also blamed Tony Abbott for undermining Turnbull. Laming figured that Abbott was not interested in resolving the internal dispute over energy, and that all he really wanted to do was destroy Turnbull.

Laming now says it would have been better if Turnbull had left the issue alone – not because no one cared about power prices, but because no one believed the government could do anything to stop them rising, and it was the one issue that Abbott could use to undermine Turnbull. He could not use tax, he could not use indigenous matters, and he could not use welfare.

Energy was Abbott's weapon of choice, and it was Turnbull's Achilles heel.

'Tony was the guy with bricks hurling them through the window. Nothing was going to stop him. Even if Turnbull had pulled out of Paris, Tony would have moved on to something else on energy,' Laming told me.

In Laming's view, the greater the focus on energy from Abbott, the more wounded Turnbull became.

Laming said the angst felt by fellow Queenslanders in the wake of Longman was both harsh and misplaced.

'I thought the Longman disaster was candidate-related,' he said. He thought Ruthenberg's medal muddle cost him and the party dearly. The only way the LNP could have won that seat, he believed, was with a stellar candidate like Wyatt Roy or Mal Brough, and Ruthenberg was a long way from that.

He also said it was the media, rather than Turnbull, that had been responsible for raising expectations.

Nevertheless, when he arrived in Canberra for the resumption of the sitting week, Laming was still hopeful, in spite of all the weekend speculation, that Turnbull could find a way through.

Early on Tuesday morning, around 7.00, Laming received a phone call from Turnbull. Turnbull told him he 'had a feeling' that something was going to happen, and if it did, asked if he could count on his vote. Laming told him that he could. In his own mind, and after having discussed it with his colleagues, Laming had concluded that if anything did happen, and if the vote against Turnbull was 20 or under, he might be able to skate through.

'Twenty was the magic number,' Laming said. He did vote for Turnbull, and was shocked when 35 others did not. At this point, Laming thought Turnbull's position had become absolutely untenable, and that another challenge was inevitable, either within a few weeks or certainly by Christmas.

That afternoon, he texted Dutton and told him that although he had voted for Turnbull for the sake of stability, if there was another ballot he would vote for Dutton.

Ultimately, Laming did vote for Dutton, although he admits that Scott Morrison made a compelling argument when he rang to lobby him.

Morrison's pitch was simple. He was the one who had stopped the boats. He was not the one responsible for keeping them stopped; he was the one who had stopped them, full stop. He had also, as social services minister, overseen important welfare reforms. Then, as treasurer, he had delivered three reasonably popular budgets. Unlike his predecessor.

Laming had vowed to himself before speaking to Morrison that he would not double-cross Dutton, and he didn't, but he could see why Morrison's support was building. He was extremely persuasive.

Unfortunately for Turnbull, the discontent with him had seeped well beyond the Queensland border.

Jason Wood was one of the few Victorian lower-house members to actively campaign and vote for Dutton. Another was Michael Sukkar, and, of course, Greg Hunt. In the Senate, it was young right-winger James Paterson. It highlighted the schism that had opened up in the Victorian Liberal Party.

On the Thursday of the previous sitting week, while he was in the Virgin lounge waiting to fly home, Wood received two phone calls from journalists asking him if anything was happening on the leadership front. Wood said there wasn't, as far as he was concerned, and then asked Queenslander Bert van Manen and West Australian Steve Irons, who were with him, if they knew of anything. They said they did not.

When he became aware of the *Daily Telegraph* story, Wood spoke to Dutton. Wood says Dutton told him, 'Mate, I am not going to challenge.'

The next morning, Turnbull rang Wood. Turnbull remembered his conversation in January with Wood. A very angry Wood had complained to Turnbull about what he saw as his neglect of marginal seats and fundraising, particularly in his own seat of Latrobe, and was unhappy that, unlike Dutton, a former fellow cop with whom Wood had bonded, Turnbull did not seem to get the 'African gang' issue then running hot in Victoria.

It was during this discussion that Wood told Turnbull he would do the numbers against him at the end of the year if things did not improve. Wood reckons Turnbull remained calm throughout that conversation, whereas he clearly did not.

Turnbull had the January discussion with Wood in mind when he rang him on that Saturday morning to ask him directly if he was now doing numbers against him. Wood said he was not. He told Turnbull who he had spoken to, and repeated that, as far as he knew, nothing was happening. He says he did make it clear to Turnbull that if there was a challenge, he would not be voting for him.

Wood's view, then and when we spoke soon after, was that Turnbull should be given until the end of the year to 'turn things around'. Wood also says he spoke to Sukkar, who told him there was no challenge.

So numbers were furiously being counted, everybody was talking to everybody else, but no one was planning to do anything. Wood was convinced by Monday night that Dutton had the numbers.

Reflecting on this later, Wood came to believe that this view had been encouraged by Morrison's men – not Morrison himself – because they wanted Turnbull gone.

Zed Seselja is a senator from the ACT, the most left-wing

catchment area in the country, only rivalled by Victoria, from where his very good friend Michael Sukkar hailed.

The Liberal's version of the glimmer twins – they were almost always bracketed together – they stuck by Abbott to the end, and were fully paid-up members of the monkey-pod group that clustered around Dutton. They remained emotionally tied to Abbott, even though Turnbull promoted both to the frontbench.

Colleagues were scathing about the monkey-podders afterwards, claiming they had dressed up personal dislike as ideology to excuse their behaviour. Sukkar's punishment was to be dumped by Morrison as assistant treasurer, and from the frontbench altogether, in the hope of appeasing outraged women MPs in particular.

It is fair to say that Seselja and Sukkar tolerated Turnbull, but never warmed to him.

Seselja was angry that a coalition government, which was supposed to be about promoting choice, had managed to get not only Catholic schools but also the independents offside. When people complained that Turnbull was too left-wing, Seselja says he did not think of energy policy or the NEG as prime examples – unlike some of his fellow monkey-podders, like Andrew Hastie or Angus Taylor – but of Catholic school funding.

And as much as he says he liked and respected the education minister, Simon Birmingham – describing him as bright, hardworking, and diligent – on this issue, putting it mildly from Seselja's viewpoint, his performance fell well short of what was required. Seselja was dumbfounded when Birmingham accused the sector of 'being bought by a few pieces of silver' in the wake of the 17 March Batman by-election in Victoria. Seselja thought he should have been moved from the portfolio.

'We had drunk the Gonski Koolaid,' Seselja told me later. 'We screwed part of our voting base.'

The by-election had been forced after Labor's David Feeney

mucked up his citizenship paperwork. It was Feeney's second transgression, after earlier neglecting to record another house on his pecuniary interest register.

The Liberals did not field a candidate in the seat, leaving it to the Greens and Labor to slug it out – the theory being that Liberal preferences would only help Labor get over the line, and that without a Liberal candidate, the Greens' Alex Bhathal would triumph. Labor had preselected the former ACTU president Ged Kearney, a good candidate, a woman with high name-recognition. The Greens were bitterly divided, and Kearney won easily.

During the campaign, Shorten had promised to restore $250 million in funding for Catholic schools in his first two years of office, if elected. There were reports that the Victorian Catholics had made 30,000 robocalls into the electorate. Shorten later gave them credit for helping deliver victory to Labor, and they were happy to claim it, even though there were doubts about the influence they had really had. Barnaby's doodle had helped make Shorten Labor look stable, united, and focussed, but it suited Labor and the Catholics to write a different narrative.

Birmingham, who is both articulate and hard-working, had helped restore the Liberals' standing on education. They were never going to beat Labor in one of its core policy areas, but Birmingham had at least removed some of the angst over cuts to funding that had lingered from the first Abbott budget. However, the overt political campaigning by the executive director of Catholic Education Melbourne, Stephen Elder (a former politician), to the effect that the government's needs-based funding system had left some Catholic schools worse off, led Birmingham to make a rare mistake.

Birmingham says that everyone except Elder in the Catholic education sector had been working constructively to fix the problem.

The image of Judas and the 30 pieces of silver began bouncing around in Birmingham's head after Shorten rang to thank Elder for helping Labor win the seat. To Birmingham's mind, this had a whiff of conspiracy around it, so when he was asked if he thought the Victorian branch of Catholic education had been constructive, out it popped. Birmingham did not mention Judas and betrayal, but said, 'There's always somebody who can be bought by a few pieces of silver.'

It sent his colleagues spare. A new inquiry was announced, which took months to report, and the problem festered. The Catholic sector turned the screws after Longman, even seeking to claim some credit there for a very late, minor intervention.

Birmingham says he went to an education forum in Longman, appearing with both Shorten and his shadow education minister, Tanya Plibersek, and reckons there were barely 20 people there.

Birmingham says it was his one mistake to say what he said. Nothing else he had done or said had escalated the dispute.

'I don't regret it because I think it was incorrect or untrue. It was a very accurate way of describing what was happening,' Birmingham says. 'But, politically, it was a misstep.' He and Elder subsequently had a number of conversations as they tried to resolve the problem.

As well as being unhappy about the Catholic funding, Seselja reckons that, for him, Longman encapsulated all the problems with Turnbull and the government. It revived memories of Turnbull's shortcomings as a campaigner; he could not understand why the party allowed itself to be outspent so badly in the final week, and the drop in the party's primary vote showed that conservatives had drifted away from the LNP. Nevertheless, he had not at this stage reached the threshold decision that Turnbull had to go. He had more or less resigned himself to Turnbull remaining.

Seselja says he didn't think too much about the reports of Dutton moving against Turnbull. He saw reports of Dutton's Thursday interview with Hadley, in which he said he would resign if he lost faith in Turnbull, as the Queenslander trailing his coat. It was also obvious to him that sections of News Corp were running aggressively against Turnbull. He thought that Friday's *Daily Telegraph* story was part of the general egging-on of Dutton by Hadley, News, and Sky.

Seselja spoke with like-minded colleagues over the weekend, and while there was aggro, he says none of the people he spoke to were talking about a challenge or counting numbers.

He called Sally Cray on Monday, they talked about Catholic-school funding, and he told her that most of the angst was coming out of Queensland.

Seselja, who usually sat between Craig Laundy and Andrew Hastie in the party room, thought, 'Oh shit' when Turnbull vacated the leadership. He says he had a split second to decide, and he went for Dutton. He was confident that Dutton could win back conservative voters and win the election. He did not think that Turnbull could do either.

When the vote was read out, he judged that Turnbull's position was untenable. Seselja thought he had a moral obligation to fess up, so he texted Turnbull after question time, asking to see him. When they met around 6.00 that evening, Seselja offered his resignation as an assistant minister. Turnbull told him he did not want to accept it, and would not if Seselja agreed to not take part in any other spill motions against him.

Seselja could not give that guarantee. Unlike other senior members of the Dutton camp, Seselja says he never thought at any stage that it was in the bag. He did not walk the petition around, and while he talked to colleagues to swing them Dutton's way, he figured a few of them were lying when they said they would vote for him.

Part of Seselja's allotted task was to go out into the media and spruik for Dutton. 'That's a shitty place to be in a leadership stoush,' he reckoned later. It would have been much easier being in the background, although in this contest there weren't too many who managed that. Seselja soon found pictures of himself with Dutton, Abbott, and Morrison, highlighting his role in the coup, featuring in ACT union pamphlets, but he was comfortably re-elected.

Once Scott Morrison entered the race, Seselja thought the three-way contest might work to Dutton's advantage, because it would split votes between Morrison and Bishop. Seselja judged that if it ended up as a contest between Dutton and Bishop, Dutton would win. As it happened, the progressives had already figured this out. 'The left was pretty ruthless,' Seselja told me later, referring to the leaked WhatsApp messages that showed they had urged their fellows to vote for Morrison rather than Bishop, because in a Dutton–Bishop contest, Dutton would win. It was a grudging compliment, but a compliment none the less.

Seselja also agreed that Hunt and Abbott were drags on Dutton's challenge. Seselja doesn't even pretend to understand the finer details of Victorian Liberal factionalism, but he knows enough to know that Hunt did not add a single vote to Dutton, and is realistic enough to accept that Abbott probably cost him a few.

Seselja reckons that Abbott was never going to be appointed to a Dutton ministry, and remains convinced that the story was put about by Turnbull supporters to damage Dutton.

Less than a week later, Sukkar said he felt emotionally and physically exhausted.

Sukkar says he would never challenge a sitting prime minister, nor advocate for it, and didn't, despite the claims that he had been urging Dutton to run.

Sukkar says that, later, he thought Turnbull had made a major strategic error in vacating his leadership, and but for that would have still been prime minister. He met with Turnbull in his office after the Tuesday party meeting to offer his resignation. He asked him why he had brought it on, and says that Turnbull replied, 'Well, they were coming after me.' Sukkar told him he had voted for Dutton, and confessed he was shocked that Turnbull had called it on.

Sukkar outlined his concerns, which revolved around energy and the Catholic education funding, which he could not believe had not been resolved, even though it had been a running sore, particularly in Victoria, for more than a year.

Turnbull told him he was not obliged to resign, because he (Turnbull) was the one who had called the spill. He told Sukkar, just as he had told Seselja, that he could stay if he undertook to support him in any future leadership challenge. Sukkar said he could not do that.

'I have never been in love with Turnbull, but he basically ran a good government. He called a spill when his stocks were at their lowest. It was like a domino effect. It's like the day after the GFC – you don't liquidate then, you don't sell at the bottom. It was the worst possible time to do it.'

Sukkar reckons the Turnbull era was marked by tenuous periods, including when Barnaby Joyce was forced to resign, and when people fell foul of the Constitution. 'There's always been some sort of fuck-up threatening the government or the leadership.

'My view always was that we were on track to lose. With all due respect, he is not a good campaigner, and we would probably lose 1 per cent in the campaign. That would be an honourable loss, not a walloping – maybe a dozen seats – but we could rebuild.

'The wheels started to fall off over energy and company tax. I felt it was going to get worse and worse, and I don't think he could have picked a worse time. The Queenslanders were agitating because they thought they were going to lose.'

Sukkar says he contributed $30,000 to the Braddon by-election campaign to fund 20,000 phone calls.

He rejects claims by colleagues that the monkey-pod room meetings were used to plot for Dutton. 'They were whinge sessions.

There were 25 people. It leaked like a sieve. Whatever happened there ended back at the prime minister's office or in the media. It was not watertight. It was a conservative catch-up. People like Dan Tehan and Andrew Wallace would come.'

Fellow Victorian James Paterson riled those of his Victorian colleagues who stuck with Turnbull. They reckoned his involvement smacked of student politics, and ignored the likely electoral consequences in his home state.

In my first discussion with Paterson in the immediate aftermath of the coup, he too was unrepentant.

'My confidence in the PM, his ability to listen to the party room, was smashed on Monday,' Paterson said. 'On Friday, when he took over negotiations from Josh, their solution was to move from legislation to regulation. I and others said we could only support it in legislation, not regulation. He went and did exactly what we warned him not to do. It did not please any of his critics. That was bad enough. On Monday, when he gave his press conference, I couldn't really tell you what the policy was.

'Even then, on Monday, I had decided this was not going to end well. I was not pushing for change; I was not advocating change. When he moved that spill, that was another bad display of judgement. I knew his leadership was toast.

'I was shocked and dismayed he moved the motion. When I heard the result, it reaffirmed the direction I was heading in the last sitting.'

Paterson decided to 'help make the transition'.

'I had no appetite for leadership change. I didn't have any conversation with him [Dutton] about leadership until the Wednesday. I spoke to Sukkar over the weekend about the policy about the leadership.'

Paterson says he voted for Dutton, and in the immediate aftermath had no regrets whatsoever about the coup. The exact opposite, in fact.

'I feel relieved about the change, particularly [because] the way he has behaved vindicated the decision to remove him. Asking for 43 signatures was a new requirement which did not previously exist. If a challenger says he has the numbers, it is untenable to require a petition. It is an extraordinary act of vandalism.'

Paterson said it was hard to know when Morrison entered the show. 'We lost people to him immediately,' he said.

Tasmanian Richard Colbeck stuck with Turnbull, like he had stuck with Abbott. In both cases, he said they went down because they were not, or their governments were not, what people had expected.

In Abbott's case, it was the broken promises that did the initial damage. Colbeck made the mistake of mentioning the government's credibility problem at a full ministry meeting in August 2014 after the May budget showcased Abbott's full reversal. Colbeck told the meeting that the government had no narrative that the backbench could unite behind. 'We said we would be a government of no surprises,' Colbeck remembers saying. 'We surprised ourselves sometimes.'

He said it was as if he had farted in a lift.

Colbeck says the first reason Turnbull was brought undone was because he was not the prime minister that people thought he would be.

And the second? 'Revenge. There were a few in the party that did not want him there, no matter what. They weren't going to rest until he was gone.'

CHAPTER TWELVE

Bullies and Co.

In the immediate aftermath of Turnbull's dismissal, the corridors and offices of Parliament House, and then the media, were filled with allegations of bullying or inappropriate behaviour. Although it was the shenanigans before as well as during the leadership week that induced women to lift the lid on some of the behaviour, the complaint eventually landed squarely on cultural problems within the Liberal Party that stretched beyond those activities and into what was then another pressing problem – the desperate shortage of women in the parliamentary party.

Prompted by details of conversations involving Senate colleagues, including Lucy Gichuhi and Jane Hume, Linda Reynolds was the first Liberal to put on the record the bullying she believed had taken place during the putsch. Reynolds rose twice in the Senate during the days of madness to call it out, without naming names, because she said she felt ashamed at what she was hearing. Later, a lot of men – mostly – seeking to justify their behaviour, told the women to toughen up, as if it was okay for them to be pushed around in the name of politics.

Julie Bishop and Kelly O'Dwyer were unequivocal that bullying had occurred. Julia Banks cited bullying as a factor in her decision, announced days after the coup, not to recontest her seat of Chisholm for the Liberals. The story – lacking names, dates, and places – morphed into one about female representation in the parliamentary Liberal Party. Their number had shrunk to a measly 12 in the House of Representatives. Liberal women were an endangered species.

Most of the angst in that leadership week revolved around Jane Hume, the first-term senator from Victoria, and the behaviour of young conservative MPs gathering numbers for Peter Dutton. Hume – bright, earthy, and tough – would later describe what happened that week as nasty, ruthless, and more like cage fighting than croquet. But she would not say it was bullying. Lucy Gichuhi was also mentioned; however, she abandoned her plan to name names in the Senate at the request of Morrison, who appealed to her not to do anything that would inflame the situation, and to give him time to look into it.

Hume's preselection had not been settled at the time of the challenge. It was made clear to her during coup week that if she voted for Dutton, it would be fixed swiftly and painlessly. The Victorian Liberal president, Michael Kroger, frontbencher Michael Sukkar, and senator James Paterson – who later regretted his part in the events of that week, without regretting Turnbull's departure – all spoke to Hume at different times. Sukkar and Kroger used her impending preselection to pressure her into voting for Dutton. Paterson did not do so, but he did tell her that if she showed her ballot paper to a colleague, it would prove she had voted for Dutton. A tearful Hume related the conversations to her colleagues after they occurred. Eventually, when it got too much for her, she locked herself in her office to get away from it all.

Victorian Sarah Henderson, who went public saying she had been offered, but rejected, a ministry to vote for Dutton, doubted that any bullying had occurred during the week, while also conceding that aggressive behaviour was par for the course in politics. She recalled she had once felt compelled to pull up a minister she thought was overstepping the mark in a conversation. She told him to stop speaking to her that way. As a former journalist and daughter of a politician, Henderson had no trouble dealing with aggressive or difficult people.

Gichuhi's concerns also centred around her preselection. Gichuhi had been a Family First candidate; then, when the party leader, Bob Day, was knocked out of the Senate after being found by the High Court to be in breach of section 44(v) of the Constitution for having 'an indirect pecuniary interest' with the Commonwealth, Gichuhi took his place in April 2017, and then signed up with the Liberals in February 2018. Gichuhi was convinced that conservative South Australian Liberals were behind the leaking of details of damaging entitlements claims in an effort to knock her out of the preselection race. She blamed them for her relegation to the unwinnable fourth spot on the Senate ticket at the beginning of July 2018, but she refused to name them.

Gichui had told other colleagues that, during coup week, Tasmanian senator Eric Abetz had approached her in the lead-up to the second ballot, saying that, as Christians, they needed to stick together. Gichui told him she did not think some of the behaviour of her colleagues was at all Christian. However, she did not regard what Abetz said as bullying – only slightly ridiculous, given the way some Liberal MPs, male and female, were carrying on. She did not believe Abetz to be part of that, nor involved personally in any bullying.

Although Banks cited bullying as a factor in August, she was mainly referring to behaviour before the spill, when she felt intimidated by both Liberal and Labor operatives.

In early June, Banks found out, after seeing photos posted on Facebook, that Dutton and Sukkar had visited Box Hill in her electorate without paying her the courtesy, as the local member, of informing her. They did a walk-through, and then met with some of her donors. After Banks complained to the prime minister's office, Dutton called her to apologise, saying he hadn't realised Box Hill was in Chisholm. He thought it was in Sukkar's electorate of Deakin. Dutton said to Banks, 'God, you're hard-core in Victoria.'

Banks took this to mean that Sukkar played it hard. Banks then rang Sukkar to chip him about the visit and also to challenge him about the speculation surrounding her preselection. Sukkar blamed that speculation on her 'mates' leaking to me. She also asked him why he had chosen Gladys Liu (subsequently selected as the Liberal candidate to replace her, who surprisingly retained the seat) as his representative at the Anzac Day dawn service at the Box Hill RSL. Organisers had told her it was a last-minute and unusual action, because Sukkar had not been represented there before.

According to Banks, after she told Sukkar he should have paid her the courtesy of informing her he was going to visit her electorate with Dutton and meet with people whom she had only recently introduced to Malcolm Turnbull, Sukkar interrupted her, saying, 'Let me just cut in there. This is a very damaging phone call for you.'

Banks replied, 'Well, it's disappointing for us to have to ...' Sukkar interrupted her again, to say, 'No, it's not damaging for me. It's damaging for you.' A corporate lawyer before she entered parliament, Banks makes notes of her conversations.

Banks says on the Thursday of spill week, Morrison called to ask her for her vote. At this stage she did not know that Bishop was running, so she said she would vote for him. When she found out that Bishop was in fact running, she called him back to tell him she would be voting for her. Fine, Morrison said, but he wanted to know if Banks would vote for him if Bishop were eliminated. Do I have your vote in the second ballot, he asked. She said he did.

Later that night, she ran into Steve Irons, who she says put his face centimetres from hers to tell her that she had to vote for Morrison, that it would be politically naïve to vote for Bishop, and that, further, if Dutton got up, he would quit. She had also seen her friend Ann Sudmalis visibly upset. Later, Irons would show a text message from Sudmalis to him, saying she had not been upset by him.

Sudmalis followed Banks in announcing she would not recontest her New South Wales seat of Gilmore, even though Morrison had gone in to bat for her when her preselection was under threat. She also cited bullying as a factor, and pointed the finger at New South Wales state MP Gareth Ward, who denied it.

In the wake of Turnbull's demise, Liberal women were damned if they complained about bullying, and damned if they didn't. If they complained, the Bullies and Co. ridiculed them for being weak, or condemned them as wreckers or liars. If they didn't, they knew that an unsavoury culture, which they obviously felt was taking hold in the Liberal Party, regardless of whether it happened inside Parliament House or outside it – before, during or after coups – would continue.

The day after the first ballot, on Wednesday 22 August, Reynolds had told the Senate she was 'deeply saddened and distressed' by what was happening on her side of politics. She was equally saddened, although not surprised, by the childish delight and hubris of Labor.

She stood again in the chamber almost exactly 24 hours later to say she was even more distressed and disturbed by what had happened inside her own party since she had spoken the day before, particularly overnight and that morning.

'Some of the behaviour I simply do not recognise and I think has no place in my party or in this chamber. Whatever happens over the next 24 hours, I cannot condone or support what has happened to some of my colleagues on this side in this chamber in this place,' she said.

'The tragedy of the madness that has taken hold of a number of my colleagues is that this has been a very good government.'

She went on to list the government's achievements, including tax cuts and jobs growth, and then came back to what was plaguing her. 'I say to everybody in this place and to anybody who may be listening. I do not recognise my party at the moment. I do not recognise the values. I do not recognise the bullying and intimidation that has gone on.'

She finished by saying she felt 'ashamed that we are letting our nation down'.

Reynolds hadn't planned on doing this. She had seen and heard things from colleagues deeply upset by what was going on.

'I was in the Senate chamber, after the House of Representatives had risen early, but Coalition senators were determined the Senate would keep sitting,' she said.

'The government frontbench was empty, except for assistant minister Anne Ruston.

'Anne was a hero. She was in the government duty minister's chair. I was in there supporting her, as was Richard Colbeck. Anne's great ability to lead shone through – with dogged determination, she almost single-handedly managed government business that most challenging of afternoons.

'The leadership consiglieres and their apprentices were trying to intimidate or bully people into signing the petition. I didn't think the petition was necessary, according to party-room rules. I was sitting in there, I was so distressed. I was tired. I looked tired. I probably sounded tired, too.

'I was incredibly upset at what I believed to be unethical behaviour that wasn't values-driven. The bullying had no place. It was men and women who were running around doing that. A number of our women were particularly vulnerable.'

Even after having spent so much time in the military, Reynolds confessed to being surprised by the tactics and the brutality of the whole exercise.

'There is a reason historically that when government power changes hands via a coup, those who lose and their supporters are executed or exiled. It's off with their heads. Human nature is human nature. Those who win have debts to pay, and those who lose have scores to settle,' she says.

Reynolds, sensible and hardworking, deserved to rank as highly in the parliamentary party as she has in the military; yet, immediately after the coup, she was only made an assistant minister.

Reynolds' problem? She was not factional – she did not play the political games. It was not until Steve Ciobo announced in early March he was quitting the parliament that Morrison gave Reynolds his slot in the cabinet as defence industry minister, promising to elevate her to cabinet as defence minister if he won the election – and he did.

Reynolds had voted for Tony Abbott in 2015, and she voted for Malcolm Turnbull in 2018. As the first woman to be promoted to the rank of brigadier in the Army Reserve, Reynolds says her behaviour was influenced by her military experience. She would not participate in any mutiny against any leader.

In contrast, Andrew Hastie, a former SAS soldier, took an active role in Dutton's campaign to unseat Turnbull. There is no suggestion at all that Hastie was involved in any inappropriate activities. The surprise, given his higher ambitions, was that he took part at all.

Hastie has the potential for bigger things, if he stays the course.

During John McCain's final visit to Australia, after he had addressed Liberal MPs, Hastie asked a deep question of the war hero and former Republican presidential candidate, 'What does victory look like?' McCain, himself handsome in his youth, responded by telling the room, 'If I looked like Andrew, I'd be president.'

Hastie immersed himself in the coup, and then did not step back from his role in Dutton's challenge. He owned what he did. He never felt he owed Turnbull anything. Hastie did not believe he had won Canning at the 2015 by-election because of Abbott's overthrow and Turnbull's ascension. He and Ben Morton always believed he was on track to win before then.

Hastie's military experience was very different from Reynolds'.

'I came from a part of the army that respects authority, and constantly chafes against it,' he told me.

'The SAS is a free-thinking, flat organisation. It's not hierarchical and rigid like the rest of the military. We operated in small teams, often in isolation.

'If people want to stereotype me as, "Yes sir, no sir, three bags full, sir", well, that's nothing I have ever been.

'I don't put my tie on in the morning and wonder what the next lily pad is to jump onto to get to be prime minister.'

Whereas Hastie was a political newbie, Reynolds had worked for both the party and politicians. She had happily been on the staff of Fred Chaney and Chris Ellison – one deeply moderate, and the other deeply conservative. She describes herself as a Menzian Liberal who believes strongly in individual freedoms – she supported same-sex marriage – but who remains conservative on economic and security issues.

No one bothered in those last few days to ring and ask her for her vote. No one lobbied her. They knew she would stick with the leader.

'Maybe it's the army officer in me. I have a fundamental problem with leadership coups,' she told me later. 'And just because you can, doesn't mean you should. After nearly 30 years in the army, in my view, the leader is only ever as good as the team.'

The root cause of the heavy-handed tactics had much to do with the changed nature of the Liberal Party, particularly in Victoria, where concerted recruitment drives targeted at churches meant that traditional conservative or progressive Liberals felt both threatened and unwelcome.

Long-serving Liberal Party members and officials familiar with what has occurred there say that prospective members from the Mormon or Dutch Reform churches were told that if they wanted the party to be more conservative, they needed to join up so they could use their numbers to make it so.

If they wanted to stop same-sex marriage, euthanasia, and safe schools – the programme developed to teach children acceptance of LGBTQI people – they had to do it from within. They were the three issues that were key to the signing-up of thousands of the religious right. This bred an intolerance of alternative views, and fostered the idea that if they got enough people into the party, they could reverse both marriage equality and abortion laws. They would turn up en masse in buses at electorate annual general meetings of sitting members to either influence votes there, or to make sure that their members were elected delegates to state assembly.

That first issue – same-sex marriage – was the one that threatened Hume's fledgling career. It had caused angst for Paterson as well, but he mitigated it by campaigning for greater protections for religious freedoms after the same-sex marriage vote, which he had supported. His preselection was sorted before the coup. Not so, Hume's.

Well before that week, Hume had asked all her colleagues, including Sukkar, for a reference for her preselection, but he refused, 'because my friends won't like it'.

Hume and Sukkar had not spoken for months, except when he called to caution her about talking to the media. Then, surprise, surprise, after the first ballot on the Tuesday, he rang her, saying, 'Mate, mate …' Her radar immediately went up. They were definitely not mates.

Sukkar told her it was time to build bridges. 'It would be really good if you were seen to be supporting Dutton,' he said to her. 'You would just be endorsed. It would save you weeks of cups of tea with old ladies in a preselection you might not win.'

Then Kroger rang to advise her she should simply tell people she was doing what Cormann was doing. At that stage – the Wednesday before question time – she believed that Cormann was sticking by the prime minister, and told Kroger this.

'Mmm, mmm. You just follow Mathias,' Kroger advised.

Hume had been to drinks in the prime minister's office on Tuesday night, and then on Wednesday night in Paul Fletcher's office, which Turnbull attended. A tearful Hume told her colleagues what Sukkar and Kroger had said to her. They all came to the same conclusion: if she voted for Dutton, the threats to her preselection would disappear.

Fletcher had set up a WhatsApp-called 'drinks' for like-minded MPs on Wednesday morning, then messaged moderates to come to his office for – you guessed it – drinks in his office that evening. This group was subsequently renamed Sensible Friends, and then Friends for Stability. It was the messages from this last iteration of the WhatsApp group urging moderates to vote for Morrison, rather than Bishop, that leaked after the coup.

Turnbull had spoken at Fletcher's drinks gathering. Hume was not reassured. She thought he looked beaten. She told him he had her loyalty, but she was worried there were no heavyweights there. Scott Morrison, for one, was absent.

'We look like the kids who didn't get picked for the team,' she said.

Hume had dinner that night in the prime minister's office. News was breaking that Cormann was set to quit. Lucy and Pyne were dismissing this as fake news, unlike Turnbull's staff, who were nowhere near as upbeat.

The next morning, Thursday, Hume recalls that everything changed very quickly. She received calls from Laundy, Birmingham, and Ruston to tell her that Cormann, Cash, and Fifield were resigning.

The message from her friends to Hume was simple: you should sign the petition and save yourself.

Paterson came to her office to tell her that Cormann wanted to see her, and he walked around with her to Cormann's office.

Cormann said to her, 'You said you trusted my judgement – this is what I am doing.' And he showed her the petition. Hume told him that Sukkar and Kroger had threatened her preselection. Cormann reassured her he was not doing that. She signed the petition. She was the 39th to sign.

As they walked back to her office, Paterson told her that, in order to protect herself, she needed to show her ballot paper to Tasmanian senator Jonathon Duniam. After this, an emotional Hume locked herself in her office and rang a few friends. Morrison rang to tell her that if Turnbull lost the spill, he would stand and he would like her vote. Bishop also rang to seek her vote. Hume told her she would not be voting for her, but thought she was brilliant. Duniam told her she didn't have to show him her ballot paper. He was as horrified by the suggestion as she was.

On Friday, Hume ended up voting against the spill, and then, after it was successful, voted for Morrison. Back in Melbourne that night, Hume and Paterson sat together at the party's state assembly meeting; then she, her partner, Nick, and Paterson, with his wife, Lydia, had pizzas and a glass of red at an Italian eatery, Ombra, in Collins St. They had all been friends before, and wanted that to continue afterwards.

However, there were those who sought to bully or shame the women into silence after the allegations became public.

Broadcaster Alan Jones told them to swallow a teaspoon of cement and toughen up. Craig Kelly said they should roll with the punches. Kroger said politics was a 'rough business', and downplayed or scoffed at the accusations when he was interviewed by Sky's Laura Jayes.

'I mean, you know, someone said that someone's brother's sister's cousin was spoken to rudely by the butcher's auntie,' Kroger said. 'I mean, seriously. Can we talk in facts here, rather than this pathetic rumour and innuendo? Am I aware of anyone who was threatened, bullied, intimidated? No.'

Reynolds later observed that, as state president, Kroger's very public comments made it (intentionally or otherwise) almost impossible for anyone within the Victorian Liberal Party to speak out.

Newly elected federal vice-president Teena McQueen, who was on the federal executive, which Morrison initially tasked to sort out the mess, advised women to put up or shut up. Ms McQueen told women to suck it up. She accused complaining women of wanting the spoils of victory without the fight.

Women nominating for preselection were also reluctant to go above the radar, fearing that if they won they would be stigmatised with accusations that they had only achieved success because of their gender. They worried that it would diminish their victory and also their sense of achievement. Then, if they happened to lose, it wouldn't be because of their gender, or because the male powerbrokers were looking after their own, of course; it would be because they were lousy candidates.

Liberals held a preselection, the first grassroots plebiscite in the bush, in the marginal New South Wales seat of Eden-Monaro on Saturday 22 September, in Cooma, where locals reported there was not an empty shop in sight – thanks, they say, to Malcolm Turnbull's Snowy 2.0. There were two women candidates – Fiona Kotvojs and Jo Leatham – and one man, Nigel Catchlove. The women had insisted on little or no media profile, because they did not want, at the end of the process – assuming that one of them won – to have anyone say that the only reason they got there was because of the gender/culture/bullying wars then playing out in the federal sphere.

Kotvojs, a good grassroots politician, won the preselection, but failed to win the seat.

Julia Banks severed all connections with the Liberals. She had held off announcing her move to the crossbench – which she had been contemplating for some time – until after the Victorian state election.

Predictably, she was vilified by the very people in the media who had applauded South Australian senator Cory Bernardi when he resigned and set up his own party, Australian Conservatives, only months after being elected for a full six-year term as a Liberal at the 2016 election. Then again, Bernardi was wounding Turnbull. They were also the very same people who refrained from criticising Craig Kelly when he was threatening to go to the crossbenches if Morrison didn't save his preselection. The same applied there: Kelly also was wounding Turnbull. They provided him with the platforms to do it.

Banks's departure greatly disappointed her friends in the Liberal Party, who said they were blindsided by her decision. Reynolds, who had been so sympathetic to Banks, was saddened and angry that she had chosen to leave without any forewarning, even attending the regular Liberal Party meeting that morning without giving a hint of what she had been planning only shortly before she made her announcement. Reynolds said she had felt 'a deep sense of betrayal'. Banks's new friends on the crossbench – Kerryn Phelps, Rebekha Sharkie, and Cathy McGowan – welcomed her with open arms. The pictures rubbed salt in raw Liberal wounds.

O'Dwyer was also taken by surprise, and felt hurt by Banks's decision, but when Banks wanted to drop by O'Dwyer's office after her valedictory speech, O'Dwyer's anger dissolved.

After her announcement, Morrison wanted Banks to visit him in his office. She refused – she was not going to respond like a schoolgirl being summoned by the headmaster. With Frydenberg acting as intermediary, Banks finally spoke to Morrison on the phone. She says his main concern was to establish that her resignation had not been precipitated by any problem she had with him.

Bill Shorten quickly sniffed an opportunity.

Very soon after Banks announced her move to the crossbench, Shorten approached her in the annexe to the House of Representatives chamber as she waited to vote in a division.

Labor had already worked out one of her options. Banks says that Shorten told her if she ran in the seat of Flinders, where her family owned a holiday home, and where they had spent most of their summers for two decades, Labor would run third in the seat. In other words, they would help her beat Greg Hunt.

Banks's nemesis, Michael Kroger, tendered his resignation on Friday 30 November, less than a week after the disastrous Victorian state election, and three days after Banks moved to the crossbench. Banks had complained loud and long of having been deprived of resources during the 2016 campaign – which Kroger hotly denies.

Banks did receive $250,000; however, MPs marvelled at how much more in the way of money and resources had gone to the seat of Bruce, where Helen Kroger was running. As well as crediting Turnbull with her victory in the seat, Banks was grateful for the financial and moral support from O'Dwyer.

The relief at Kroger's departure, which had been demanded immediately after the state election by women like O'Dwyer, was palpable.

In his first incarnation as president, decades before, Kroger had made a valuable contribution, helping to get good people into politics – Petro Georgiou and Peter Costello, to name but two. The second time around, he was seen as divisive: he hogged the limelight; he was accused of briefing against MPs, including O'Dwyer; he allowed branch stacking to run rampant; he fostered the activities of Marcus Bastiaan, whom he protected and promoted as he recruited the religious right; and he would tolerate no questioning or criticism of his decisions or activities, belittling (or bullying, depending on your definition) any man or woman who dared take him on.

According to party officials and long-serving staff alike, his second term was a disaster. Much of the blame for the party's decay was laid at his door. Several men and women who spoke to me for this book – all unwilling to be quoted by name, either because of fears of retribution, or because they did not want to cause further damage to the party – were highly critical of his presidency, accusing him of abusing members of the party's administrative committee, and of creating 'trauma and chaos'.

One former party official who had served during his second tenure summarised his approach: 'Michael Kroger was not a consultative president; he did not respect the Constitution; he did not attempt to investigate the branch stacking, as it benefitted his presidency; and he used the media to his own advantage and to undermine the reputations of those he disliked. He openly backed his preferred candidates at each annual general meeting where the election of admin committee members took place – something previous presidents would never have done.

'Michael Kroger's presidency saw the Victorian division ripped apart, and factionalism become the focus.'

Over the summer, there was a fightback of sorts to try to recast the narrative that had taken hold, which was that the Liberal Party was anti-women.

Reynolds, who had kicked off the bullying stories, also kicked off the counter-narrative, to explain why she was against quotas, and to outline what the party was doing to improve its female representation. Sarah Henderson joined in, as did others.

Reynolds felt insulted by the notion that Liberal women were hapless victims of misogynistic men who were directing and controlling them. Stuff that, she thought. She did not think her remarks in December were in conflict with her remarks in August;

in fact, the opposite. Reynolds was not denying there was a problem with female numbers in the party. Far from it. She had campaigned for more than four years for action to increase them. Her hope – her intention – was to force people to focus on making it better.

'I was heartily sick of trying to make ourselves a small target,' she said later. 'We left ourselves wide open to attacks from Labor; they were just going to keep hounding us.'

Reynolds does not believe quotas would work in the Liberal Party, and while Labor boasts it has worked for them, she reckons what has really worked for Labor is the steady pipeline of women coming through the trade union movement.

So while once again it highlighted how few Liberal women there were, Reynolds wanted to use that very fact to underline the urgent need for the party to be more proactive in finding and then mentoring suitable women candidates.

Around this time, Julia Banks announced she was going to run as an independent against Hunt in Flinders. People who refrained from criticising Morrison when he chose Warren Mundine to run in Gilmore, after the man preselected to replace Sudmalis had been elbowed out, continued to vilify Banks and to condemn her for seat-shopping. Jane Hume regularly attacked Banks on social media. Mundine, marketing himself as a conservative indigenous man on Sky, had certainly party-shopped – from Labor, to the Liberal Democrats, and eventually to the Liberals, which he joined only hours before Morrison announced his candidacy.

The sole candidate for the Gilmore preselection had been Grant Schultz, son of the quirky former federal member for Hume, Alby, who had said he was going to challenge Sudmalis before she quit. He was voted in 40 to 9 by preselectors, and then refused a request at the end of 2018 from the New South Wales state president, Philip Ruddock – at the behest of Morrison – to withdraw.

Morrison then insisted that the state executive disendorse

Schultz so that Mundine could have the seat. Using loose language, Morrison, who had previously clamped down on women making accusations of bullying, made veiled accusations of bullying against Schultz, even though Sudmalis had not named him. It seemed as if Morrison was equating challenging a sitting member with intimidation. It all left a very bad odour. During the campaign, the former long-serving Liberal member for Gilmore, Jo Gash, joined the campaign of the Nationals' candidate, Katrina Hodgkinson, against Mundine. Neither of them won the seat, which fell to Labor.

The fracas over Mundine also diverted attention from another attempt by Josh Frydenberg to swing the debate back on to the economy, and it left other MPs scratching their heads about what the Liberals stood for if the party selected a candidate for a must-win seat who had first tried two other parties, and if the prime minister sought to equate a preselection challenge to bullying.

Banks had separated mentally from the Liberal Party on the day that Turnbull lost the prime ministership. She made the physical break in stages, finally deciding to run as an independent in Hunt's seat after a Christmas Eve church service at St John's Anglican church in Flinders in his electorate. Banks had been leaning towards leaving parliament altogether. After announcing her move to the crossbench, she had received low-level death threats, to go with all the high-level abuse from the hard right of the Liberal Party. She was genuinely fearful of the impact it would have on her family if she decided to run as an independent against a sitting Liberal. Her mother, Helen Lolatgis, who had always encouraged her high-achieving daughter, was now telling her to wave goodbye to politics because it was too brutal.

On Christmas Eve, they went to the same Anglican church in Flinders that they had been going to for 20 years, and the vicar stopped Banks on the way out to thank her for what she had done. 'The whole community is talking about you and what you said about refugees and climate change,' the vicar told her. 'It's so good to have a strong, independent woman.' Mrs Lolatgis overheard the conversation.

The next day, as they were preparing Christmas lunch for the family, her mother told Banks she had changed her mind. She should run.

Kelly O'Dwyer announced her decision not to recontest her seat of Higgins on 19 January, with Scott Morrison standing beside her. She cited her desire to have a third child, and the important times in the lives of her first two children, Olivia and Edward, that she had missed.

O'Dwyer ended her political career with dignity, but her friends believe that if it were not for Turnbull's removal, the pendulum might have swung a bit the other way, and perhaps she would have served one more term. O'Dwyer struggles with this question. She had a good relationship with Morrison; however, there is no doubt she had an even better one with Turnbull. O'Dwyer always gave it her all. She was used to working hard, she had grown accustomed to dealing with lots of stress, and she was adept at arguing with colleagues; however, there is a big difference between making the sacrifices involved in being a key part of the government, and struggling through in opposition.

There was also self-awareness involved. In her valedictory speech, O'Dwyer said politics was a brutal business. It is not necessarily true, therefore, that only brutes survive, and that nice guys and gals finish last; but it is truer these days, given the increasingly hostile nature of the environment, that those with double or triple layers of rhinoceros hide are better equipped to make it. It seems that, in order to survive, politicians have to be even harder and tougher than before when they either take it or dish it out. O'Dwyer knew that she would have to change to survive in that environment, and she didn't want to change.

Her greatest concern about leaving was the message it would send to other women about choosing a political career. Her experience showed them what they could expect, both good and bad. If they were good enough, they could make a terrific contribution, and then at some point they would have to make a choice. Men have had to make it, too. Tim Hammond was the promising young member from the seat of Perth, tipped for big things in a Labor government, until he quit in 2018 because the constant travel back and forth was interfering with fatherhood. Or so he said. His choice wasn't questioned, whereas Kelly's was.

Soon after, on Australia Day, Zali Steggall, a former Olympic ski champion turned barrister, announced she was running as an independent against Tony Abbott in Warringah. Abbott's delcons mobilised, just like they did against Turnbull, to try to destroy her. When I asked Steggall during her campaign if she had been warned in advance what to expect, she laughed. She said that, as someone who had lived in the electorate for 25 years and had watched Abbott over that time, she knew exactly what to expect. She did not wilt. She was used to the mind games of competitors at the elite-sport level, and the sledging techniques of fellow barristers.

In the space of a few days, for different reasons, the Liberals lost, failed to keep, or could not recruit a number of smart professional women who should have been an integral part of their rebuilding. To the surprise of no one, a few weeks later, Julie Bishop also announced she was leaving.

CHAPTER THIRTEEN

The spillover effects

On the day he announced he was resigning from parliament after 26 years, Christopher Pyne maintained the same sprightly demeanour he had when he first arrived as a 25-year-old. That was the public Pyne. The private Pyne had confessed to friends that he had come to see parliament as a hateful place. Turnbull's removal factored into his decision to leave, although he maintained he probably would have gone anyway, even if Turnbull had survived.

Pyne felt then that he was going out on a high, when people were sorry to see him go. Always leave them wanting more, he would say. Despite efforts by others to claim he had been in the thick of it, in 2015 he was not involved in the coup against Abbott. In 2018, he was instrumental in whipping his factional enemies on the right, even if he could not save his very good friend, and he had to do it by sacrificing Julie Bishop. For a long time afterwards, he was completely unsympathetic to Bishop for taking it so personally; later, he realised how devastating it must have been for her, and how difficult it would have been to deal with such a public humiliation. This does not mean he regretted his actions. His objective and that of the other moderates was to defeat Dutton and to give the right a belting they would long remember.

After Turnbull's defeat at the Friday party-room meeting, all

Pyne wanted to do was get out of the place as fast as he could. He shared a quick glass of champagne with his staff in his office to celebrate Dutton's demise and Morrison's victory. Yet Pyne, who loved politics, with all its intrigues, was miserable. He left Parliament House an hour after the vote. He was crying as he left the building, cried all the way to the airport, and was still wiping away tears on his flight back to Adelaide. He was shattered.

Pyne has been friends with Turnbull for decades. They had first met at the constitutional convention called by John Howard in 1998 to debate the republic. Turnbull was leader of the Australian Republican Movement. Pyne, along with Andrew Robb, was co-convenor of Conservatives for an Australian Head of State. Pyne was also Peter Costello's proxy when he couldn't attend.

Pyne recalls his first impressions of Turnbull: 'Charismatic, articulate, determined.' Also, back then, headstrong. 'He was convinced that his way ahead was the right way, and he didn't bring the direct-elect republicans into the tent. As a consequence, the referendum was doomed from the start. A number of the direct-election republicans, many of whom were my friends, were aghast that he left them a choice between the parliamentary model or to campaign against the referendum. Sadly, many of them chose the latter.'

It was the start of a beautiful friendship. Pyne's proud boast is that he voted for Turnbull in every ballot. Pyne had been through nine leadership changes. This one left him distraught. He wasn't the only one. 'I haven't cried so much since my father died,' he told me later when I interviewed him in his Parliament House office. Then he choked up again. He wasn't the only minister who teared up during post-coup interviews.

Pyne had a four-word explanation for Turnbull's denouement: personal ambition, revenge, hatred.

'The right hated him, and they were prepared to destroy the

government to get rid of him. They never ceased from the moment he became prime minister,' he said.

A few days after the coup, at the swearing-in at Government House, Pyne was seated next to Mathias Cormann. Pyne could not bring himself to look at Cormann, nor even to speak to him. He had admired the finance minister, but could not understand why he had behaved as he had. Pyne says he was 'incandescent' with rage at Steve Ciobo, whom Turnbull had appointed as a shadow minister, who had been dumped by Abbott, and was then rescued again by Turnbull and promoted into cabinet, only to be betrayed by him – twice in the space of a few days. 'Ciobo stabbed him in the back,' Pyne said.

Morrison appointed Pyne as defence minister. He stripped Ciobo of the trade portfolio, which he loved, kept him in cabinet, and then, without even a hint of irony, made him Pyne's assistant minister for defence.

Ciobo understood the anger of his colleagues. However, for him it wasn't just about political friendship; it wasn't just about political loyalty. He also cried from the stress of it all, but waited until he got home. His son, Asher, had been born with a heart defect, and that ranked as the worst time of his life. Dutton had provided moral and physical support during that awful time, so their relationship went well beyond a political alliance.

After his son's illness, that week in August 2018 was the next worst in Ciobo's life. He has been through it in his mind over and over, any number of times since, trying to work out if he would do anything differently in retrospect. It was so fraught, whichever way he went, that he was done for.

'Either way I jumped, I would have been stuffed,' he said later. 'It's like Sophie's choice. I was close to Malcolm, and close to Peter.'

He knew he owed Malcolm, but he says he was trying to weigh up who was best to unite the party, who was best to ensure its supporters held firm, and who would be best-placed to win the election. He feared Shorten would glide into office and implement policies that would take years to recover from. He decided that the person best equipped to handle this was Dutton, not Turnbull – a choice that would cost him dearly.

Ciobo resigned from parliament, only a couple of weeks after a candid interview with me in his office, saying he had been weighing up his future for a while. There is no doubt, however, that events in August influenced his timing, before an election that the Coalition seemed destined to lose, and the limited career prospects that would follow for him if he stayed and went into in opposition.

There was a fine symmetry to the separate announcements made on the same day by Pyne and Ciobo that they were quitting parliament. Both of them wanted out while they still had time to build other careers.

Yet each of them will carry the scars of what happened that week. Pyne, at least, left knowing who his friends were and who were not. As far as any politician can.

The swearing-in of the Morrison ministry had been incredibly awkward. For those watching, it made for uncomfortable viewing. Josh Frydenberg, the new treasurer, now ranking second in the Liberal Party, had many reasons to feel proud, and perhaps one not to. He hugged his old friend Greg Hunt and gave him a peck on the cheek. It was stilted, and to this day their relationship has not been properly repaired.

Michaelia Cash wore a broad, fixed, determined smile for the cameras. As well she might. Cash should have been dropped long before. She had been a great asset, and then turned herself into a giant liability.

Cash had been unable to do media for months. Not only was

she under a cloud over the tip-off by her office to media about an impending raid on the AWU by the Australian Federal Police, but she had threatened, when Labor was questioning her about the role of her staff, to talk about rumours involving some of Bill Shorten's younger female employees.

Her threat to relay salacious scuttlebutt was made in anger after provocation; however, Cash refused to apologise, ignoring advice from friends and colleagues alike, including Cormann, urging her to admit in the cool of the day that she had made a mistake. Her intransigence compelled them all to defend her, even though their hearts weren't in it. She was the perpetrator of another bleak period for Turnbull, who was forced to back her, and then she betrayed him even after he had confided in her about the darkness that had enveloped him after he lost the leadership in 2009. He had told her that if it happened again he would leave.

Morrison kept her in the cabinet, even though there were other good women who should have been promoted ahead of her. Cormann had insisted on this, just like he insisted that she walk out with him and Mitch Fifield to tell the world that Turnbull was done for. Turnbull staffers watched, shaking their heads in disbelief. They said later that Cash had received more help from their office than any other cabinet minister, down to them writing her lines for her press conferences.

Six weeks after the swearing-in, at the beginning of the parliamentary week in the third week of October, Pyne had mellowed enough to invite Cormann to dinner at Canberra's exclusive Commonwealth Club.

When I asked Pyne why he had issued the invitation, he replied, 'I felt sorry for him. He has shredded his reputation. He has suffered personally immeasurably. I can see it on his face.

'I am a nice person. I could see how broken he was by the catastrophe he was involved in. I couldn't add to that pain any longer. I had frozen him out for six weeks. I wanted the world to swallow me up [at the swearing-in]. I couldn't bear to talk to him.

'I couldn't keep adding to his pain. He made an incalculable error of judgement.'

It was a difficult dinner. Pyne asked Cormann why he had done what he did. Cormann replied they had convinced him they had the numbers to topple Turnbull. 'So what? Who cares?' Pyne said. 'Malcolm made you. It was your responsibility to stay with him to the end.'

Pyne also says he told Cormann that night he had overheard their conversations in the monkey-pod room. He told Cormann he had heard him say he was going to sound him out about being Dutton's deputy. Pyne says Cormann responded by saying, 'I wouldn't know, mate – I was never in the monkey-pod room.' Pyne insisted he was. 'I said, "I heard you talking in the monkey-pod room."'

It sounded like two fibs from Cormann. Dutton supporters also confirm he was in the room, and while he told Pyne subsequently and others during the days of madness that he was convinced Dutton had the numbers, he told a different story to Ciobo over dinner in January 2019 in Davos at the World Economic Forum – he never thought Dutton had the numbers, and he had not been involved in planning the challenge.

It left Ciobo questioning everything and everybody he thought he knew.

Beyond his comment about his close friendship with Cormann, which says it all, Dutton is reluctant to give a blow-by-blow account of what happened before and during the coup, including whether Cormann voted for him in the first ballot – although the strong inference is that he did.

While Cormann was in Davos, his lunch buddy, factional ally, and fellow Dutton backer Michael Keenan quit on Australia Day. To those who knew Keenan, it was not a surprise. He cited family reasons, including the birth of his fourth child, for not recontesting his seat of Stirling, which Liberals at that stage feared they would lose, along with a slew of other seats in the west. They ended up holding them all after a last-minute rush of undecideds to the much-safer harbour provided by the Liberals.

The friendship between Ciobo, Keenan, and Dutton was strained, to say the least. In the immediate aftermath of the coup, Keenan was white-hot with rage against both Dutton and Cormann. According to what he told others, both of them had assured him that all the planning and numbers were solid. He felt humiliated, and believed the events would leave a stain on his career that would never be erased. He was shattered.

They all insist their friendships have now repaired. All is forgiven, if not forgotten.

After revelations that her colleagues had banded together to block her leadership bid – with not a single MP from her home state of Western Australia voting for her – Julie Bishop quit as foreign minister, and then in February 2019 announced her resignation from parliament altogether. The two most popular Liberals were gone. Bishop was humiliated by her low vote for the leadership, felt betrayed by the strategy that had wrought it – which, she says, blindsided her – and then was infuriated by Morrison's decision to keep Cormann and Dutton in the cabinet in their previous positions.

According to Morrison, Bishop quit the frontbench because she could not bear to sit in the same room as Cormann and Dutton. Bishop herself was not convinced that Morrison really wanted her there, and admits she was furious that Cormann and Dutton had paid no penalty for destroying Turnbull and wrecking the government. She blamed them for the catastrophe, and then watched them get off scot-free. She was convinced that Cormann had been part of it all along, and that Dutton had been plotting for months, and yet no punishment was meted out for what they had done.

'I was disillusioned by the fact that those who tried to bring down Malcolm Turnbull's leadership, who didn't have the numbers to do so, were prepared to continue, and there were no consequences,' Bishop told me.

'There's no message sent to those to say, be very careful when you embark on such an exercise.'

This contrasted with Morrison's offer for her to stay in her foreign affairs portfolio, which she regarded as lukewarm and half-hearted. Her strong impression was that her services were no longer required. Before the coup, Turnbull had shunted her aside, preferring to rely on Cormann and Dutton, and then she felt Morrison regarded her as surplus to requirements, even though she remained the most popular Liberal, and one who worked tirelessly for marginal-seat holders to raise money and get votes.

'By that stage, I didn't want to be part of the cabinet,' she said. 'I understood Dutton and Cormann were going to retain their positions, there were no consequences.' She decided not to accept Morrison's offer on principle, and then, after turning it down, held a press conference in a striking pair of red heels that became an elegant piece of political history – like their owner – and retreated to the backbench. Relations with most of her West Australian colleagues were frosty, with other MPs saying she barely spoke to them after the coup.

Morrison never had any intention of punishing either Dutton or Cormann. He calculated that he needed them both more than he needed her to keep the government together; not because he valued their counsel as much as Turnbull had done, and not because he relied on them as conduits to conservatives, but to provide some semblance of unity, particularly for the all-important base.

When I spoke to him, Morrison conceded that Cormann had been damaged by the events, saying that was why he had warned him against defecting. But, he said, he has helped Cormann with his 'rehabilitation process'.

He described Cormann as a 'bloody good minister' and a very important minister in the government, stressing that his job as prime minister was to 'put the show back together quickly, and the show needed him'.

While he was disappointed with the decision that Cormann took that week, Morrison asks himself, 'Do I think that he was plotting for months, and all of that? No, I don't. I take him at his word that none of this began for him until, at the very earliest, that spill on Tuesday.

'I don't believe that he was either aware or involved up until that point. Now, I may have been naive, I may have believed him too much, I don't know. And frankly, now, it doesn't matter to me. It just does not matter; it's irrelevant. He took some decisions that week, like a lot of people took decisions that week in the circumstances, and that's politics, and you've got to get over it and move on and work together, and that's actually what has happened.'

Morrison says he and Bishop got along very well that week. He understood why she was running, and there was no antagonism. They had an 'affable' conversation the night before the ballot.

But he says it's 'rubbish' to say his offer to her to stay in cabinet as foreign minister was half-hearted. He says he wanted her to stay.

'I wanted her in – I wanted her to be foreign minister,' he said.

'She told me that she couldn't sit in a room with Dutton and Mathias. And that's why she couldn't take the job. And I said,

"Well, if not you, who should the foreign minister be?" And she said, "Marise", and I said, "Good, because that's who I would have given it to." But I was fair dinkum in asking her, and she said no.'

Morrison says Bishop did not put it to him that it was either her or Dutton and Cormann, because she knew they were in and did not ask him to rethink that.

'I had no beefs with anybody. I mean, I wasn't – they weren't running against me,' he said.

'My point was, look, Malcolm's lost. I was sad about that, but I ran, Peter ran, I won. So why would I want to carry on the venom? There was no venom between Peter and I [*sic*], at all, or Mathias and I. I was annoyed at the decision Mathias had made, but, you know, Mathias and I have had our disagreements over the years, we get over them – we're professionals.

'To rebuild the party, you have to bring everybody in. And I wanted her in, but she chose not to be in.'

In February, when Bishop announced she would quit parliament, she gave a short, dignified speech, and then bolted from the chamber without staying to hear Morrison and Shorten respond. Subsequent comments she made that she was the one who could have beaten Shorten were deemed by some of her former colleagues to be unhelpful to the government, and even Warren Entsch said he regretted having voted for her.

Bishop was wrong in one important respect about Cormann and Dutton. They might have kept their cabinet positions, but they had each lost a lot. Cormann was a much-diminished figure. His influence in the government had waned. He was hollowed out, and was not expected to stay in parliament for long.

Dutton's prospects of re-election were not helped early on by his dumber-than-dumb accusation that his Labor opponent, Ali France, an amputee, was using her disability as an excuse not to live in the electorate. France gave as her reason the fact that she could not find a suitable house, but would move into the electorate and renovate one if she won the seat. Dutton apologised but, incredibly, it took him a couple of days to do it. A concerted campaign by GetUp! to dislodge him failed miserably. On election night, he quoted Paul Keating from 1993 to describe his win as 'the sweetest victory of all'.

Not content with killing him, the delcons also wanted Malcolm Turnbull dismembered. Turnbull did not help himself by refusing to tweet or even do a robocall in favour of his preferred candidate, Dave Sharma, for his old seat of Wentworth during the by-election campaign, and then by appearing in a special *Q&A* on the ABC as the sole guest.

He stayed mute during the campaign. However, when friends, former colleagues, and former staff cautioned him against doing *Q&A*, he told them he was not going to be a 'trappist monk'. And he began writing a book about his own life and his own version of events. It was never in his nature to stay silent or avoid the spotlight, but he was in danger of wrecking his legacy and becoming another Abbott, or another Rudd.

Apart from registering his initial support for Sharma, who was a former diplomat and generally regarded as an outstanding candidate – the sort that the Liberals would need to rebuild – Turnbull refused pleas from everyone, from Scott Morrison down, to do something to support Sharma.

Turnbull's son, Alex, made a number of interventions, all against the Liberals, which did nothing to help his father, and created turmoil in the family. It put Turnbull in an invidious position. He could come out in support of Sharma and fuel the soap opera surrounding his family, or stay silent and face the accusations of not wanting to help or, worse, of acting in concert with his son to sabotage the campaign.

Morrison, his office, and other Liberal MPs were 100 per cent convinced that the leaking of the Ruddock report on religious freedom in the latter stages of the Wentworth campaign was the work of former Turnbull staff. The staff denied it was them. They pointed the finger at members of the review committee.

The leak was very unhelpful because it alerted people to existing legislation, passed by the former Labor government, that not only allowed schools to ban gay teachers, but gay children, too. The report actually recommended making it more difficult for children to be banned; however, the fact they were able to do it at all – and ban gay teachers as well – played very badly, not just in Wentworth.

The government also didn't help itself with a series of blunders. Morrison jumped into the middle of a dispute incited by Alan Jones doing his bully-boy routine against the CEO of the Sydney Opera House, Louise Herron. Jones, well known for his love of the sport, wanted the opera house to be used to advertise the Everest horse race. Morrison agreed with Jones, describing the opera house as Sydney's biggest billboard. Morrison was thinking like the marketing man he used to be, not like the prime minister.

Equally crass was Morrison's announcement only days out from the Wentworth vote that the government would consider moving the Australian embassy in Israel from Tel Aviv to Jerusalem. It was a crude attempt to appeal to the 12 per cent of Jewish voters in Wentworth. It had nothing to do with Australia's national interest – he knew the Indonesians would not like it – yet he announced it anyway. Cabinet ministers were both appalled and fearful. It did not win Sharma, a former ambassador to Israel, a single vote. The blatant politicking behind it probably cost him votes, when he already had that section of the Jewish vote locked up. Sharma had written an opinion piece months before suggesting the move, but it was Morrison's call. It was Sharma's first outing as a candidate, and although he was consulted about its merits, after putting the case for and against the move, he was happy to leave the decision on whether to throw it into the middle of the campaign to the supposed experts. Morrison made the wrong call. It rattled his MPs because it looked panicked and desperate. Which it was. It reminded them of the Gillard government's abrupt ending of the live-cattle trade with Indonesia after the *Four Corners* documentary on the cruel treatment of the animals in abattoirs.

The day before Morrison announced the possible move of the embassy, Coalition senators had voted for a motion sponsored by Pauline Hanson stating that it was OK to be white, a slogan with racist antecedents she pinched from the Ku Klux Klan and the American alt-right. It was a monumental stuff-up, and they had to have another vote to reverse it. This incident would play out very badly for the government in the later debate on the emergence of white supremacists in Australia following the murders by an Australian man of 50 Muslims at mosques in Christchurch.

One of Morrison's less believable lines – as the third prime minister in five years from the same party – was his plea to Wentworth voters not to plunge the Coalition into minority government by voting against Sharma, because it would create instability.

Around the same time, just to add to the sense of crisis permeating government ranks, the Nationals were imploding.

It's a close-run thing, but Michael McCormack was one of the least charismatic leaders the Nationals had ever had. First prize would have to go to Warren Truss, who was nevertheless well regarded for his breadth of knowledge and his sage political advice, particularly in cabinet.

McCormack failed to fire. The Nationals felt he was being walked over by the Liberals on every issue, but particularly over agri-visas, which farmers were pushing to address worker shortages, and the so-called big-stick energy legislation, which would force energy companies to divest. So leadership speculation, which had been rumbling, erupted. In the run-up to Wentworth, Barnaby Joyce declared on TV that if they offered it to him, he would take it. Those who like Joyce say he stuffed up by putting it out there in the middle of the by-election. Those who don't like him say he never had the numbers, and that no one was offering it to him anyway. It was too soon – he hadn't spent enough time in rehab, and he was a big negative for women. National MPs said their wives didn't like the idea, so if they didn't, other women wouldn't like it either.

David Littleproud, a notable absentee from a media event featuring Morrison and McCormack in South Australia to talk about getting more unemployed to work on farms, was keen, and rightly mentioned in despatches as a future Nationals leader, but was way too green – in terms of experience, that is. Nobody had the numbers. McCormack didn't have enough to secure his position beyond question, Littleproud wasn't putting his hand up, and Joyce, who was, didn't have enough support to knock him off, while Darren Chester stuck with McCormack.

Joyce's frustration built, boiling over in the party room, in the week after the Wentworth vote, against Kevin Hogan, who had gone to sit with the crossbenchers after Turnbull's ousting. It was a curious arrangement. Despite leaving cockies' corner for the crossbench, Hogan continued to attend Nationals meetings, and had been preselected again for the Nationals for his seat of Page. Hogan reckons his people loved the fact that he was a quasi-independent. It was all too much for Joyce. 'You are sitting with the fucking Labor Party,' he exploded at Hogan. It was duelling f-words as Hogan fought back.

The dissatisfaction with McCormack continued, with eruptions every few weeks, and with Joyce usually at the centre of them. The instability showed no signs of abating until the day after the election. The Nationals had held all their seats, even Cowper, which they had thought they would lose to Rob Oakeshott because of Luke Hartsuyker's retirement. McCormack's leadership was safe for the time being, at least from Joyce.

The week leading up to the Wentworth vote was one of the worst of the Abbott–Turnbull–Morrison government. Unsurprisingly, it ended with a swing against the Liberals of 19.2 per cent in the primary vote, handing the seat to Independent Dr Kerryn Phelps, who once upon a time had been a prospective Liberal candidate. The final two-party-preferred result, at 52.5 to 47.5 per cent, was a bit more respectable, but it did little to diminish the anguish or the anger at Turnbull's dumping and around his refusal to help the party.

For the first time that Liberals could remember, in 20 years of volunteering at booths in the electorate, Wentworth had to call for help from interstate so the booths could be staffed on polling day.

As much as he loved and admired him, calling him 'a great man', even Pyne was exasperated by Turnbull's refusal to help out in the by-election. He spoke to him four times in the week leading up to the poll on 20 October. In the end, even Pyne was left wondering whether Turnbull wanted the Liberals to win it.

Dutton said, 'I think that Turnbull sabotaged Wentworth, and will do his best to sabotage us at the election.'

Turnbull's argument was that he had left politics, and that if he intervened it would be a distraction. Which, of course, ignored the fact that his refusal to publicly support Sharma was also a distraction. Pyne was convinced that if he had said something, Sharma – who lost by 1,500 votes – would have won the seat. He thought Turnbull's arguments for not stepping in were ridiculous.

Turnbull's enemies needed no excuse to hound him – they would have done it anyway – but he gave them reason to. Perhaps he would have changed the result, although it is doubtful. Voters were so cynical by then, they would not have believed anything any of them said, least of all accepted that the wounds were healing.

Occasionally, when his discipline lapsed, Turnbull threw his enemies a bone to keep them in the hunt. From New York, where he sat out the Wentworth campaign, he tweeted that Peter Dutton should be referred to the High Court, and then he was taped describing Tony Abbott and Kevin Rudd as embittered (true) and as miserable ghosts (also true).

Turnbull remains deeply unapologetic about his 'miserable ghosts' remark. After all, he never said he would never say anything. He just didn't stay in parliament to do what Tony Abbott and Kevin Rudd had done.

Turnbull made the off-the-cuff remark in New York to a group of young Australians. It was supposed to be off the record, showing once again that there is no such thing. He was trying to explain why he got out rather than hang around. He was not the first nor the last former prominent politician to offer advice to his successors. John Howard and Paul Keating did it regularly, and Peter Costello would pop up around budget time to critique the Coalition's budgets.

In one notorious interview with Leigh Sales on the ABC's *7.30* on 7 May, the night before the 2018 budget, Costello disparaged the economic performance of his successors, saying that national debt as a proportion of the GDP, 19 per cent, was at about the same level as when he became treasurer in 1996.

'It took us 10 surplus budgets to pay it off last time. You'd be doing well to pay it off in 10 surplus budgets this time,' Costello told Sales.

'If I may say so, Leigh, I think the probabilities are we'll never get back to where we were. You and I will die before that happens.'

Morrison as treasurer had always been careful to pay tribute to Costello for his work, and often described him as a mentor. He was both hurt and infuriated by what Costello said. He had been disappointed before by other Costello interventions, but swore that he would never forgive him for what he said in 2018. Undeterred, after the 2019 budget, Costello criticised the Coalition for offering tax cuts beyond two elections, expressing doubts that people could believe they would ever be delivered.

Turnbull's interventions were pretty mild, compared to his predecessors. Nevertheless, the point of escaping to New York had been to remove himself from politics.

He came home the day after the Wentworth by-election, declaring he was retired and would not be involving himself in 'partisan politics'.

Days later, Morrison sent Turnbull as his envoy to Indonesia to attend a conference on oceans, and to use his friendship with President Joko Widodo to smooth over the tension caused by the embassy decision. Barnaby Joyce and Abbott were furious.

President Widodo, like so many others, had been blindsided by Turnbull's removal, and was then taken by surprise by the embassy decision. He asked for Turnbull to attend the conference, seeing that Morrison couldn't, and then Morrison asked Turnbull to try to smooth things over on the subject.

After his meeting with Widodo, a liberated Turnbull offered his own view that he thought moving the embassy was a bad idea. Even though it was, Turnbull saying so publicly did not help either Morrison or himself.

Alan Jones goaded Morrison into poking Turnbull, and it rebounded, provoking a damaging spat between the former prime minister and his successor. Morrison told Jones on air that Turnbull had exceeded his brief. Turnbull corrected Morrison and the record publicly by saying he had received formal and informal briefings from Morrison and the government on the embassy decision before he left for Indonesia. Whatever relationship they had left was badly frayed.

In that first long-form interview on ABC's *Q&A* with Tony Jones, when a member of the audience asked him why he was no longer prime minister, Turnbull said he did not know why – it was up to those who had dislodged him to answer.

Turnbull did not criticise Morrison, but while he did not blame him for what happened, it left a chink.

Asked if Morrison was a Steven Bradbury or Niccolò Machiavelli, Turnbull replied, 'I take Scott at his word. The insurgency was led by Peter Dutton, was obviously strongly supported by Tony Abbott and others. Scott did not support it.

'I assume you mean he took advantage of a situation that was created by others. Well, I suppose, you know, that is how he's presented the circumstances himself, and I'm not in a position to contradict that.'

So the next day, when Morrison was again asked why Turnbull was no longer there, he took a stab at it, saying that his colleagues had felt Turnbull was out of touch with core Coalition supporters. Morrison also defended the right of the parliamentary party to change leaders at any time.

'Those who had advocated that [change] made points about the need to better connect with the values and beliefs of Liberal, National, and LNP members across the country,' he said.

Turnbull was growing increasingly suspicious about the role of Morrison's lieutenants in the coup, and Morrison was angry that Turnbull was going out of his way to either not help, or to be deliberately unhelpful.

This reached a peak in early December 2018. From Argentina, where he was attending a meeting of the G20, Morrison called Liberal powerbrokers in Sydney to secure the preselection of disruptive backbencher Craig Kelly, who was threatening to sit on the crossbench and then run as an independent if he was disendorsed.

The government had had another horror week with the defection of Julia Banks to the crossbenches.

Turnbull contacted members of the New South Wales state executive to insist that Kelly – whose preselection he had saved in 2016 – should face the local preselectors. The moderates had already chosen a candidate, and they had the numbers to dump Kelly. Turnbull's remarks were leaked, including that he had said Morrison should go to an election on 2 March, as he had planned to do by calling it as soon as the Australia Day weekend had finished, in order to save the New South Wales government of Gladys Berejiklian. As it transpired, Gladys saved herself.

Turnbull was quoted as telling New South Wales Liberal Matt Kean, 'We should force Scott to an early election because all he's about is keeping his arse on C1 [the prime minister's car].'

Turnbull's ill-advised intervention guaranteed that Kelly was once again, incredibly, saved – this time by Morrison – even though he, along with Abbott and senator Jim Molan, had vigorously advocated for greater democracy in the party when Turnbull led it. Despite the fact that Kelly had to be saved twice from his own preselectors, the executive was not about to side with a former prime minister against a serving prime minister. Once again, it showed there was no penalty for bad behaviour.

Molan, who had been dropped to an unwinnable spot on the Senate ticket, below Hollie Hughes and Andrew Bragg, asked Morrison to intervene on his behalf, too. Even though Molan had lost at a preselection attended by more than 500 people, he attributed his loss to factional vote-rigging and to false assurances from Morrison's factional powerbrokers. Morrison's patience had been worn out by Turnbull, and he was irritated with Molan for blaming others for his failure. There were conservative voters, supposedly supporters of Molan's, who had not bothered to turn up for the preselection ballot. Besides, Morrison's friends pointed out that Molan had voted for Dutton – so why, they asked, would Morrison go out of his way to help him? Molan was privately scathing about Bragg, and pitched for Liberals to vote number one for him below the line.

This sparked an unwelcome spat with the Nationals during the campaign because of a threat to their third spot on the agreed Coalition New South Wales Senate ticket. Both Hughes and Bragg were duly elected. Molan, whose term expired at the end of June, wasn't. He was then tipped to take the senate vacancy created by the appointment of Arthur Sinodinos as ambassador to Washington, but moderate liberals wanted him punished for what he had done during the campaign, and – again – Morrison let it be known he thought Warren Mundine should get the slot.

After Turnbull's remarks about Morrison had been leaked, Turnbull tweeted to confirm his intervention. He then went on Radio National and said it all again, repeating his call for Morrison to go early, dobbed in Kean as the source of his 'arse' comment while not directly confirming it, and did a brief doorstop as well.

Friends, as well as enemies, were on fire, and his friends were angry and exasperated. He was wrecking his legacy, as well as looking like he was out to wreck the government. Even though he hotly denied he was behaving in any way like Abbott, he was causing himself needless damage.

Incensed by Turnbull, despite his earlier claim that the party room was entitled to change leaders when they wanted to, that night Morrison called a special party-room meeting to change the leadership rules in order to make it harder to organise coups. Under the new rules, an elected prime minister could not be cut down unless two-thirds of MPs voted for a spill. Such rules would have saved both Turnbull and Abbott.

It was supported near-unanimously, albeit not necessarily 100 per cent enthusiastically. In an effort to quell criticism after the spill, Trevor Evans, the member for Brisbane, sent detailed, thoughtful responses to constituents who emailed him. In response to one on leadership rules changes, Evans said he was in two minds.

'I understand the aim perfectly, but I'm also conscious that a prime minister being "first among equals" has been part of Australia's Westminster traditions, as well as every other commonwealth country who inherited this system over the past few hundred years, and it hasn't seemed to have been a problem for much of that time,' he wrote.

'I'm reflecting on whether the root cause is fundamentally a weakness in the system that has become evident only after the breakdown of the traditional media model, or whether the root cause is something peculiar to this current generation of leaders in Australia.'

Good point, and one that other Liberal MPs agreed with, even though they were not game to say it. Evans thought Morrison's change was useful 'at least for the purposes of the public looking to draw a line under the leadership change in 2018', and proved to some people that the government and the party room was listening to feedback and responding to it. Still, he remained unconvinced about its efficacy.

'Whether the rule change ultimately works remains to be seen. For instance, it is interesting to hypothesise what happens to a future leader's position, in practice, in the event that a spill motion achieves less than the required two-thirds majority, yet reveals that the leader's support is less than 50 per cent of the party room,' he told me.

'I suspect, ultimately, nothing beats majority support.'

Too true, and something that both past and prospective leaders need to reflect on, particularly those who believe that comebacks are possible, particularly if MPs forget and forgive what happened yesterday.

Which brings us back to Abbott. The internal hostility towards Abbott intensified after the spill. From the top to the bottom, they wanted him gone. They wanted an end to the Turnbull–Abbott wars that had ripped them apart. One cabinet minister who had stuck with Abbott, and then stuck by Turnbull, was disappointed by Turnbull's subsequent behaviour, but conceded that he, at least, had left parliament.

Angry and exasperated by Abbott's continuing interventions, he asked, 'Now how do we get rid of Abbott?'

Abbott finally dropped the pretence that his guerrilla/gorilla campaign was some high-minded battle to save the soul of the Liberal Party.

He admitted it was all deeply, deeply, personal between himself and Turnbull. Writing in *The Australian* on 29 October 2018, where a cavalcade of commentators and opinion writers had wittingly, willingly, supported his charade that he was putting forward constructive alternative policy prescriptions for the Liberal Party, Abbott said, 'In my judgement, it's much less a philosophical divide that's hurt the party over the past five years than a clash of personalities. I'm confident that the internals will be better handled now that some leading players have changed.'

At least that rang true, unlike what he reportedly told Tasmanian Young Liberals on 20 August, when he was trying to bring Turnbull down over the NEG, after he had held every conceivable position on climate change under the (warming) sun.

'It is not about personalities, it is not about him, it is not about me, it is about what is going to give Australians the best possible energy system that delivers affordable, reliable power,' Abbott said four days before Turnbull was deposed.

'What we have got to get is a contest. The only way we can win the next election is to have a contest over policy, not over personalities. We have got to be the party that is on the side of getting prices down and let Labor [be] the party all about getting emissions down.'

This charade was further exposed in early March during a debate with Zali Steggall and other candidates for his seat of Warringah, when Abbott said he no longer believed that Australia should pull out of the Paris agreement, because there was now a new prime minister and a new energy minister.

This coincided with another intervention from London by Turnbull, when he said he had been deposed because of fears he would win the election, not lose it. He described it as a peculiarly Australian form of madness. It did sound mad.

What he should have said was that there were people who hated him so much they were prepared to do everything in their power to destroy him, even if it meant destroying the government.

Abbott was more upfront about his motivations when he told David Speers for his book *On Mutiny* that one of Turnbull's fundamental mistakes was not to hold out an olive branch to him after the 2016 election.

'[Mr Turnbull] made it absolutely crystal clear that as long as he was leader, I would never be in his cabinet,' Abbott told Speers. 'I said, "Fair enough, Malcolm, that's your decision, but I'll do my thing on the backbench. You've got more to lose than I have."'

Then he confessed that he went on to make life tough for Turnbull, regularly critiquing him in media interviews. Everybody knew exactly what he was doing, while the delcons, the delusional conservatives, maintained the fiction that Abbott had been trying to help. Abbott's belated admission was a statement of the bleeding obvious.

Abbott's admission did not come as a great surprise to Turnbull. Abbott had made threats along those lines to him a number of times. Turnbull was never going to reinstate Abbott. He always believed that as prime minister, Abbott – or his office – had briefed against his own ministers and leaked from the cabinet. Further, he suspected that if Abbott were to be reinstated he would find a reason to resign from his portfolio, ostensibly on a matter of principle, with the aim of plunging the government into crisis. Bottom line: he could not be trusted. In Turnbull's judgement, it was better to have Abbott outside rather than inside, and most of his ministers agreed with him. Beyond Abbott's band of delcons, no one was twisting Turnbull's arm to reinstate Abbott.

When Turnbull was gone, Abbott zeroed in on a new target.

Ignoring his promise not to wreck or undermine, he switched his attention from Turnbull to Morrison. Peter Hartcher reported in Nine newspapers an anecdote from 2015 in the wake of the disaster of the 2014 budget, saying that Morrison had told Abbott to dump Hockey as treasurer and replace him with ... Morrison himself. Morrison denied this, although he would not have been alone in telling Abbott to dump Hockey. Dutton had, too.

Abbott was also keen to remind people – sotto voce, of course – about the messy battle for Cook, which saw the disendorsement of the preselected candidate, Michael Towke, after allegations of branch stacking. Morrison replaced Towke, and then Towke was later cleared. Abbott thought Morrison was tainted by the whole thing and that it showed a lack of integrity. Fancy that.

Abbott also experienced a second empty-chair moment on Friday 14 September at the Balgowlah RSL at a meeting of the Warringah Federal Electorate Council to endorse his preselection for the 2019 election.

With a beer in front of him, Abbott gave an eight-minute speech, during which he paid tribute to the Turnbull government for its achievements, quickly followed by his declaration that he felt 'entirely vindicated' by the policies of the Morrison government. At that point, one of those present later confessed he felt like throwing up. Abbott stressed the importance of everyone rallying around the government and staying united, especially as he still had 'a good deal of public life left in me'.

Everyone took that to mean he wanted to be opposition leader after the election, which pretty much everyone believed they would lose.

Certainly, as he fought to keep Warringah, he made it much clearer – in subsequent on-the-record interviews with journalists, including Troy Bramston – that, yes, he did want his old job back.

When the time came for preselectors to tick off on his endorsement, a significant number showed what they thought of him, his behaviour over the past three years, and his policy positions. The official vote was 68 for him, 30 for Anybody But Bloody Abbott (ABBA), and two informal. The first time that something like this had happened was in February 2015, when two disgruntled backbenchers decided they had had enough and moved a spill motion. The empty chair got 31 votes. Six months later, his prime ministership was over.

By all accounts, the preselection meeting was boisterous. The chairman on the night, Greg Smith, refused to announce the result, rejecting a formal request from former Liberal senator Chris Puplick to announce it, prompting endless speculation about the numbers against Abbott being much higher.

Smith accused those demanding the numbers of being out to wreck the government. Teena McQueen argued it was for the good of the party to withhold the numbers. His opponents said that the failure to disclose the figures rendered Abbott's preselection illegitimate, as well as making a mockery of his campaign for greater democracy and transparency.

The strength of anti-Abbott sentiment was accentuated by subsequent votes, where Abbott's candidate, Walter Villatora, who did have competitors, was smashed for the position of vice-president in two ballots. In the first, he went down 66 to 44, and in the second, 62 to 22, with 17 for 'other'.

Abbott and the delcons downplayed the significance of that

night, although it was a clear warning that a grassroots revolt was brewing against the local member. Abbott's colleagues, who were not thanking him for what had transpired three weeks before, could see what was coming. The Abbott haters in Warringah had decided months before not to formally challenge his preselection for the 2019 election. They had not wanted to create even more trouble for Turnbull by turning Abbott into a martyr. Nor did they want the prospective challenger – including one well-credentialled woman – subjected to the media Bullies and Co., who responded venomously to any whiff of criticism of Abbott or their own loopy agendas.

Nevertheless, the Abbott critics wanted him gone, so when GetUp! and others began mobilising against Abbott, they were a long way from distressed. Disgruntled Liberals and others coalesced around Zali Steggall, who had been stressing her Liberal history, which sounded good until she admitted she had never voted for Abbott. She did, however, vote Liberal in state elections.

Officials, MPs, and party members all agreed that Abbott was in deep trouble. Even family members of prominent Liberals who lived in Warringah were not prepared to vote for him. As it turned out, there was a massive 12.5 per cent swing against him on primaries. Steggall garnered 57.4 per cent of the two-party-preferred vote, leaving Abbott with 42.5 per cent. The people of Warringah, who had voted overwhelmingly for same-sex marriage, supported action on climate change, and generally wanted Liberal governments to succeed, no longer believed that Abbott stood up for them or any of the things they believed in. Although Abbott congratulated Steggall on her win, he said on election night that he would rather go out a loser than a quitter. The fact is that he lost in September 2015, and a dignified resignation then would have spared himself and the party a lot of grief. He sacrificed respect for the sake of revenge.

Craig Laundy was gutted. He had been considering quitting before Turnbull was deposed, and had foreshadowed this with Turnbull. His youngest daughter, Analise, had been diagnosed with a serious illness, and his father, Arthur, was getting older. The family, along with the family business – a string of hotels – needed him. What happened confirmed his inclination to get out.

Only a few days after the coup, as he talked about what happened, he was raw, his emotions spilling over.

'I came to Canberra with a business, not political, background. I came here with a good heart, believing in people. I am a loyal bloke. Everything I believed to be right and wrong has turned to crap. I have had enough. I have a career to get back to,' he told me then.

'My old man says, "Leave, they are a bunch of pricks", and he is right. After being nothing but loyal to the end, then to turn around and watch bastardry rewarded! I worked my guts out. At midday on the Wednesday, I texted Mathias to say, "Please can I come and see you, I need your help." I knew what Malcolm's numbers were. He [Cormann] said he had a press conference to do, and he would ring me after. He never rang. I texted him at 4.00 pm Friday to say, "If only you had rung" – very, very, sad day.

'He is supposedly a hard-headed politician, and he stabbed the prime minister in the back. I had the numbers to say, "Stay with us."

'My theory: I think Morrison put his numbers – about 10 votes – he put them with Dutton so he could come up through the middle.

'What I have seen in the last week is enough to last me a lifetime. It's been an absolute privilege being there to see it. I have had a real chance to see something that was a moment in history.

'I have been disheartened for five or six months – just the fact everyone was trying to tear Malcolm down. It's just so brutal. I have had his back since day one. It's a full-time gig. It's been mentally, physically, and emotionally exhausting.

'Suse came down on Thursday afternoon, and as soon as she walked in the door I burst into tears. I said to her, "I couldn't save him. I let him down." She hugged me and told me I hadn't, but I feel I have let him down.

'As a publican, I have met plenty of people in my time who have done well and done nothing. All this stuff about him being rich, aloof, out of touch is a disgrace. He is one of the most humble and down-to-earth people I have ever met.'

Later, after vicious pieces appeared, ripping into Turnbull, Laundy appealed to Turnbull's critics to back off. 'The job is finished. Be gracious in victory. Let him be gracious in defeat.'

Pretty soon, though, Laundy was appealing to Turnbull to temper his criticisms, to think of his legacy, not to wreck, not to be like Abbott. Fearing Laundy's seat of Reid would be lost to Labor without him, Morrison made a strong pitch to Laundy to get him to stay, but he resigned in mid-March. Laundy threw his heart and soul, not to mention his own money, into helping child psychologist Fiona Martin retain his seat of Reid. Despite a 1.4 per cent drop in the two-party-preferred vote, Martin held on

The emotional and physical toll continued. Mitch Fifield was not alone in lamenting what he had done.

A few months after the vote, Dean Smith said he regretted voting against Turnbull – not because he had come to forgive him for what he says was Turnbull's belittling of him at a party meeting over same-sex marriage, but because of what followed his ousting. Smith says he underestimated the transactional cost of the change, and the extent to which Liberals had relied on the contrast between 'Labor leadership shenanigans and our lack of shenanigans, and the lack of depth among frontbenchers to handle such a tumultuous change – the lack of integrity around all that, the immaturity, the naivety. The people who resigned then pledged loyalty, then resigned again, only to remain in the cabinet. They have kept the same faces around the table.'

Smith was not critical of Turnbull's post-leadership behaviour. 'I totally understand it,' he said, although he believed it would have been better for Turnbull if he had behaved better. A few months later still, Smith had come to terms with what he had done. He had no control over those events. He had to make a snap decision on the Tuesday morning, and was glad he had voted for Dutton. As he keeps saying, being popular is not everything.

Smith says the challenge now for the Liberal Party is to find ways to communicate its traditional values in a contemporary way.

'When you look at the last six or seven years of the coalition government, the very strong theme is this: why did it take the Liberals so long to accept the changing nature of community views on climate change, same-sex marriage, the need for a banking royal commission,' he asks. Good questions.

Smith says the Liberals have to talk to modern Australian about small and family enterprises, their support for families, about choice for education, health, and aged care, and care for the environment.

In early October, after Morrison spent three days in the West campaigning instead of just flying in and flying out, Ken Wyatt detected a turnaround in the mood. People were reconsidering their vote. Fundraising was going well. He was also personally buoyed by the decision to call the royal commission into ageing. He doubted it would have happened under Turnbull.

MPs on the west coast were sounding more optimistic than those in the south-east. However, that optimism crashed in the New Year, and pretty soon they were rattling off five seats they feared would fall: Pearce, Stirling, Moore, Hasluck, and Swan. They were on a roller coaster. Ultimately, though, the Liberals held all their seats in the west.

Immediately after the change, James Paterson was comfortable with his role. A few months later, though, he too had softened; he was regretful. He admitted that, 'with the benefit of hindsight', he should have been 'more careful' about what he had signed up to.

He also admitted to underestimating the cost of the transaction, even though people had warned him beforehand about the after-effects of a spill. He says not being there to witness it first-hand in 2015 had influenced his pre-coup assessment of the possible flow-on effects.

'It hasn't worked in the way that I hoped it would,' he said. That was partly because Dutton didn't win, but also because 'the change of leader hasn't improved our political prospects'.

Paterson remained critical of the Turnbull operation and its policies; however, while he had hoped for a change in the 'trajectory', it hadn't happened, especially in his home state of Victoria.

He says he thought it would be unpleasant for a few weeks, and then it would pass. He knows now how wrong he was about that.

He says he also underestimated how badly Turnbull would behave. The second time we spoke, in January, he was pessimistic about what lay ahead.

'I think it's going to be pretty bad,' he said.

Andrew Hastie was unforgiving, particularly resentful over slights or perceived acts of disloyalty going back before his preselection. Given what he must have seen and done as a soldier, he sounds bruised by the brutality of politics.

It confirmed his view of just how important friends are, and reminded him that few true friends are to be found in politics. So he puts in an extra effort to stay close to his family and friends outside.

'I might seem naïve to some people, but I am taking on these lessons and internalising them, and remembering them,' Hastie says.

He was convinced that Turnbull would lose the election, and although it takes him by surprise, there is no hesitation when he answers the why-question.

'There was a failure of leadership both internally and politically. Internally, we had lost confidence in his leadership, his ability to sell our values and our narrative. There was an ongoing and lingering dispute between the two sides of the party.'

He said John Howard had been able to bridge the divide, and he was confident Peter Costello would have if he had stayed. He wished Costello had stayed, because if he had, so much of what had happened since 2007 could have been avoided.

'The NEG was the final straw,' Hastie said. 'If we didn't stand up now, we were just going to get shot down. I didn't come to parliament to sacrifice my principles.

'People were angry and disappointed with Turnbull. The Longman by-election was evidence that Newspoll might be saying one thing, but on a seat-by-seat strategy there was no pathway to victory under Turnbull.'

Hastie was not alone in being reminded about the value of true friends. Trent Zimmerman, on the other side of the political divide from Hastie, who turned 50 in October, remembered precious advice he had received from former Nationals leader Tim Fischer when he was first elected.

Fischer told him to make a list of the people he considered his 10 best friends from inside as well as outside politics, and then to check at the end of each month to see how many of them he had spoken to. Zimmerman resolved to try harder to stay in touch with them.

CHAPTER FOURTEEN

Getting to know Scomo

When the whip, Nola Marino, announced that Scott Morrison had beaten Peter Dutton by 45 votes to 40, a loud cheer, a foot-stomping roar, erupted in Malcolm Turnbull's office. Morrison was never the most popular minister among Turnbull's senior staff, yet it was a brief moment of euphoria in the most trying of days. Morrison's triumph meant the demise of the by-then much-hated Dutton.

The one question that Morrison couldn't answer later, which Bill Shorten kept asking, because he knew full well that Morrison could never answer it truthfully, was why? Why was Morrison prime minister, and not Turnbull? It was not a question he could answer honestly without triggering a civil war, or inviting questions about his own role and that of his supporters in Turnbull's downfall. Which is why people kept asking it. In his first question time, he dramatically quoted American general Norman Schwarzkopf, who led the coalition in the first Gulf War against Saddam Hussein: 'When placed in command, take charge.' Yes, but why was he in command? Sometimes it sounded like he was doing everybody a favour. I stepped up, I am Stormin' Norman. I am in control.

Morrison would have also had to say, among other things, that Turnbull took too long to make decisions. Howard consulted, and then acted in quick time. Whatever Howard lacked in strategic thinking, he made up for by capitalising to the fullest on events. He made a number of cracking mistakes, but he knew instinctively where to land on an issue once it erupted.

That was the way Morrison saw himself, too. Except, while he shared some of Howard's characteristics, he fell short on others. His judgement as prime minister, as opposed to campaigner, was sometimes awry, and he didn't always land on the right spot.

Like Howard, he was dogged. Like Howard, he worked hard. Unlike Howard, he did not always take or seek the advice of the experts around him, although he did take the time to consult Howard himself.

Morrison liked nothing better than flying solo. He could be stubborn, and he could be dismissive of colleagues to their faces, or of them to other colleagues – even offhand about people like Alex Hawke and Stuart Robert, without whose help he would never have made it. When he was told Hawke was keen to be rostered to ask a question in parliament, Morrison said, 'The spearchucker will do what he's told.' Spearchucker was his nickname for Hawke.

One of Morrison's worst periods came during his dodging and weaving over One Nation preferences. He neglected both his moral and political duty as a leader to do what was right for all Australians in his anxiety to placate or woo the deep north. It was always bound to arise as a problem. The timing was both fraught and opportune. It was in the lead-up to the budget when he wanted the focus on the economy, but also after a fine speech from him in the wake of the Christchurch massacre about bringing Australians together – something that Hanson has never sought to do.

Morrison tried to avoid it for days, arguing initially that it was the job of the party organisation to decide where One Nation would be preferenced after nominations closed and they could see who else was on the ballot paper. Journalists were unkind enough to remind people that the party's processes had not deterred him when he jumped in to save Craig Kelly or impose Warren Mundine.

Morrison and Frydenberg were cautioning colleagues to avoid saying anything that would cause ructions inside the Coalition – code for not upsetting the Queensland Nationals.

They were ignoring the angst it was causing Liberals, and failed to twig to the damage the New South Wales Labor leader Michael Daley inflicted on himself and his party after footage of him emerged in the final week of the state campaign saying young educated Chinese were taking the jobs of Australians and forcing them to flee Sydney.

Even after that, Morrison refused to criticise Hanson when he was asked by broadcaster Neil Mitchell if he thought she was racist. At the very least, he could have said she had made racist remarks; he didn't even do that. All he could say was she had not said inappropriate things in her conversations with him. As if that was what mattered, rather than what she had been saying to the rest of us for 20 years. Instead of treating Hanson as the enemy, and her voters as his friends, by explaining in graphic detail where and why she was wrong, he sounded like he was playing footsie with her.

Although he toughened up his language, he kept waving his fig leaf about the party organisation having to decide, even after the first episode aired of an Al Jazeera sting, replete with hidden cameras and microphones, showed her chief of staff, James Ashby, and her Queensland Senate candidate, Steve Dickson, had the begging bowls out seeking cash from the American gun lobby so they could change Australia's tough gun laws. And this was after the massacre in the New Zealand mosques by an Australian white supremacist.

Two Liberal MPs – Victorians Tim Wilson and Kelly O'Dwyer – declared openly that they would put One Nation last, and cabinet ministers, including Simon Birmingham, were urging him to switch. Morrison finally relented when news of part two of the Al Jazeera documentary broke, showing Pauline Hanson propagating the evil notion that the Port Arthur massacre was really a conspiracy to change Australia's gun laws, enacted by John Howard in 1996.

Morrison's decision to preference One Nation after Labor was not supported by the Nationals, who regarded the Greens as a greater threat to Australia. Hanson called him a fool who had handed Shorten the keys to The Lodge. Talk of conspiracies flourished, as Alan Jones agreed with Hanson and accused Morrison of betraying conservatives.

There is no doubt it would have been much worse for Morrison if he had not moved at that point. There would have been a full-blown rebellion inside the Liberal Party, and the issue would have dogged him and every other Liberal all the way to the election, making it impossible to get any other message out.

He gained little credit for the decision, because he took too long to make it – he went too far for some, and not far enough for others – and even then had only got to that point kicking and screaming, forced by his colleagues and the weight of public opinion.

Until the preference debacle, war-weary Liberal MPs had suffered in (media) silence over his captain's calls, while they privately feared they were heading for annihilation.

In the early days, Morrison's keenness to accentuate the differences between himself and Turnbull looked natural. Then it looked as if he was trying a bit too hard. By the end of 2018, the whole Scomo thing, including a bus tour in Queensland on the Scomobile, was beginning to wear thin. He was losing the prime ministerial aura. The ordinary-bloke persona only works up to a point. First, no truly ordinary bloke gets to be prime minister; second, there is nothing wrong with having a prime minister a little less ordinary than yourself. He or she has to be all things to all people – someone in touch with the community, with their thinking as well as their needs, a good neighbour who also looks at ease on the world stage, and just that cut above the pack.

Morrison showcased his family, and he talked about his passion for cooking seafood curries, which was only exceeded by his passion for the Cronulla Sharks. His religion became an issue. Someone released footage of him praying. Rudd would do doorstops outside churches on a Sunday, which rubbed people up the wrong way because it looked – like everything else he did – too staged. With Morrison, it was genuine. Which was also disconcerting in its way, at least outside the Australian bible belts. Modern Australian had never had such an overtly religious prime minister before.

After having campaigned vigorously against same-sex marriage during the plebiscite, he followed up by advocating for greater protections for religious freedom, and early in his prime ministership, he promised he would press ahead with legislation to deliver on it. Morrison quietly dropped the idea before the election because of the internal divisions that it threatened to incite.

Initially, coalition MPs were encouraged by Morrison's performance. He was doing as well as could be expected under incredibly difficult circumstances. But was his best good enough?

Four weeks in, Morrison was determined that no one could say he wasn't giving it his best shot. In one of our early conversations, he was convinced he could replicate Paul Keating's feat when he won the unwinnable election against John Hewson in 1993. Morrison was hoping that Bill Shorten would be his Hewson. It took him a little more than two weeks to overtake Shorten as preferred prime minister, but a wide gap opened up in the two-party-preferred vote.

The first post-coup Newspoll showed support for the Coalition at its lowest for a decade, trailing Labor 44–56 per cent, which would see a loss of 30 seats. Given the government's instability, that poll was always bound to be a cracker, but it had a sobering effect. And it came two days after the Liberal vote in the New South Wales state seat of Wagga Wagga by-election had plummeted by 30 points. Although Gladys Berejiklian was having her own problems in New South Wales, part of the drop was attributed to the bloody Canberra games, which had gone from the parlour to the dungeon. Suddenly, the 10-point drop in Longman didn't seem so bad.

It stayed like that for the next Newspoll, which, if anything, was worse for the Coalition because Labor's primary vote had lifted. Gradually, the gap widened. Labor appeared, in those early stages, to be headed for a landslide victory.

Morrison's first outing as prime minister was to drought-affected parts of Queensland. Unlike Turnbull, who has a cattle property in the Hunter Valley, he freely confessed to not knowing one end of a sheep from another. And also unlike Turnbull, who had bought a new Akubra in Charleville (only to have people ridicule him by saying he bought it in Rose Bay) to wear when he was out at drought-stricken properties, Morrison visited Quilpie in south-west Queensland on 27 August, three days after the coup, wearing a baseball cap. The comparisons were irresistible.

Morrison was determined to present a different image, and the media helped him do it. It wasn't too long before they began to ridicule him for the baseball caps.

Where Turnbull went slowly, Morrison speeded up. As well as trying to model himself on Howard, he also saw himself as the political equivalent of former dual-code international rugby player Ray Price, aka Mr Perpetual Motion. There were blizzards of announcements and marginal-seat visits.

Where people thought Turnbull dithered, Morrison wanted to be seen as decisive. Sometimes it was impulsive, sometimes it worked, and sometimes he didn't give people enough time to absorb one good announcement before he swamped it with another.

Labor watched without worrying too much. They suspected he would either do himself in, or be done in by his own.

Morrison also overdid the empathetic daggy-dad bit. He was laying it on too thickly.

His language was direct and his messages were clear. People could understand what he was saying, but there was a feeling that something was missing – the mystique of office.

'He's the sort of guy you would get to do your books, not make prime minister,' was the acid assessment of one of his cabinet colleagues.

Another MP, summoned to a meeting late in the day, found himself watching the prime minister in his office eating a burger, still wrapped in foil, and chips. He found it unbecoming. Stories began appearing about his poor diet. Over summer, he appeared to put on weight.

Howard's signature walks in his newest track suit set a good example. Abbott's obsession with body image meant regular visits to the gym. Turnbull kayaked on the harbour or walked with Lucy. Shorten, overweight as a child, and chubby as an adult, took up running. All of them were better for it. The job is all-consuming, making exercise essential for physical as well as mental wellbeing. A few months later, Morrison let it be known that he was swimming regularly. He looked healthier, and his relaxed manner with people put them at ease.

Three months after Morrison's swearing-in, the Victorian election on 24 November 2018 sent tremors through the federal government. After the Wentworth by-election loss, there had been a good-riddance-to-bad-rubbish attitude from the mad right and the Turnbull haters, as if those voters were no longer needed nor welcomed in the Liberal Party. Guess what? They knew that. That's why so many of them had deserted. They did it again on a grander scale in Victoria.

Before the coup, Victorian Liberals said their research showed they were not travelling too badly. But as soon as Turnbull was deposed, the Victorian Liberal leader, Matthew Guy, knew he was in for it. Guy thought to himself, 'That's it.' Game over. He believed Turnbull's best bet after the first meeting was to call an election. No doubt that would have also helped Guy. The party's internal polling showed the coup had trashed the Liberal brand. Its net favourability rating fell to minus 17 per cent from the small positive rating it had held only a few months before. It never recovered. Bill Shorten had a favourability rating of minus 30, while Morrison's fell gradually from minus 2 to minus 8 to minus 15. The Victorians didn't want Morrison in the state campaign. He was scheduled to make one visit, which initially was to talk about funding for the East–West link; however, this changed after the Bourke St terrorism attack when Sisto Malaspina, the founder of Pellegrini's, was killed. Morrison and Guy went together to the famous Melbourne landmark to pay their respects.

Labor's giant billboards and advertising featured Morrison, Dutton, and Abbott with Guy. Just to give one example: opposite the suburban Frankston pre-poll on the side of a tall building was a giant photo of the state liberal leader, Guy, flanked by Morrison and Dutton with the slogan: *This Saturday stop liberal cuts to Frankston schools and hospitals.* Up and down the sandbelt seats, on the Frankston train line, there were swings to Labor of 10 per cent.

Even in his own electorate, at polling booths that were once his stronghold, Guy copped verbal abuse from voters about leadership instability. Guy had been leader for four years, with a united team. It didn't matter; they got splattered. As the election approached, the gap between the major parties narrowed, but there was still around 8 per cent undecided. They broke Labor's way.

Of course, it was not the only factor responsible for such a devastating loss. A poor campaign was not helped by a lack of money to run a mini-campaign in advance to build, or reshape, Guy's image, battered by the Lobster with the Mobster saga, when stories broke that he had dined with an alleged gangster at the Lobster Cave restaurant. Thanks to Michael Kroger's suit against the party's principal donor, the Cormack Foundation – a stroke of genius precipitated by the foundation's insistence that the party president should not also chair the finance committee – which polarised the party, and cost a fortune in legal fees, the cupboard was bare. The foundation had insisted on the change in the wake of the $1.5 million fraud conviction against the party's former state director Damian Mantach. The theft had occurred before Kroger's election, but his insistence on keeping both positions did not sit well with governance changes that the foundation believed were now essential. His suit against Liberal stalwarts Hugh Morgan and John Calvert Jones, who had spent a lifetime serving the party, and were original directors of the foundation that had been formed as an investment company in 1988 to raise funds for the Liberals, was costly both politically and financially.

It was not until Josh Frydenberg intervened and brokered a peace deal in October 2018 that the money began to flow again, but it was too late.

Months later, Labor staffers in Victoria were boasting that they were going to zero in on those Liberal MPs who had plotted against Turnbull to capitalise on the lingering anger. They were singling out seats like Flinders, where they believed Greg Hunt was especially vulnerable because of his role. Michael Sukkar was also looking shaky after state seats like Ringwood, which fell within the boundaries of his seat of Deakin, swung to Labor.

The party's research had shown that while Turnbull was a disappointment, he was not hated. He had clawed his way back to a positive rating, to the point where one state Liberal said he believed Turnbull's chances of winning were greater federally than that of the state Liberals in Victoria. Turnbull had sunk to around minus 8 as the end of 2017 approached, then swung back up in 2018 to plus 10. After their unsustainably high expectations of Turnbull waned, people had learned to live with their disappointments. There was a suspension of doorknocking and cold calling in some areas for a couple of weeks, because all that householders wanted to talk about was what had happened in Canberra.

It would be wrong to attribute a loss of that magnitude solely to Turnbull's demise; however, there is no doubt it was a significant factor. The fury over the coup, combined with a bad campaign, led by an inexperienced director and a state president who came across as remote from reality, were a deadly combination – particularly after Kroger had tried to shop around to the media phone footage of the police minister, Lisa Neville, at lunch the day after the Bourke St incident.

Media spurned it as a non-story. Neville, who had already fronted the media twice, turned up on the Saturday for lunch at a restaurant called Trunk, where Kroger was also lunching with the state director, Nick Demiris, and long-serving Liberal operative Ian Hanke, so they filmed her. They argued to Guy's media advisor, Tony Barry, that it fell into the same category as former police commissioner Christine Nixon visiting the hairdressers and then going to dinner during the catastrophic Black Saturday bushfires in 2009. Barry argued that there was no comparison, and refused to have anything to do with it. State political reporters refused to touch it. The premier, Daniel Andrews, was furious when he heard that Kroger himself was shopping it around.

On *Insiders* the day after the election, Andrews said he hoped Kroger stayed president for life. 'I don't often commentate on our political opponent [Kroger], but you know, swanning around the suburbs that you've never been to in your Burberry trench coat, lecturing people about the cost of living – people pick fakes, and they pick nasty fakes from a long way off,' Andrews said.

The Liberal Party's broad church appeared to be crumbling.

Too often, it chased what it called the base, a dwindling, ageing membership. In Queensland, many of them were One Nation outcasts; in Victoria, refugees from Family First, or recruited directly from Mormon churches, where they were promised that their conservative views would gain prominence through their force of numbers. In Western Australia, veteran Liberals complained that the 'happy clappers' had taken over. The acquisition of these ultraconservatives encouraged the desertion of the traditional small-l Liberal voting base.

As one senior Victorian Liberal put it, 'We not only lost the doctors' wives, we lost the doctors, too.'

The dominance of the hard right, if not numerically then in its exercise of power, was threatening to turn the party into a rump, retaining only a cluster of seats north and west. The party seemed incapable of speaking to young people and women.

After the Victorian election, Morrison did the smart thing politically by calling a meeting of the state's federal Liberal MPs to allow them to vent, and vent they did. Kelly O'Dwyer warned that the party was seen as homophobic, anti-women climate-change deniers. 'It has to stop,' she said, regretting the demise of the-live-and-let-live philosophy of the Liberal Party she had joined as a teenager. O'Dwyer demanded Kroger's immediate resignation as state president, even though there was no obvious replacement. After years of bitter rivalry, coupled with his culpability for the loss, she wanted him gone.

Scott Ryan was sick of the delcons, and sick of the lectures from the hosts on Sky after Dark. He put it only a little less bluntly when he pleaded for greater tolerance, saying that Liberals did not want views rammed down their throats, nor to be subjected to litmus tests for what it meant to be a real Liberal. Michael Sukkar thought they were all getting carried away with themselves, until one of his and Kroger's allies wrote a blistering email about the party, the president, the state director, the leader, and the election result, which leaked. Kroger had been angling to stay on until March, when his term expired, but after federal vice-president Karina Okotel – one of his ultra-conservative protegés, who authored the email – called it the worst campaign ever, and accused everyone involved of driving them off a cliff, Kroger resigned.

Victorian state voters had ripped the heart out of the Liberal heartland. A 71-year-old living in a retirement village beat John Pesutto, a leadership contender in the blue-ribbon Liberal seat of Hawthorn. In the blue-ribbon seat of Brighton, a 19-year-old spent $1,750 and almost beat newbie Liberal James Newbury. These were not high-profile, cashed-up independents. In Malvern, the swing was 10.1 per cent; in Ringwood, 7.9 per cent. Nepean was lost with a swing of 8.6 per cent. On those figures, Josh Frydenberg, Greg Hunt, Michael Sukkar, and O'Dwyer were about to experience a world of pain. These were not omens – they were messages. Voters were well informed about which of their MPs had been involved in the August coup. It wasn't so much because they liked Turnbull, although clearly many Victorians did. Those who didn't were nonetheless fed up with the game-playing that had delivered three Liberal prime ministers in three years. If MPs were busy plotting, it meant they were not concentrating on governing.

Newbury said later that voters were sick of the spin, and sick of the internal games. He had clung on with a margin of 1.1 per cent, in a seat held by the Liberals or their historical predecessors since 1856, partly because he had worked the electorate hard for two years. Liberals voted for him through gritted teeth, but one in five who did so said they would not be voting Liberal federally.

State Liberals believe that Labor collected data from the same-sex marriage plebiscite to target Liberal voters. The vote had been highest in many safe Liberal seats, so Labor rightly guessed that those voters might be more sympathetic on issues like safe schools and injecting rooms. Conservatives would later rail against the folly of the plebiscite. The problem was that right-wing MPs in Canberra had been violently opposed to a free vote, which would have been cleaner, safer, and cheaper. They insisted on a plebiscite, hoping it would never happen, even though they knew it would show their opponents in Labor and GetUp! where their soft voters were.

Afterwards, Morrison sent Guy a long text, commiserating, urging him to look after himself, and finished by saying his 'thoughts and prayers' were with him.

Then the year ended as badly as it had begun, with another National MP with doodle problems.

Hopes of finishing the year on a positive note vanished with publication of the revelations of Andrew Broad's crude sexting of a sugar babe. Broad gazumped what was billed as the best economic news in a decade. As luck would have it – and, in politics, everyone needs at least a grain of it – *New Idea* revealed Broad's attempted dalliance with a Hong Kong–based young woman looking for a sugar daddy on the same day that Josh Frydenberg and Mathias Cormann released the Mid-Year Economic and Fiscal Outlook, which projected the first surplus in more than 11 years, healthy economic growth, more-than-respectable jobs growth, and even a tick-up in wages growth. Spending was down, welfare payments were down, and tax receipts from companies and people in work were up.

All of this was swept away by Broad's inability to keep his mind on his day job, which of course he ended up losing as a result. It was made worse because McCormack knew it was coming, as did the prime minister's office.

They didn't have all the gory details, including text messages sent by Broad, such as: 'I'm an Aussie lad, I know how to ride a horse, fly a plane and f..k my woman. My intentions are completely dishonourable.'

Perhaps too squeamish to ask Broad all the tough questions, it looked as if, once Broad had given them the broad outline, they had all sat down in the middle of the tracks waiting for the train to arrive.

Broad's colleagues, Libs and Nats alike, didn't know whether to laugh or cry. Broad, another vocal opponent of same-sex marriage on the grounds that it would weaken traditional marriage, who had lectured Barnaby Joyce on the importance of character, resigned as an assistant minister, and then announced he would not be recontesting his hitherto ultra-safe seat of Mallee at the election.

The timing made talk of a possible return of Joyce to the leadership untenable. In January, Joyce and Campion let it be known they were having another baby; then, undeterred, he resumed his quest to regain the leadership.

Just as Nationals MPs were asking if it could get worse (and the answer is yes, always) stories appeared soon after about the frequent travels to Asia of George Christensen. Christensen was cleared of any wrongdoing by a police investigation, but there was a follow-up a few months later stating he had spent 294 days over four years in the Philippines. For a whopping 11 weeks every year, this marginal-seat holder was absent from his electorate. He was called the Member for Manila, and the story broke while Morrison was dodging the One Nation preference issue. Christensen was one of those desperate for a preference deal with One Nation to save his backside, when perhaps closer personal attention to his electorate was what was needed.

The loss of New South Wales Nationals' seats to the Shooters, Fishers and Farmers party in the state election showed how damaged their brand was.

None of it augured well for the upcoming federal election.

The Reverend Bill Crews, whose work feeding the homeless and caring for the poor has brought him into contact with countless politicians, summed it up aptly, if depressingly, by saying that when it came to sex or greed or power – or the prospect of power – ethics and rules fell by the wayside.

The government had hoped that the release of the Mid-Year Economic and Fiscal Outlook that day would gazump Labor's national conference, which began on Sunday 16 December. Labor had switched to December after the Turnbull government decided to hold the super Saturday by-elections the same weekend as Labor's conference, scheduled in July.

On Saturday 15 December, Morrison announced his inelegant dismount on Australia's embassy in Israel, saying that even though his government now recognised West Jerusalem as the capital, the embassy would stay in Tel Aviv until a peace agreement was reached between Israel and the Palestinians.

At the same time on Sunday as Bill Shorten was timed to deliver his keynote conference speech, Morrison announced that Australia's new governor-general would be the serving governor of New South Wales, retired army general David Hurley. Morrison emphasised that Hurley was his first and only choice. It was safe, it was predictable, it was dull. It was exactly what he and his advisers wanted – a story that would disappear in a day.

Hurley was widely respected. He was a decent man with a lovely family. But Morrison missed an opportunity to heal rifts in his own party and to show women that a Liberal prime minister could find a place for them in the country's highest offices. Julie Bishop would have been a great choice, but Morrison wanted no bar of her in the job. In any case, if not her, then why not another woman?

There were more than 12 million of them – more women than men in Australia. Surely one of them was capable of doing the job? Instead, it went to another bloke who already had a job. The leading Liberal in the country could not see, again, that his party had a problem with women, and that just maybe here was an opportunity to correct that. He finally got the message and redressed the balance when he decided over summer that he would appoint Ita Buttrose as the new chair of the ABC after the head-hunters had given him a choice of three men. Following the resignations of male ministers, he appointed more women to the cabinet – a record seven.

Then, to cap off a great year, a Newspoll analysis in *The Australian* on 26 December showed that, on almost every measure, Turnbull and his government had been ahead of Morrison and his government. It all pointed to a wipe-out in Queensland, all the way down into Victoria. Happy Christmas, prime minister.

The Liberal brand was so damaged that internal polling in some seats in late 2018 showed that without the candidate's name, the Liberal vote dropped 13 per cent. Some lucky Liberals found that with their name attached, they had a slight swing to them; others, that their name added more than 10 per cent to the primary vote, although in some cases they feared that would not be enough.

Morrison decided to kick off the election year by restarting the debate on Australia Day celebrations. He was insisting that 26 January should be the one-and-only date on which councils could conduct citizenship ceremonies – neither the night before nor the day after – or lose the right to conduct them at all. On top of that, he said he thought there should be a dress code.

The fashion police were going to run the nanny state.

This was the same bloke who turned up for his official shoot for his official Christmas card in a crummy pair of sneakers that public servants felt needed some whitening to look decent. Morrison, who had played no part in the photoshopping, which also gave him two left feet, joked that they should have started at the other end to give him more hair, but social media was flooded with shots of him in lairy, striped daggy-dad shorts.

'He was never a policy guy, never an ideas guy. And nobody wants to be lectured to by someone who wasn't elected,' said one former party official who knew Morrison well, stretching back to his time as New South Wales state director, when he ran the losing election campaign for John Brogden. Morrison had a poisonous relationship with Brogden. They had to communicate via intermediaries, including Brogden's chief of staff, David Gazard, who went on to become one of Morrison's best friends.

Others who worked closely with Morrison also referred to his detachment from policy formulation. The suite of policies that stopped the boats was put together by Jim Molan. The budgets that he delivered were largely of Turnbull's and Cormann's making.

According to someone who worked closely with Morrison in government, 'The only thing I have ever known him to show passionate belief in is his opposition to same-sex marriage.'

Morrison's effectiveness as a politician lay in his ability to barrel through. Give him a mission, and he devotes all his energy to bringing it home. His forceful personality, plus his single-minded determination to achieve his objective, were two of the reasons why, in April 2010, in a column published by *The Australian*, I became the first to nominate him as a future leader for the Liberal Party. Of course, there was no knowing then how or when, but from where I sat, it seemed he had the talent, the ambition, and the drive to get there.

The government was bracing for a torrid time when parliament resumed in February, but it went better than expected. In the first week of the sitting, Labor's decision to vote for a crossbench bill to bring refugees on Manus and Nauru to Australia for medical treatment, the so-called medevac bill, was manna from heaven.

On 12 February, for the first time in 90 years, a government was beaten on a substantive motion on the floor of the House, but Morrison skilfully managed to turn a tactical defeat into a strategic victory on boats.

If he had deemed the bill a confidence motion in the government, he could have called a snap election. He argued to his MPs that the government needed more than the boats issue; it needed the budget as well. However, without the election, the government's rhetoric lacked heft, and sounded like what it was – a scare campaign. There was too much huffing and puffing, and an ill-advised stunt with a visit to a briefly re-opened Christmas Island.

On 13 February, the night of the Minerals Council annual dinner, Labor frontbencher Kim Carr was only slightly taken aback when one of his companions at the table told him, 'Don't you stuff it up like we did.'

That remark confirmed for Carr that the skirmish over asylum-seekers had done nothing to change the political fundamentals. Even more so because the person who uttered it was the Liberal Party's former federal director, Brian Loughnane, who was there with his wife, Peta Credlin. The tenor of the conversation, at that table at least, was that the government was finished and that Labor would soon be governing.

Elsewhere, Labor MPs from further north, while agreeing that the government was 'cooked', were not convinced that Shorten's support for the medevac bill was all that smart. Every day we spend talking about boats is a bad day, Queenslander Graham Perrett said. Nevertheless, Perrett's assessment of the mood up his way was 'not as good as 2007 (when Rudd won so handsomely), and not as bad as 2013 (when Abbott won so handsomely).'

Inside the government, morale was up – a few even dared to think victory might just be possible – when, in the second week, the government was hit by the Helloworld scandal. It was revealed that Mathias Cormann had not paid $2,700 for tickets for himself and his family to Singapore in mid-2017. It was bad enough that Cormann claimed he hadn't noticed he hadn't been charged. It was made worse by the fact he had personally rung the Helloworld chief executive, Andrew Burnes, to ask him to make the bookings, saying he had given him his credit-card number. Burnes also happened to be treasurer of the federal Liberal Party.

It was a resounding fail on the pub test for Cormann, followed by more grief for the government after it transpired that Australia's ambassador to the US, Joe Hockey, also a very good friend of Burnes, had intervened on behalf of Helloworld in discussions about the travel requirements of the embassy.

The national accounts in March showed there was a per capita recession, which few people had ever heard of before, but it sounded bad, and came after Morrison was warning that Labor would tip the economy into recession if elected, and now it looked like it could happen under his watch. Turnbull and Abbott reignited their climate wars, and Morrison went backwards when he said in a speech to mark International Women's Day that their advancement should not come at the expense of men. How else exactly that would happen, he did not make clear. He often mucked up his words or grabs, and this was a premeditated doozy.

Hopes of a slight recovery in Newspoll were dashed, and morale plummeted again, only to be revived on 23 March with a stunning victory in New South Wales by Gladys Berejiklian, the first woman to be elected premier of the state.

Berejiklian won because she was competent and hard-working, and avoided the culture wars that plagued the Liberal Party to govern from the centre. And because her opponent, Michael Daley, self-destructed in the final week of the campaign. Again, local Liberals did not embrace Morrison in the campaign. He was invited to Berejiklian's launch, but was not allowed to speak.

No matter. The lessons were obvious. The result showed that with an effective campaign, a resilient economy, a record of delivery, a respected leader, and a weak opposition leader struggling with the detail of his own policies, anything was possible.

The Liberals went into the election campaign not only thinking that they might get out of it with a respectable loss, but that, in spite of everything, they might even manage to stumble over the line. For the first time, many of them could see the pathway to victory that Morrison always believed existed. It gave them the one ingredient that had gone missing months before. Hope.

CHAPTER FIFTEEN

In God's hands

On the night before the election, as he prepared to fly to Tasmania to make one last pitch to voters in Braddon and Bass – two seats that Labor didn't even consider to be in play – Scott Morrison sent a text to Josh Frydenberg.

Morrison, who had spent every day on the campaign trail declaring it a contest between himself and Bill Shorten – burying the tainted Liberal brand, hiding unpopular members of his cabinet (like his environment minister, Melissa Price), and erasing memories of the bloody recent past – paid a glowing tribute to his deputy for his work as treasurer, for his loyalty, and for contributing to the party's latter-day unity and stability.

He finished by declaring, 'It's in God's hands,' adding, 'I believe in miracles.'

And so it came to pass. That night, when he claimed victory, as he stood on the stage with his wife, Jenny, and their two daughters, Lily and Abbey, the children they had struggled to have, Morrison told exuberant Liberals, 'I have always believed in miracles! I'm standing with the three biggest miracles in my life here tonight – and tonight we've been delivered another one.'

Apart from his family, faith has been the constant in his life. It is an integral part of his physical and emotional infrastructure, the source of his infinite self-belief. His confidence that he could win never waned, and it was the one thing about him that made the biggest impression on colleagues, staff, and friends as he criss-crossed the country day and night for months, drinking beers, eating pies, meeting voters, and schmoozing with journos.

Despite all the published polls, all the predictions, all the darkest fears of his colleagues, he single-handedly, single-mindedly won a slim majority by making the choices clear. Voters could either have him, or Bill Shorten, he kept telling them. They could have a strong economy with him in charge, or Labor's $347 billion in extra taxes. He never deviated. Beyond the personal income tax cuts that had been included in the budget, and a late plan for the government to go guarantor for deposits from young first-home buyers, he did not promise anything, other than himself – always accompanied by verbal or visual images of disaster if Shorten were to win. It was the most effective negative campaign, executed brilliantly by Morrison, co-ordinated by Andrew Hirst, the federal director handpicked for the job by Malcolm Turnbull, now elevated to hero status in the Liberal Party, who would have had the same mechanics in place and who would have run the same ground campaign for his old boss.

It was a stunning victory, against all the odds, especially in the wake of the trauma triggered by the events of August. The desire to win is a powerful motivator. Or, as Samuel Johnson famously said, back in the 18th century, 'When a man knows he is to be hanged in a fortnight, it concentrates his mind wonderfully.'

Morrison was transformed into a Liberal legend, winning enormous authority in the party and over the government, equal to John Howard after he wiped the floor with Mark Latham in 2004, even though the nature of Morrison's campaign did not even provide his MPs with a clear idea of where he would lead them, or what his plans were. When Leigh Sales asked him on ABC's *7.30* who would have the upper hand in driving policy if he were re-elected, Morrison replied meaningfully with two words: 'I will.'

That sent a shiver up the spines of more than one government MP, particularly those who had been on the receiving end of his temper. Whether in opposition or in government at the most senior levels, politics is a high-pressure, high-stress environment, and Morrison has not succeeded as well as he has in such a short space of time by being faint-hearted. But this also meant he had few close friends in the government.

One cabinet minister who had gone toe to toe with him a number of times confided that a few of his colleagues felt intimidated by him. Turnbull could be cutting, but colleagues also found the good Malcolm warm, and excellent company. Sometimes they did not know what to make of Morrison.

Tony Eggleton was fond of describing Turnbull as the prime minister from central casting, and it is true he always looked the part. He was highly intelligent, charming when he wanted to be, generous with both his time and money, and amusing – occasionally when he didn't intend to be. Like when he had just finished reading a fascinating article in *Le Figaro* on a global issue and offered to share it, saying, 'You can read French, can't you?' *Er no, I can barely read English, but thanks anyway, just a one-par summary would be great.*

The delcons aside, Turnbull was not hated by voters. They were disappointed by him, not repelled. He had a shyness about him that made him seem aloof, and he often displayed a certain diffidence in groups. He exuded intellectual superiority, but once at ease or engaged, he could win over a room or an interviewer. While his critics were profoundly irritated that he knew so much about so many things – and condemned him for always being the smartest person in the room and making it so obvious that he was – others were impressed by the breadth and depth of his interests, and were drawn to him because of it. His style and personality was in stark contrast to Morrison's, who is described by those close to him as a decent, 'big, boofy guy' with a big, boofy personality to match, who fills a room, and bounds around hugging and back-slapping, looking natural and in touch, but with an ego that can bruise people or topple furniture.

Like Turnbull, Morrison has a much less charming side witnessed often by colleagues; however, after he was elected in his own right, senior frontbenchers were confident (or hopeful) that he would keep his temper in check; that if he was presented with facts that contradicted his view, and people stood their ground with him and were able to swing him around, he would not hold a grudge or punish them for it. They believed he had a good strategic sense of where he wanted to position the government in three years' time. Morrison might not have been a policy guru, but he had always been clear about his objectives and what needed to be done to achieve them.

Perhaps sensing the nervousness aroused by his constant campaign refrain of 'Me, me, me,' Morrison reassured people he would govern from the middle for quiet Australians. As the campaign drew to a close, he ventured that it was not about him – it was about them.

He showed both his political smarts and the extent of his authority when he announced his cabinet and ministry. In his first post-election meeting with public service chiefs, he ordered them to concentrate on service delivery, and then structured the portfolios accordingly on his frontbench.

Those who helped him get there were kept close. Despite his magnetic attraction for controversies, Stuart Robert went into cabinet, Alex Hawke became a minister, and Steve Irons became an assistant minister. Morrison kept Ben Morton even closer as assistant minister to the prime minister and cabinet. Michael Sukkar was partially rehabilitated, and others close to Dutton, such as Trevor Evans and Luke Howarth, were also rewarded with assistant-minister positions.

Arthur Sinodinos could have had a cabinet post, but when Morrison offered him the American ambassadorship, he took it. Mitch Fifield, already in cabinet, could have stayed, but chose instead to accept Morrison's offer of ambassador to the United Nations in New York. Both men had been involved in politics, one way or another, for decades. The time was right for them to go. Their departures robbed the government of two safe pairs of hands, but enabled Morrison to move another friend, Alan Tudge, who had backed Dutton and who was also another true believer in the true sense, into cabinet.

The Liberals' woman problem evaporated after Tanya Plibersek withdrew from the Labor leadership race and Morrison appointed a record seven women to his cabinet. More Liberal women and more Nationals women had been elected to the House and to the Senate, quietening, for the time being at least, the debate about the party's ability to attract women.

Ken Wyatt's appointment as the first indigenous person to be promoted to cabinet and to be made minister for indigenous Australians was generally well received, raising hopes that a conservative government would take up the challenge of Aboriginal reconciliation. However, despite Wyatt's assurances that he would not rush into anything, conservative commentators were already on guard, warning Morrison he risked inciting divisions if he pressed ahead with any plans for indigenous recognition in the constitution, or for a separate voice for indigenous peoples.

Morrison had moderates on his frontbench, but it was clearly weighted to the right.

There was also a whiff of the Howards about Christian Porter's new roles. Porter remained attorney-general, with the addition of industrial relations. He also became Leader of the House, the high-profile position left vacant by Christopher Pyne's departure. Any one of those positions is a full-time job. To other Liberals, it looked like Morrison had set the scene for creative tension between Porter and Frydenberg, whose leadership ambitions were also well known and never denied. It worked well for Howard to have Peter Costello and Peter Reith competing for years, rather than to have one clear rival whenever the question of succession came up. Morrison knew his history.

Regardless of the party-room rule changes that have made it difficult to remove sitting prime ministers, and despite his unexpected victory, the political parlour games will never stop. They are a fact of life for every any leader in whatever party. They will intensify for Morrison whenever the government suffers the inevitable stresses of office, particularly with so many vexed issues remaining unresolved after the election: climate change, energy, religious freedoms. Economic and industrial reforms were also left untouched. Governments do not have the luxury of marking time. Nor can they get away with leaving vacuums, or with thinking that perpetual campaigning can substitute for governing, or keep pointing at what the opposition is doing wrong and profiting from it. Unfortunately, Morrison's lack of an agenda during the campaign also meant that he lacked a governing mandate, beyond personal income tax cuts, other budget measures, and the home deposit scheme. So in a parliament where every independent or crossbencher claimed a mandate simply by virtue of being there, where the government's improved position in the Senate had still fallen short of a majority, and at a time when the economy appeared to be softening, tough times beckoned.

Even with the tax cuts, there was a bit of trickiness involved. Morrison used them as fall-back on the rare occasions on the campaign trail when he was asked about his plans for government, saying they would be legislated immediately after the election was over. Within days of his re-election, he had to fess up and admit that in fact they couldn't be legislated immediately. Parliament could not be recalled in time to have them dealt with before the beginning of the new financial year, because the election writs would not be returned until 28 June.

Obviously he knew this when the election was called, so somehow forgetting to mention it was a very shabby beginning for Morrison. Worse followed, then much worse. Burned by its decision to increase interest rates during the 2007 election campaign – which was actually a sign of the economy strengthening – the Reserve Bank held off cutting interest rates until after the election, helping the government avoid pesky questions during the campaign about whether the economy was tanking.

The cut came in the middle of raids by the Australian Federal Police on journalists. The home of News Corp's Annika Smethurst was raided more than a year after she had broken an important story about plans to give spy agencies additional powers to spy on Australians, and the ABC was raided over an equally important story two years before by Dan Oakes and Sam Clark on allegations of unlawful killings and misconduct by Australian special forces in Afghanistan.

If there was an upside for the government, it was that the raids smothered the bad news about the economy. Morrison, in a familiar tactic (it was the pastor who let the cameras into the church; he didn't authorise Stuart Robert to count numbers for him) initially tried to argue it had nothing to do with him, and that the cops were simply upholding the law. Then, when all Australian media groups condemned the raids and the chilling effect they would have on news gathering, press freedom, and the media's ability to hold the government to account, and the controversy became worldwide news, he said he was open to having another look at the laws over which he happens to preside as prime minister.

Morrison's first nine months as prime minister had generally been lacklustre. His captain's calls (moving the embassy in Israel, imposing Warren Mundine in Gilmore) backfired, and he could be shouty in parliament.

As a campaigner, he was near faultless. But campaigning is not governing. Different rules apply; different skills are needed. Initially, Coalition colleagues are so grateful to be returned, they are prepared to – briefly – forgive almost anything. Then, whether Liberal or National, they get resentful if they feel they are being overlooked or taken for granted, and then turn hostile if the leader fails to consult them or mishandles issues. Victory restored Morrison's prime ministerial aura, but there was no knowing how long it would last.

Besides, even those who believed in miracles knew how much work had been undertaken behind the scenes by earthly beings to deliver them.

The party organisation had done everything it humanly could to help him win, and to avoid a repetition of 2016. In February 2019, after conducting regular reviews of Andrew Robb's recommendations, a final internal assessment of the Liberals' preparedness was presented to the party's federal executive meeting in Canberra, and endorsed. Under Nick Greiner as president (also chosen by Turnbull), and Hirst as federal director, the executive had combed through Andrew Robb's review. With three months remaining until the election, they had all been listed and implemented. Greiner, who had a good political and business brain, was the chairman of the board; unbelievably, the hard right, with its penchant for self-harm, would have dumped him if it had been able to muster the numbers.

Hirst loved election campaigns, despite the fact that as a young junior staffer he had spent his first one in 2004 proofing transcripts in John Howard's press office before going on to work for a succession of Liberal leaders. His father, Gordon, and his mother, Jan, had also been political staffers, so he had a genetic predilection for politics. Bright and eager, he reckons his first campaign experience taught him the importance of accuracy in grunt work.

As the political year – an election year – got under way, party officials were confident there would be no repeat of the great mistakes of the previous election. Shorten would be well defined, and the negative campaign would be prominent and unrelenting. They could always do with more money, but fundraising was continuing apace; in fact, despite a pause after the leadership switch, fundraising resumed well under Morrison – perhaps even better than under Turnbull – and there was enough money to fund a vigorous negative advertising campaign. Marginal-seat polling had been undertaken, a data-analytics unit was established, and clear-cut messaging would ensure that voters would be left in no doubt about the choices they faced.

And so all that came to pass, too. The campaign would prove how well prepared they were, how accurate their polling, and how deadly their research.

After inviting tenders, the Liberals chose KWP! Advertising, which had run the successful South Australian state election campaign. The campaign was headquartered in Brisbane, a symbolically important gesture that also gave them instant access to local media and electoral hotspots. All was right with the world when former Howard advancer Jodie Doodt found a coffee shop that would open for them at 5.30 am. With more than 100 people at headquarters desperate for regular caffeine hits, it was a smart move by the small-business owner.

Around Australia, the party had at its service a blend of the experienced and the battle-hardy, such as Chris Stone, who had just completed Gladys Berejiklian's winning campaign. In Victoria, newly appointed state director Simon Frost was picking up the pieces of a shattered party, while Sam Calabrese in the west had found his feet. Tasmania, with popular figures like the premier, Will Hodgman, and senator Richard Colbeck, was continuing to move towards the Liberals. In South Australia, the premier, Steve Marshall, seldom left the side of Nicolle Flint, who was under extreme threat in Boothby in the wake of her role in the coup.

The organisation had done everything it could to ensure that the big things they were responsible for could be controlled. The personalities, the normal tensions, and the stuff-ups of every campaign, overlaid by the lingering bitterness of the 2018 coup, could not. But a narrowing in the polls as the campaign was called, along with recent proof from New South Wales that campaigns can win elections, encouraged warring MPs to call a truce.

A number of Liberals took other precautions. On a giant billboard in his electorate of Deakin, where Shorten kicked off his campaign, Michael Sukkar could not find room to inscribe the word 'Liberal'. Sukkar, recognised as one of the party's best on-the-ground campaigners, easily held on to his seat. With people dressed in dinosaur suits campaigning against Tony Abbott in Warringah, candidates like Dave Sharma in Wentworth and Tim Wilson in Goldstein decided it was prudent to cast themselves as 'Modern' Liberals.

On the day of Morrison's official launch, which turned into a celebration of him and his family, the Liberal logo was barely visible, tucked away in the bottom-left-hand corner of the screen behind him, hardly ever in shot during his long speech. You needed binoculars to see it.

The Coalition's essential message was crystallised in its advertising in print and across all media platforms. Distilled from focus-group research, it became the bunting wrapped around every polling booth in the country on election day, which in turn had been reinforced by Morrison at every press conference, in every speech, in every debate, every day, from the beginning. Featuring an unflattering photo of Shorten, it warned of 'The Bill Australia Can't Afford. Higher taxes, more debt, a weak economy.'

While this worked a treat as a negative, it also played in a positive way into the coalition's greatest strengths: the economy and budget management.

Frydenberg's 2019 budget themes and content were pre-tested, perhaps more than any of its predecessors. Staff looked up Peter Costello's quote from his 1998 budget, shamelessly plagiarising it word for word to frame Frydenberg's. 'Back in the black, back on track' worked as well 21 years later as it did for Costello – even if, on the night, Frydenberg's surplus was a forecast, not an outcome.

After Frydenberg's confident delivery, the prime minister, his office, and the treasurer's office had their traditional late-night phone hook-up with the Crosby Textor polling team to go through the focus-group reaction to the speech. The surprise hit was the package of assistance for mental health. It registered on two levels: because it was a good idea, and because people were surprised it had come from a Coalition government.

'It is a national tragedy that we lose so many people to suicide and that so many people live a life of quiet desperation,' Frydenberg said (in another steal, this time from Henry David Thoreau) in announcing the $461 million package for a youth mental-health and suicide-prevention strategy. The package, drawing on Morrison's own interactions with groups like Lifeline, and his concerns as the father of two girls growing up in the fraught environment of social-media influences, had been developed inside his office.

Nine days later, at 6.30 am, Morrison's chief of staff, John Kunkel, arrived at The Lodge. Ben Morton was already there. Morrison had flown in the night before, and word had already seeped out he was set to visit the governor-general to call the election for 18 May. Morrison tweaked his themes with Kunkel, Morton, and others before his press conference: a strong economy, more jobs, both without the burden of higher taxes, and a choice between him and Shorten.

'You will get to decide between a government that has fixed the budget, or Bill Shorten's Labor Party that we always know can't manage money,' he said. 'You will have a choice between a government that is lowering taxes for all Australians, or Bill Shorten's Labor Party that will impose higher taxes that will weigh down our economy. It's taken us more than five years to turn around Labor's budget mess. Now is not the time to turn back.' He did not deviate from these lines for the entire campaign, all 38 days of it (from 11 April to 18 May). Morton, who never thought Turnbull had the discipline to stick to a message, stuck like glue to Morrison while he did it, as did Morrison's chief political adviser, Yaron Finkelstein. Kunkel spent most of the campaign at party headquarters.

Senior Labor figures were torn between admiration and anger. They tipped their hat to his discipline and his success in making Shorten the issue, but reckoned it was shameless nonetheless that he could get away with not announcing any policies or vision.

Shorten's chief of staff, Ryan Liddell, who was well liked and well regarded, later admitted that the opposition leader got off to a shaky start, with a couple of early stumbles, but regrouped. Nevertheless, Liddell was frustrated because everyone, including journalists, believed that Shorten was assured of winning, and were therefore tougher on him than on Morrison. He reckoned they let Morrison get away with not answering questions, not producing any policies, and not coming under any pressure for it.

In other words, it was a reversal of 2016. And it was a role reversal in another important sense: Morrison was behaving like an opposition leader, rolled up into a small target, while Shorten was presenting himself as the prime minister in waiting, with a huge reform agenda.

At no point during the campaign did Morrison or his team believe they were done for, or that Labor appeared set to win – although when Newspoll on the last day showed Labor had gone up slightly on its two-party-preferred vote, hearts skipped a few beats.

They were taken aback at how bad Labor's campaign was on the ground and in the air, how inaccurate its polling was, and how poorly Shorten was performing.

After his early blunders, Shorten rallied for a bit, and then continued to make mistakes in the final days. Morrison went out of his way to get the travelling media onside with regular off-the-record drinks sessions and even a game of mini-golf. Shorten had a different approach. After he was told that Channel 10 reporter Jonathan Lea had been assigned to cover him, Shorten unwisely whispered in the ear of another journalist that Lea was a 'c…'. Shorten had also previously asked one of Lea's superiors when he was going to get rid of that 'dickhead'. Nervous staffers told the executive that Shorten was only kidding.

Then came a fateful press conference.

Lea created damaging headlines for Shorten in the very first week of the campaign by angrily persisting with questions to him to reveal the cost of his climate-change policies. Shorten could not or would not answer. Combined with his mucking-up of a question from Sky's James O'Doherty about any future action on superannuation, which betrayed his poor grasp of his own policies, it was a rocky beginning for the opposition leader. It showed again how, with just a few questions, journalists can derail the most carefully planned campaign.

Shorten also did not know how much electric vehicles cost, nor how long it would take to charge them, despite announcing that he wanted a million of them on Australian roads by 2030. From then on, he was surrounded at media events by frontbenchers with a grasp of policy detail. He tried to make a virtue of necessity by promoting his team, but Liberals chortled that this only emphasised his weaknesses and Morrison's strengths.

Labor's launch, which again showcased his team and its unity, with the presence of Julia Gillard, Kevin Rudd, and Paul Keating, was derailed by Keating with an impromptu interview with the ABC's Andrew Probyn, when he said the heads of security agencies were nutters who should be sacked to repair Australia's relations with China. The arrogance of Labor's campaign was twice highlighted by Penny Wong – first in her launch speech by referring to the 'small men' of the Liberal Party, and then by refusing to shake Simon Birmingham's hand after a debate in which he dared mention Keating's nuttiness.

Shorten steadied, and then made a few very bad calls.

He won the first two debates against Morrison, then went on to win the final debate, narrowly, hours after an emotional press conference in which he took *The Daily Telegraph* to task over its treatment of his account of his mother's life. Voters paid attention to big moments – the debates, the soap opera surrounding Pauline Hanson's Senate candidate Steve Dickson succumbing to Strippergate, the party launches. In the humdrum of the campaign, the story about Shorten's mother, Ann, penetrated. Although he had told the story of her life often, he had omitted a detail when he retold it on ABC's *Q&A* a few nights before. The *Telegraph* splashed with a cutting headline: 'Mother of Invention'.

The previous day, Labor's campaign headquarters had received what was later described as a 'relatively innocent' email from the author of the article, Anna Caldwell, asking basic questions about Shorten's mother. Later, Shorten's team was tipped off by another journalist that the story was going to be a 'hatchet job'. They spoke to the paper's editor, Ben English, who told them it would be a front-page story with a double-page spread inside. Shorten, described as 'incredibly upset' by what he saw as an attack on his dead mother, prepared a statement that was posted online as soon as the story appeared.

Shorten's office maintains the story was pushed by a Liberal press secretary, without the full knowledge of senior Liberal campaign officials. When questioned the next day, Morrison and Frydenberg denied the party was behind it, and Morrison also criticised the *Telegraph* story. Increasing the frustration of the Shorten team with the media, other journalists claiming they had also been approached to run it refused to publicly name the press secretary responsible, because they felt it would be dobbing in a source.

Tabloids will be tabloids, but the treatment of the story became a story itself, raising questions of bias. During a 10-minute answer, when he choked back tears, Shorten went after News Corp as he recounted his mother's life and career.

It was his finest moment in the campaign. For someone so often described as wooden, programmed, or insincere, he was raw and emotional, speaking from the heart. 'It humanised him,' one Liberal campaign staffer said later, admitting that it was one of the big moments that broke through. The story, defended by the paper and its author, was clearly not designed to help him, although there is no doubt it did – maybe too much.

Either emboldened by his trifecta of wins in the debates, or fired up because he thought the Liberals were behind an attack on his dead mother, Shorten took the fight up to Morrison.

Morrison's religion had been bubbling away as an issue well before the campaign began.

There was the look and sound of the evangelical preacher as he revved up his audience. 'How good is Australia/Jenny/Sarah/Gladys?' he would often ask the crowd, depending on who or what was before him. He described people as 'agents of God's love', and in his final major address at the National Press Club used a phrase favoured by Pentecostal Christians when he promised voters, 'I will burn for you.' He used it again, in his victory speech, and again, arms uplifted, when he addressed his first joint party-room meeting after the election. 'We must burn for the Australian people, every single day,' he told his MPs as he promised to govern with humility.

According to Labor insiders, the contrasting Morrisons had been showing up in the party's research. Before the campaign began, when he was an unknown quantity, senior Labor figures reported voters were using that old-fashioned Australianism 'bible basher' to describe him. Voters were finding it hard to reconcile his religion with his political persona. Contributing to this was Morrison's decision to allow cameras to film him at two starkly different events during the campaign.

The first was when he invited journalists in to watch with him, on a big screen, the first episode in the final series of *Game of Thrones*, a show renowned for its gratuitous sex and violence. Hawke and Howard had invited the cameras in to watch them watching sporting events – not shows that were rated for mature audiences only, because of their 'strong brutal medieval warfare and violence throughout including scenes of rape and torture, grisly and gory images, strong sexual content, graphic nudity, language and brief alcohol use'. That was seriously weird.

The second, soon after, was to invite the media into his Pentecostal church in Sutherland on Easter Sunday. The photos of him singing, with arms raised in praise in an evangelical pose, were like nothing Australians had ever seen from a prime minister. They were deeply unfamiliar images. Many people, including many of his own MPs, felt this was something to be kept private, not paraded. Liberals recalled Kevin Rudd's penchant for holding doorstops outside church on a Sunday, which drew criticism at the time. They stayed quiet, but felt queasy.

A few days later, Shorten made a number of not-so-subtle references to Morrison 'preaching' and 'parading his morality'. Tackling suggestions that the Liberals were about to do a preference deal with Clive Palmer, whose vote had shot up following Hanson's decline and a reported $22.5 million advertising spend, Shorten on 27 April posed the question this way: 'How is it that this bloke, this Mr Morrison, who's always up on the high ground, always on his soap box, you know, parading his morality, yet, you know, when it comes to doing a deal with Mr Palmer, he puts all of that aside, gets to the bottom of the barrel?'

Over at Liberal Party headquarters, where there was also some nervousness about the reaction to the shots of Morrison inside his church, there was uncertainty about how it might play out. They thought Shorten's comments were designed to get the news bulletins to run the footage again, so obviously Labor had decided they were helpful to them, which conversely caused Liberals to worry it might not be helpful to them.

Subsequently, after Morrison joked that Shorten should not allow himself to be filmed running, devout Catholic Kristina Keneally let loose on 29 April with a couple of pointed tweets:

> I'm just wondering if @ScottMorrisonMP, who criticises @billshortenmp for running in public view, has read Matthew 6:5–6: 'When you pray, don't be like the hypocrites. They love to stand in the synagogues and on the street corners and pray so people will see them.'
>
> 'When you pray, you should go into your room and close the door and pray to your Father who cannot be seen. Your Father can see what is done in secret, and he will reward you.' – From the Gospel according to Matthew, Chap 6, verses 5 & 6.

Keneally's tweets received little coverage.

In the second-last week, on the night of the final debate, Shorten and one of his staffers were in the boardroom of the National Press Club. Morrison had been standing with his back to them, and when he turned to face them, he was in what seemed to them a prayerful pose, his hands together. They were struck by the image, convinced he had said a quiet prayer before the big moment.

Then, four days before the election, the issue blew up. While campaigning in Perth, Morrison was asked two questions by two journalists, which gave Shorten a pretext to jump in. Despite some muttering in Morrison's camp about media conspiracies, there was none – it was journalists doing what they do, trying to think of questions that have been asked but not answered hundreds of times during the campaign.

The Australian Financial Review's Tom McIlroy asked Morrison if he was still personally opposed to same-sex marriage, and if his position had changed since it had been legislated. Morrison fobbed off the question by saying the issue was now law, he was glad the change had been made, and people could get on with their lives.

Sky's James O'Doherty then asked him if he believed gay people would go to hell. This was a reference to the controversy that had been running throughout the campaign surrounding the Rugby Union's Israel Folau, who had been dropped from the game for saying that gays, adulterers, drunks, and other assorted sinners would go to hell if they did not repent. Morrison had earlier criticised Folau, but, for whatever reason, he chose to dodge O'Doherty's question, again by saying he supported the laws of the country.

If he had said 'No', the story would have disappeared. The next day, Shorten, without being asked specifically about Morrison's responses, decided to give him a bash below the bible belt.

'I cannot believe in this election that there is a discussion even under way that gay people will go to hell,' Shorten said. 'I cannot believe that the prime minister has not immediately said that gay people will not go to hell. This country needs to really lift itself, and the political debate and coverage needs to lift itself in the next four days,' he said.

Morrison had to do a bit of mopping up, saying he did not

believe gay people would go to hell, that he was disappointed Shorten had stooped to this level, it was grubby, and in any case he was running to be prime minister, not pope.

Everyone ran the footage again of Morrison in church. He succeeded in reaching the high moral ground, Shorten damaged himself because he looked clumsy and opportunistic, and religious believers were reminded that Morrison was one of them. While those close to Shorten believed his intervention was justified, and that he was making a legitimate point, senior Labor MPs thought he had mishandled the issue. In their view, if it had to be done, it should have been done by someone else, probably Keneally. Simon Birmingham, who had argued in cabinet against Morrison's push to keep the individual-seat votes on same-sex marriage secret, because revealing them would expose Labor MPs who were compelled to vote Yes even if their electorates voted No, was proved right. Chris Bowen, one of the first of a succession of Labor MPs to say after the election that Labor had to learn to speak to people of faith, suffered a large swing against him in his seat of McMahon, which had also recorded a 65 per cent No vote on marriage equality.

Later, one experienced Labor campaigner thought Morrison's decision to allow the cameras in was a deliberate attempt to woo people of faith. Another thought it was calculated to appeal to the anti-Muslim vote, particularly among One Nation followers in Queensland.

Either way, it appeared to work. Early research, based on two-party-preferred swings, by Ben Phillips, associate professor at the ANU's Centre for Social Research and Methods, found signs it had paid off.

Phillips found that out of the 30 most Christian electorates (aside from the small number of electorates where independents dominated), only two swung to Labor. One of those was Gilmore, the only seat picked up by Labor, although more likely this was because Morrison's decision to impose Warren Mundine as the candidate upset local Liberals. In Herbert, regained by the Liberal National Party, where 58 per cent of voters identify themselves as Christian, the swing to the government was 7.62 per cent. In Flynn, which Labor had hoped to win, where 62 per cent of voters identify as Christian, the swing to the LNP was 5.25 per cent.

Phillips noted that the top 20 electorates which recorded the highest swings have higher populations of Christians. The highest swing of 11.26 per cent was secured by George Christensen in Dawson, despite the fact that he had spent almost as much time in Manila as he had in Mackay. The Christian population in his electorate is 62 per cent, 10 per cent above the national average.

All top-10 swing seats – seven of them in Queensland, and three in New South Wales – have above-average Christian populations. In Queensland, Labor's primary vote dropped below 30 per cent.

Phillips's research was based on the count before it was fully completed, and relates to the two-party-preferred swing; however, he did not believe that the story of the election, with its surprising swings, would change in any meaningful way.

'At the electorate level, the main factors that correlated with a swing to the Coalition on a two-party-preferred basis were a low level of education, lower income, a higher share of persons who identify as Christians, and a larger share of blue-collar workers,' he said.

'This was a somewhat surprising result, as the Labor policies, at least with regard to the hip pocket, were heavily based around higher personal income taxation, compared to the Coalition, and cracking down on tax concessions – such as negative gearing, franking credits, capital gains, and trusts ... The majority of the impact of these policies would have been felt by high-income and high-wealth households.

'Those groups who appear to have swung to the Coalition were unlikely to be impacted by the Labor policies. Those groups most impacted adversely by the Labor tax policies actually have swung to Labor.'

Trying to work out why will keep researchers, pollsters, and campaigners occupied for years.

From where they sat in Brisbane, armed with their superior research, those at Liberal campaign headquarters had a fair idea where Labor was going wrong. They were incredulous when Shorten paid his homage to Gough Whitlam in Blacktown, in the same place that Whitlam had delivered his iconic 'It's time' speech. They did not think Shorten was helped by the presence of former prime ministers at his launch, because it reminded people how many of them there had been. No former Liberal prime minister, including John Howard, who had campaigned tirelessly in marginal seats, attended Morrison's launch in Melbourne. It was one out, all out. If Howard couldn't be there, nor could Abbott. (Turnbull was in New York, so couldn't have been there, in any case.) Abbott was toxic in Victoria especially.

They also believed that Shorten's Blacktown speech would revive memories of how poorly Whitlam had managed the economy. In his speech, Shorten told voters that if they wanted to 'change the nation forever', they needed to vote Labor. Those listening, particularly those who did not remember Whitlam fondly, who were confused or frightened by what he proposed, could only wonder what else he might do. They were not reassured.

Then, when the news broke on Thursday night that Bob Hawke had died, Liberal campaigners were amazed that Shorten stopped campaigning altogether, except to talk about Hawke.

The news of Hawke's death came as a terrible shock to Shorten. He had visited Hawke not all that long before, and he seemed better than the previous time Shorten had seen him, months before. The news rattled him. He was told around 5.00 pm on the day, but was sworn to secrecy to give his widow, Blanche d'Alpuget, time to tell members of the family and other friends. The only person in his team who knew was Liddell. At 5.45, Shorten was scheduled to do a pre-recorded interview with Leigh Sales for *7.30*, his final one for the campaign. He went ahead with it, understandably upset, but did not tell Sales. She announced the news after the interview aired, following the release of the formal statement announcing Hawke's death, as the program drew to a close.

Liddell rightly says that they would have been criticised whichever way they went after the news broke about Hawke's death – whether they changed the nature of the campaign to make it more low key, or continued full pelt. After debating the pros and cons, Shorten and his campaign team decided it was best to pull back and to stay in Sydney, where there was a massive outpouring of grief for Hawke, instead of spending the final day in Brisbane as planned.

It was a most unusual ending to a most unusual campaign. The entire focus of the last 48 hours of the campaign switched to Hawke.

The view of the commentators and most of the politicians was that Hawke's death would help Shorten, that it would be his final gift to his beloved Labor Party. The view was that if Morrison had momentum, it would be stalled because of the brief cessation of hostilities. The media was swamped by glowing retrospectives of Hawke and his achievements, leading people to believe this would also help Shorten because it would remind people just how good Labor governments could be. That sounded logical.

Slight problem: Shorten was no Hawke. They were both creatures of the trade union movement, but Hawke's life and career rested on bringing people together, working with business and the union movement through the Accord to expand the economy and create jobs. He did not run class wars. And, for good or ill, Hawke was the most authentic of politicians. All the early footage reminded people how dynamic and charismatic he had been, and how much they loved him, despite his flaws. Shorten looked puny, disingenuous, and divisive.

When seasoned Labor operatives and frontbenchers looked back later, it was a case of everything going wrong that could go wrong. The policies were wrong – there were too many of them, so they could not be sold properly – the messaging was wrong, the advertising was wrong, the leader performed badly in the first two weeks, and then he pulled back at the critical time. A record 4.76 million Australians voted before polling day, posing enormous challenges for campaigns. Early analysis by the Liberals was showing pre-polling had gone 53–47 per cent their way; then, when the undecideds were heading to the booths, it was all about Hawke.

Labor had so many policies that offended one interest group or another, or different groups in the community, and every day there was a different message, with no convincing narrative to tie them together.

'There was a sense of complacency and confusion around what we were trying to say,' one senior Labor man said later.

'You can't blame any one person – we all had a part to play. No one opposed those policy positions. They were all carried without dissent. Once we settled on policies, we then had to pay for them, and then we had to deliver a surplus.

'There was a view we could afford to lose support here or there because we were confident that our polling was showing we could still win.'

Another, confirming that there had been no dissent inside the shadow ministry on either the direction Shorten was taking or in the policies formulated, said they all seemed to forget they were the opposition, not the government. Their confidence only grew as they watched the Liberals tear themselves apart. They convinced themselves that shifting to the left with a raft of big-bang policies, rather than hugging the centre with a less ambitious agenda, would overcome Shorten's unpopularity, which wouldn't matter anyway because the Liberals were dysfunctional.

Asked why Labor didn't grandfather the franking-credits changes, for instance, in an effort to mitigate some of the backlash or offset the scares, one frontbencher replied that they needed the money to pay for the big spends like an extra $14 billion on education. And to double the surplus. One begat the other, which finally begat losing the unloseable election.

'We bit off more than we could chew on tax,' he admitted. 'Voters felt they couldn't trust Shorten, and the campaign was ungovernable.' They couldn't get a grip on it.

Later, Liddell echoed Shorten's complaint about the sheer weight of 'vested interests' running against Labor, which he believed overwhelmed their campaign. He said the volume and content of the combined advertising of the Liberals and Palmer was a major factor in the defeat. The messaging was effective – simple and highly negative, if misleading.

However, he also recognised the great weight of their agenda. 'Bill wanted to be elected in his own right, with his own policy agenda,' Liddell said. 'We were trying to do a lot of things.'

Because they presented such a brew of tax policies, the gate was opened to scares about others that would follow. Labor MPs were bombarded with questions about their (non-existent) plans to introduce death taxes, or to cut pensions. Once these scares took hold on social media, it became impossible to fight them or kill them off. Another scare, in another sign of the rise of the religious right, was the leafletting of western Sydney alleging – falsely – that Labor was planning to allow late-term abortions. Labor MPs later claimed this had cost them votes.

While the issue of franking credits hurt Labor, what hurt almost as much was the shadow treasurer, Chris Bowen, saying that if people didn't like the policy, they didn't have to vote Labor. So they didn't.

Shorten's policies to redistribute income seemed to belong to another era or in another country, or designed to run against another leader. He modelled himself on Bernie Sanders and Jeremy Corbyn, neither of whom had won anything. Hawke and Keating had talked about aspiration, jobs, and the economy; they had instituted major reforms on every front, including the workplace. Shorten offered soft socialism, seldom talked about jobs or what needed to be done to create them, and he and Labor seemed incapable of pivoting from a campaign formulated during the Liberals' civil wars, which underestimated Morrison's campaign skills and the Liberals' tougher approach.

It bred complacency, and it delivered catastrophe. Labor failed to make the charge of continued chaos or dysfunction stick, despite the gift of the country having had to endure three Liberal prime ministers in three years.

The Liberals were not without their problems. Their worst time during the campaign was when candidates dropped like birds from trees with heat stroke.

In one day, less than three weeks before the election, the Liberal Party was forced to abandon two candidates in Victoria – Jeremy Hearn in Isaacs because of an Islamaphobic rant, and Peter Killin in Wills over his homophobic rant. Incredibly, in a sign of the increasing presence of the religious right in the party, a couple of members of the party's powerful administrative committee voted against Hearn's dumping. In their view, he could apologise, and everybody would soon move on. Not only did this reveal a lack of sensitivity, but it also showed a complete lack of appreciation of political realities in a campaign.

The new state director, Simon Frost, helped mitigate the damage by digging up rape jokes and other unsavoury comments on social media by Labor's candidate for Melbourne, Luke Creasey. Although Creasey had deleted his social-media postings, new software developed by the Liberals enabled them to find damaging posts he had sent to friends. Shorten had to sack him soon after he stood up and backed him.

A week out, the Victorian Liberals were forced to dismiss a third candidate, Gurpal Singh in Scullin, after his inappropriate comments on rape. They had held out against sacking Singh for almost a week after it became known he had also made homophobic comments. The sequence played out very badly for the Liberals. Members of focus groups, unprompted, raised the problem of candidate selection.

The party had suffered badly from a poor campaign at the 2018 Victorian state election, but had regrouped after the departure of Michael Kroger as state president and Frost's appointment as state director. Despite the problem with the candidates, a more rigorous campaign and a less polarised party was credited with saving seats they believed were gone.

In January, Liberal polling showed the party could lose as many as eight seats in the state, including Corangamite and Dunkley, already notionally Labor through redistribution. The Victorian premier, Daniel Andrews, who had swept to victory only a few months before, had a favourability rating of plus five. Josh Frydenberg was at minus 9, Morrison was at minus 16, and the federal Liberals were at minus 20. Ominously for Shorten, in his home state, he topped the pops on unfavourability at minus 26. But Labor men and women told each other that unpopular leaders had won elections before. The most recent prime example was Abbott.

At the beginning of the campaign in April, Labor believed it would win between four and eight seats in the state. It didn't win any, and it even had to battle to wrest Corangamite from Sarah Henderson.

The Liberals were never going to win the Victorian seats in which its candidates were dumped, but their polling showed they were on track to win a third seat in Tasmania, that of Lyons. This was until the anti-Muslim social-media posts of their candidate, Jessica Whelan, were exposed.

In a further tribute to the enhanced research capabilities of the Liberals' dirt units, Labor was also forced to ditch two candidates for unsavoury comments, including the number two on Labor's Senate ticket in the Northern Territory, Wayne Kurnoth. This spread the hurt around, particularly when Shorten claimed he had never met Kurnoth, and pictures of the two of them together soon miraculously appeared, making Shorten look like a liar. Not surprisingly, vetting processes focussing on social media as well as citizenship issues are now set to be the focus of internal reviews by the major parties.

Candidate selection aside, the contrast in the two campaigns and the two leaders was as stark as it could possibly be. Labor was dragged down by an unpopular leader struggling to sell unpopular policies, the detail of which he did not know. But Labor also ran a poor ground campaign, it was hampered by bad polling, and it left itself open to scare campaigns that it then failed to rebut. Having mastered the art of the scare in 2016 with claims that Turnbull was going to privatise Medicare, experienced Labor campaigners watched as Shorten and his team left themselves exposed to multiple scares, flailed around in their responses, and then jumped from issue to issue with no consistent theme or narrative. Labor's by-election campaign in Longman was fought with sharp, targeted messages, uncluttered by alternative policy prescriptions, focussing instead on the government's proposed company tax cuts. That template was thrown out as Labor forgot or ignored every campaign rule, just as the Liberals had in 2016. Labor's national campaign director, Noah Carroll, resigned in July.

Although Mark Textor sat this one out, the Liberals stuck with Crosby Textor. They brought out Michael Brooks from the UK, who had run the Tory campaigns of 2015 and 2017. The fact that he was a Pom posed no impediment to his ability to sift through data to determine what made Australians tick and where they sat. The Liberals' polling was spot on.

As well as believing it could win between four and eight seats in Victoria, two or three in Queensland (including Petrie, Forde, and Flynn), and two or three in the west (perhaps Pearce, Swan, and Hasluck), Labor believed it could hang on to most of the seats it already held.

A week out, senior members of Shorten's campaign team said they were 'cautiously confident' that they remained on track to win. Told that the Liberals were claiming Bass and Braddon as likely gains, they said their polling did not show any movement against them in Tasmania. At that stage, they were still confident they could hang on to most of their seats in New South Wales, believing they would probably lose Lindsay but pick up Gilmore (which they did), and gain others in Queensland and Western Australia (which they didn't).

Queensland became the new killing fields for Labor. It was ironic that retaining Longman and Braddon at the by-election in July had saved Shorten's leadership from a planned onslaught from Anthony Albanese (and provided the impetus for the move against Turnbull), only for them to lose both those seats and more in the general election.

In Queensland, Labor lost both Herbert and Longman, did not pick up another seat, and fell further behind in seats once considered marginal. The party now holds only six out of the 30 seats in the state.

Over in the west, Liberals reported that former Labor leader Kim Beazley was telling them that his daughter Hannah, running in the seat of Swan, was getting smashed over franking credits. (As it turned out, the sitting Liberal member, Steven Irons, held on to the seat relatively comfortably, suffering a swing of only 0.7 per cent against him.)

The Liberals had had a path to victory under Turnbull, which was amended slightly after the switch. They judged early on that Abbott was gone in Warringah, and that they were in with a chance to regain Wentworth from independent Kerryn Phelps; to win back Lindsay; to hold all their New South Wales seats, including Reid, despite Craig Laundy's retirement; and to retain Gilmore, despite local hostility to Mundine. Laundy worked unstintingly to help his successor, Fiona Martin, keep the seat, including pouring in a reported $100,000 of his own money, and he did this in the face of malicious criticisms from hard-right Liberals who were angry that he had stuck by Turnbull and then resigned his seat.

The Liberals were reasonably confident about Tasmania, knew Queensland was swinging back with Herbert and then Longman – their polling even picked up the shift in Lilley, held by Wayne Swan, who was retiring – and judged that things had settled down in the west. Although it appeared that Corangamite and Dunkley would be lost, the wildcard had always been Victoria.

On the night before the election, the Liberals' tracking poll showed its primary vote in key marginals had ticked up to 44 per cent. The pathway to victory, thought impossible after Turnbull's demise, and then possible, was now likely.

Shorten resigned on the night of the election. Rather than the party signalling a new direction with a new generation of leaders – say, with Queenslander Jim Chalmers at the helm — Anthony Albanese replaced him unopposed.

Albanese's job of building bridges and convincing people that Labor had understood why it had been so comprehensively beaten was made difficult by Shorten's bitter farewell speech to caucus.

Shorten failed to accept responsibility for the loss and the reasons for it. Instead, he blamed 'corporate leviathans', 'financial behemoths', and 'vested interests' in the media who had opposed him. In other words, it was the fault of the big end of town – Palmer and News Corp – not his policies, and not his inability to sell them.

Morrison was blessed by Labor's brawling, as well as by the departures, voluntary and involuntary, of most of the older Liberal warriors. It meant there was the feel and look of a new government, although the civil wars have left scars.

Very soon after the election, key figures in the attempted Dutton coup were seeking to justify their behaviour – or maybe it was their way of seeking forgiveness – telling friends and colleagues that Morrison's victory had vindicated their actions in August. They got slapped around because everybody knew they had wanted Dutton as leader and that they had done whatever they could to block Morrison. And as far as many serving and former Liberal MPs were concerned, if the plotters and the delcons had succeeded in installing Dutton, the Liberal Party would have been annihilated pretty much everywhere, except in Queensland.

Dutton and Cormann stayed close. Like brothers. After the election, they rented an apartment together in the inner-Canberra suburb of Kingston.

The band of delcons also moved quickly to try to rewrite history, overlooking the fact they had wanted Dutton, had called Morrison 'Turnbull-lite', predicted his decision not to preference One Nation would cost him the election, and moaned that Abbott was still the Liberals' best leadership option. They blamed GetUp! and the unions for Abbott's defeat, despite large swings against him in the most conservative booths in Warringah, never at any point acknowledging that he might have brought it on himself by offending mainstream Liberals. They also sought to blame Turnbull's son, Alex, who had contributed financially to independents, and by implication blamed

Turnbull himself, as if a parent can direct an adult child which way to vote or spend their money. Together they had done all they could to destroy Turnbull and then block Morrison – and then they either basked in his victory or sought credit for it.

It took Morrison from September 2018 to May 2019 to get the two-party-preferred vote back to where it had been when Turnbull was dumped. The polling that Morrison used to guide his campaign was conducted by the same pollsters who prepared the marginal-seat polling which showed Turnbull the previous July that he was in a winning position. Showing once again the perversity of expectations, Morrison's victory was roughly the same in terms of the number of seats won as Turnbull's in 2016, yet he was exalted, while Turnbull was demonised. (Morrison ended up with 77 seats, compared to Turnbull's 76, and Labor with 68, down one from 2016.) In fact, there have been numerous examples of governments – including ones led by Bob Hawke and John Howard – losing seats at their first re-election bid, and then stabilising or improving at the second.

Turnbull might not have been as disciplined as Morrison on the campaign trail; however, the election campaign would have been much shorter in 2019 than the 55 days in 2016, the Coalition's ground game would have been the same, as would the negative advertising, which would have hammered home the same message about Shorten – warning of his policies and the risks Labor posed to the economy.

Turnbull, who did not consider the NEG dead, might even have had an energy policy. He would not have done as well in Queensland as Morrison, where once-marginal seats have now been rendered safe, although internal polling showed that Herbert would flip back to the Coalition. On the other hand, Turnbull would have done better in Victoria. Holding on to Dunkley and Corangamite was not beyond the realms of possibility, nor was picking up Cowan in the west, as well as the Tasmanian seats. Voters would not have gone into the campaign thinking Turnbull was certain to win, which had worked to Shorten's advantage in 2016.

Sensible Liberal MPs recognised all of this, just as they recognised the futility of pursuing any of these arguments, because that way madness lies. And they had had far too much of that already.

Acknowledgements

When I wrote 10 years ago that I thought Scott Morrison would one day lead the Liberal Party, it never occurred to me that it would happen so soon, under such extraordinary circumstances, and that I would still be around to write about it. I thought I would be out of the game well before then – just like I thought, after Tony Abbott won, I would never write about his road to ruin.

Then, on 24 August 2018, when the Liberals seemingly went mad and installed their third prime minister in three years, I followed suit by deciding to write a third book. I only ever thought I had one book in me; then, after the second, I told friends and family to feel free to slap me if I ever looked like writing another. To be honest, I never thought the need would arise; I was sure that events would spare me the physical and mental ordeal of trying to reconstruct the destruction of another prime minister. It seemed to me that Malcolm Turnbull would lead the government to the 2019 election, that he would more than likely win it, that afterwards there would be little to say about it, and that by the time he was gone, I would be gone, too.

But, like many other Australians, after it happened, I wanted to know why it had happened. Why, with so much at stake, would they risk everything to remove another prime minister? As bad as

Abbott was, they had only just got away with it when they ditched him. Surely they risked retribution from the gods? Wrong. The heavens sided with Morrison.

Most of my interviews and conversations with politicians, staff, and officials occurred before the election, with the explicit understanding that nothing would appear until after it. I offered that guarantee in the hope that they would be more honest and more forthcoming about what happened. Many of them were, and I am grateful to them for that. While I had been speaking to people during the week of the coup and in the weeks before for my column for *The Australian*, I also began speaking to key people for this book from the very next day, the Saturday, the day after Turnbull was deposed, because I wanted their recollections to be fresh. And raw. And unaffected by the result of the election, whatever it was. I thank them for that, too.

They were such difficult days for many of them. I have done my best to convey that, because too often we think of politicians as robots, devoid of emotion, programmed to react a certain way, rather than as human beings with the foibles and flaws, ambitions, and emotions that we all have. There were those reluctant to speak, particularly after I also told them I was not interested in quoting anonymous sources. Gradually, most of them relented. A few, particularly in those early stages, told me their sessions with me were like therapy. Some (such as Mathias Cormann and Tony Abbott) refused to even respond to requests for interviews, and others (such as Barnaby Joyce) said they would speak, but somehow couldn't find the right time. Malcolm Turnbull, writing his own book, agreed only to check a couple of facts with me.

My great good fortune has been to have the same cast and crew around to help and support me this time as I did a decade ago when I wrote my first book, *So Greek* – except, of course, for the late, great Elpiniki Savva. Elpiniki would have described my compulsion to keep writing as a sickness, the same one that drove her to never give in or give up, while our darling Christina, who has inspired so much of everything I have done, would have been as lovingly supportive as always.

Henry Rosenbloom, the founder of Scribe, has published and edited all three books. After *The Road to Ruin*, I told him, like I told others, that I was never writing another book, and begged him not to even think about asking, but Henry is nothing if not persistent. And a dream as an editor. I know this one was the hardest. Because of the number of characters involved, and the number of incidents to recount, it was the most difficult to write. Thanks to Henry, it makes sense. And also thanks to my great friend and mentor, and the best political journalist Australia has produced, Laurie Oakes. He was the first person I told I was writing this book, and the first to tell me what I already knew: that I was mad. Nevertheless, Laurie did what he has always done for me: helped me with advice, listened to my whingeing (not always sympathetically), and then became the first person to read and correct my manuscript.

Computer genius Matt Peacock, my personal Mr Fixer, was available for the third time to help me through all the glitches and essential rearrangements of chapters and notes, as well as transcribing two extended interviews. The most common phrase heard around our house for months was, 'Thank God for Matt.'

My husband, Vincent Woolcock, after an initial harsh but true assessment of my state of mind, soon rallied, more confident than I could ever be about the final product. My brother, Steve; his wife, Dana; my nephews, Andrew, Peter, Thomas, and Christian; and my nieces, Laura and Maria, were on board from the get-go, loving, supportive, and enthusiastic – all of which is made easier because they don't have to live with me or even close by me during the production process. Then just as *Plots and Prayers* was completed, came the best gift of all, a baby girl for Peter and Maria – Nicki

Christina, born on the birthday of her late paternal grandmother, Nicki, and named after her and her aunts.

My great friend Elissa Fidden, with dry good humour, provided valuable moral support and acute political observations, and gave me the best piece of advice any author could have when I was immersed in writing *So Greek*, and that was to polish, polish, and then polish some more. I wish I could have done better, but ultimately you can only do your best. Elizabeth McCabe, all class, came through with some much-needed photographs and empathy. Payment will be made on the next Hawaiian excursion.

Sue O'Leary produced another delicious Christmas cake, as she should after once again insisting I had to write the book. Showing no sympathy whatsoever, she would simply urge me to keep writing. My friend Jack Kunkel has grown into the most amazing young man, brilliant at everything he does; he even helped keep me going with a batch of delicious amaretti. Pretty soon, I will stop cooking for him, just like I stopped playing Scrabble with my nephews when they got too good. Knowing when to quit is important. Thanks to so many other dear friends – Denis and Denise Page; Lajla and Beat Sidhu; Chris and Rob Hunter; Charles Mailler; Eric and Georgina Koundouris; Laura Grande; Laura Tingle; and Kerry-Anne Walsh – for their interest, encouragement, and confidence in the outcome.

The final clearance for this project was provided by Antonio Didio and Walter Abhayaratna, who between them care as best they can for my various declining body parts. That came at the beginning of September 2018, when they were out on their regular Sunday walk. My adrenalin rush had worn off, and by that time, confronted by the enormity of the task, I was hoping they would say no. I have cursed them both many times since for their enthusiastic go-ahead, which I suspect came because they – like me – are full-on political tragics.

I remain grateful to *The Australian*, particularly Christopher Dore, John Lehmann, and Alan Howe, for having run my column for almost a decade. Apart from one quibble several years ago, no one has ever told me what to write or taken issue with what I have written, even though at times I have been out of sync with the prevailing sentiment.

After watching others in envy for years, I began appearing on *Insiders* in February 2011. When Kellie Mayo and Barrie Cassidy rang to invite me on, I thanked them, and told them I had been hanging out for a year after my re-entry into political journalism, waiting, hoping, to be asked. It was a blast, a terrifying one, to get a gig on one of my favourite programs and to work with such wonderful people, from Kellie to Barrie to Sam Clark, Robyn Powell, and particularly all the cheery magicians in the make-up room – Thelma, Sarah, Claire, Esther, Justin, and Sylvie.

Having a platform, whether in print or on screen, to express a point of view is an absolute privilege. Because nothing lasts forever, it will all come to an end one day. While I will be devastated, I will do my best to dwell on how lucky I have been that it has lasted so long; that for so many decades, people have been willing to pay me to do something I love. Thank you one and all, from beginning to end.